The FIRST WORLD WAR
on the HOME FRONT

The
FIRST WORLD WAR
on the HOME FRONT

TERRY CHARMAN

**SENIOR HISTORIAN AT
IMPERIAL WAR MUSEUMS**

ANDRE
DEUTSCH

Text copyright © Imperial War Museums 2014
Design copyright © André Deutsch Limited 2014
Photographs copyright © Imperial War Museums 2014

First published in 2014 by André Deutsch
an imprint of the Carlton Publishing Group
20 Mortimer Street, London W1T 3JW

A CIP catalogue record for this book is available from
the British Library

10 9 8 7 6 5 4 3 2 1

ISBN 978-0-233-00429-7

Imperial War Museums image reference numbers, in order
of appearance: Q81832, PST414, Q111826, Q53266,
Q57077, Q53464, PST12052, Q53359, HU52451,
Q61348, Q109912, Q56276, Q54729, Q54144,
Q54019, Q54384, Q53999, Q31229, Q47894

Printed and bound by CPI Group (UK) Ltd,
Croydon, CR0 4YY

*To the memory of my beloved grandparents
Alfred and Nellie Newman, two warriors
on the home front 1914-1918*

CONTENTS

It is not the critic who counts; not the man who points out how the strong man stumbles, or where the doer of deeds could have done them better. The credit belongs to the man who is actually in the arena, whose face is marred by dust and sweat and blood; who strives valiantly; who errs, who comes short again and again, because there is no effort without error and shortcoming; but who does actually strive to do the deeds; who knows great enthusiasms, the great devotions; who spends himself in a worthy cause; who at the best knows in the end the triumph of high achievement, and who at the worst, if he fails, at least fails while daring greatly, so that his place shall never be with those cold and timid souls who neither know victory nor defeat.

THEODORE ROOSEVELT

INTRODUCTION

Writing in his 1916 holiday diary almost two years to the day after Archduke Franz Ferdinand had been assassinated in Sarajevo, 50 year old Brighton businessman Henry Peerless noted:

It is a year since I last penned lines in a similar book to this. What a year! We have lived day by day obsessed with one thing – WAR. Every placard on the street is something about the War. Soldiers everywhere – wounded soldiers, poor creatures without limbs, jar on one at every turn. Sensation after sensation comes on us every day. I wonder if I can recollect all the things that have assailed us – submarine warfare waged by Germany in a most barbarous manner – zeppelin raids on east coast of England, London, and once or so on the Midlands, Brighton has hitherto escaped, but we have had several "alarums and excursions".

In his classic autobiographical work *Soldier from the War Returning*, Great War veteran Charles Carrington, whom I had my privilege of meeting during my first summer at the Imperial War Museum forty years ago, wrote: "The First World War hardly came to Britain." It is a verdict with which I am afraid I cannot agree. As Peerless wrote on the day after the bombardment which preceded the Battle of the Somme began, in nearly two years of war the country had experienced:

Military service bills–military compulsion–Derby recruiting schemes–income tax raised to five shillings in the pound–war loans– Exchequer bonds–military tribunals–loss of ships...rebellion in Ireland by the Sinn Feiners–women tram and 'bus conductors, ticket collectors on railways, porters, postmen, milkmen and munition workers–paper money...suspension of bank holiday at Whitsuntide– early closing of public houses–no treating in many places–forms for employers employing men between 18 and 41 years of age–trade union rules in many cases overridden–dilution of skilled labour… Munitions we now manufacture on a colossal scale…the adoption of "British Summer Time".

And all this even before the Gotha and Giant air raids on London of 1917/–18, and the introduction of rationing in February 1918. No wonder the "pompous and over-fastidious" Peerless, who "did his bit" both as a Special Constable and a part-time soldier in the 1ˢᵗ Battalion Sussex Home Protection Brigade, could write:

What a revolution for dear old England." A year later, he was still bemoaning the fact that: "At every turn we run against some restriction of the Defence of the Realm Act…They take away our beer, the blessed birth-right of every free-born Briton…Potatoes and sugar are difficult to get… Tobacco, that boon of mankind, has a further tax clapped on it…" Yet despite the "hundred and one other galling little pin-pricking things that get on one's nerves…up until now the people bear them wonderfully well, playing the game as I never expected they would…

Today, a century after it began, the First World War to most people conjures up the imagery of trench warfare on the Western Front; the mud, the rats, poison gas, the rotting corpses all of which loom so large in the poetry of Owen, Sassoon and Graves. Conjured up too are the "butchers and bunglers", the unfeeling generals, personified by Haig, safe in their chateaux and callously sending millions of men to their deaths. Unlike the British perception of the Second World War, the home front between 1914 and 1918 hardly impinges on the national consciousness at all. Yet, everything that is so familiar to us about the 1939–45 home front had a precursor in the earlier conflict; rationing, communal feeding, blackout, digging for victory, internment of aliens and air raids (during which double the number of Londoners sheltered in the Tube than in September 1940). And when the war was finally won in November 1918, the celebrations were far more enthusiastic and far less restrained than they were in May and August 1945.

Yet in a strange way there is a perception in twenty-first century Britain that we "lost" the First World War, and that it was all one huge blunder and the men who fought it and the civilians who supported it were all duped into doing so. Of course the war was a terrible catastrophe, and the loss of life and suffering enormous, but I agree with Harold Mellersh who fought with the East Lancashire Regiment and whom I was privileged to accompany back to Ypres in September 1977. In his First World War memoir *Schoolboy into War*, published the following year, he wrote:

> One of the curious things about a nation at war – one of the tragedies too – is that life is intensified. There is much happiness in wartime, much that is spirited, much that is admirable, much even that is just jolly…[Furthermore]…I and my like entered the war expecting an heroic adventure and believing implicitly in the rightness of our cause; we ended greatly disillusioned as to the nature of the adventure but still believing that our cause was right and we had not fought in vain.

After researching this book, I firmly believe that this was true of the civilians too.

Of course in a nation of 44 million, not everyone was an angel, but not all were villains either. And while there were certainly many who did not "do their bit", there were countless others like my Uncle Ted, who as a very young teenager, and with his father fighting in France, went out to work to help support his mother, brothers and sisters. In 1964, the fiftieth anniversary of the outbreak of war, I was near enough the same age as Uncle Ted had been when he became the Charman family's breadwinner. I can vividly recall that spring pleading (successfully), with my parents to get a 625 line television set in order to see the new BBC2 flagship series *The Great War*. And I also remember buying and lapping up that summer the nine volumes of *The War Illustrated* (£2) and the 13 volumes of *The Great War* (£3. 3s 0d) with my birthday money. I then had a large extended family of great aunts and uncles, and I listened fascinated to their reminiscences of 1914–18, of what my grandmother always called the "Kaiser's War". But the same year I also bought the Pan paperback of William Shirer's *The Rise and Fall of the Third Reich* and that started me off on another and more enduring trail. But now, fifty years later, I have returned to the Great War, and hope that in the following pages I have done justice to the enormous effort that the British home front made to the Allied victory in 1918.

THE LIGHTS GO OUT: AUGUST 1914

*A SILLY GERMAN SAUSAGE THOUGHT NAPOLEON HE
WOULD BE, HE WENT AND BROKE HIS PROMISE, IT
WAS MADE IN GERMANY.*
(From the 1914 song "Belgium Put the Khibosh on the Kaiser".)

"In retrospect, the moment before a storm breaks is found to have been
heavy, lurid, pregnant with foreboding. So it is with the summer of 1914,
which seems to have been lived in a breathless pause before the storm.
Actually at the time it was like every other summer there ever had been
or ever would be."

At 3.15 pm on the afternoon of Friday 24 July 1914, a cool and
gusty summer's day in London, the Cabinet met at 10 Downing Street.
A conference at Buckingham Palace on the seemingly insoluble question
of Irish Home Rule had just broken down. Now the Cabinet, presided
over by Prime Minister Herbert Henry Asquith, "with the head of a
Dickensian character and the nature of a Roman", met to discuss what one
member described as "the inconceivably petty" issue of the boundaries of
Fermanagh and Tyrone. "There was", the 62-year-old premier reported
to his much-adored, and much younger, confidante Venetia Stanley, "a
lot of vague & not very fruitful talk about Ulster … but the real interest
was Grey's statement of the European situation, which is about as bad as
it can possibly be."

Archduke Franz Ferdinand, the heir to the Austro-Hungarian throne,
and his wife Sophie had been assassinated in Sarajevo by a young Bosnian
Serb nationalist on 28 June. Now, Asquith told Venetia, Foreign Secretary
Sir Edward Grey had told his colleagues that:

Austria has sent a bullying and humiliating Ultimatum to Servia, who cannot possibly comply with it, and demanded an answer within 48 hours – failing which she will march. This means, almost inevitably, that Russia will come on the scene in defence of Servia & in defiance of Austria; and if so, it is difficult both for Germany & France to refrain from lending a hand to one side or the other. So that we are within measurable, or imaginable, distance of a real Armageddon, which would dwarf Ulster & Nationalist Volunteers to their true proportion. Happily there seems to be no reason why we should be anything more than spectators. But it is a blood-curdling prospect – is it not?

Asquith's young, thrusting First Lord of the Admiralty, Winston Churchill, was not as sanguine as his chief. He too had been struck by the "quiet, grave tones" of Foreign Secretary Sir Edward Grey reading out the terms of the Austrian ultimatum. "The parishes of Fermanagh and Tyrone," he was to write later, "faded back into the mists and squalls of Ireland, and a strange light began immediately, but by perceptible gradations, to fall and grow on the map of Europe." Churchill was not only the civilian head of the world's greatest navy, but he was also a "swashbuckler ... [who] knew what war was like", and one of the few European ministers that summer "who had personal experience of soldiering at the front". Back in November 1912, he had had a gloomy conversation with newspaper proprietor George Riddell. Speaking of the most recent Balkan crisis, Churchill told Riddell:

... it all depends on Austria and Germany. If the former maintains her position regarding Servia, war is inevitable unless Germany declines to support her, which she may do as she has all to lose and nothing to gain. England may be able to keep out of trouble, but if she stands aloof, and if Germany and Austria are successful in their combat with Russia and France and the Balkan states, we should be left alone in Europe. It might therefore be better for her to join France, Russia and the Balkan States so as to ensure their success.

Now, with the Austrian ultimatum, sent with Germany's backing, it looked as if Churchill's prophecy was about to be fulfilled.

That Friday afternoon as the Cabinet met, the vast majority of Britain's 43 million people were almost completely ignorant of the fact that Europe and their own country were potentially facing

Armageddon. Their reaction to Franz Ferdinand's assassination had been fairly underwhelming, although there was much sympathy for the aged Emperor Franz Joseph at this latest tragedy to befall the House of Habsburg. Beatrice Kelsey, a 26-year-old Warwickshire governess to a Viennese family, was holidaying with them in Budapest on Sunday 28 June 1914, a day of "grilling heat". That morning they had gone sightseeing, returning to their hotel for a jolly lunch eaten to the accompaniment of gypsy music. Then, "suddenly halfway through the meal, the music stopped and a hush fell over the room. The headwaiter moved about, speaking in a low voice and, when he reached our table, it was to tell us that the Archduke Franz Ferdinand and his wife had been assassinated." Beatrice was struck by how rapidly the Hungarian capital changed to "a city of mourning"; returning to Vienna, she found that there, too, were "signs of mourning on every hand", coupled with "anxious questioning about the new political situation which would inevitably follow the Archduke's death". Compton Mackenzie, author of the recently highly acclaimed novel *Sinister Street*, was on the Italian island of Capri when he heard the news. "Whether it was to create an impression of knowledge for simple folk," he later recalled, "or because I had a moment's illumination of the future I do not know; but I declared that this murder would mean a European War."

At Eton College, the news from Sarajevo sounded ominous to 17-year-old future Foreign Secretary and Prime Minister Anthony Eden, who was already showing a precocious interest in foreign affairs. But his foreboding at the Archduke's death was "soon thrust in the background for the Eton and Harrow match in July". For Eden and his fellow Etonians, the early summer days all seemed full of "gaiety, sunshine and good food". His exact contemporary Bernard Newman of Ibstock, Leicestershire, was hoping to go up to Cambridge University in 1915. He recalled that Franz Ferdinand's fate "attracted little attention. People in these outlandish places were always getting murdered; they should have the sense to get themselves born in a law-abiding country like England. So the Archduke was dismissed in trifling paragraphs in obscure columns, and nobody was quite sure where Sarajevo was."

On hearing the news, Archibald Gordon, the Duke of Wellington's private secretary, recalled Franz Ferdinand's visit to London to attend King Edward VII's funeral in May 1910, when he had stayed at Apsley House: "The Archduke could neither speak French or English. His appearance and figure were not prepossessing, and his manner was rather abrupt, but I knew that he was not a lover of England, though he loved its flowers and the Chelsea Flower Shows, and with me this told in his favour."

Sarah Macnaughtan, a populist novelist and friend of Field Marshal Lord Roberts VC, the Empire's most renowned hero, recalled with feeling:

> *On a certain radiant morning before the hay was mown, we learned that a man and a woman had been murdered in a distant country. Murder has a particularly horrible sound about it on a summer morning with red roses in bloom. We felt deeply for a great family who had known many tragedies, and we said sorrowfully that here was another awful happening to an ill-fated house. For a woman done to a violent death also we felt pity and horror. But the murder was an historic event and not a personal one, and after a time it was forgotten or left undiscussed.*

Even junior Foreign Office clerk Owen O'Malley, newly married and with "few thoughts to spare for anything but the organization of our private lives on a bare £650 in a maisonette at 72a Lexham Gardens", was blissfully unaware of the potential danger of the Saravejo murders. He was holidaying at the small community of Skipness, overlooking the Isle of Aran on the Argyllshire coast, where the daily papers only arrived in the late afternoon. And so,

> *returning for tea on Monday 29ᵗʰ June from a day's sailing, I walked up from the boathouse to find Bertie Graham [a cousin] reading* The Times *on the bench outside the billiard room windows. He told me that the Austrian Archduke Francis had been murdered in Sarajevo and that the news had made a stir in London which then seemed almost as far away as Serbia. If I had still been in the Western Department I might have possibly foreseen more fully the events which were shortly to follow, but I had by then been transferred to the African Department of the Foreign Office.*

So Owen went in to tea "without realizing that the death sentence of innumerable Skipnesses and all they stood for had already been pronounced. In a few days, however, I was recalled from leave and from then on my personal life was carried away on a flood of portentous events."

The "portentous event" of Sarajevo made little impact on the consciousness of most other Britons as they scanned their daily papers.

Of much more interest was Jack Johnson's victory after 20 rounds over Frank Moran in a contest for the World Boxing Championship in Paris. Britain's own Bombardier Wells achieved a similar triumph at Olympia when he knocked out Colin Bell of Australia in the second round of the British Empire Heavy-Weight Championship. Daring airman Harry Hawker had a close shave when his plane crashed as he attempted to loop the loop at Brooklands. Safe on the ground at Lords, the Royal Navy beat the Army by 170 runs, while at the Oval Surrey scored 502 runs for six wickets against Middlesex. At Trent Bridge, Yorkshire just saved the game against Nottinghamshire, and at Sandown, Sir Eager romped home first in the Sandringham Foal Stakes. Over the weekend there had been some mysterious fires at Peckham; incendiarism was strongly suspected, with militant women suffragettes, campaigning to get the vote, the principal suspects. Another fire at Hatton Garden had caused thousands of pounds' worth of damage. There was the usual disquieting news from across the Irish Sea, where a "Defence of Ireland Fund" to raise money to buy arms and ammunition for the Nationalist Volunteers had been announced. But from Germany came good news. A British naval visit to Kiel had proved a great success. Both the British commander Vice Admiral Sir George Warrender and Herr Liebermann, Kiel's mayor, had delivered speeches in praise of Anglo–German friendship and "peaceful rivalry" which had been warmly greeted. British "Jack Tars" and their German hosts "filled with the same spirit of mutual respect and esteem" were said to have got along like a house on fire, with everybody looking forward to a return visit in 1915.

In November 1913, only a few months before Sarajevo, Franz Ferdinand and Sophie had been the guests of King George and Queen Mary on a private visit, with both men indulging their passion for shooting. The King had found the archducal couple "both charming" and "very pleasant", and so he dutifully made a private visit of condolence to the Austro-Hungarian embassy in Belgrave Square. To Vienna, Sir Edward Grey sent both the British Government's assurances of deep sympathy and his own personal condolences. Out of respect, a Buckingham Palace Court Ball scheduled for 29 June was postponed until July, and in the House of Commons on 30 June, Asquith delivered, as he told Venetia Stanley that evening, his own "'obituary' on the Austrian royalties".

In early July, the ultra-conservative *Morning Post* had delivered a warning that the Austrian reaction to the assassination might well lead to a European War. But this was not a view shared by the press as a whole. On the day that the Court Ball should have been held, there had been a debate on the Foreign Office Vote in the Commons and Sir Edward Grey delivered a statement on foreign policy. Commenting on the debate, *The Nation* observed with some acidity, "Parliament gave nearly as much time on Monday to its annual survey of foreign affairs of a world-wide Empire as it bestowed on the municipal dispute between Purley and Croydon." In its report of the debate, the *Yorkshire Evening Press* opined that the "normal man" cared more about the activities of the household cat than he did about foreign affairs. As long as his own domestic tranquillity was undisturbed, he was unconcerned. Interest in foreign affairs was really confined to students, speculators and politicians. Moreover, to show any interest in events such as "Sunday's crime in the sordid capital of Bosnia required an experience of knowledge, a breadth of vision and a measure of disinterested enthusiasm wholly absent from all except a very limited minority".

It was not long before Sarajevo disappeared from the news altogether. In any case there was so much more of interest nearer home. For one thing the weather was becoming more bearable. Summer storms had battered parts of the country and there had been several deaths from the heat and from lightning strikes. But now temperatures were down from the high eighties Fahrenheit to the more acceptable mid-seventies.

The papers themselves made news. Press magnate Lord Northcliffe, "The Napoleon of Fleet Street", had launched the *Daily Mirror* in 1903 as "the first daily newspaper for gentlewomen, written by gentlewomen for gentlewomen". The first day's sale topped a quarter of million, but then slumped rapidly to 25,000. So the next year Northcliffe re-launched the *Mirror* as "a paper for men and women, the first halfpenny daily illustrated publication in the history of journalism". By the end of June 1914, it achieved a circulation of one million and received a telegram of congratulation from King George and Queen Mary. That same week Their Majesties had an unwelcome visitor when police at Buckingham Palace detained and placed "under observation as to her mental condition" an armed woman intent on selling "His Majesty two houses which she thought might be a good investment". Italian inventor Signor Marconi was reported as being optimistic in establishing "before the end of the year wireless telephonic communication between London and New York". A burning question of the day, much exercising correspondents to the papers, was the desirability of female attendance at boxing matches. But "A Mere Man," writing in *The Times* the day after, commented:

> *Is it not an historical fact that the most enthusiastic and appreciative spectators of the gladiatorial contests of ancient Rome were Roman ladies? Is it not true that the bullfights of modern Spain are graced by the most beautiful and elegant ladies of that country?... Are not our most sacred and ancient buildings almost daily desecrated or burnt to the ground by women? Why then so much squeamishness about a little blood at a boxing match?*

Herbert E. Hayes of the Egypt General Mission was also concerned about the moral welfare of women. He hoped that *The Times* could

> *spare space for a warning against the subtleties of the pernicious 'white slave' traffic. Women dressed as nuns frequent Continental docks and stations and deceive the innocent and unprotected by pretending they represent certain religious orders who are deputed to take care of girls and young women travelling alone. I was in Naples a few days ago and was able to prove that the system of deceit is widely practised there.... I trust you will utter some warning that will set the various vigilance societies to deal with the matter.*

And on matters of the nation's moral welfare, there were many who deplored the pernicious influence of American ragtime music and the supposed immorality of the new-fangled tango dance. The great days of British music hall, when George Leybourne had delighted mid-Victorians with his spirited rendition of "Champagne Charlie", were already past and it had been musical comedies like *The Quaker Girl* and *The Merry Widow* that had proved so phenomenally successful with Edwardian audiences. Then in 1912 from America came ragtime, seen as both a result of and a response to a new social atmosphere, "charged with excitable unrest". At a matinee performance at the London Hippodrome on 23 September 1912, Peter Bernard, a member of the American Ragtime Octet, sang Irving Berlin's "Alexander's Ragtime Band" for the first time in Britain. "What a night!" Peter recalled. "The audience went crazy for the new music," and the octet packed the Hippodrome for 12 weeks. They were followed by *Hullo, Rag-Time!* starring the vivacious and daring Ethel Levey, who, in a publicity stunt for the show, made her first aeroplane flight at Hendon piloted by pioneer aviator Claude Grahame White. *Hullo*

Rag-Time! ran up 451 performances and was seen by poet and "darling of the gods" Rupert Brooke at least a dozen times. A flood of ragtime songs, the most popular of them all seemingly penned by Berlin, swamped the country: "... the butcher's boy on his rounds whistled 'That Mysterious Rag' and Young Britain thumped out 'The Ragtime Suffragette' on parlour pianos which had never known such wild treatment."

But there were many who were not so keen on this musical invasion from "Yankeeland". *Punch* featured a cartoon of the muse "Music" trying to shut out ragtime music – "A present from the U.S.A." – with the caption "Time, gentlemen, please!". Others were even less delighted with the arrival of the tango. The Duchess of Norfolk, writing to *The Gentlewoman*, was in no doubt: "In my opinion such dances are not desirable, for the tango in itself and in the comments that it leads to is surely foreign to our English nature and ideals, of which I hope we are still proud." Lady Layland-Barratt went even further: "I consider it an immodest and suggestive dance altogether, impossible for any girl of refinement or modesty." In contrast, Lady Troubridge had "no radical objection to the tango if properly danced ... it is far more refined than many other modern dances lately in vogue." The dance had already been denounced by the pope, and now the fashionable and outspoken Jesuit priest Father Bernard Vaughan, who regularly inveighed against the sins of London smart society, weighed in to the tango debate: "It is not what happens necessarily at a tango tea that so much matters as what happens after it. I have been too long with human nature not to know that like a powder magazine, it had better be kept as far as possible fireproof." From Vienna, still in mourning for the Archduke and his wife, came the news that the officers of the Austro-Hungarian Army were now forbidden to dance the tango while in uniform.

In any case those officers had another and more serious matter on their minds, and were preparing to teach the Serbs a lesson. On 23 July, with Germany egging her on, Austria-Hungary dispatched an ultimatum to Serbia in which a punishing and humiliating restitution was demanded for the crime of Sarajevo. A reply was expected within 48 hours. The following day *The Times* reported that "The gravity of the situation created by the presentation of the Austrian ultimatum to Servia is indicated by the fact that the Austrian Minister in Belgrade has been instructed to leave Servia, unless the Servian Government complies with the Austrian demands by 6 o'clock this evening. It is stated that Russia has decided to intervene on behalf of Servia."

But the Balkans still seemed a very long way away to British holidaymakers as they sang along with seaside pierrots the summer's big hit from America, "Get Out and Get Under":

A dozen times they'd start to hug and kiss –
And then the darn'd old engine it would miss,
And then he'd have to get under,
Get out and get under,
And fix up his automobile!

In Europe armies might be beginning the process of mobilization, but holiday crowds in Britain were reading that only one out of every three ex-soldiers from the British army had been successful in finding a job in the past year. They also read how

a novel but unsuccessful method of deserting was adopted by a
private of the 2nd Worcestershire Regiment. Dressed as a woman
and accompanied by his wife and her brother, he left his house
and proceeded to Farnborough … trouble arose and the party were
taken to the police station. The police sergeant, touching one of the
"woman's" curls, found that it came away in his hands. The "woman"
thereupon confessed to being a man and to an attempt to desert. He
said his wife had cut off some of her hair so that he could wear it. The
wife was also arrested, charged with the illegal pawning of bedding.

But within days such "silly season" stories began to be edged from the news by the chain of sombre and threatening events taking place in Europe. On 28 July, the *Yorkshire Herald* told readers that it hoped "the terrible catastrophe of a European war" might yet be averted, but the same day Austria declared war on Serbia, and the next day Austrian monitors on the Danube began bombarding Belgrade. On 30 July, the *Herald* now believed it would be "something approaching to a miracle if a terrible explosion does not follow". In the high echelons of Whitehall, Chancellor of the Exchequer David Lloyd George told George Riddell, his newspaper-proprietor confidant, "I am fighting hard for peace. All the bankers and commercial people are begging us not to intervene. The Governor of the Bank of England said to me with tears in his eyes, 'Keep us out of it. We shall all be ruined if we are dragged in!'"

On Saturday 1 August, 25-year-old civil servant Percival Trenerry had hoped to return for the Bank Holiday to his parents' home in Bristol, but

"During the morning, however, I learned that I might be required at the Office at short notice in connection with the war scare. Our addresses were taken, and also the telephone numbers of those who have telephones." Instead of going to Bristol, Trenerry decided to spend his Saturday half-day holiday at the Rectory Ground, Blackheath watching the finish of the Kent versus Surrey cricket match. "Surrey nearly always lose this match," he recorded in his diary, "but this time they were on top. Except for the batting of Woolley, the cricket was rather slow, Kent endeavouring to confine their loss to a defeat on the first innings. About tea-time, the play was stopped by rain and I came away." Before rain stopped play, Trenerry had been sitting next to a German who "understood English county cricket thoroughly". He told the young civil servant that "he had received a notice to hold himself in readiness to return to Germany in the event of war". But he "did not want war as he had business interests in England which would suffer in consequence".

In the small village of Kennington, near Ashford in Kent, author and journalist Albert Kinross noted how in normal times

> *our chief interests at this time are hops, cricket and the fruit crop. Till Friday, July 31, we were unconscious of anything unusual; then, only then, did the better instructed among us begin to take the prospect of war with any seriousness. In the evening I went off to the local cricket club for some net practice. It still seemed impossible that this calamity could break. At home we had suffered from so acute a strain that a little distraction was a godsend. On the cricket ground all the "locals" were discussing Kent's chances against Surrey. A message had come through, duly discussed, in the window of the leading newsagent that Germany was under martial law. "Was she?" said the cricketers, and went on bowling.*

Writer Eveleen Culling shared Kinross's anxiety about the prospect of a European war that weekend as she holidayed at Horley, Sussex, with the actress Evelyn D'Alroy and her journalist husband Malcolm Watson of the *Daily Telegraph*. She recalled: "… as the political tension increased, the anxiety and uncertainty became almost unbearable. Life had become suddenly unreal; it had become indefinite, muddled; there was a sensation of some mysterious brooding force, some unknown, sinister influence drawing closer and ever closer, and the bright future had become obscured and dark."

Harold Balfour was a 17-year-old public school boy at Blundell's in the West Country and a member of the school's Officers' Training Corps. In July 1914, the OTC was at camp near Birmingham but "our week was cut short by the European crisis. The first news we had of the seriousness of the outlook and the first taste I had of war was when the cooks left, and I had to cook for my tent." On 31 July, impatient with what he saw as the "dilly-dallying" of his political masters, regular army officer George Macmunn came up from his home in Cheam, Surrey to "live in my room at the War Office, as I saw we would be overwhelmed with work. With me I brought a suit-case of uniform and another of flannels for the Broads, where I had a wherry for the next week, if it did not come to war." The day before, social reformer Ben Keeling, just returned from a walking holiday in Germany, wrote gloomily to a friend: "How horrible this threatened war is! Where is the sense of the human race?" But he was optimistic too: "I can't help thinking that we and Germany will settle it somehow. I can't believe in the Russians and the French politically or strategically. I am sure that the Teuton and Anglo-Saxon are going to dominate the world politically. Both from a sentimental and from a logical point of view, I detest our position on the Franco-Russian side." A view shared by no less an authority than scholar-statesman Lord Bryce, former ambassador to the USA, who, two days after Sarajevo, had told political journalist C. P. Scott that it was Russia he feared; "Germany ... was right to arm and she would need every man."

Nine-year-old John Macnamara was travelling by train to Cornwall with his parents on 29 July. "My father", he remembered, "was looking at the latest edition of the paper. 'War between Austria-Hungary and Serbia,' he said gravely. 'I do not see that it will affect us,' said my mother. Europe is a very dry place now,' he continued, 'a match could set the whole place alight. I do not like the look of it.' With that he lit his pipe and threw the match out of the window." Oxford graduate, prospective barrister and member of the Inns of Court OTC Alexander Gillespie, writing the next day to his parents, thought much the same. "It is pitiful," he told them, "that the blood of the Archduke should need the blood of so many others to wipe it out – though I suppose his murder was just the match to the powder magazine." With remarkable prescience he continued:

> *I don't see any means except a war to decide whether the Austrian or the Serb will have the ruling voice in the Balkans, and I don't see*

where the war will stop once it has begun. Instead of being a frame to hold Europe together, it seems that this system of alliances is just a net to entangle us all. Europe will be crippled for thirty years if a great war comes – it might be worth paying such a price to have it driven into the head of every man in Europe that our present armaments are insane – but that, I'm afraid, is just what a war won't do, because of the passions it will leave behind.

On Saturday 1 August, Albert Kinross went off to play cricket at a country house near his village and

again I realized the tremendous gap that yawns between our leaders and our led. The villagers and servants who formed the bulk of the two sides were all intent upon the game; to them it was the one reality, this unseen thing of no account. Over us others hung a cloud. We tried hard to be cheerful, to keep our thoughts on the game, but inevitably they came back to the one topic. There was talk of the swearing-in of special constables; the price of food might rise.

Later in the afternoon, a car drew up: "… it contained an officer in mufti. 'How many horses are there in the stables?' he asked. He was told, and stayed to tea with us." Impatient to find out what was happening, Albert biked to Ashford to get an evening paper and found the town "full of people similarly bent; but the London train had not come in; the Bank Holiday had upset it". Albert saw a Territorial Army officer sitting in his car, also waiting, and noted how the larger houses in the district had sent a maid or footman to collect the papers. "We waited and talked. Kent had made a draw with Surrey – that was something to talk about…. The evening papers came at last. It was War – it could mean nothing else but war. I shared my paper with half a dozen strangers. I read it spread out on the counter of a little shop which I had entered because a good lamp burned there. I dare say some of us bought things in that shop, but it never occurred to me that it stood open for that purpose."

In Newcastle Methodist minister James Mackay wrote in his diary: "Great excitement prevails all over the country. News has come that Russia is mobilizing and Germany has presented an ultimatum. People are alarmed everywhere. People are buying large quantities of foodstuffs. Grave fears are held by our own country. People are talking in hushed whispers everywhere. Great anxiety prevails."

In London that Saturday night, journalist Ferdinand Tuohy was ordered by his editor, "Go out and write up the war scenes in the West End. This is the goods." Arriving at Piccadilly Circus, Tuohy saw:

> *The theatres just emptying on the surging, twinkling scene; on the pavement a London crowd ... young men what we liked to call "bounders"; "gay" women in longish dresses and picture hats, freely from Berlin and Vienna; a few frothy, giggling flappers running the domestic gauntlet for an hour or two; old treading roués, eyes alone alert; "Varsity Youth" "just down" and bent on a wonderful night; opera-hatted "Johnnies" sauntering with magnificently knobbed sticks, white gloves, and an air of benign tranquillity; intermingling with it all, the Babel and jostle of Soho.*

Then a newspaper van "drew up with a skid outside the Tube. 'Germany Declares War on Russia. Speshul!' The news flashed from lip to lip. People paid a penny to see it blurred in the stop-press. Passers-by formed in knots. Yes, this was 'it'." Outside the Pavilion in Coventry Street, a band of young Frenchmen swept by Tuohy singing their national anthem, "a challenge which met its match in an answering chorus" of "The Watch on the Rhine" from a group of young Germans in the Haymarket. Tuohy continued on his assignment and found that

> *down in the cafés and beer halls of Soho it was Bedlam, while wine and lager, but chiefly lager, flowed in unending gallons. German students were doing the goose step behind portraits of the Kaiser; reservists marched up and down; and deep-lunged Lieder, student songs and* hochs *for mighty sons of the race* (Es lebt Bismarck! Hoch, hoch, HOCH!) *mingled with Strauss and Lehar and deafening shouts of "Prost!".*

Trying to compete with the uproar, a young German bawled out to Tuohy, "There're twelve hundred of us going back to-morrow. France closed. Holland, of course. We must finish *la belle* France in a fortnight. It only took a month in 1870. But your Fleet? That is the point ... it must stand clear, yes?" Outside, in the fresh air, Tuohy saw a young German carrying a sword and goose stepping up and down Panton Street before "an ugly movement engulfed him until two or three policemen broke up the circle and escorted the cause of it back to his flat". One of the policeman told Tuohy, "We've got to go carefully tonight. They're ten thousand of them blarsted foreigners from every country on earth in about a square mile 'ere and 'arf of 'em 'ave gone mad already. Not drink neither – just excitement-like." By the statue of Eros, Tuohy saw a large crowd "patriotically chairing a solitary Red-coat who was bellowing something about Spion Kop. The figure was to head a midnight procession to the Palace. We'd show the Kaiser! That was about the native temper that Saturday night."

The next morning, down in Kent, Kennington's tiny church was packed. "All of us," Albert Kinross wrote, "high and low, seemed to have come together with one object; to gather strength and fortitude, to feel and find our solidarity. Luckily our padre is the best Christian of us all. If ever the village thought and felt as one man it was on last Sunday." At his OTC camp at Rugely near Birmingham, Harold Balfour attended a church parade in the camp's canteen tent. It was a boiling hot day as the padre delivered his sermon on the war crisis. Speaking of the imminence of war, he told the assembled soldiers and schoolboys: "… it may be that some of you here will be called upon to lay down your lives for your country." But, as Harold was later to write, "neither the preacher nor his congregation could have visualized that … many of those who listened to his words, and who light-heartedly thought that the premature break-up of camp and upset of daily life was 'rather a rag', would within a few weeks themselves be dead, and that within four years there could be but a few survivors from that packed tent of boys."

The Reverend James Mackay, coming home from Sunday school in Newcastle bought "a war edition (my first Sunday newspaper). The situation is very acute…. The feeling in the country is electric…. I preached at Worley Street in the evening. I had the national anthem sung." Also attending church that day was the devout but prim and priggish civil servant Percival Trenerry. He noted in his diary:

We had special "war time" hymns to-day. The sermons, morning and evening, were on the subject of war. The Vicar's sermon in the evening was well-delivered but rather hackneyed. He propounded the trite but unsatisfactory idea that the war is allowed by God for some good but mysterious purpose – possibly to chasten us for our sins. He also pointed out that one day the reign of peace would come as prophesied in the Old Testament. I thought to myself that this was not much consolation to those who have to put up with war now. Moreover, the idea that war is to punish us for our sins in neglecting

Sunday observance, etc.., falls rather flat, for the burden of war falls probably more heavily on the just and comparatively innocent than it does on the guilty.

After Evensong, a special service of intercession was held, with most of the congregation staying to attend. At the morning service it had been announced that Germany had declared war on Russia. Now came the news that "the Germans had invaded Luxemburg. The general opinion seems to be that Germany is responsible for the conflagration, but I think Russia is to blame."

Similar services were taking place "throughout the length and breadth of the land and prayers were offered for the nations in the crisis through which they are passing". At Westminster Abbey that afternoon, Archbishop of Canterbury Randall Davidson "delivered a striking sermon on the duty of the nation and the citizen in the troublous time before us", and offered up prayers for those "whom the providence of God it has fallen to hold, at a great and sudden juncture, the trust for Britain's well being and for Britain's honour". But the service at the Abbey, as well as those at St Paul's Cathedral and a number of churches, was marred by "particularly humiliating scenes" when, "following on their denial that they intended to suspend their campaign of militancy, the irresponsible section of suffragists created disturbances".

Writing in her diary the night before, a Londoner had noted that there was "among the public a certain annoyance that England might be dragged into war on Serbia's account, as they cannot grasp that Serbia is a pretext in the balance of power". The next day, meetings protesting against the war were held all over the country. In Edinburgh, the anti-war demonstration held on the Mound in the city centre was broken up by what the *Scotsman* described as "an antagonistic element in the large crowd". Croydon teenager Harold Bing heard that the London anti-war demonstration was to be held in Trafalgar Square that afternoon and that Labour leader Keir Hardie was going to be one of the speakers. So he made the journey – 11 miles (18 km) – on foot, listened to Hardie and the other speakers, "and of course walked home again afterwards which perhaps showed a certain amount of boyish enthusiasm for the anti-war cause. It was quite a thrilling meeting with about 10,000 people there and certainly very definitely anti-war." Marmaduke Walkington, another teenager, had dreams of martial glory that Sunday, albeit "with a haunting fear that I wouldn't be able to get into the Army because of my youth. I was painfully conscious of the fact that I didn't look a day older than my 17 years. My face was very round, very red and quite babyish. It would be terrible if the War did happen and I couldn't enlist!"

At the War Office, military bureaucrat George Macmunn took a more jaundiced view of the Trafalgar Square meeting which had so enthused Harold Bing, recalling: "All Sunday I was in the office, and looking out at the great Peace Meeting called in Trafalgar Square. About 3.30 pm there came down the hardest thunder shower I've ever seen outside the tropics. Mr Cunninghame Graham and all the speakers got the sign from Heaven that, alas! It was too late to talk of peace. The square was as empty in ten minutes as at dawn." In Cardiff the previous day, a special meeting of the executive council of the South Wales Miners' Federation had passed a resolution calling upon the Government "to continue its position of neutrality, and to use all its powers in the attempt to limit the area of the present conflict and its speedy termination". Copies of the resolution were to be sent to Asquith, Churchill and Sir Edward Grey, who were already being bombarded with gratuitous advice from interested parties on how to steer Britain through the crisis. One was the venerable international jurist and Quaker Sir Edward Fry, who wrote a brief but heartfelt letter to *The Times*: "For God's sake, before England joins in the horrible war, let her be sure that she does so only in the case of dire or absolute necessity."

At the same time as Fry was penning his earnest plea, at the Inns of Court OTC camp at Persham Down, Alexander Gillespie was writing to his parents to tell them: "I have just sent in my name through the Colonel for a Commission in the Special Reserve of Officers in case of mobilisation.... There was no time to consult you and Mother first, but I felt sure that, if the want comes, you would wish me to do anything that lay in my power to help, for I am free, and my career at the Bar would not suffer from waiting for six months or so." At the camp, where Alexander and the rest of the men were "training and manoeuvring for all we are worth", no news had been received of the crisis that evening, "and so I hope that there may still be some honourable way to peace. I don't want to fight the Germans, for I respect them, but if the country is drawn in, I feel I must go in too, and do the very best I can."

That Sunday the Cabinet sat twice in emergency meetings. The first lasted from 11.00 am through to 2.00 pm and the second from 6.30 pm to 8.00 pm. Asquith was disconsolate that no letter had arrived for him that day from Venetia Stanley and wrote: "Apart from that it has been pretty black. Germany is now in active war with both Russia & France, and the Germans have violated the neutrality of Luxemburg; we are waiting to know whether they are going to do the same with Belgium."

While Asquith and his ministers argued back and forth, his brilliant but erratic second wife Margot paid a visit to the German ambassador's residence. Prince Karl Lichnowsky, an enlightened Silesian aristocrat, had been *en poste* at the Court of St James since October 1912, and had worked hard for an Anglo–German rapprochement. He and his wife Mechthilde, who wore eccentric clothes and had a passion for playing the piano, although not always at opportune moments, were popular in London society, though Asquith himself thought them "rather trying". That Sunday Margot "found Princess Lichnowsky lying on a green sofa with a dachshund by her side; her eyes were red and swollen from crying, and her husband was walking up and down the room wringing his hands. He caught me by the arm. 'Oh say it is not true, there's going to be a war! Dear Mrs Asquith, can nothing be done to prevent it?' The Princess got up and looked out the window and said: 'Look at this beautiful England, and to think that we are going to fight against her.'"

That evening, from the Bachelors' Club in Piccadilly, Sir Edward Hulse Bt, a Scots Guards officer, wrote to his mother his own, not always strictly accurate, appreciation of the situation. He had found that the

General opinion is as follows:- Asquith, [Lloyd] George and Churchill are in favour of intervention and whole-hearted support of France. Haldane and all the rest are against it, and are ready to work hard (with the power of Labour and Syndicalism and threat of national strikes, etc.) to get Asquith to climb down. Overwhelming opinion amongst the "man in the street" is that we must help France.

Hulse felt that that it was not now just a question of national honour, but of "national welfare and actual life in the future". He was afraid that: "If we climb down (which is thought almost impossible, as it is completely unthinkable) then we must be done. Canada might join the U.S.A., Australia set up on its own, anything, in short, might be the outcome of such a degrading performance. As you will see, abroad all socialists and syndicalists have regretted mobilization, but state that, as it is an accomplished fact, it is the duty of every man, etc. – in fact, patriotism. If we can't do the same, we had better go to bed!" Old Etonian

Hulse was of the opinion that large numbers of soldiers would not be needed to aid the French, writing that "ten boy Scouts and the British flag is all that is wanted…. [but] As a matter of fact, 120,000 or 160,000 troops from us at Maubeuge would mean a very real help to France, although people talk about our army as a drop in the ocean." During the crisis, Sir Edward told Lady Hulse: "Churchill has leapt up by bounds in popularity, and as his action and war-like spirit is compatible with his popularity and personal advancement, I imagine he is to be trusted to do the right thing absolutely. There are fears of his resigning tomorrow, if things go wrong in the Cabinet and in the House." Less impressive, Hulse thought, was Churchill's colleague Foreign Secretary Sir Edward Grey: "As you know, they say that Grey has been playing the double game, threatening Germany with all our forces thrown against her, and holding out to France, at the same time no hopes of help. He must decide soon, and is at present for climbing down."

He voiced the frustration felt by many that weekend concerning the apparent tardiness of Britain's preparations for war:

> *Prevalent opinion is that the Stock Exchange closed down three days too late, and that we have done everything three days too late. Why the devil we can't get our mobilization orders out, instead of talk, talk, talk and nothing done, goodness only knows. No one can any longer say that it is an aggressive action as everyone else has done it, and it would merely be precautionary; we have not got the practice in handling big things that France and Germany have, and the sooner we get a move on, the better prepared we shall be for being in the right place at the right time, if events demand it, instead of putting in an appearance a fortnight later, as we probably should do.*

But Woolwich had mobilized that day with "everything going well and in shipshape order there", despite the fact that on the marshes "the mosquitoes have assembled in myriads, and are peculiarly poisonous, and very painful".

That night at the club among Hulse's fellow diners were staunch anti-Home Ruler and leading barrister Sir Edward Carson and the dour, austere Conservative leader Andrew Bonar Law, "the former determined and very serious, the latter rather flustered to look at". Hulse heard that "there will be a big scene in the House to-morrow as war and peace parties about equal. It makes one hot all over to think of the peace-at-any-price party being so strong at this juncture." Before signing off, Hulse, who was to be killed in action the following year, aged 25, at the Battle of Neuve Chapelle, told his mother: "Probably things will have happened to modify or alter the gist of this letter by to-morrow," and added a postscript: "Large crowd just passed Piccadilly cheering a French Tricolour!"

Hulse may have been clear in *his* mind what Britain ought to do, but a London lady diarist noted the same night that:

> *Popular feeling that war will be dreadful & England would do better to keep out of it; uneducated people cannot understand what is at stake, nor obligations of national honour. Neither can they grasp we must fight Russia against Germany. No idea that we may be invaded; even educated people find it unthinkable.... Many people still more interested in the Bank Holiday & August holiday than the war; general annoyance at their arrangements being upset.*

One of those whose August Bank Holiday arrangements had been upset was Percival Trenerry, who despite the crisis found that his presence at the Board of Trade was not required that day. At a friend's office he encountered one of Sir Edward Grey's private secretaries who told them "that war between Great Britain and Germany is almost certain". Another colleague had been to the Government printers, to find it "carefully guarded because of the confidential printing in connection with mobilization, etc., which is being done there". On leaving his friend's office, Trenerry joined the crowds watching the ministers arriving for the 11.15 am cabinet meeting. Ferdinand Tuohy was there, too:

> *Whitehall was thronged; scenting crisis, Londoners paraded the very heart of Empire, from early morn to midnight, letting off steam by cheering every passing Minister and a number of people in cars and taxis who weren't Ministers at all. Winston, afoot, came in for the most cheers though none knew then how he had circumvented, defied, a disintegrating Cabinet, and kept the Fleet mobilized, on his own. He was just "good old Winnie".*

If Churchill received cheers, there were boos for Lord Haldane, the Lord Chancellor, already being attacked for calling Germany his "spiritual home". Later that morning, Trenerry saw Haldane, who had been helping Asquith out at the War Office in Whitehall: "No one seemed to recognize him. He is very ponderous, both features and build

19

being heavy. He seemed deep in thought, and, as usual, had one hand behind his back. He shakes his shoulder in a most peculiar manner when walking."

Trenerry lunched at an ABC tea shop, where he had had two pieces of shortbread and two of chocolate, all for 6d (sixpence). Deciding to make the most of the Bank Holiday, he "went by tram from Vauxhall Bridge road to the Oval to see Surrey play Notts. Hobbs made the highest score of his career – 226. He started his innings at noon, and was out at 5.30 pm.... He seemed to get out through sheer weariness, hitting recklessly at a ball from Iremonger who must have had quite a shock when he saw the ball hit the wicket at last." Throughout the afternoon "frequent editions of the papers were brought round the ground with the latest news about the war and England's probable attitude towards it". Outside the Oval, Trenerry heard one of the newsvendors calling out, "Mob-ilization of the fleet, Sir. *Sprechen Sie Deutsch?* Germany in the North Sea, Sir."

While Trenerry's presence may not have been required in Whitehall that Bank Holiday Monday, a day of clear skies and hot sunshine, at the War Office George Macmunn was working hard helping to get Britain's army ready for war. He was able to get away for a short time to see what was happening in the capital. Because

all the excursion trains had been cancelled ... all the Bank Holiday boys and girls were thrown back on the London streets, in their white skirts and their coloured sports coats.... They formed long lines and marched throughout the day, arm-in-arm, singing up and down Parliament Street, or went off by thousands at a time to Buckingham Palace to cheer His Majesty or any visitor to the War Office of importance. That marvellous body of great enterprise, the London hawkers, and those who cater for them, rose to the occasion. Enamelled buttons with portraits of the King and Queen and British and French flags appeared. The Union Jack and the Tricolour in paper on sticks, French gendarmes' cocked hats and plumes were in great demand and exactly what the holiday folk wanted. Pork pies were doing a hot thing and amid the crowd was the constant throng of lines of mobilizing details crossing London and threading their way from one terminus to another and Mr Apprenrodt pasted up on his [Coventry Street] restaurant windows: "We are British subjects".

The London lady diarist also noted that: "… there were crowds in Whitehall, Downing Street & Buckingham Palace all day. Very ordered, but a feeling of nervousness as to whether the Government would play the game & support France. The King & ministers greatly cheered. Belief among the more educated that England would take her part, but fear among the poor at the rise of price of food & the time the war might last."

Up in Newcastle that morning, Methodist minister James Mackay and 45 mission members left the city's Central Station for a Bank Holiday excursion to Stocksfield. In his diary he recorded: "The weather was splendid but the great dark war cloud hung over us. We could not dispel our anxiety try as we would. Despite this however we had a very enjoyable outing." En route, "At every railway station … a military guard is stationed. The whole community seems alive with uniformed men. Several trainloads of soldiers passed us on their way to the city." Back in Newcastle, "news has come to hand that the Naval Reserve have orders to mobilize. War between France and Germany has been declared. Things look very black. Germany's high-handed action makes our interference almost inevitable." In Chepstow, Monmouthshire, the Agricultural Show was taking place as usual, but one of the judges noted in his diary: "All the Gloucestershire Yeomanry officers who were at the show were recalled by telegram about four o'clock, and left at once."

The sudden train cancellations caused large numbers of would-be holiday-makers to be "stranded" in the capital, noted *The Times* the following day, "and so men in flannels and women in light dresses suitable for a promenade by the sea spent a large part of the day in the Strand and Westminster: and lunches that were to have regaled them on the sea-shore were eaten in London parks." The Anglo-American Exposition at White City, "Sunny Spain" at Earl's Court and Madame Tussauds all did well, but London's museums less so. The British Museum had 3,573 visitors compared to 6,044 in 1913; at the Science Museum there were 2,154 visitors, down from 3,878 the previous year, and the Victoria and Albert Museum 3,440 as against 4,895.

The railway companies may have cancelled their Bank Holiday excursions, but there were still quite a number of rail travellers that weekend, although those at Victoria were predominantly "Frenchmen, Italians, Spaniards and a few Germans … their exceedingly grave expressions testifying to their anxiety". At Charing Cross, according to *The Times*, *travellers were much more in evidence than at Victoria.... The trains for Dover, Ramsgate, Margate, Broadstairs, Deal and other favourite resorts were well filled, but their passengers gave one the impression of people going away without enthusiasm, even without object.... As a small indication of the trend of feeling, it is worth mentioning that scarcely half a dozen bags of golf clubs were to be seen on the platforms at Victoria and Charing Cross. The holiday-makers seemed to have forgotten their pleasures in their great anxiety. Up to the very moment of leaving they bought up the latest editions of the morning papers eagerly, and instantly became engrossed in the news from abroad.*

But despite all the anxiety and the cancellations, Southend still received over 60,000 Bank Holiday trippers by train over the weekend, and even more travelled to Brighton, including 21-year-old Alfred Newman and his fiancée Nellie Payne from Kingston upon Thames, who had daringly made the journey on Alfred's brand-new Douglas motorcycle. In Yorkshire, there were only eight special Bank Holiday excursion trains to Scarborough instead of the anticipated 28 or 29, and it was estimated that the number of visitors to the resort, where the general mood was said to be one of "uneasiness and anxiety", was down by 15,000. "Everywhere there was sunshine," *The Times* reported, "but over all hung the war cloud, and saying that Englishmen take their pleasures sadly was for once justified."

Despite the gathering war clouds, there were plenty of diversions that weekend. Cowes Regatta may have been abandoned, but the Royal Southampton Yacht Club went ahead with theirs, and the rest of the "heavy programme of sporting events has not at present been curtailed on account of the crisis in Europe", *The Times* reported. There was racing at Sandown, Birmingham and Ripon, and polo at Cowdray Park where Cowley Manor defeated Capron House by nine goals to five. In addition to the Surrey v. Nottinghamshire cricket match that Percival Trenerry attended at the Oval, Yorkshire and Lancashire played at Manchester and Canterbury Cricket Week opened as usual on Bank Holiday Monday with a match against Sussex. But even there, where The Old Stagers had acted in plays during Canterbury Cricket Week for 72 consecutive years, it was not certain that performances would go ahead as a number of army officers due to take part in *Priscilla Runs Away* had been recalled to their regiments. More professional acting was to be found at Stratford-upon-Avon, with Frank Benson as Benedick in *Much Ado About Nothing* at the Memorial Theatre. Stratford was reported as already being full of visitors, but: "Some of the many people who are prevented from going abroad, or the many foreign visitors from foreign countries unable at the moment to return home, might do worse than contemplate a visit to Stratford-on-Avon and its beautiful neighbourhood during the four weeks of the festival." Lighter theatrical fare graced London's Princes Theatre, where the Ruritanian melodrama *Queen at Seventeen* had just opened. Starring Jean Cavendish as the Queen, the play's action took place in one of "those bustling little imaginary kingdoms in Southern Europe, where all the prizes are open to youth and valour". Henry C. Hewitt played the male lead, "a young lieutenant, infelicitously named Von Hapsburg", noted *The Times*, and "the smart uniforms and picturesque scenery contributed a good deal to the effect of what was, on the whole, a stirring play".

There was non-war news from overseas too. On 30 July, Lieutenant Tryggve Gran of the Royal Norwegian Navy made the first flight of the North Sea. Leaving Aberdeen at 1.00 pm, he arrived near Stavanger four hours and ten minutes later. The 400-mile (640-km) flight, sponsored by air enthusiast Lord Northcliffe's *Daily Mail*, was made at an average speed of 96 miles an hour (154 km/hr) and Lieutenant Gran had had to wait over a week for suitable weather. The *Mail* was proud to announce that during the flight the gallant Gran "carried in his pocket a letter addressed to Queen Maud of Norway, asking her to graciously accept a copy of yesterday's *Daily Mail*, the first newspaper to be carried by air from Scotland to Norway". Two days later, and despite grave misgivings about leaving Britain at this time, home-grown hero Sir Ernest Shackleton and his Imperial Trans-Antarctic Expedition set sail on their ship the *Endurance* for the first stage of their journey to the South Polar region. A large crowd of spectators gathered early that Saturday morning at South India Dock to see them off and they "raised hearty cheers" as the *Endurance* cast off just after 8.30 am.

From Paris the same day came a dispatch from *The Times*' fashion correspondent:

It is difficult to write about fashion when all the world is thinking and talking of war. Yet fashions, like all other things in daily life, must go on; they are a cog in the wheel, and for smooth running the cogs must all do their duty. Nevertheless, when war scares us, we feel more like Red Cross uniforms than new creations from a dressmaker, and if we spend money at all we want to put it into bandages, flannels, and surgical instruments rather than into new hats and fanciful footgear.

But despite the gloomy talk of war, the dispatch ended on an encouraging note. For the ladies of the Paris fashion world, "like the rest of the world, stand face to face with public and private disaster, and they, like the rest of their countrywomen, are meeting it bravely with their heads held high and a smile". But there were frowns of puzzlement in France too. There was much concern about Britain's position and what she proposed to do if, as seemed all too likely, the Germans went to war with France, Russia's ally since 1894. Sir Frederic Cardew, a former Governor of Sierra Leone, writing to family in Paris on the morning of 3 August, told them: "The war is the most awful calamity that has visited Europe, I should think, as all the newspapers say, since the fall of the Roman Empire and I fear much that we shall be drawn into it for it seems a point of honour with us. There is no doubt that the French look to us to assist them and will have a very low opinion of us if we don't." But in the French capital it was an open secret that there were quite a number of Asquith's cabinet, including Chancellor of the Exchequer Lloyd George, who wanted Britain to remain neutral in the European War. Meanwhile, French official circles looked forward to a positive statement of Britain's intent when the official announcement was made in Commons on Monday afternoon.

At 4.00 pm, just as the crowd at the Oval were watching Jack Hobbs notch up his second century, Foreign Secretary Sir Edward Grey, "a recluse by nature, seldom seen in society … a lover of birds, a keen fisherman and consequently a man of patience and foresight", rose to deliver his statement on Britain's position. His speech that afternoon was, in the view of the Speaker James Lowther, "the most moving I ever heard in the House". Grey had had hardly any time to prepare, but as his Parliamentary Private Secretary Arthur Murray recalled, "during the morning he had snatched a little time from the mass of work and interviews to dictate hurriedly a few brief notes". Then, together with Murray and his Private Secretary Sir William Tyrrell, Grey walked down to the House, saying very little on the way. The Commons was so crowded that for the first time since Gladstone had introduced his

Second Irish Home Rule Bill in 1893, chairs had to be brought in and placed along the floor. Murray still remembered with emotion 30 years later the occasion when Grey

> *rose to speak in a packed, tense and troubled House. Only ten days had passed since Austria had thrown her dagger at the valiant Serbs and Germany had already drawn the sword. The House hung on his words. An occasional break in his voice, and a characteristic movement of hand to head, betrayed his emotion. But his tale was straightforward, and his counsel faltered not. From his lips fell the unadorned sentences that proclaimed for all time the justice of the cause for which the British Empire stood ready to spring to arms.*

Lobby correspondent Alexander Mackintosh was impressed too. "Feeling was acute", he recalled,

> *as the Foreign Secretary described the situation and the obligations that we had assumed. His speech was in form simple and plain, almost conversational, but so much faith was placed in his character and judgment that his words were convincing. The temper of the audience, although its silence was seldom broken, became more and more distinct as Grey proceeded, and when he sat down the Government knew that the House would be with it in armed resistance to German aggression. There was no Jingoism, but there was firm, solemn determination.*

Afterwards, Murray spoke to Grey: "how deeply moved the House had been by his speech.... I told him that no-one could have done more than he had done to prevent war that was bursting upon us, and that thanks to him we stood with honour before the world. He talked quietly and sadly – the past was behind; the future lay ahead, beginning with a war which might shatter civilization as we knew it. We must win this war, and then make sure that Germany was never allowed to do this terrible thing again." Grey returned to the Foreign Office where Permanent Under-Secretary Sir Arthur Nicolson congratulated him on the speech. Grey, leaning gloomily by the window, did not answer but moved into the centre of the room and raised his hands with clenched fists above his head. Bringing his fists with a crash onto the table he groaned, "I hate war. I hate war."

Later that afternoon, 61-year-old former Indian civil servant Charles Robert Thomas Balston, now retired and living in Dulwich, had read "the garbled account of Sir Edward Grey's speech in the House of Commons as it came through the tape in the vestibule of my club, in which he was represented as explaining the situation & showing how unfettered the country was by any definite promise and I remember how I broke away and started impatiently homewards to hear from a French lady on the top of a bus a plainer & much shorter summary of the situation. It was 'But Monsieur your honour!'." When Balston obtained a published account of Grey's speech he saw "that in the Foreign Secretary's carefully guarded language the assurance was given that if the German fleet came into the Channel or through the North Sea to attack France, the British fleet would give her all the protection in her power. Further he said the Belgian King had appealed to England to uphold the integrity of Belgium, and here at least, the promise was definite and written. We were pledged to defend Belgium...."

Margot Asquith had been to the House to hear the speech: "... when we returned to Downing Street the crowd was so great that extra police had to be brought from Scotland Yard to secure the way for our motor." Arriving at No 10, she found herself "too exhausted to think, I lay sleepless in bed. Bursts of cheering broke like rockets in the silent sky, and I listened to snatches of 'God Save the King' shouted in front of the Palace all through the night." A crowd of about 20,000 people had gathered in front of Buckingham Palace earlier in the day and had been entertained when "a party of urchins marched up to the Palace carrying a monster Union Jack. The cheekiest of them made the crowd roar with his imitation of a policeman on point duty directing traffic." That night at around 10.00 pm, the King and Queen with the Prince of Wales made an appearance on the Palace balcony, to be given, in the words of one spectator, "an enthusiastic and loyal reception by the crowd".

Ordered by his paper to go Belgium the next day, Ferdinand Tuohy "looked in on that delicious revue *The Passing Show* at the Palace. Elsie Janis and Basil Hallam were singing *For you're here and I'm here/So what do we care?* That was roughly how we felt about things that Monday night. Yet the lamps were going out in Europe, one by one."

The same evening Alexander Gillespie wrote again to his mother and father, The Inns of Court OTC had returned to London by train in the early hours and "we were kept at H.Q. waiting for orders, but are now dismissed till to-morrow morning". Alexander had got news of Sir Edward's speech and told his parents, "I'm afraid there is little doubt that we shall be at war tomorrow." All day he had been thinking of them "and wondering what you were doing and saying, for I feel that your part in these troubles is so much the hardest of all. We have so much excitement to keep us busy, and so many cheerful companions that it isn't hard for us to see the bright side of everything." At midnight, writing from the National Liberal Club, Ben Keeling, a passionate Germanophile, was unable to see the bright side. He was

> *amazed at the lack of feeling and interest about the war everywhere – even now. I have just passed by a ring of guffawing fools sitting over their whisky in the smoking room. The holiday people at Cowes and in the train simply didn't seem to grasp the fact that we are on the edge of the greatest abyss in history.... I had not seen an English Bank Holiday scene for many years and I was glad to be mixed up with it. The patient, courageous, placid stolidity of the crowd was amazing. But, the insularity, the inability to get a glimmering of this appalling situation!... And these smug Liberals – ugh!*

Keeling had long looked forward to a "predominantly Teutonic Central European State stretching from Antwerp to Trieste", but now recognized, "I am enough of a Liberal and Constitutionalist to object to the foundations of such a State being laid upon a blood-and-iron policy. It is not good for England or for Germany which I feel to be my own country after England." But the real villain of the piece, in Keeling's view, was Russia. "I believe firmly that Russia has provoked this war, and that without Russia's intrigues it might never have taken place," he wrote, and hoped that in time there would be a "Western combination against these accursed barbarians, Jew-baiters, and upholders of gross medieval Christianity ... they are the enemies of civilization."

Keeling also fulminated at the "old-womanish platitudes" and "smug insular pietism" he had detected in Grey's speech that afternoon. But he was very much in the minority. The overwhelming response to the speech had been positive, with it receiving an enthusiastic press in the morning papers on 4 August. Even the *Morning Post* joined the praise, telling its readers how foreign diplomats had looked down on "an assembly of British representatives which, while inwardly swayed by powerful emotions, nevertheless presented that outward aspect of dignified restraint which is one of the proud possessions of the British character". The *Daily Mail*, hardly a Government supporter either, told its readers that "the proceedings in the House of Commons yesterday was worthy of a tremendous occasion. They will fill the nation with fresh courage and confidence." The *Daily Mirror* declared, quoting Grey, "'We could not stand aside!': Britain will not allow Germany's fleet to batter France's undefended coast.... The thoughts of all Britishers went out to sea yesterday, for with the statement of Sir Edward Grey in Parliament, the safety and sanctity of the Empire may easily again depend upon the Navy which has given us such heroic a history." But there were some discordant notes, too. The *Manchester Guardian* hoped that Britain would remain neutral, as she had done in the 1870–71 Franco–Prussian War: "Europe in arms watches Great Britain. Italy has asserted her freedom to keep the peace, will England follow the good example?" But despite reporting that "war and rumours of war seem to have made no diminution of the happy holiday crowds," the paper acknowledged that Britain was now faced with "the greatest calamity that anyone living has known".

One lady diarist in London noted how Grey's speech had produced a "strong feeling against Germany & opinion is that her methods of procedure are mean and crooked", but Austria, the cause of it all, was "disregarded now". In his diary Percival Trenerry recorded how at the Board of Trade nobody could settle down to do any work "owing to war excitement". Throughout the day news trickled into the office: "In the afternoon, we learned that Germany had declared war on France and Belgium. In the evening papers came the news that Great Britain has sent an ultimatum to Germany with regard to Belgium, an answer being demanded by midnight." On his way home that night, Trenerry saw armed sentries guarding railway signal boxes and bridges. And already the first war rumours were spreading. That morning Trenerry heard that the Admiralty had lost sight of the German fleet "and did not know where it was. Also that Sweden would side with Germany against England." Ben Keeling had seen that, to get to grips with the French, "Germany naturally determines to strike as hard as she can and as soon as she can – and that involves invading Belgium. But the practical inevitability of this first step ... doesn't make it any more acceptable."

Just like Percival Trenerry, 22-year-old Territorial Army soldier George McGowan of the National Telephone Company had reported for work on Bank Holiday Monday and again on Tuesday but got very little work done either day. At his chambers in Lincoln Inn, barrister Francis Buckley was not surprised at the turn of events: "Ever since 1904 it was reasonably clear to me that our country would have to fight the Germans or go under." But he found the atmosphere oppressive: "… it was as though a terrible thunderstorm was hanging overhead, ready to burst; gloom and foreboding on the faces of all. There is no doubt that most of our people were taken by surprise and that they were aghast at the sudden gathering of the war cloud." Yet there were flashes of understated British humour throughout the day. *The Star* recorded a conversation in a suburban train that morning:

> First Traveller: *Looks pretty threatening, eh?*
> Second Traveller: *Yes, I think we are bound to have some showers before the day is out.*

Professional soldier Arthur Hanbury-Sparrow, an officer in the Royal Berkshire Regiment, was exasperated with the Government. He believed that "the war will be so short that every hour is precious. Already we're days behind, thanks to our rotten Government's weakness … at Downing Street the great ones sat wobbling, vacillating … how absurd … to act as if we were free to choose! How could we keep out on a technical quibble when we had been morally committed to France for years?" George Harbottle, a clerk with the ship-owning firm of Cairns, Noble & Co. since leaving school in 1910, had gone on Bank Holiday Monday to the South Northumberland Cricket ground at Gosforth to play a team from another club. They failed to turn up, and so George and his team mates "sat there in the sunshine and discussed what our personal action be if, as already seemed certain, war would be declared next day". George decided to join the Territorials and on Tuesday morning went to St George's Drill Hall in Newcastle, only to be told that there was no authority as yet to accept recruits but to come back in the evening. This he did, "and with a number of others … we were accepted, given our uniforms, and a medial inspection of a somewhat rudimentary character and told to report at 9 am the following day in uniform."

While George was waiting to join up, the Cabinet received definite news that the Germans had invaded Belgium. News which Asquith told Venetia Stanley "simplifies matters". So at 2.00 pm Sir Edward Grey telegraphed an ultimatum to Berlin. The German Government were asked to furnish assurances that they would respect the neutrality of Belgium, which had been guaranteed by all the powers, including Prussia, by the 1839 Treaty of London. A reply was requested by 11.00 pm (midnight in Berlin). If no satisfactory reply was received, the British ambassador in Berlin Sir Edward Goschen was to ask for his passports and to tell the Germans that the British Government would feel bound to "take all steps in their power to uphold the neutrality of Belgium and the observance of a Treaty to which Germany is as much a party as ourselves". In Whitehall there was little hope that the Germans would comply, and a declaration of war was drawn up and signed by Grey ready to be taken to the German Embassy. Asquith went down to the House to tell MPs the latest developments. As he and Margot left Downing Street by car, it "was full of anxious and excited people … some stared, some cheered, and some lifted their hats in silence". Asquith reported to Venetia Stanley, "The House took the fresh news to-day very calmly & with a good deal of dignity and we got through all the business by ½ past 4…. We are on the eve of horrible things." The Prime Minister's sang-froid that day was admired by Maurice Hankey, Secretary to the Committee of Imperial Defence: "All day long telegrams were pouring in, not arranging themselves in an easy and clear sequence but confused by a medley of rumours and reports from every quarter. During these events I was … in close personal touch with Asquith; and I was very much impressed by his clear, orderly mind, his coolness, courage, and decision, and his amazing powers of seizing on essentials. He inspired me."

That afternoon the thought of war was very far from the mind of future Labour junior minister six-year-old Joseph Mallalieu. His father Frederick had taken the family to Old Trafford to see the three-day Lancashire v. Yorkshire cricket match, which Yorkshire won by ten wickets. In later years Joseph could recall little of the match, but vividly remembered that his father, a Liberal politician, had insisted on buying the evening paper outside Exchange Station to catch up on the latest news of the crisis. Even more vividly, Joseph recalled that he was "sick after eating a custard tart and … we nearly missed the train home".

Meanwhile back at the Foreign Office that afternoon and evening, junior official Harold Nicolson, son of Sir Arthur, noted how the staff was now working at full pressure under the blaze of countless electric lights. The Committee of Imperial Defence mobilization scheme, prepared for the most part back in 1910, was working without a hitch. All that remained to be done was to send out telegrams at 9.00 pm warning every British diplomatic and consular mission throughout the world that war was imminent. The telegrams had, Nicolson recalled, "already been printed in advance and had reposed for years in what was known as the 'war press' of the Western Department. All that was required was to affix with the rubber stamp provided the one word 'Germany' in the blank space."

At 10 Downing Street, Margot Asquith joined her husband, Sir Edward Grey and Liberal grandee Lord Crewe in the Cabinet room where they sat in silence smoking cigarettes as they waited for the ultimatum to expire. "The night was hot," Margot remembered, and "all the windows were wide opened … from the Mall came the sound of thousands of people who were gathered outside the railings of Buckingham Palace". Among the crowd outside the Palace was Sister Emily MacManus of Guy's Hospital. With friends from the hospital, "we made our way through the evening crowds of restless, anxious people, to the great space in front of Buckingham Palace. War! Yes, it had come.… I was exhilarated; England had done the right thing. She would have been disgraced had she waivered or failed." Evelyn Needham, a City businessman and an officer in the Special Reserves, was dining that night with his cousin:

After dinner we went out and joined the enormous crowds of people throngingdown the Mall towards Buckingham Palace. I do not think I have before or since seen such as an amazing sight. The whole of the Mall from St James's Palace to Buckingham Palace was one seething, solid mass of people – very orderly and quiet on the whole as if they realized the seriousness of the situation. But every now and then would ring out a roaring chant "We want the King". His Majesty, accompanied by the Queen and many other members of the Royal Family, came out time after time on to the balcony, and were greeted with uproarious cheering and the singing of the National Anthem. By this time, special editions of the evening papers were out with the posters "War Declared". After watching this wonderful sight for about an hour, we walked back by Trafalgar Square and Piccadilly Circus. Everywhere were dense crowds of people, some cheering, but the majority quiet and seriousness.… Newspapers boys were running about with scare posters. "Great Naval Battle in North Sea" was one; "Gallant French Aviator Rams Zeppelin and Sacrifices Himself" was another. Both absolutely untrue!"

Also untrue was the report received at the Foreign Office at 9.40 pm that Germany had declared war on England. In undue haste, the prepared British declaration of war had to be amended, retyped and then taken round to Prince Lichnowsky at the German Embassy by junior official Lancelot Oliphant. No sooner had Oliphant returned at 10.15 pm than a message came from Berlin stating that Germany would not reply to the British ultimatum and, to the "infinite regret" of German Chancellor Theobold von Bethmann-Hollweg, "a state of war would arise at midnight". The message sent Foreign Office mandarins into a panic and yet another declaration had to be quickly substituted and the previous one retrieved. Harold Nicolson, "grasping the correct declaration in a nervous hand", was given the task and got to the embassy at 11.05. After much ringing of the bell at a side door, Nicolson was eventually let in by the butler, only to be told that Prince Lichnowsky had already retired for the night. Nicolson refused to be put off and told the butler that he was the bearer of an important communication from the Foreign Secretary. At that the butler left Nicolson on his own for five minutes or so, then asked the young diplomat to follow him by lift to the third floor, where "the butler knocked at a door. There was a screen behind the door and behind the screen a brass bedstead on which the Ambassador was reclining in pyjamas." Nicolson explained his mission and Prince Lichnowsky, pointing to the writing table, said: "You will find it there." Nicolson saw that "the envelope had been but half opened, and the passports protruded. It did not appear that the Ambassador had read the communication in which the passports had been enclosed. He must have guessed its significance and have cast it on his table in despair." But the 28-year-old Nicolson, destined to become one of the greatest diarists of the twentieth century, had to complete his mission.

A receipt had to be demanded and signed. The blotting pad was brought across to the bed, and the pen dipped in ink. While the Ambassador was signing, the sound of shouting came up from the Mall below, and the strains of the "Marseillaise". The crowds were streaming back from Buckingham Palace. Prince Lichnowsky turned out the pink lamp beside his bed, and then, feeling he had perhaps been uncivil, he again lighted it. "Give my best regards," he said, "to your father. I shall not in all probability see him before my departure."

The next day at 3.00 pm, American ambassador Walter Hines Page found his German colleague still in pyjamas, "a crazy man. I feared he might go literally mad … the poor man had not slept for three nights." Page also saw the King, who "declaimed at me for half an hour and threw up his hands and said 'My God, Mr Page, what else could we do?'"

On the night of 4 August, King George had dutifully written up his diary:

I held a Council at 10.45 to declare war with Germany. It is a terrible catastrophe but it is not our fault. An enormous crowd collected outside the Palace; we went on to the balcony both before & after dinner. When they heard that war had been declared, the excitement increased & May & I with David [the Prince of Wales, future King Edward VIII] went on to the balcony; the cheering was terrific. Please God it may soon be over & that he will protect dear Bertie's life [the future King George VI]. Bed at 12.0.

In York that evening, a large crowd had assembled outside the offices of the *Yorkshire Herald* in the city's Coney Street to hear the news, and when the declaration of war was announced there were "loud and prolonged cheers ... and the National Anthem was heartily sung". In Newcastle a similar crowd had gathered at the Central Station and in front of the *Chronicle's* office waiting to hear that Britain was at war. Mary Coules, on holiday in Worthing, Sussex, recalled:

During the first three days of August everybody was asking "Will England join in? and we were beginning to dread that we should have been ashamed of our country – or rather our government ... we were listening to the band on the parade on the night of August 4ᵗʰ – there was a queer, subdued flutter of excitement among the crowd, and we youngsters guessed that something important was happening. The band struck up – for the first time – the National Anthems of the Allies, except the Belgian, which nobody knew. At the close of "God Save the King" there was an outburst of cheering and caps thrown in the air.

But in London and over the country "on the whole the crowds which received the news that we were at war behaved quietly, being oppressed, and with reason – although with how much reason they did not yet know – by the gravity of the event. Outside Buckingham Palace, however, loyalty to King George provided the motive for hysterical displays of patriotic fervour."

Most of King George's subjects only learnt that they were at war the next day. In Hornchurch, Essex, housewife and mother of five Annie Purbrook jotted down in her "diary scribblings" how: "… just a week ago I don't think that, in spite of newspaper scares, any one of us, the uninitiated public, thought there would be war – and certainly they never really imagined that England would be in it." When her 22-year-old daughter Constance returned from her job in the City "and told us that it was officially announced that England had declared war on Germany we were actually glad … Edward [the Purbrooks' eight-year-old son] rushed into the garden shouting 'England has declared war! Hurrah! Good Old England! Three Cheers for England!'" Annie looked at all her offspring's eager faces and smiled too, "but inwardly I selfishly prayed that my dear children might never know the horror of war." Barrister Francis Buckley, who had tried to join the Territorials back in 1908 but had been rejected on account of weak eyesight, found that "when the stroke of fate fell and we were committed to the war, there was a curious sense of relief in many hearts. Better death and ruin than dishonour. A shameful peace or neutrality is for most Englishmen harder to bear than all the horrors of war. Besides this struggle for freedom had to be fought out." In Newcastle, where "great excitement and sorrow" prevailed, Reverend James Mackay noted:

> *There were no great demonstrations of excitement. The people took things very calmly.… It is awful to think, that, the greatest countries in the world, the countries representing the highest forms of culture, are engaged in bloody warfare. But it is true. War is upon us in the fullness of its horrors. The nations, enlightened as they are, are flying at each other's throats. The Prince of Peace is forgotten. Oh! How this must wound His great loving heart. Nevertheless, now that war is with us the thing we must do, however much we deplore it is to fight – and fight to win. Germany must never have the power to plunge Europe into war again. But oh! One grudges the fine young lives that must be sacrificed to this Moloch of war.*

Mackay went to the city's Central Station where "the sights are heartrending. Weeping women and children are everywhere. There is no cheering, no great ovations, no wild enthusiasm, just a great stricken mass of humanity broken hearted as a mother who has lost her only child. How will the Kaiser answer for the sorrow of these hearts on that great day?"

The *Daily Express* may have had as its headline that morning Nelson's immortal signal before Trafalgar "England expects that every man will do his duty", but in Whitehall on the first day of war, Board of Trade civil servant Percival Trenerry gloomily recorded an atmosphere of "great depression and nervousness everywhere" which was not improved by the torrential rain that hit the capital that day. Then at "about noon, without warning, there was a terrific clap of thunder. No one had seen any lightning, and there was no rain at the time, and many of us thought for a few minutes that it was the sound of a cannon.... There appears to be a feeling of uneasiness lest a German airship or aeroplane should drop explosives on London – a contingency which civilians did not need to fear in the past." Equally gloomily, the next day he wrote that "probably not since the time of Napoleon has there been such a feeling of uneasiness as there is in England to-night".

But if there was uneasiness, there was also a feeling of resolution too, combined with an ever-growing loathing of Germany, with "people ... indignant at her hypocrisy, her mean dealings & her lies". "Much ink," Sarah Macnaughtan wrote,

has been spilt in explaining why we went to war with Germany.... Probably a schoolboy, briefly and simply, might be able to put the matter as concisely as anyone else, and his creed, for all its simplicity, is a national one: "When you see a little chap being downed by a big one you cut in as soon as you can. And if the big bully says it's your turn next and begins to swing his arms about, you take him on for all you're worth." England has never allowed her friends to be bullied, and no one who knew her dreamed that she was going to allow it to happen now. Her children – unexpectedly for those who did not know her – began to stop quarrelling with each other, and buckled on their swords to meet the common foe. We were not ready – we did not pretend to be ready – but we meant to fight whether we were ready or not. Also, we meant to go on fighting till the end.

CHAPTER TWO

"YOUR COUNTRY NEEDS YOU"

WE DON'T WANT TO LOSE YOU BUT WE THINK YOU OUGHT TO GO, FOR YOUR KING AND YOUR COUNTRY BOTH NEED YOU SO.
  (From the 1914 song "Your King and Country Want You".)

To Lord Kitchener alone must be attributed the impetus which by May 1915, had enrolled 1,700,000 men in Britain's voluntary armies. Such was the magic of his name, that he had but to state the cause in which his New Armies were enlisted to be noble and right, for the flower of Britain's manhood to believe him implicitly, and unmurmuringly, unquestioningly to give their blood in that belief. Whether this vast army could have been built up more rapidly had Kitchener based his New Armies on the nucleus of the existing Territorial force is a technical controversy which will never be cleared; that until his death he was the greatest force behind the British management of the War is a point indisputable.

This tribute to Kitchener appeared 20 years after his death in a 1930s partwork aimed principally at ex-servicemen. But it encapsulated well what the vast majority of British people felt about him during the war. On hearing of his death at sea in June 1916, Ethel Bilbrough wrote in her diary:

The worst news we have had since the war began reached us today, and all England is electrified with shock – sudden & awful – that Lord Kitchener is drowned. He and his principal staff were on their way to visit Russia, and when off the Orkneys at night, and in a rough sea & gale of wind, some evil German submarine [sic]

37

*torpedoed and sank the vessel they were on, and none were saved
except two of the ship's crew, who were unable to throw any light
on the disaster. It has been a sad blow to England, for Kitchener
was a fine man & who but he could have raised a* voluntary *of
five million* [sic] *men. Everyone is feeling depressed and downhearted, for the war lord was so trusted, and in a fierce struggle
like the present war which is a struggle to the death, it is a bad
thing to lose a trusted leader.*

Charles Balston in his war diary recorded:

*... the tidings came as a great shock and a profound grief to the
whole country and the King voiced the national feeling in an Army
Order in which he called his loss a "disaster" and said that he would
be "mourned as a great soldier, who under conditions of unexampled
difficulty rendered supreme & devoted service to the army and the
state". His body lies in the sea; but on Tuesday the 13th June the nation
paid tribute to him in a service at St Paul's Cathedral at which the
King & Queen were present: and on 17th at Ladybank Mr Asquith,
addressing his constituents, pronounced his eulogy. In Germany
even, with some outbursts of joy and insult, there was sorrow at his
tragic fate and the expression of the opinion that this was the most
distinguished career of any English officer since Wellington.*

In an earlier entry reflecting on the events of 1914, Balston wrote,

*Lord Kitchener at home was laying down the foundations of a mighty
army.... He was the man who conceived the project & won the
British people to carry it out. The masses trusted him and rushed to
the standard raised in their midst. When he said he wanted 100,000
men they came. When he asked for 600,000 they came. When he
asked for a million they came. He said they were necessary and they
believed him. The British soldier is great. The wealth and power of
Britain is great. Our statesmen are great. But Lord Kitchener was
the great Englishman of his day.*

At 64 years old, Kitchener was on leave in England from his post
as British Agent in Egypt when war broke out. He had first attracted
attention in 1885 during the abortive attempt to relieve General Charles
Gordon in Khartoum, then shot to fame with his re-conquest of the
Sudan 13 years later, culminating in the victorious Battle of Omdurman.

Despite criticism over his treatment of enemy wounded in the book *The River War* by brash 25-year-old army officer-cum-war correspondent Winston Churchill, Kitchener was the nation's hero – a position consolidated during the Boer War, although again he was a target for criticism, this time for establishing concentration camps, in which over 20,000 Boer men, women and children died. As Commander-in-Chief in India between 1902 and 1909, Kitchener clashed with the Viceroy, Lord Curzon, over control in military matters, and won. After India he visited Australia and New Zealand, advising their governments on defence organizations, before taking up his Egyptian post in 1911. Only his old Boer War chief Lord Roberts VC enjoyed greater prestige, and there was a great deal of truth in *Punch's* couplet:

> *When the Empire needs a stitch in her,*
> *Send for Kipling and for Kitchener.*

An aloof and autocratic "confirmed bachelor" with a taste for fine porcelain, Kitchener was intolerant of interference and criticism, and distrusted politicians. It was said that Queen Victoria had remarked of him, "They say he doesn't like women, but he's always been very nice to me." Along with his undoubted military skills and expertise, Kitchener had an enormous capacity for hard work and long hours, but also an inherent inability to delegate, acting as his own chief of staff and military secretary. And, having served abroad for most of his military career, he was, on his own admission, ignorant of home conditions. He told Ulster statesman Sir Edward Carson: "I don't know Europe; I don't know England, and I don't know the British Army."

Kitchener was about to return to Egypt when he was recalled from Dover by Prime Minister Asquith on 3 August 1914. Although there were still misgivings on both sides – "May God preserve me from politicians," Kitchener remarked to industrialist Sir Percy Girouard – two days later it was announced that "K of K" had accepted the post of Secretary of State for War. It was a very popular appointment. Kitchener was, one paper claimed, "the man who gets things done and his appointment as War Minister was greeted with satisfaction throughout the Empire". Furthermore, he was "the man the Kaiser fears". And certainly he wasted no time at the War Office in taking steps to expand Britain's army, so tiny when compared to those of her French and Russian allies and of her German foe.

The regular army in Britain and the Empire on the eve of war numbered 156,110 with an additional 78,400 British troops serving in India. The regular reserve of trained men numbered 146,000 while the special reserve of partially trained men stood at 63,000. In addition there were nearly 270,000 men in the Territorial Force of part-time volunteers. But the latter Kitchener contemptuously dismissed as a "Town Clerk's Army", telling the Prime Minister's daughter Violet: "I prefer men who know nothing to those who have been taught a smattering of the wrong thing." On 6 August 1914, his first morning at the War Office, Kitchener was handed a pen which failed to function. "Dear me," the new War Secretary was heard to mutter, "what a War Office! Not a scrap of army and not a pen that will write!" But despite these shortcomings an appeal was drafted, approved and published in the press on 7 August. Under the heading "Your King and Country Need You" there was the announcement that "an addition of 100,000 men to His Majesty's Regular Army is immediately necessary in the present grave National Emergency. Lord Kitchener is confident that this appeal will be at once responded to by all who have the safety of our Empire at heart." Men between the ages of 19 and 30 were called to join up for general service for "a period of three years or until the war is won". A few hours after the appeal was published, Kitchener was telling his Cabinet colleagues that British sea power alone would not win the war, and that the country must be prepared to raise armies of millions and keep them in the field for several years. This sombre assessment, or in Churchill's words "inspiring and prophetic truth", was received by Asquith and his ministers in silent assent.

Kitchener's confidence in the response to his appeal for 100,000 men was not misplaced. The papers were soon enthusing, as was the new magazine *The War Illustrated*:

Since Oliver Cromwell, by an appeal to the religious spirit of the Puritans, created in his model army the finest engine of war in the modern world, our nation has never responded so quickly and sternly to an appeal from a commander as it has done to the call made by Lord Kitchener for the immediate creation of a new Army of Freedom. Our forefathers had to use press-gangs, and recruit from every prison in the kingdom, in order to win Trafalgar and Waterloo. Now the flower of our young manhood was seen last week fighting in friendly fashion outside the recruiting stations in order to win the honour of being the first to join the new army. All told, the British Empire has already nearly one million men under arms, and a million more will surely come forth if they are needed in the last and greatest of wars for establishing peace and free government throughout the world. Roll up! Roll up!

Reports of the British Expeditionary Force's first action at Mons and the fact that it was frankly admitted in *The Times* that the "battle is joined and has so far gone ill for the Allies" boosted recruitment figures. On 25 August, the day the Battle of Mons was reported, 10,019 men enlisted and the totals for the next three days were 10,251, 11,396 and 12,789. Between 23 and 29 August London yielded the highest number of recruits, 10,334, Birmingham 3,516, Manchester 3,141, Glasgow 2,220, Newcastle 2,126, Cardiff 1,544 and Liverpool 1,469. But in Dublin, where British troops had fired into a crowd of demonstrators on 26 July 1914, only 398 men joined up.

To accommodate those men who joined up to be with their friends and workmates, Pals Battalions were formed, more often than not on the initiative of a local worthy like Lord Derby in Lancashire. The 15th Battalion of the Highland Light Infantry was made up of men from the Glasgow tramways with the 16th Battalion formed out of former members of the city's Boys' Brigade. The 17th Battalion of HLI was raised by Glasgow's Chamber of Commerce. One of its four companies was composed principally of former pupils at Glasgow Academy and the city's high schools, while another was made up of ex-students of the Royal Glasgow Technical College. The two remaining companies consisted of young men from the city's offices and businesses. The 11th Battalion of the Welsh Regiment was known as the "Cardiff Commercials", while the 17th Battalion of the Northumberland Fusiliers consisted of men from the North-Eastern Railway Company. The 10th Battalion of the Royal Fusiliers was dubbed the "Stockbrokers' Battalion" and 10th Lincolnshires the "Grimsby Chums". The Pals Battalions had a tremendous *esprit de corps,* but there was also criticism in some quarters of what appeared to be their seemingly highly selective recruiting policy. On 29 October 1914 the *Labour Leader* complained: "The middle-class and professional classes form exclusive companies, they do not hasten away to the nearest recruiting office, for fear they would rub shoulders with their less polished fellow-beings. Their patriotism does not run to that."

But patriotism, along with a love of adventure, an urge to escape a boring job and a dull, domestic routine, and wanting to be with friends, remained a potent reason for joining up. In February 1915, the Young Men's Christian Association ran a competition in which soldiers were asked to submit a short piece on "Why I Enlisted". The first prize of 10s 6d (ten shillings and sixpence) went to Driver John Delves, who wrote from Wellington Barracks, Lichfield: "My two younger brothers enlisted at the outbreak of the war; I enlisted immediately realizing that my place was not at home." Runner-up Lance Corporal J. Smith of Cleethorpes, Lincolnshire, "having once served my country for twelve years (I resided in Australia), on the outbreak of war I came to England and enlisted, to serve my King and country and the Empire." Another runner-up, Lance Corporal G. Stimson of Braintree, Essex, had joined up "because I think every Englishman capable of doing so should enlist to protect home and country, and be prepared to go anywhere to do so". From Portobello Barracks, Dublin, Private George Wakefield enlisted "because, as an Englishman and a lover of freedom, I thought it was my duty at this time to give my services to the King and country for the reparation of Belgium and the defence of British policy". The final runner-up, Private R. Poole of Blandford, Dorset, told the YMCA: "The reason I enlisted was to fight for my God, my King, and country, and because I could not bear to walk along the street at night and see the boys in uniform, drilling to go and fight. I was only seventeen when I joined."

Looking back on August 1914, Ulric Nisbet, a Marlborough public schoolboy who joined the Royal West Kents, reflected:

It wasn't a matter of "our Country, right or wrong". Our country was 100 per cent right and Germany 100 per cent wrong. We were fighting for King and Country and Empire and Gallant Little Belgium. We were fighting to uphold the principles of justice, freedom, and international morality and to smash Kaiserism and German militarism.... We had been taught to worship God one day a week but to worship Country and Empire seven days a week. The British Empire was the greatest empire the world had ever known, and its greatness was due to the superior qualities of the British. Foreigners weren't just cast in the same mould.

Former Merchant Taylors' schoolboy W. T. Colyer thought much the same sitting at his office desk on the first day of the war and fuming over the Germans: "I wish to goodness I were in the army. I felt restless, excited, eager to do something for the cause of England. And then the impulse came, sending the blood tingling all over my body; why not join the army now?" Nor were these patriotic sentiments confined to those who had been at public school. George Morgan, who served in the West Yorkshire Regiment, was to recall, "… history taught us at school showed we were better than other people … and now all the news was that Germany was the aggressor and we wanted to show the Germans what we could do."

A 31-year-old social worker, Clement Attlee, future Labour Prime Minister and Churchill's deputy in the next war, took a cooler view, recalling:

> *I could not accept the ordinary cry of "Your King and Country need you", nor was I convinced of Germany's sole guilt. On the other hand it appeared wrong to me to let others make a sacrifice while I stood by, especially as I was unmarried and had no obligations…. I realized that some people had to serve and perhaps be killed and that I was partially trained already. I had no real conscientious objection.*

After a few initial difficulties due to his age, Attlee, as a former public schoolboy, managed to secure a commission in the 6th Battalion South Lancashire Regiment and fought at Gallipoli, in Mesopotamia (present-day Iraq) and on the Western Front. Two other future Prime Ministers eventually found their way into Kitchener's New Armies. The 20-year-old Harold Macmillan was caught up in the emotion of the hour, and recalled, "Our major anxiety was by hook or by crook not to miss it." But a serious operation for an inflamed appendix prevented him from joining up until October 1914, when he was commissioned a second lieutenant in the King's Royal Rifle Corps before transferring to the Grenadier Guards in March 1915. At 17, Anthony Eden was underage, and in any case, as his Eton housemaster told him, "You won't be use at the war, but you could be some help in the house four." It was not until October 1915, and after the death in action at Ypres of his elder brother Jack, that Eden was able to gain a commission in a newly raised battalion of King's Royal Rifle Corps. He went on to become, at the age of 20, the youngest brigade major in the British Army and to win the Military Cross in June 1917 for rescuing his platoon sergeant from no-man's-land.

While Eden had to wait over a year before he could enlist, one of the very first recruits was 30-year-old H. C. Meysey-Thompson, who had a legal post in the City of London. In his diary entry for 5 August 1914 he noted: "the British ultimatum to Germany expired at midnight and war certain". He now decided to

try and join something, if possible "Inns of Court" OTC. Go up to London by morning train and go straight to Inns of Court armoury in Lincoln's Inn. Find that the adjutant has left for luncheon, so go and lunch at "Cock", returning directly afterwards. Find a long string of would-be recruits, waiting to interview second-in-command. Finally my turn comes, and I go before an elderly gentleman disguised as a major, who, in spite of his uniform, boots, spurs, could be nothing but a Chancery barrister. My age, and the fact that it is twelve years since I performed any form of military duties make him reluctant to accept me, but I impress upon him that I was a marksman at Marlborough, and carefully suppress the fact that I never attained the rank of lance-corporal, and am finally passed.

Meysey-Thompson eventually got a commission in the Royal Berkshire Regiment and served on the Western Front.

Another young man most eager to "do his bit" was Edward, Prince of Wales. On 6 August the Prince, who had only just turned 20 a week before Sarajevo, noted in his diary: "… asked [my father] for a commission in the Grenadiers stating that I could no longer tolerate being unable to serve my country. And dear Papa never hesitated a moment & immediately instructed Ld. Stamfordham to notify this to the War Office…. It was a happy moment for me & now I am an officer & going to do active service!!" Writing to a friend on 9 August, the Prince was more candid: "It has been awful for me as up till Thurs, as I was sitting in this bloody great palace absolutely devoid of any job!! It was more than I could stick, so my father was good enough to give me a commission…. It will be hard work but I like that as you know. I do so hope to get out & have a go at those bloody Germans who are getting it in the neck, thank God!!" But the Prince's hopes of serving at the front were soon dashed in an interview with the Secretary of State for War himself:

Face to face with this immense, fierce-looking man, one would have said that all the slow, stubborn purpose of Britain was

*concentrated behind his somewhat florid countenance. He listened
to my case. "What does it matter if I am killed?" I insisted. "I
have four brothers." Lord Kitchener's steely blue eyes met mine. He
answered: "If I were sure you would be killed, I do not know if I
should be right to restrain you. But I cannot take the chance, which
always exists until we have a settled line, of the enemy taking you
prisoner."*

Despite further entreaties from the Prince, "there was no budging
Lord Kitchener. He vaguely mentioned something about a staff job in
France later on, but that was little consolation."

Further down the social scale, 22-year-old Bruce Seymour likewise
petitioned his father for a chance to serve: "I feel I shall never be happy
again if I do not at least do that," he wrote on 31 August.

*Nothing would please me better than to die fighting for my country.
If I am not fit they will not have me, but I shall have at least tried....
Do please say I can do this or I shall never respect myself again. It is
worrying my conscience a very great deal.... You can depend on it I
shall not disgrace myself if I am accepted.... I would love to have a
go at the Germans.... Do please say I can take my chance.... It is for
the old country Dad.*

Bruce got his way. He joined the Wiltshire Regiment and served
chiefly in Mesopotamia.

But there was to be initial disappointment for ex-Kingston Grammar
School boy R. C. Sherriff, who thought of himself to be officer material:
"An officer, I realized, had to be a bit above the others, but I had a sound
education at the grammar school and could speak good English. I had
had some experience of responsibility. I had been captain of games at
school. I was fit and strong. I was surely one of the 'suitable' young
men' they were calling for." But when it was his turn to be interviewed,
Sherriff received a tremendous shock:

*"School?" enquired the adjutant. I told him and his face fell. He took
up a printed list from his desk and searched through it. "I'm sorry," he
said, "but it isn't a public school." I was mystified. Until that moment
I knew nothing about these strange distinctions. I told him that my
school, though small, was a very old and good one – founded, I said by
Queen Elizabeth in 1561. The adjutant was not impressed. He had*

lost all interest in me. "I am sorry," he repeated. "But our instructions are that all applicants for commissions must be selected from the recognized public schools, and yours is not among them."

Sheriff did eventually get a commission in the East Surreys, serving in France before being invalided home in 1917. He was to write the greatest of all war plays, *Journey's End*, the royalties from which he left to his beloved Kingston Grammar School after he died in 1978.

Shortly after Sherriff failed to obtain his commission, there was another innovation in recruiting, which quickly caught the public imagination. This was the creation of "Bantam" battalions made up of men between 5ft and 5ft 3 in (152–160 cm) in height. In October 1914, a miner from Durham had walked all the way to Birkenhead in an attempt to enlist, but although otherwise fit and healthy, he was turned down on account of his small stature. At Birkenhead he caused such a rumpus he had to be forcibly ejected from the recruiting station, but his story came to the notice of Birkenhead's Member of Parliament, Alfred Bigland. Without more ado, Bigland approached the War Office and got permission to recruit a battalion of men below the minimum height. Within a few days around 3,000 men from all over Britain had come forward and were enrolled in the 1st and 2nd Birkenhead Bantams (the 15th and 16th Battalions of The Cheshire Regiment). Kitchener saw the value of the idea and sanctioned the nationwide raising of Bantam battalions, which eventually totalled 24. The whole of one division, the 35th, was made up entirely of Bantams, and two-thirds of the 40th Division was also composed of them.

If height was no bar to serving, neither was a man's religion or lack of it. A recruit was asked what his religion was:

"Ain't got none," came the reply.
"Well, you must have one," he was told by the recruiting officer. "What do you do on a Sunday morning?"
"I goes rat catching with me dad."
"Put him down as R.C., sergeant major."

Later in the war, after being sentenced to three years' penal servitude for a purse robbery, a 43-year-old man asked to be allowed to join the army instead. He told the court that he had never had a chance and over half his life had been spent in prison. "I want to die a clean death," he said, but his request was refused.

There was no shortage of encouragement, professional and amateur, for young men to enlist. Ethel Bilbrough pasted in her war diary a typical appeal from September 1914:

Men and Women of England.
A ruthless and relentless foe seeks to grind under its heel your Country and your Liberty.
You are called upon to light your lamps of sacrifice.
To send every fit man to the Front – your Sons, your Brothers, Your Friends, and to pray to God that they may return unharmed.

Soon recruiting posters were appearing everywhere, as *Times* journalist Michael MacDonagh noted:

Posters appealing to recruits are to be seen on every hoarding, in most windows, in omnibuses, tramcars and commercial vans. The great base of Nelson's Pillar is covered with them. Their number and variety are remarkable. Everywhere Lord Kitchener sternly points a monstrously big finger exclaiming "I Want You". Another bill says: "Lord Kitchener wants another 100,000 men." ("My word," remarked a lonely spinster according to a current joke, "one would do me!")

Nelson himself appeared on one poster: "1805 'ENGLAND EXPECTS'. 1915 ARE YOU DOING YOUR DUTY TO-DAY?" So too, after his death in November 1914, did Kitchener's old chief Lord Roberts: "He did his duty. Will YOU do YOURS?"

Over 200 poster designs were issued by the Parliamentary Recruiting Committee, but the most famous of all was one based on the front cover of the 5 September 1914 issue of the magazine *London Opinion*. Designed by Alfred Leete, it bore a portrait of Kitchener pointing over the slogan "Your country needs you" and was intended "to draw men to the colours and inspire them with the belief that their heroism was being devoted to a just and holy cause". The image immediately caught the public's fancy, and the next week the magazine was offering postcard-sized copies at 1s 4d (one shilling and fourpence) a hundred. The Parliamentary Recruiting Committee obtained permission to use the design for one of its posters, and they started appearing at the end of September and became one of the best known posters in history.

It was soon found that "one of the greatest aids to recruitment was the Church, which from the pulpits of all denominations preached the military cause with a fervour that made a deep impression on those who heard the stirring Christian call". Typical was an address "Shall I enlist? An appeal to Christian men in the hour of England's need", delivered at Sheffield's Victoria Hall Of Brotherhood and Sisterhood by the Reverend George N. McNeal on 20 September 1914. The Reverend McNeal was in no doubt what the answer should be:

For every able-bodied, able-minded man, whose burden of home responsibility can be laid down for a time, the path of patriotism is obvious and open – "Go and fight your Country's battles".... The war will certainly take months – it may take years.... England does not trouble to ask what the cost may be. No price can be too high to pay when honour, freedom, civilization, and Christianity are at stake.... Our British casualties already probably number 30,000. Some of you have been plunged 'ere now into sorrow for the loss of those you love – cut off in the springtime of their young lives. Thank GOD they died for their Country. Do not mourn overmuch for them. But these gaps must be filled.... If it is necessary, will you go? You are strong in body and mind. You are unmarried; you have no one dependent on you; will you go? You tell me that you have a good situation. What has that to do with it? Go, not because you are out of work, not in order that you may rid yourself of responsibilities; go from the highest motives of patriotism and Christianity.... Do not go merely out a love of adventure, but as a result of thought, conviction and prayer. And fathers and mothers, let your boys go; do not try to keep them back. Urge them to go as Christians, not merely to fight for King and Country, but to fight for the principles of the religion of JESUS CHRIST, and to uphold the banner of His Cross.

Religion also was a staple ingredient in the recruiting speeches of Horatio Bottomley, described by counsel at a pre-war bankruptcy trial as "the cleverest thief in Europe", and on his own confession "an oratorical courtesan. I sell myself to the man with most money." His first recruiting rally took place at the London Opera House on 14 September 1914. So great was Bottomley's appeal that 5,000 people filled the opera house while 15,000 more waited outside trying to get tickets. That evening for the first time he delivered his "Prince of Peace" speech:

It may be – I do not know and I do not profess to understand – that this is the great audit of the Universe, that the Supreme Being has ordained the nations of the earth to decide who is to lead in the van of human progress. If the British Empire resolves to fight the battle cleanly, to look upon it as something more than an ordinary war, we shall one day realize that it has not been in vain, and we, the British Empire, as the chosen leaders of the world, shall travel along the road of human destiny and progress, at the end of which we shall see the patient figure of the Prince of Peace pointing to the Star of Bethlehem that leads us on to God.

This near-sacrilegious tear-jerker was accompanied by Bottomley's usual violent verbal abuse of the "Germhuns". He then called on every man capable of bearing arms to join up and help "hasten the glorious time of peace". Criss-crossing the country, delivering recruiting speeches and giving "lectures", the charismatic Bottomley was well paid for some of his appearances and within a year could claim to be the most popular speaker in Britain.

Such efforts were supplemented by a band of unofficial and amateur recruiters. As early as 31 August 1914, Bruce Baily had written to his father about "those white feathers some ladies are going to present to fellows they see loafing about". Back in 1902 A. E. W. Mason, "one of the favourite novelists of the day", had published *The Four Feathers* which told the story of young army officer Harry Feversham who resigns his commission just as the prospect of war in Sudan looms. On his resignation, Feversham receives four white feathers as symbols of cowardice. Three are from brother officers, and the fourth from his fiancée Ethne. It turns out all right in the end, with Harry covering himself with glory on the battlefield. But the image of a white feather as a symbol of cowardice stuck, and on 30 August 1914 at a recruiting rally in Folkestone retired Admiral Charles Penrose Fitzgerald "gave thirty women the duty of handing out white feathers to men who were not in uniform". The Admiral looked upon such men as "deaf or indifferent to their country's need", hence in need of public shaming by patriotic young women. This would prove to be, the Admiral had no doubt, "a danger … far more terrible than anything they can meet in battle". The idea caught on, and along the coast at Deal on 1 September, the *Daily Mail* reported that the Town Crier had shouted out, "Oyez! Oyez! The White Feather Brigade. Ladies wanted to present to young men of Deal and Walmer who have no one dependent upon them the Order of the White Feather for shirking their duty in not offering their services to uphold the Union Jack of Old England. God Save

The King." In response to the Town Crier's efforts, according to *The Times*, "several young women went round fixing white goose feathers in coat lapels and hat-bands of young men lolling on the beach and the promenades."

Inevitably, the White Feather Brigade, men as well as women, as often as not handed out their "badge of dishonour" to discharged soldiers or those on leave who had chosen to wear mufti, or indeed to young munitions workers. In January 1915, Bombardier Henry Joseph Wilding of the Royal Field Artillery, winner of a Distinguished Conduct Medal, found himself in court after a fracas in High Street, Finchley. Wilding had punched Arthur Houghton, who fell and hit his head against a wall, in the belief that Houghton had put a white feather in his hat. The magistrate told Wilding that he could return to his battery in France, but if Houghton died "he would be sent for". Henry Wallace was also home on leave, after being badly wounded in France, and was travelling on a bus when a woman gave him a white feather. Much surprised, Wallace asked her what it was for, to be told, "You're a coward." Incensed, Wallace replied, "Excuse me, I'm not a bloody coward, if you'd like to look at my leg, you can find the other piece which is lying on the Fricourt battlefield on the Somme." Another passenger threatened to intervene, and to save a scene, Wallace told the woman, "The best thing you can do, madam, is to get off or you might find yourself in trouble." She stopped the bus and got off. Injured Royal Flying Corps pilot Collie Knox's reaction was far less restrained:

> *An attractive young girl with a weak mouth had handed me a white feather at the Carlton Grill. She also handed one to my companion. As he had only two hours previously received the Victoria Cross at the hands of the King at Buckingham Palace, the gesture did not go too well. This information, which I imparted to her with withering calm, knocked the girl even sillier than she was normally. Most of the White-Feather girls should have been horsewhipped.*

On occasion the white feather found its mark. Frederick Henry Broome had joined up underage, but after being invalided back to "Blighty" his true age was discovered and he was discharged. "I got a job in civvy street," he was to recall some fifty years later, "and … I was walking across Putney Bridge when I was accosted by four girls who gave me three white feathers. I explained to them that I'd been in the army and had been discharged and I was still only sixteen years of age but they didn't believe me." By now several other people had gathered round Frederick and the girls and he "felt most uncomfortable and awfully embarrassed and said something about I'd a good mind to chuck them in the Thames and eventually broke off the conversation feeling very humiliated. Finished the walk across the bridge and there on the other side was the 37th London Territorial Association of the Royal Field Artillery. I walked straight in and rejoined the army."

Throughout 1915, men continued to enlist although now in worryingly diminishing numbers. But German "atrocities" such as the *Lusitania* sinking, Nurse Cavell's execution and the Zeppelin raids tended to stimulate recruiting, as the no-nonsense, ultra-patriotic editor of *Aeroplane* Charles Grey recognized: "At a very modest estimate I should say that every bomb which falls on British soil is worth fifty recruits and every death caused by a bomb or shell from a Zeppelin is worth a thousand; so if the Zeppelins will only keep on coming they will considerably hustle that extra 300,000 recruits that Lord Kitchener wants." Grey went further:

> *It is rather a pity that arrangements cannot be made for airships to be guided by bogus signals to some of the districts where recruiting is slack. A few bombs here and there would probably wake things up a bit, and fetch in some of the "slackers"; for as a matter of fact, quite a number of so-called "slackers" do not enlist for the simple reason that they cannot see yet that the war is any particular affair of their own; it is not that they really "funk" fighting.*

The press continued to publish features on how magnificent remained the response throughout the country to voluntary recruitment. In September 1914, Cardiff had claimed the honour of having enlisted the heaviest recruit to "Kitchener's Mob", a 19-stone (266-lb/120-kg) former police constable. A year later, over 100 employees at Kew Gardens had joined up and four of them had been commissioned. And in the small village of Stretton-under-Fosse in Warwickshire, 24 men out of a population of 150 were "serving with the Colours ... leaving the village without a single young man eligible for military service". The following month it was reported that, "with six sons serving in the Army, Mrs Eliza Welch, of Bishops Lydeard, Somerset, has just said goodbye to a seventh son, who has left home to follow his brothers' example". The Bishop of Willesden, preaching at Holy Trinity Church, Paddington, on 28 November 1915, "referred to the striking fact that had come to his notice – that out of two streets containing 210 houses in the very poorest part of Edmonton, 201 men had joined the Army." By May 1918, Mr John Barker of Bonner Hill Road, Kingston upon Thames, Surrey, had had no less than 34 members of his family – sons, grandsons, nephews and sons-in-law – serving in the armed forces, six of whom had been killed. The King himself sent congratulations to another cleric, the Reverend Cox, rector of Dartington, Devon, whose five sons had all enlisted and been given commissions. Two of them had come back from Argentina to join up. William Muir, a former sergeant in the Black Watch, travelled all the way from Dawson City, in the Yukon, northwest Canada, to join up. Unfortunately, in celebrating his return to Britain he had a drop too much to drink and found himself before the Thames Police Court charged with drunkenness. But happily, on hearing of the reason for his inebriation, the magistrate allowed Muir to go free. And from Singapore to Kingston upon Thames, travelling at his own expense, came magistrate Arthur Milthorp to join the East Surrey Regiment. Sadly, he was to be killed in action on the Somme in August 1916. Another long-distance recruit was Noel Savage, who travelled from Borneo to Bangor, via Japan, Russia, Finland and Sweden.

Age appeared to be no bar to serving King and country. Sidney Watson, a Hitchin grammar school boy, enlisted at 15 and served for nine months in France with the Royal Fusiliers in charge of a Lewis gun team. His true age then became known and he was sent home. As soon as he could, Sidney joined up again, and in June 1917 became a second lieutenant in the Royal Flying Corps. At 15 years old, Harry Davis from Camden Town also enlisted in the Royal Fusiliers as soon as war was declared. He spent his 16th birthday at Gallipoli and his 17th in the trenches on the Western Front before being wounded on the Somme. William Young, from Woking, Surrey, enlisted in the Royal Sussex Regiment at the even earlier age of 14. He returned home from France in September 1916, "suffering from shock after being buried by the explosion of a German shell". That January, *The Times* had reported: "A Sussex boy named Jannaway has been discharged from the Army on his 15th birthday. He enlisted in the Artillery 12 months ago, went to France in May, and was at the Battle of Loos and other engagements." Private John Masters of West Ealing, whose father was also a private but in the Royal Army Medical Corps, joined the East Surreys when only 13 years and 8 months old in September 1915. And when Arthur William Peyman was charged at Greenwich in October 1915 with being an absentee from his regiment, Mrs Peyman produced his birth certificate which showed that her son was only 14 and not 19 as he had claimed when he enlisted. The same month, at the other end of the age scale, William Hearn, a 54-year-old park keeper at Bushey Park, Middlesex, who had already served 30 years with the East Surreys and had four sons in the army, was commissioned as lieutenant and quartermaster in the 2nd Battalion of Royal Welch Fusiliers.

Sometimes there were financial and material inducements to enlist. Lord Aberconway offered a bounty of £5 for every recruit to Kitchener's Army from families on his estates in the Vale of Conway. Men of the North-Eastern Railway Company who joined up received the assurance that they would "have their places kept open for them". Furthermore, "the Company will give allowances to their wives and families or other dependents, and, so far as possible, will let their families continue to occupy the company's houses". Likewise the South Metropolitan Gas Company assured employees who enlisted that no appointments to the permanent staff would be made until the end of the war and that "when peace is declared applicants for such positions will be required to produce satisfactory evidence of what they have done for their country in her hour of need". The West End sporting tailors' firm Aquascutum told its customers that they had sent a notice to all their firm's employees that read: "We think it is absolutely necessary for every single man between nineteen and thirty to answer his country's call. We shall be pleased to pay half his present salary to any of our present employees while serving and will keep his situation open for him on his return. In the event of a parent or parents being dependent on the volunteer, full salary will be paid him during his service." Reginald Loder, squire of Maidwell Hall, Northamptonshire, offered a village cross to the parish in the county showing, in proportion to population, the greatest number of volunteers: 224 parishes were qualified to compete for the honour; 115 entered the lists, with Church Brampton winning the cross, Castle Ashby coming second and Wadenhoe third.

Back in August 1914, Kitchener had deferred to Asquith when the Prime Minister told him that the introduction of compulsory military service might very well threaten the country's unity at such a crucial time. The very idea of conscription was anathema to most Liberals, to Labour supporters and to not a few Conservatives. But eventually, in January 1916, and despite the fact that a staggering 2,466,719 men had volunteered between August 1914 and December 1915, conscription had become inevitable. A register taken in August 1915 revealed that there were over two million single men of military age still not in the army. That autumn Lord Derby, the Director General of Recruiting, launched a scheme to attract more volunteers, but the number of men coming forward remained insufficient. And so on 5 January 1916, Asquith introduced the Military Service Bill. It was finally approved on 24 January after a heated and often bitter debate, with opposition coming not just from pacifists but those who were against it on legal and moral grounds as well as from a humanitarian standpoint. Sir George Fordham, Chairman of Cambridgeshire County Council and prominent Liberal, went as far as resigning his party post as he "could not support a coalition government which has brought about compulsory military service". So too did Home Secretary Sir John Simon, who resigned his Cabinet post and joined the Royal Flying Corps.

Under the terms of the Military Service Act, from 2 March 1916, all single British male citizens aged between 18 and 41 were now liable to be called up. On 25 May, a second bill, extending the call-up to married men, received the Royal Assent. Exemptions were granted for those engaged on work of "national importance", the sole supporters of dependents, the medically unfit and approved conscientious objectors. Tribunals were to consider applications for exemption and to test the sincerity of those conscientious objectors – soon to be dubbed "conchies" – who refused to bear arms.

Back on 6 December 1915, Frank Lockwood had been canvassed under the Derby Scheme: "I had to say whether I was willing to join, or the reason why I had not done so. The reason I gave was that I was not physically strong enough for a soldier's life." Now, at the beginning of March 1916, he was less than impressed with the Military Service Act which he thought was far from fair: "... the very way in which it was gradually introduced was shady. The Registration Act – though little notice was taken of it at the time – was the first step. The Irish, who were not included in this registration, saw the shadow & flocked back to Ireland in boatloads & in the Bill their 'patriotism' is rewarded by their exemption. The first groups have had their calling up notices. The result is that they are

'whining' and 'squealing' & finding fault with everything and everybody."
At the end of the month Lockwood noted: "The majority of single men
have now resigned themselves to the provisions of the Military Service Act
& are ready to be called upon. The greater portion of shirkers now are
the married men, who besides being 'slackers' are also 'wrigglers'." And
in August he was still fuming: "While national service has been forced
upon the English people & the tribunals have had instructions not to give
exemption except in case of absolute necessity, Irishmen can come over &
earn the high wages which are now the rule, while our lads are sent away
to face death & hardship of all kinds for 1/- [one shilling] a day."

A month later, on 2 September, after bemoaning the lack of freedom
in wartime Britain, Lockwood noted:

> During the past week or so, the police have been conducting systematic
> round ups of shirkers, laggards and slackers, as the papers call them.
> Theatres, Music Halls, Parks, Football Matches etc. have come in for
> their share. The idea has been to catch every man who visited the
> above places & ask him to produce papers or registration card showing
> why he is exempt from military service. They have even gone as far
> as to lock the exits, while the search is on. Men who fail to produce
> satisfactory reasons are taken to the police station pending enquiries.
> Such a position is not nice for any man to be in.

As well as "shirkers, laggards and slackers", there were those who
sincerely believed that the war was wrong and wished to have no part
of it. Back in late July and early August 1914, the Labour Party had
opposed the war in principle, but with the German invasion of Belgium
and Britain's declaration of war, the party divided. Its small group of
Parliamentary pacifists were now led by James Ramsay Macdonald. In
January 1924 Macdonald was to become Britain's first Labour Prime
Minister, but ten years earlier, on 2 August 1914, he over-optimistically
predicted, "In three months there will be bread riots and we shall
come in." A year later a petition was got up in Macdonald's Leicester
constituency which expressed its "detestation of his attitude, utterances
and writing" and repudiated "his claim to represent Leicester, and calls
upon him to resign his seat forthwith". Macdonald's future Chancellor
of the Exchequer Philip Snowden was also, "owing to his views on the
war", barred from speaking at a temperance meeting at Holmirth, near
Huddersfield, in December 1915. Other Labour leaders like George

Lansbury and the party's founder Keir Hardie, dubbed "Keir von Hardie" by *Punch*, continued passionately to denounce the war, and the Union of Democratic Control called for a negotiated peace.

In November 1914, the No-Conscription Fellowship was created, with Clifford Allen as its chairman and Fenner Brockway as honorary secretary. It was open to men of all political and religious persuasions liable for call-up, who would refuse to fight on grounds of conscience. The following month, the Fellowship of Reconciliation, an association of Christian pacifists of all denominations, was founded. Now, with the passing of the Military Service Acts, members of all these organizations soon found themselves up before tribunals.

One of the first to appear was Herbert Stanley Morrison, who within three days of his birth on 3 January 1888 was found to be totally blind in his right eye. As such he would have been automatically exempt from military service, but the rising London Labour politician chose to make a stand on the issue. Back in September 1914, Morrison had denounced the war in the *Labour Leader* in a series of articles, the most infamous appearing in the issue of 3 September:

> *"Your King and Country Need You"*
> *Go forth, little soldier! Though you know not what you fight for*
> *– go forth! Though you have no grievance against your German*
> *brother – go forth and kill him! Though you may know he has a wife*
> *and family dependent on him – go forth and slay him; he is only a*
> *German dog. Will he not kill you if he gets the chance? Of course he*
> *will. He is being told the same story! "His King and Country Need*
> *Him!"*

Now he told the tribunal at Wandsworth that he was a socialist by religion and a member of the Independent Labour Party. As such he had a deep conscientious objection to taking part in a war that he believed to be a result of the capitalist system. Previously he had been forthright in denouncing anyone who had assisted in the war effort, even those who knitted balaclavas for the troops. But now he agreed to undertake alternative service, offering to be a dustman in Wandsworth. This generous offer was turned down and Morrison was directed to work on the land. For his "compromise" Morrison was attacked on both sides. Fellow conscientious objectors thought that he had sold out and should have gone to prison for his principles, while at the same time he was considered a cowardly "conchie" by "super patriots". But now, as he told a friend, instead of prison or the trenches, "I'm off to pick currants." Morrison, one of Churchill's most inspired appointments as Home Secretary in the next war, did his agricultural work at Letchworth Garden City, while still conducting London Labour Party business. His skills as a politician were obviously greater than as a gardener; on one occasion he pulled up recently planted flowers and cabbages while leaving the weeds.

Morrison was one of the 16,000 conscientious objectors to military service during the war, a small enough number when compared to the nearly six million men who did serve in Britain's armed forces during 1914–18. Although small in number, they attracted both a disproportionate amount of space in press and Parliament and almost universal public obloquy, as did those who publicly supported them. As early as February 1916, *The Times* reported: "… the name of Mr Arthur Sherwell, the local member of parliament, has been struck off the list of vice-presidents of the Huddersfield Liberal Club owing to his hostile attitude towards the Military Service Act and his general political conduct during the war." In May 1916, Godstone Rural District Council in Surrey unanimously decided to refuse to employ conscientious objectors to military service. Two months later London County Council's Education Committee proposed that conscientious objectors should now be considered ineligible for the Council's scholarships. Home on leave from France, Captain Harold Wilberforce-Bell noted that in the streets of London there were: "… a great number of young men – known as 'Fetch Me's' – about, many more than there should be. These are England's cowardly and most useless people – its conscientious objectors." A view shared by a Yorkshire farmer who, in September 1917, told conscientious objector John Boast to "go and hang himself". In Chislehurst, Kent, Ethel Bilbrough declared: "Naturally every coward and slacker thinks fighting is 'wrong'! and the most ludicrous reasons are being put forward by men who want to get exemption owing to their conscientious (?) principles. The other day a man who said he was an artist, claimed exemption on the grounds that he 'could not mutilate anything so beautiful as the human form'!!" At Knutsford, Cheshire, shopkeepers refused to serve conscientious objectors housed in the local prison, "and they were compelled to go long distances to buy foodstuffs. On their return, the crowd met them, and their cycles were smashed and their clothing torn." And Irishmen, not subject to conscription, were likewise treated in a hostile fashion. In July 1917, farmers in West Lancashire were refusing to employ Irish labourers of military age during the potato harvest as "strong feelings prevail against these men".

The tribunals, some 2,000 in number by the end of March 1916, often gave a very rough ride to conscientious objectors, despite the stipulation that their members should be of "impartial and balanced judgement". Howard Marten found his local London tribunal "pretty hostile", and Stephen Winsten complained of the attitude of the military representative on his tribunal who asked him, "Don't you think, Mr Winsten, that this country that's provided you with work, given you a good job as a teacher, don't you think you *owe* something to such a country?" Winsten, who found it difficult to label himself as either a religious political objector, was told, "… we'll put you down as a political objector. And therefore you can't get exemption. We can only give it to religious objectors." On the other hand, Wilfred Littleboy had to admit at the Birmingham Tribunal that the chairman – Lord Mayor and future Prime Minister Neville Chamberlain – was "within limits, entirely considerate". After hearing Littleboy's case, Chamberlain told him, "Well, I'm proposing to adjourn this case for a month to give you time to think it over, to come back with a further suggestion in a month's time." Littleboy told Chamberlain, "I can't give to you the slightest expectation that I shall make any change." To which the Lord Mayor replied, "Well, nevertheless I'm going to give you that opportunity." Littleboy, who as an "Absolutist", was unwilling to accept anything short of the absolute exemption that tribunals could give, received repeated prison sentences and was not released until April 1919.

Both in prison and in the army, treatment of "conchies" varied. Howard Marten was an "Alternativist" who rejected military service but was prepared to accept alternative form of employment. In the event, he was called up and, while serving in the army at Rouen, claimed that "we were forever being threatened with the death sentence. Over and over again we'd be marched out and read a notice; some man being sentenced to death through disobedience at the front … all done with the idea of intimidating us." Nearly half a century later, Absolutist Harold Bing was to tell an interviewer: "I saw a couple of warders drag this C.O. [conscientious objector] down several iron staircases feet first, with his head banging on each iron step as he came down. I suppose he'd been ordered to come down to interview the governor or something, and he refused to move and they just dragged him down." G. A. Sutherland, a former master at Harrow School, was sentenced to 12 months' hard labour by a district court-martial at Dublin for refusing to obey military orders. He told the court-martial that he believed return to prison was "the best service he could render", and added, "I am proud to think I shall never be anything but a disgrace to any army in which I may be deemed to be enlisted." George Easton positively welcomed a prison sentence. At West London Police Court in February 1916, he was charged with breaking a shop window. It was his thirteenth appearance for such an offence, and when arrested he told the police: "If they treat me as well as they have done in prison, I shall go on breaking windows. I would sooner be in prison than fighting in the trenches."

The tribunals also had to give judgement on men seeking exemption on other grounds. Some of the cases they heard were out of the ordinary, to say the least. The sexton and grave digger at Dulverton, Somerset, was granted four months' exemption after the vicar told the tribunal that an able-bodied man was needed for the job as the graveyard was a mass of rock. At Wealdstone in June 1916, a successful application was made by a firm of cabinet-makers for temporary exemptions for three employees. It was given because the firm were wholesale coffin-makers and sadly "the demand was now very heavy at home and abroad". In January 1917, a 19-year-old unsuccessfully claimed exemption at Spring Gardens Tribunal, London, on the grounds that he had had two attacks of pleurisy 13 years before. More fortunate in more than one respect was a machinist who told the Birmingham Tribunal that he had come into a legacy of £10,000 and had legal affairs to settle. He was granted a month's exemption. But the Hendon Tribunal refused exemption to Bernard Dillon, husband of the reigning queen of the music hall Marie Lloyd and a well-known jockey, despite the fact that he claimed to have his parents and four brothers all dependent on him. Dillon became a private in the newly formed Machine Gun Corps, but got into trouble in October 1917 when at the Café Royal he hit a waiter over the head with a soda-water bottle. Up before Mr Allan Lawrie at the London Sessions, Dillon pleaded guilty to common assault and was bound over for two years. The court heard that "the military authorities wished Dillon to come back to his regiment and be available for draft". Upon which Mr Allan remarked he "was glad to hear that there was a likelihood of Dillon's going to a place where violence was permitted".

Sir Charles Cayzer of St Lawrence, Isle of Wight, was much more fortunate. He obtained exemption for both his house steward and secretary at the Isle of Wight Rural Tribunal. This was because, a tribunal member opined, "Sir Charles deserved well of the country as one of his daughters was the wife of Admiral Jellicoe and another the wife of Admiral Madden". With no such useful connections, Rutland Boughton, Director of the Glastonbury Festival School and organizer of the August 1916 Festival of Music Drama, was refused exemption by the local tribunal. This despite the rather optimistic claim that his work would draw in money formerly spent at Bayreuth and Oberammergau. In Rochester, a local dentist was given six months' exemption after producing models of jawbones to demonstrate the restorative work he was doing for wounded soldiers. And Mrs Norton of Altrincham, Cheshire, was granted total exemption for her eighth son, having already seven serving in the army, one of whom was a Boer War veteran and a sergeant major with the Grenadiers. But a man with 11 children, one already serving in the army, and with four brothers also in uniform, was refused exemption by the Hitchin Tribunal. So too, at nearby St Albans, was Gilbert M. Dunn, sixth son of gentlemen's outfitter and hatter George Arthur Dunn. Gilbert Dunn, described at his hearing as "a fruit and vegetable grower", was an Absolutist conscientious objector, telling the tribunal that he would not even kill a worm. Neither he nor his five non-combatant brothers would enter their father's business, as felt was used there. Since infancy Dunn had lived on a non-flesh diet and, while refusing to bear arms, he was willing to continue to work on the land. At Carlisle Tribunal, without realizing the comic double meaning, the local paper reported: "... the Military Representative appealed against the exemption of William Blake, aged 35, unmarried, a slaughterman in the employment of Mr George Rigg, pork butcher. The Military Representative suggested that Mr Rigg should slaughter himself. Mr Rigg stated that he could not slaughter himself."

At the City Local Tribunal in March 1917, the Principal Registrar of the Province of Canterbury made an unsuccessful appeal for his 40-year-old managing clerk, claiming that the man was "indispensable owing to his knowledge of the marriage law". Equally unsuccessful was a Cheshunt man who told the local tribunal that he was "the sole support of his two dwarf sisters, whose heights were 4 ft and 3 ft 9 in". In July 1917, a week before the costly Third Battle of Ypres began, Mr Bettesworth Piggott at the House of Commons Appeal Tribunal granted an exemption to a cat's-meat man, but told him that he "must find work of greater national importance. There were too many cats about. They drank milk, which would be all very well if they caught mice, but they did not do so." A month later a member of a firm of confectionary manufacturers requesting exemption told the Southwark Tribunal his supply of "bull-eyes" to the army was "an absolute necessity to the men at the front". In September four months' exemption was given to the music hall comedian Whit Cunliffe by the Kent Appeal Tribunal. In claiming exemption, Cunliffe told the tribunal that since the war began he had sung at more than 700 concerts for wounded soldiers and other war charities without asking for any fee. And at the Shoreditch Tribunal a firm appealed for exemption for an employee who was "a director, traveller, buyer, manager, acted as cashier and costs clerk, loaded the vans, kept the place clean and made himself generally useful". *Punch* commented, "… it is just as well that they added the last item, or people might have thought he was one of those slackers we hear so much about." The same number of the magazine noted that: "A woman at West London Police Court has been sentenced for masquerading as a man. Several conscientious objectors are now getting very nervous on sighting a policeman."

There were men who resorted to most extreme measures to avoid serving King and Country, as in the case of John Henry Brown, a Bristol carpenter. On 17 June 1918 he was fined £10 for maiming himself to evade military service. The court was told: "He had placed the first two fingers of his right hand through holes in a piece of wood, and put them under a circular saw in motion, both fingers being severed." Also up before the magistrates at Bristol was Alfred Goodman Dunn, described as "a conscientious objector who dressed as a woman in order to evade military service". He had also posed as deaf and dumb. He was fined £2 and handed over to the military; in imposing the fine the magistrate said "it was the limit of cowardice for the defendant to pose as a woman and as deaf and dumb". At Little Dean in Gloucestershire, Rosina Lewis was sentenced to seven days' imprisonment in May 1918 for aiding her deserter husband Sapper Lewis of the Royal Engineers. The police had found him sewn up in a mattress cover when they searched the Lewis home. At Barton-on-Humber police court, the wife of merchant seaman Frank Hoodless received a fine of £5 with £1 8s 6d (one pound, eight shillings and sixpence) costs for altering her husband's birth certificate, "to aid him in evading military service". In West Hartlepool, a man about to be arrested by the police as a deserter shot himself rather than serve in the army. His own step-sister had "shopped" him, telling the subsequent inquest that she was ashamed that "the man should stay in bed everyday till dinner-time, while her mother went out to work on munitions". More tragic was the fate of 30-year-old Thomas Weedon, his wife and seven-year-old son. On 9 February 1917, they were found dead in their beds with the gas taps full on at their home in Morland Road, Croydon. Weedon, who was just about to be called up, left a letter behind saying that rather go into the army he had decided with his wife "to end everything". Equally sad was the case of Anna Maria Wilmington, a 65-year-old grandmother of Gittisham, near Honiton, Devon. In June 1916, she was charged with the murder of her grandson William Franks. "Worried about the prospect of the boy having to join the Army", she had shot William as he lay in bed. Anna was found insane and was ordered to be detained at His Majesty's pleasure.

In September 1916, Frank Lockwood, soon to be called up himself, noted in his diary: "During the last five or six weeks complaints have been made throughout the country about the various medical boards & their passing unfit men. The charges are quite justified, if they refuse a man, well, he *must* be in a bad state." As these complaints were aired and blunders came to light, the press revelled in stories such as that of Private A. Brown of Holbeach, Lincolnshire, a blind veteran of Mons, who in July 1917 received, for the third time in two months, a call to be re-examined. And a month after the Battle of Jutland in which he had played a gallant part, Petty Officer E. G. Jones of Brentford, Middlesex was served with papers calling on him to report for military service. In Hull when call-up papers were served on a five-month-old baby, his exasperated mother took him along to the recruiting office and there finally "satisfied the military authorities than an error had been made".

For those patriotic Britons who, due to their age or other reasons, were unable to serve in Kitchener's New Armies, there was no shortage of other ways and organizations in which they could do their bit for King and country. And "no movement showed the public spirit of the maturer men of Great Britain and their willingness to do service for the nation in its war needs than the Special Constabulary". And as early as 22 September 1914, Charles Balston was recording in his war diary that: "The King expressed his satisfaction at hearing that 30,000 citizens of London had enrolled themselves as special constables for the

Metropolitan Police District and the patriotic spirit and sacrifice evinced in the performances of their duty." One of them was John Alfred Newman, who had served with the police in Jamaica and was now enrolled with "V" Division of the Metropolitan Police at Kingston upon Thames. And at 91 years old, Luke Langley of Little Chart, near Ashford, Kent, was the country's oldest special constable, and in May 1917 was still going out on duty "when emergency arises".

A younger colleague was 45-year-old Hubert William Ord, a teacher at Blackheath Preparatory School. In his memoirs, which bear a more than passing resemblance to George and Weedon Grossmith's *The Diary of a Nobody*, Ord recalled, "On the declaration of war I was some time much puzzled where my duty lay; whether to throw up my work and endeavour to enlist…. However, I was able to do some direct work which seemed to be suitable for persons of my age as special constable." Ord joined "R" Division, "and in this I was particularly fortunate … as part of its charge had to look after Shooters Hill. For almost the whole of war-time my beat was there and in the surrounding district." Ord's duties, except during the Gotha daylight raids, were

> *at night, the beats being of four hours' duration at varied times between 8 pm and 6 am, when the regular police took over our work. Duty came along once every three weeks; this arrangement enabled one to do one's job with fair preservation of health. Otherwise the constant lack of sleep would have rendered teaching impossible; for one week it was endurable. The amount of time expended was, of course much more than four hours, as one had to make preparation for the night, don one's uniform and get up to spot, at times when often no conveyance was available."*

As the war went on, "air raids produced a considerably greater strain, since we were expected to go on duty whenever the raid occurred, whether it was our week or not, and I naturally hoped that the raids might occur on my nights of duty, but I am afraid that the enemy was not always considerate in that respect."

He was on duty both the night of "the first Zeppelin invasion" – 31 May 1915 – and again on Whit Sunday 1918 when London suffered its last air raid of the war. On the first occasion Ord was guarding the water reservoir at Woolwich Academy when he heard "the bugles from the military fort not far off sounding the alarm call" and saw "the long, luminous cigar-shaped outline" of the Zeppelin. It was, Ord reflected, "a strange thought to realize that we were watching the first time London had been attacked by an enemy since the time of the Danes". During the last raid in May 1918, he was detailed for duty at Goodge Street Underground station, where on arrival he found the platforms already filled with "people of all conditions of life, most of them of the poorer classes, and a large number of children". With them were "Mattresses of various styles … from light straw affairs made for light carriage, to the ordinary bed flock, which had been brought by the early ones, who, I gathered, were regular frequenters when the weather was 'Zeppelinish', and a profusion of miscellaneous provisions and papers such as one sees on a common on a holiday".

Ord's chief duties that night were to maintain order, to assist the sick and those feeling faint, and above all, "and this was the hardest task", to keep people from the edge of the platform. But the Specials undertook many other tasks including ambulance and salvage work after raids as well as the guarding of key installations such as railway bridges and gas works. And "it is worthy of record in history that the traitor Sir Roger Casement was transported across London to Brixton prison in a Special Constabulary car, in control of a Special Constable in uniform." Like Kitchener's initial recruits, the early Specials were not at first issued with a uniform, and at the state opening of Parliament in 1914, the Specials who lined Pall Mall and St James's Park were seen wearing all sorts of headgear from silk toppers and bowlers to cloth caps. Uniform caps were then issued which, according to the 1914-18 partwork *The Great War*, went "a long way to giving the Special Constabulary of the Metropolis an official appearance, and this at the time seemed as much as necessary. But the anti-German riots that broke out in the early summer of 1915 showed that there were many people, especially in the East End, and other poor parts of London, who would pay but little respect or obedience to 'Authority' so long as its representatives was not clothed in full uniform." So, after the usual wrangling about the cost, Specials were issued with plain blue uniforms with black buttons bearing the crown. The uniform was not only serviceable "but smart in appearance". And "the difference in the respect accorded by simple people to the wearers was noticeable from the start.… Such is the psychological effect on simple minds of a uniform."

An early appeal in Manchester for 5,000 Specials yielded 6,300 men, and by August 1917, 12,000 Mancunians had trained as Special

Constables, releasing 700 regular police for military service. Specials in Manchester also provided a force of mounted men, "some of whom had hunted in the days of peace with various hunts of the neighbouring county, Cheshire", for traffic duties. Leeds had "a Special Constabulary force of a very efficient kind, well adapted to the needs of that industrial centre". It included a motor section of 127 officers and men, and an observation unit of 181 men on the lookout for enemy aircraft. In addition Leeds boasted a corps of 93 "amateur firemen ... a valuable additional safeguard for the city in the event of fires whether caused by enemy acts or otherwise". Bristol's 483 Specials had the reputation of being the "best dressed" in the country. In Liverpool the port's Deputy Head Constable was to tell a reporter: "Apart from the consistently good services rendered day by day by the special police, probably their usefulness was most apparent during the anti-German riots following the sinking of RMS *Lusitania*. I have no hesitation in saying that had it not been for the excellent work done then by the corps the city's heavy bill of about £60,000 for damage done during the riots would have been very much greater."

When it came to policing Wales's capital there was a problem "differing very considerably from that of most British cities, for in proportion to its size Cardiff had probably a bigger alien population than any other". On and beyond the city's Bute Road, that "alien population" inhabited "mean little shops and rows of cottages contained boarding-houses, restaurants, saloons, and lodgings for almost every race. Some streets were given over to Dutch and Scandinavians, others to negroes and Chinese, and other Asiatics." At the best of times it was a hard task to police "Tiger Bay", but the war brought with it heavy additional tasks. Between August 1914 and August 1917, over 300,000 aliens had to be examined, registered and "filed for reference". Quite a few of the 1,149 Specials recruited by the end of 1916 were detailed to work in Cardiff's Aliens Registration Department while others did normal police duties. Of these, 36 elected "to act as mounted constables". Trained by an ex-cavalryman police sergeant, "they provided their own horses, free of all expense to the city".

In Glasgow, where a third of the regular police had joined the army, 3,000 Specials were initially recruited. The city's Chief Constable J. V. Stevenson told a writer that he believed that the Special Constabulary "is really a democratic movement: it shows that the laws carried out by the police are in full accord with the sentiments of the members of the community, and I have no doubt that it has had a moral effect in other countries than our own. The Continental countries wondered at our voluntary military system. Here they will see great numbers of men over military age coming forward to undertake police duty in order that fit men may be released for military service. It helps to show the spirit in which we entered this war."

Throughout the war *Punch,* in its usual fashion, poked gentle fun at the Specials. Another target was the Volunteers, the "Dad's Army" of 1914–18. Writing in July 1916, an anonymous platoon commander of the Volunteer Defence Force drew attention to the fact that the organization "throughout the country supplies an excellent example of how the spirit of patriotism can survive the blight of official discouragement and win recognition at last". In August 1914, the same writer continued, "There were a few far-sighted people in the country who realized that sooner or later every available man under forty-one would be required at the front, and that upon the surplus male population above and below this age would ultimately devolve the task of providing troops for home defence." With its hands more than full "with the tremendous business of raising a vast army and keeping it supplied", the War Office had little time or indeed inclination to take on the task of activating yet another military force. And so in the time-honoured British way, the job was left to well-meaning amateurs. Prominent among them was Percy Harris MP, secretary to the Central Association of Volunteer Training Corps from which "the Volunteer Defence movement derived its inspiration and its machinery of organization". Despite official indifference, it could boast some aristocratic backers like Lord Desborough, "the presiding genius of the 1908 London Olympic Games", and the Marquess of Lincolnshire, a distinguished ex-Cabinet minister. Soon, all over Britain, "men of every age banded themselves into platoons; these were linked up into companies, which finally in their turn, were merged into full-fledged battalions." Training was undertaken by retired officers and NCOs, and by March 1915 it was estimated that "over a quarter of a million men were voluntarily submitting themselves to military training and discipline". In London, the response was said to be "extraordinary" and quaintly titled units like the City Guards, the United Arts, the Inns of Court, the Old Boys, the Pharmacists' Corps and the London Volunteer Rifles sprang into existence.

The early days of the new force, sometimes known as the Volunteer Training Corps and on other occasions as the Volunteer Defence Corps, had an air of organized chaos, which was to be seen again in May and June 1940, when the Local Defence Volunteers (later the Home Guard) was called into being. One of its officers recalled, "At first I was platoon commander without a platoon. I had to find the men whom I was going to command. To do this I had to organize meetings in my district, canvass from house to house, and demonstrate the seriousness and utility of the undertaking." One difficulty he encountered was that "The Special Constabulary had already 'cornered' most men over military age.... But gradually I got together my platoon." Training took place in barns, deserted workshops, village halls and schools. The men were woefully under-armed: "At first we only had three rifles among fifty men – rifles borrowed from a local – and we had, generally, to be content with wooden dummies. Ultimately, a subscription list was opened, and a few more rifles were provided." Then there was the question of uniforms: "Many of my men were agricultural labourers who could not be expected to provide uniforms out of their own pockets. By various methods I obtained money sufficient to purchase uniforms for all the men, and it was a proud day when I saw my platoon in their grey well-fitting clothes." The War Office "looked askance at the whole movement" and banned the use of khaki but, after pressure from the Marquess of Lincolnshire in the House of Lords, finally and "half grudgingly" issued the men an armlet. It was red with the letters "G. R." on it and gave the Volunteers, in a very small way, official status as combatants: "The idea ... was that if the Germans landed in this country and we were called up, we could not, according to international law, while wearing these armlets, be shot as civilians in possession of arms. Encouraging, wasn't it?"

Many men became disheartened and started leaving, but then there began to be seen signs of improvement. In December 1915, at a concert in aid of the Kensington Battalion of the VTC, the Mayor announced that a royal seal of approval had been given, with Princess Louise, the Duchess of Argyll, accepting honorary command of the battalion. Some weeks later, in March 1916, the Volunteer Act of 1863 was revived and the Volunteer Forces were formally constituted and recognized for home-defence duties, and in December placed under the Territorial Force Association. The Volunteers now provided an umbrella for other quasi-military organizations including the National Guard and the Royal Defence Corps. The latter, created in April 1916, was mainly made up of old soldiers, and serving in its ranks was the father of Battle of Jutland hero Jack Cornwell VC. Their main tasks were "guard duties at prisoners-of-war camps, and also for the protection of vulnerable points such as railways and bridges". More important, perhaps, was the National Motor Volunteers, whose "private cars are placed at the public service". By the spring of 1918, the London corps of the NMV alone had reached a strength of 520 men and 433 vehicles. In two years they had transported no less than 668,000 soldiers who had come to the capital on leave or were returning to the front.

The King's uncle, the Duke of Connaught, became the Volunteers' Colonel-in-Chief, and the distinguished soldier General Sir O'Moore Creagh VC their Military Adviser. The effect of such formal recognition was "at once noticeable", a platoon commander noted. "I got my full platoon, and not only that, but I got rifles for them, and ammunition." The men of his platoon had been "splendid – they belong to all classes – we even have a judge who is a private in our ranks, and a very good private, too". When they took part in a full county battalion parade in the early summer of 1916, "I don't know how the other officers felt, but I know I was conscious of a certain pride when I saw those thousand men, properly armed and uniformed, going through their evolutions like tried soldiers, and remembered that all this had been done without asking the Government for a single penny!" Lord French, home defence supremo (*see* page 217), was in no doubt of their importance to his command, telling a City audience in November 1917, "I do not quite see how we can undertake the defence of this country now without the Volunteers."

In late 1917, a bleak time for the Allied cause, popular journalist Harold Owen attempted an assessment of the British national psychology and social changes after "three years of anguish". Owen was struck most of all by the change that had come over the pre-war "nut" or "knut". "The nut," Owen wrote,

> *was the finest flower of youthful male fashion. He was an elegant idler, strenuous only in getting "the last ounce" of his motor car. He smoked incessant cigarettes. He cultivated a manner almost effeminate. He made harmonies of neckties and symphonies of socks. Golf was too strenuous for him, and most things "too much fag." His chief attitude to life was to be "fed up" with everything that imposed any strain, physical, moral or mental. To social observers, he was quite a perplexing portent ... an apparently decadent type*

of masculinism... He furnished a text for many homilies and when the "flapper" emerged in the public limelight to keep him company, there did in truth seem every justification for pessimism concerning the future of the race if "nut" and "flapper" were to be the parents of the next generation.

But then, in August 1914, the country went to war and

the "nut" vanished and the Young Briton leapt to life. The call of his race was answered in his blood, and his fripperies dropped from him. He now lies under a many a white cross in the fair land of France – shot as he rode his despatch rider's motor-cycle in those early days of still moving armies, or brought to earth from Icarian flights high in the blue above the smoke and din of the battle-front – so that the despair of many a father's heart became one of the glories of his race.

An ex-soldier taxi driver told the Bishop of London, "What astonishes me is them 'knuts'. They used to be so tired that I had to drive them across from one side of the road to the other. But I've seen 'em now under fire, and they share with you the last cigarette and sandwich they have got." But not all were "nuts". In 1912, 186,147 emigrants had left the British Isles for Canada. One of them was 17-year-old Philip Woolfitt, elder brother of the future actor-manager Sir Donald Wolfit (who changed the spelling of the name to Wolfit). On the declaration of war, like so many others, he immediately returned from Canada to join up, and served with the Royal Engineers on the Western Front. Wounded during the Third Battle of Ypres, he died of his injuries in St George's Hospital, London. His obituary, which is typical of the undemonstrative yet proud manner with which the deaths of those fighting for Britain's freedom was met, appeared in Philip's old school's magazine:

PHILIP WOOLFITT

There was not a boy in the school who knew Phil Woolfitt who was not cut to the heart when he heard that he too had died of wounds. Leaving us in April 1912, he had spent a couple of years in Canada and was doing well when the war started. Like so many of our gallant lads he heard the call of the Mother Land at once, and eventually he was sent across to France. It was a joy to see him on his way out; the same bright, cheery, open-hearted fellow that had left us, but developed wonderfully and quite a man. He had not been in France long before he was badly wounded, and he died in hospital in London. It was with sore hearts that we laid him to rest in Newark Cemetery, and we grieve for his parents, but there was a curious thrill of pride and confidence as we look back on his splendid young life.

CHAPTER THREE

STOKING THE HOME FIRES

KEEP THE HOME FIRES BURNING
(Alternative title of Ivor Novello's "Till the Boys Come Home",
lyrics by Lena Guilbert.)

In the early weeks of the war, Ernst Lissauer, a German Jew "with the chameleon-like versatility of his race", composed the soon-to-become notorious "Hymn of Hate":

French and Russian they matter not,
A blow for a blow, a shot for a shot;
We fight the battle with bronze and steel,
And the time that is coming Peace will seal.
We will never forego our hate,
Hate by water and hate by land,
Hate by head and hate by hand,
Hate of the hammer and hate of the crown,
Hate of seventy millions, choking down.
We love as one, we hate as one,
We have one foe and one alone –
ENGLAND!

In September 1914, as Lissauer's composition was having its first public airing, the newspaper *Kolnische Zeitung* outlined a bleak future for a defeated Britain:

There will be no such country as Great Britain in existence at the end
of the war. In its place we shall have Little Britain, a narrow strip
of island territory peopled by loutish football kickers, living on the
crumbs that Germany will deign to throw them. Certain it is that the

laughable and childish military system of Britain will shortly fall to pieces. The once-mighty Empire, with her naval strength represented by the few old tubs which Germany will have left her, will become the laughing stock of nations, the scarecrow at which children will point their fingers in disdainful glee.

The feeling of hatred was mutual. By October 1914, Frank Lockwood was writing in his diary: "In this war the Germans have proved themselves veritable savages instead of the cultured nation which they led us to believe they were. They have broken nearly all the rules of warfare. They have destroyed cities & villages, butchered the inhabitants & thus rendered thousands of people homeless. Belgium has had to suffer severely for the check they inflicted on the Germans."

For the Purbrook family of Hornchurch, Essex, as for most people in Britain, the German invasion of Belgium had provided a clearcut reason and cause with which to go to war. When the family heard the news, "we were all actually glad," Annie Purbrook recorded in her war diary, "that sounds dreadful, but the English people can't stand bullying; it is not in our nature, and so far as we could judge that was what Germany had been doing in Belgium." As retired Indian civil servant Charles Balston noted in his diary: "Not content with violating the neutrality of a friendly country, the Germans at once, as a matter of policy, commenced to wreak their vengeance on the people of Belgium for daring to oppose them." After Balston had listed all the reported atrocities, culminating with the "sack of the University town of Louvain and the inhuman deeds at Dinant and Termonde", he reflected:

One has only to read the short abstracts like these to get some idea of the violence and callous brutality of the German army – and if one can only imagine for a moment our own English towns & villages, our women and children, our sick and old, subjected to such treatment one can realize in some small measure the debt we owe our Statesmen and our sailors and soldiers for saving us from such degradation and such horrors. Think of it men and women of England ... the German soldiers, whether officers or men, were no respecters of rank or persons – think of it and consider what would have been our feelings as a race if we ourselves had gone through such dire experiences.

Lord Roberts VC, the Empire's most distinguished soldier, "believed that German barbarism was a byword among civilized people", telling his friend Sarah Macnaughtan: "I have fought in the Indian Mutiny, and against Afghans, and Zulus, and Kaffirs, and Hill tribes, but none of these have ever committed such deeds of savagery as the Germans have done." Sarah herself was to recall: "… we were near enough to stricken Belgium to catch the echo of women's cries and the shrieks of young girls; we were near enough to know all about unarmed helpless people who were not spared by the soldiers in gray coats."

The popular press was soon awash with tales of the German atrocities. In the 5 September 1914 issue of *The War Illustrated,* an article entitled "Horrible Stories of German Fiendishness" informed readers: "The things done to Belgian girls and women, before their tortured, lifeless bodies with battered faces were thrown into a ditch, are so unspeakably dreadful that detail cannot be printed." More specifically: "An old man of the village of Neerhenpen had his arm sliced in three longitudinal cuts. He was then hung head downwards and burnt alive. At Orsmael, young girls have been ravished and little children outraged, and the inhabitants suffered mutilations too horrible to describe." The next issue of the mass-circulation magazine featured an artist's impression of the claim that near Charleroi, Belgian miners were forced to form a "living shield" for the German invaders. "Had Belgian soldiers fired upon the column they would then have shot their own friends. This may be Teutonic cunning," the caption continued, "but who can imagine the Allies adopting such barbarous methods?"

But a lady diarist in London had noted only a week before, following the Russian invasion of East Prussia:

> … *there seems to be the greatest hope & faith that the Cossacks will exact from the Germans the uttermost farthing of vengeance; it is hoped that the British soldiers will restrain themselves despite this provocation & maintain a high standard of humanity, but equally it is not thought brutal or lowering that the Cossacks should take their toll. Partly this is due to English people still believing that Russians are half-barbarians & it will be natural to them.*

The atrocity stories fuelled a wave of self-righteous indignation, anger and occasional violence towards Germans and their property in Britain. On 12 August *The Times* had reported:

> *That German residents and commercial houses in all parts of London are feeling a not unreasonable anxiety is evident in a variety of ways.*

One sees it in the West-end, where 10 offices of the German steamship companies are shuttered; where bakers and other tradesmen who have grown familiar to their customers under honest German names are now appearing as "Stewart and Co." or "Harris"; where the words "Deutsche Apotheke" are mysteriously disappearing from chemists' shop fronts, and the best-known purveyor of German Delicatessen has placarded the windows and walls of his various establishments with notices which say in large type that "The proprietor is a naturalized British subject" and as further insurance, that "During war-time 25 per cent of the takings of all my shops will be given to the British Red Cross Society".

The article reported that German-owned shops in Stepney had been attacked: "in two cases German bakers' shops have been wrecked in the night, and in one case a grocer has similarly suffered." One reason for the attacks was the "wicked stories that have gained currency of the intention of German bakers and purveyors of food to poison their provisions". Happily, "so far the evidence goes to show that the perpetrators of such acts of violence have not been Englishmen, but the more lawless of the other foreign elements, between some of whom and the German residents feelings always run high." In the war's first weeks enemy spies were supposed to be everywhere, and as late as August 1916, four soldiers were charged at Dover with assaulting a deaf-mute whom they took to be a German secret agent. One of them told the court that before the assault "he had questioned the deaf-mute in English, French, Dutch and German and the reply to the German question sounded like '*Ja*'."

British firms soon seized the opportunity to capitalize on the disappearance of competition from their German counterparts. "No more German Eau de Cologne," read an early wartime advertisement from Boots the Chemists,

What Cologne "where the Eau comes from" cannot supply, BOOTS, The Chemists, are prepared to furnish – the best Eau de Cologne, prepared with the finest genuine oils in Boots laboratories. Boots British Eau de Cologne entirely supersedes "4711", "Gegen-uber dem Julichs-platz", and the numerous other German colognes, and is, quite apart from patriotic reasons, preferred by the discerning.

And Cater, Stoffell & Fortt of Sulis Springs, Bath, demanded of potential customers: "Why mix German water & Scotch whiskey? The right Table Water to add is the British Table Water – Sulis." To Britain's motorists Dunlop addressed: "An appeal to PATRIOTISM. Will YOU answer it? Continental tyres are made in Germany by the enemy. Their purchase here assists him, while the use of *any foreign tyre* diminishes the employment of British workpeople. BRITISH-MADE DUNLOPS are far superior in quality, and can be supplied in unlimited quantities at usual prices. Fit them to your motors and cycles and help to keep the flag flying. What is your answer?" Meanwhile Sanitas sternly admonished British households: "<u>DON'T</u> USE GERMAN DISINFECTANTS USE THE ALL-BRITISH 'SANITAS' PRODUCTS." For those suffering from all forms of gout, rheumatism and other ailments, "Your annual Cure at Carlsbad, or Homburg, or Bad Nauheim, may have been interfered with this year and you are anticipating the winter with some concern. Try a BRITISH CURE this autumn at BATH, the historic British Health Resort."

Any hint of a commercial connection with the enemy was seen as business poison, and firms with German-sounding names were quick to assure potential customers that they were British, Allied or at least neutral in origin. At the end of August 1914 the Jaeger Co. published a notice to the public:

> To dispel all doubts which may have arisen in consequence of the name of a German Scientist forming part of the title of this Company, we point out the following facts:- The Jaeger Co was founded here with British Capital in 1883 to acquire the sole rights throughout the British Empire in connection with the System of Pure wool Clothing originated by Dr Jaeger. The Company has always been British, entirely under British control, and the greater part of the Company's goods is made in the United Kingdom.

At the same time an "Important Notice to the British Public" appeared in the papers announcing:

> It has been brought to the notice of Hahn's Corsets Ltd that unfair advantage is being taken of the present European crisis by some unscrupulous commercial rivals to spread a report that the principal and founder of this company – Robert M. Hahn – is a GERMAN.

This is a deliberate Lie and evidently done with a purpose to wrest the reputation which it has taken Mr Robert M. Hahn 25 years to attain as that of the GREATEST LIVING AUTHORITY ON PERFECTLY ANATOMICALLY FITTING CORSETS.

In reality, Mr Hahn was an American citizen, "belonging to one of the leading Southern families". So prospective customers could now buy his corsets, not only without fear that they were "injuring their delicate internal organs" but also in the knowledge that they were not helping the enemy.

A month later, Schweppes – "Always ask for Schweppes Malvern and leave alien waters alone" – was provoked to offer a £100 reward in order to track down those spreading false and malicious rumours that the firm was German. J. Lyons & Co was forced to go even further, bringing a libel action against rival grocers Lipton Ltd for suggesting that the Lyons directorate was "composed of Germans, and that by purchasing their commodities the public is assisting the enemies of Great Britain". The public were assured that the company, its directors, shareholders and shopkeepers were "ALL-BRITISH". Less convincingly, a barber's in Kentish Town was proud to announce: "This is a Ingelische Shopp". And rather smugly, the makers of Bovril were in the happy position to point out: "When you buy Bovril you can be sure you are getting the product of a genuine all-British and <u>always British</u> company. Bovril <u>always has been British</u> and consequently there has been no need to make any change in the constitution or directorate of the Company <u>SINCE THE OUTBREAK OF THE WAR</u>." A list of directors, which included one prince, three earls, a lord and a Victoria Cross winner, was included, as it afforded "the best guarantee of the entire absence of any alien influence or control". The advertisement concluded: "Insist on having Bovril, BRITISH TO THE BACKBONE."

Firms, commercial establishments and other organizations were quick to dismiss their German and Austrian employees and proud to announce the fact. On 26 August 1914, the Committee of Management of the Society of Automobile Mechanic Drivers of the United Kingdom passed a resolution expelling all members of Austrian and German nationality, "with the exception of those who are natives of Alsace and Lorraine". A fortnight later *The Times* announced: "Messrs. Spiers and Pond (Limited) inform us that at the earliest possible moment after the outbreak of war they discharged from their employ all un-naturalized Germans,

Austrians and Hungarians and have no intention of re-engaging them or of engaging any subject of the German and Austro-Hungarian Empires." At the beginning of November, *The Graphic* announced: "With reference to the recent campaign regarding German and Austrian staff in hotels, we may mention that the directors of the Alexandra Hotel, Hyde Park Corner, were among the first to make a clearance of alien enemy staff in all departments". And the decision to retain Hanover-born Mr J. Gottschalk as manager of the Northampton Corporation Tramways caused a veritable storm in the municipal tea cup that October.

On 21 November 1914 *The Graphic* ran a feature on "The Hated Name – and its British substitute": "Since August 10 (when they began) scores of advertisements have appeared in *The Times* announcing that people bearing Teutonic names have changed them." Up to 16 November, 164 names were listed, with *The Graphic* commenting: "What's in a name? The Germans, with all their love of Herr Wilhelm Shakespeare, cannot agree with him that a rose by any other name would smell as sweet; for many of those who live in this country are getting rid of their uneuphonious Teutonic names. In the changes effected there is room for laughter – and for the future bewilderment of genealogists." Among the first to change their names were Percy and Felix Rosenheim of Liverpool, Michael and Samuel Siegenberg of Holloway and Alfred Schacht of the Stock Exchange. The Rosenheims changed their name to Rose, the Siegenbergs to Curzon, while Schacht became Dent.

It was not just people's surnames that were "de-Teutonized". A spate of other name changes took place in 1914, and the process continued right up until the end of the war. Hanover Buildings in London's Tooley Street became Devon Buildings, and Mayfair's Coburg Hotel was renamed the Connaught Hotel. In Effingham, Surrey, the Blucher Hotel became the Sir Douglas Haig in June 1917, while Farnborough District Council went as far as to erase "the name 'H. Fehrenbach' from the dial of the clock in the Town Council chamber because of its Teutonic origins". And although Lewisham residents voted 41 to 17 against changing the name of Berlin Road to Belgian Road, Islington Council was petitioned to rename Giesbach Road, Upper Holloway, "as residents in the road object to the name". In November 1916, there was a minor crisis in London County Council over changing the name of Bismarck Road, Highgate, to Cavell Road after Nurse Edith Cavell, who had been shot by the Germans the year before. Her execution had been almost universally condemned and she had by now gained international martyrdom. Unfortunately, 14 Bismarck Road had been the scene of the murder of Margaret Lloyd, one of the victims of "Brides in the Bath" serial killer George Joseph Smith. In the summer of 1915, the public's morbid fascination with Smith's arrest, trial and execution had almost pushed the war news off the front pages. Thus "the name Cavell was objected to on ground that the road had obtained notoriety by a sensational murder trial." And so instead Bismarck Road became Waterlow Road.

In March 1915, the Harrogate Corporation refused to recommend the changing of the name of the "Kursaal" to "Coliseum" despite the Mayor's urging the change "on the grounds of patriotism and the effect on the revenue a German name might have". The Mayor's suggestion was ridiculed by Councillor Rowntree, who asked "if German music, Turkish baths and several treatments in the Harrogate cure bearing German names were to be abolished". With Italy still neutral, Rowntree warned the council against adopting the Italian name "Coliseum", as "those not for us might be against us". But "German music" had already come under attack. In *The Graphic* on 21 November 1914, readers were advised: "Be British! is a motto which is benefitting our musicians. Thus at the Queen's Hall concert on Saturday we were able to listen to Dr Walford Davies playing on a Broadwood piano his charmingly gay 'Conversations'. Germanic 'Kultur' has dominated the concert-room too long." And in May 1916, the sixth British Music Convention meeting at Harrogate had as one of its main objectives to find "means of ousting the Germans from the music trade of this country".

From the start, individual enemy aliens and their movements were closely monitored, as 19-year-old Teresa Kalman found to her cost. On 26 August 1914, Teresa, a music-hall artiste of German nationality, was fined £1 at Guildford for "being an unregistered alien enemy and travelling without a permit". The court was told that "the defendant, who is performing at the Guildford Theatre Royal as 'Tessie Tate, the Scottish dancing belle' stated that she had thought that her brother had registered her at Bethnal-green". A fortnight later, it was announced that none of Teresa's compatriots or any Austrian would now be permitted to enter the London Corn Exchange. Nor would they be allowed on the Weston-super-Mare golf course or in the club house.

Throughout the late summer, autumn and winter of 1914, the British public were fed a steady diet of German atrocity stories from both the Western and Eastern fronts. One told of how three dying and starving British soldiers had been tortured by the Germans on 9 October: "You want food. We will beat you to death. That is all you will get from us." On Boxing Day, *The War Illustrated* devoted four pages to German atrocities under the title "The Crown of Infamy on the Brow of 'Kultur': Civilization's Christmas account rendered against the Nation of Organized Barbarians who have drenched Europe in blood". But however horrific these events were, they were taking place a comfortably long way away. Then, "on Wednesday forenoon, 16 December, the British public were startled, but not dismayed, by the news that German cruisers were bombarding the towns of Hartlepool, Scarborough and Whitby." Nine soldiers, 97 civilian adults and 37 children were killed and in addition 466 soldiers and civilians were wounded during the bombardments. The youngest victim was a six-month-old baby and the oldest an 86-year-old lady. Frank Lockwood noted in his diary that day: "The Germans have again broken the recognized rules of warfare, this time by the shelling of unfortified towns." Churchill thundered: "Whatever feat of arms the German navy may hereafter perform, the stigma of the baby-killers of Scarborough will brand its officers and men while sailors sail the seas." In Chislehurst, Kent, Ethel Bilbrough bristled with anger. The German navy's action was "apparently their idea of valour and chivalry! Over 100 lives were lost – or rather massacred ... it is horrible to think that such things can take place in these enlightened [?] days, but then the Germans are proving every day that they have no sense of right or justice, or morality, or honour."

Charles Balston thought much the same. In his diary, after detailing German atrocities in Belgium, he noted: "The men who did these things were rightly called Huns. But who gave them that name? Who was it that urged them to emulate Attila and his Huns?" The answer came in the *Daily Telegraph* of 9 September 1914, in which a parallel was drawn "between Attila the German Emperor of AD 457 and his successor of today". Balston was forcibly struck by the way

> *Attila's proclamations to his troops before battle sound as if they were falling from the lips of the Kaiser ... that the Kaiser sought to emulate his progenitor there can be no doubt. Even so as far back as 1900 when he sent his brother Henry to China* [sic] *he enjoined him "to strike out*

with his mailed fist and spare not". To strike like Attila and his Huns. Did he not also invoke the grace of God & did he not allow his armies to strike as the Huns did when he had the Belgians at his mercy. The term was not of enemy origin. It was the appellation expressly chosen for his troops by the Kaiser – and it suited them. *

Writer Beverley Nichols, in 1914 a multi-talented and sensitive pupil at Marlborough College, recalled:

My father's reaction to the war was typical. The word "German" was forbidden in the house, a German was a "Hun" and as such must be described. This made intelligent conversation about the war even more difficult than in most British households, particularly for my mother. The least vindictive of women, the word "Hun" came uneasily to her lips, and she was constantly offending him. When she did, he would stick in his eyeglass, and stare at her, asking her who these "German friends of hers" might be? He knew no "Germans". He only knew "Huns".

John Nichols would undoubtedly have approved of the sentiments of retired colonial governor Sir Frederic Cardew, who hoped "that if the Allies win the Kaiser and Prince Rupert [of Bavaria] will be held personally responsible for the atrocities which have been committed & I hope they will be hanged". A view shared by Weedon Grossmith, co-author of the classic *The Diary of a Nobody*. In a letter of condolence to a friend whose brother had died he wrote: "That the poor dear boy should have been gassed and passed away in great pain distresses me so much and if *possible* increases my hatred to that scoundrel The Kaiser and his Court. That this cursed villain The King of Germany will come to a terrible end there is little doubt. Probably by his own people, but I am afraid it will be a quick end with a bullet instead of being shamed and disgraced before the end."

---

*On 2 July 1900 at Bremerhaven, Kaiser Wilhelm II addressed a contingent of the German expeditionary force to China which was sailing to help put down the Boxer Rebellion. He told the men: "Just as the Huns, a thousand years ago under the leadership of Attila, gained a reputation by virtue of which they still live in historical tradition, so may the name of Germany become known in such a manner in China, that no Chinese will ever again dare to look askance at a German."

The year 1915 was to bring a fresh crop of outrages by the "Huns", prompting Charles Balston to write: "The aims of Germany and her methods of warfare give a clear indication of the fate that would befall the Empire if we lost." January saw "demented Germany gloating over the proof that their Zeppelins can cross the North Sea and kill English children of four years and English women of seventy". In April, during the Second Battle of Ypres, came the first use of poison gas on the Western Front. Having "little hope of winning by fair fighting, the enemy developed the inhuman, forbidden methods of asphyxiation in preparing his diabolic method of attack". The poisoning of wells in German South West Africa [present-day Namibia] and the use of liquid fire on the Western Front were just two other examples of "this system of murder and brigandage" that Balston recorded in his diary. And then, on Friday 7 May 1915, came what the *Daily Express* the next day would headline as "The World's Greatest and Foulest Crime", the sinking of the crack Cunard transatlantic liner *Lusitania*.

Ethel Bilbrough's reaction to this latest example of the "Kaiser's bloodlust" was typical in Britain:

On the 7th May 1915 all Europe was thrown into a state of consternation at a diabolical act of the German fiends! They actually torpedoed (and sank) one of our largest liners, the Lusitania *coming from America; and twelve hundred civilians – Americans, English, and many other harmless people were drowned without a chance of escape. Words entirely fail to express what all England ... felt at this unparalleled outrage ... the relentless wickedness of such an act has not its like in all history I should think. But the Germans become more inhuman every day."*

Charles Balston noted that in Queenstown mortuary, the bodies of 30 babies were exhibited, and made "a harrowing & ghastly sight which filled those seeing them with an insensate desire for vengeance". He quoted with approval a speech made by Rudyard Kipling at Southport a few weeks after the *Lusitania* sinking: "After stigmatizing their crimes Kipling declared 'that there was only two divisions of mankind today Human beings and Germans' and that the world was sick of them and everything connected with them and all they do, say, think and believe."

Hard on the heels of the *Lusitania* sinking came the publication of the Bryce Report on Alleged German Atrocities. Lord Bryce was the epitome of the Great and Good, enjoying universal respect on both sides of the Atlantic. He had been British ambassador in Washington and his word carried enormous weight in the USA, to where many copies of the Report were immediately dispatched. It concluded, often on the flimsiest of evidence: "Murder, lust and pillage prevailed over many parts of Belgium on a scale unparalleled in any war between civilized nations during the last three centuries." On a more exalted plane, Lord Bertie, Britain's ambassador to France, confessed: "I began by not believing in German atrocities," but now, on reading the Report, felt "that I myself would, if I could, kill every combatant German that I might meet".

Charles Balston wrote that there was now a "National loathing of Germans": the business world and the country as a whole shared Kipling's anger and disgust "and were determined to have done with all German traders. The Stock Exchange led the way in excluding Germans; the Royal Exchange, the Baltic, the Metal Exchange, the Commercial Sales Room, Smithfield Cattle Market, Covent Garden and the Provincial towns followed suit." In Bristol a resolution was passed that "No German or Austrian-born subject shall *ever* be eligible for election as a member of the Bristol Stock Exchange".

The "anger and disgust" turned violent, as Frank Lockwood recorded in his diary on 14 May: "As a result of the outrage on the *Lusitania* there has been looting & destroying of German property in all parts of the country." In London, anti-German rioting began in earnest on Tuesday 11 May, and in the next 48 hours it was estimated that in Camden and Kentish Town over 150 shops were attacked. At first the police "seemed powerless to check the excesses of the mob, and thousands of men, women and children marched from shop to shop taking their fill of destruction, and stripping each place they attacked of everything it contained. The looting was not checked until mounted constables arrived and drove back the rioters." One shop that came under attack was Adolph Schoenfeld's tobacconist at 136 Chrisp Street, Poplar. Schoenfeld had been resident in Britain for over 40 years and his son Adolph Jnr was to serve in the Middlesex Regiment. Another long-term German resident was a baker who had been in business for 32 years. His shop "was filled with looters, who tossed loaves of bread into the streets. Bags of flour were flung in the faces of those who fought to get a share of the spoil. When the shop had been emptied, some of the women found a way into the living rooms at the back and brought out chairs, carpets and even baking tins." The initial cost of damage was put at £20,000, and *The Times* reported: "Several policemen were slightly injured by stones or cut by falling glass. One of the rioters had to be surgically treated for a severe gash on his arm. English bakers, fearing that the crowd might attack their shops in mistake, in several instances hung out Union Jacks from their windows." In the Commercial Road area most businesses remained shuttered as the mob moved from shop to shop and then house to house: "A sudden rush … a shower of stones, and a mad rush through broken windows or battered-down door; and the house was surging with shouting people. Ten minutes later the place would be empty and nothing of value left." *The East Ham Echo* reported that Goetz's pork-butcher's shop at the junction of High Street North and Harrow Road had seen "on many occasions threatening crowds gathered outside the shop, although no damage had previously done". But in the early evening of 14 May, a large crowd gathered and "stones began to be thrown, eventually shattering all the windows. Even the police were powerless to stop it – the stones just whistled over their heads."

How much of all this was due to righteous anger at the *Lusitania* sinking and how much just a heaven-sent opportunity to get hold of some loot was and remains a moot point. *The Times*, after reporting how a tailor's goose or flat iron had been thrown through one German's window with the inscription "Revenge for the *Lusitania*", noted: "the disturbances seem to have degenerated into quite indiscriminate looting by drunken crowds". It was in Poplar, where the crowds were reckoned to be the most violent, that: "Before the constables were able to attempt to disperse the mob, horse-drawn carts, handcarts, and perambulators – besides the unaided arms of men, women, and children – had taken everything away from the wrecked houses. One saw pianos, chests of drawers, dressers and the heaviest type of furniture being carted triumphantly through the streets. 'Here is wealth for the taking,' said one man who had possession of several spring mattresses, and was calmly driving his overloaded donkey cart down Chrisp Street." At Smithfield meat market "the few German butchers who ventured to seek supplies in the early morning speedily repented their rashness". The meat porters were determined "that no man of enemy nationality or origin should buy meat there. On discovery each German was chased as far as High Holborn by the mob."

The riots were not confined to the capital. From Liverpool the McGuire sisters reported to their sibling in Boston, Massachusetts, the "dreadful riots" there and at Seacombe "against the Germans. The Scotland Rd. women I believe were just like the women of the French Revolution, so I was told by an eyewitness.... Of course they will be punished but I think we all feel the same only we are more restrained." Arthur Askey, a 14-year-old pupil at the Liverpool Institute, had already heard how the headmaster, a German named Henry Victor Weisse, had changed his name to Whitehouse. Arthur now saw the German pork-butcher's shop owned by a school-friend's father being looted and then set on fire after the family's prized piano had been flung out of the top window. In Birkenhead's Watson Street the police tried unsuccessfully to protect a butcher's shop but were overwhelmed by the sheer weight of numbers of rioters. Thomas Lincoln's fish and chip shop in Price Street was smashed up and looted by a mob made up of women and boys on the flimsy pretext that he had sold fried fish to a German.

The *Newton Guardian* reported that in Earlestown: "Anti-Germanism centred almost entirely on one point ... this was the establishment of Mr Reiss, Earlestown's most highly patronized pork shop. Mr Reiss has been a most inoffensive citizen ... and for many years a naturalized Britisher, but the human passion is a dangerous thing when roused, and such events as the dastardly deed of Friday night [*sic*] are calculated to arouse the passions of everyone against all things Germanic." The police, although sympathizing with the outraged feelings of the mob, did their best to protect the shop and "edibles that were in the window were snatched out in the rushes, but the crowd could not get a footing inside the premises". The paper commented: "Even these situations were not without their ludicrous touches. 'Hey up,' said one woman to a 'special', brandishing half-a-brick in her hand, 'just let me heave this through them windows.' 'All right,' was the retort, 'but mind you aim at Johnny Riley's [a neighbouring shop], perhaps you'll stand a chance of hitting Reiss then.' This was almost worthy of *Punch*."

In Everton, the police had their work cut out when, after arresting 20 rioters, they found themselves jostled by the mob "in an endeavour to rescue their comrades, and the police had to use their batons to quell the disturbance". The cost of the damage in Liverpool, where 200 properties were attacked and gutted, was reckoned to be over £40,000. Other major disturbances were reported in Southend, Manchester, Nottingham, Bradford, Cardiff and Glasgow, where "in the Royal Restaurant, West Nile-street, a notice has been issued that no Germans or naturalized British

Above: "There were large crowds cheering the King at Buckingham Palace and one could hear the distant roaring as late as 1 or 1.30 in the morning. War or anything that seems likely to lead to war is always popular with the London mob."

Above: "Lloyd George said that Elizabeth Asquith had described Kitchener as 'a big poster'."
The new Secretary of State for War's image on an early recruiting poster.

Above: "All good pals and jolly good company." Albert Knowles, (on right with pipe) and his comrades of the Leeds Pals at their camp in the Yorkshire Dales, September 1914. Their uniforms did not arrive until November.

Above: "I was not exactly nervous about my speech today: I am very rarely that; but…the Guildhall…was absolutely crammed…and the atmosphere almost like that of hell." Asquith speaks at the Guildhall, Friday 4 September 1914.

BOROUGH OF DOVER.

NOTICE

THE INHABITANTS OF DOVER ARE INFORMED THAT
UNDER MILITARY ORDERS THEY ARE TO

Evacuate the Town

IMMEDIATELY

All Civilians resident in the District described on
the Annexed Sheet must meet at the PLACE OF
ASSEMBLY, at

and there await orders to leave for the country
together on foot.

Vehicles will as far as possible be provided
for those unable to walk.

Each person must carry warm clothing and
food and drink for 12 hours.

Mr. A. C. Leney will act as Evacuation Officer
with Headquarters at the Town Hall.

MAYOR.

G. W. GRIGG & SON, PRINTERS AND PUBLISHERS, "ST. GEORGE'S PRESS," DOVER.

District No. 8

Priory Hill, Tower Hamlets,
Tower Hamlets Road, De Burgh
Hill, De Burgh Street, Templar
Street, and all intermediate
places

PLACE OF ASSEMBLY :

EAST STREET

Above: "If William Comes."
Poster prepared for the
evacuation of Dover in the
event of a German invasion.

Left: "The most noteworthy
feature of the whole affair was
an entire absence of panic…
so that Germany may be said
again to have broken the laws
of civilised warfare in vain."
John Shields Ryalls,
aged 14 months and
Bertha MacIntyre of 22
Westborne Park, two
victims of the bombardment
of Scarborough, 16
December1914

IT IS FAR BETTER
TO FACE THE BULLETS
THAN TO BE KILLED
AT HOME BY A BOMB

JOIN THE ARMY AT ONCE
& HELP TO STOP AN AIR RAID

GOD SAVE THE KING

Above: "At a very modest estimate I should say that every bomb which falls on British soil is worth fifty recruits...so if the Zeppelins will only keep on coming they will hustle that extra 300,000 recruits that Lord Kitchener wants."

Above: "…All enemy aliens should be locked up…our people in the Army and the Navy should not be stabbed in the back by assassins in the shape of spies": German internees housed in horse boxes at Newbury Racecourse, October 1914.

Above: "The anti-German riots in the East End are assuming big proportions… thank goodness the people are fighting this danger themselves, instead of waiting for the Government to take slow measures…even your peaceful Mummy cries hurrah!" Rioters smash the windows of a German-owned shop in the East End of London following the sinking of the *Lusitania*, May 1915

Above: "Sex has nothing to do with patriotism or with the spirit of service. Women are just as eager to work for the nation as men are." A London bus conductress taking the fare from a member of the Royal Flying Corps.

Above: "In the ultimate analysis it is the nation with the best women that's going to win the war." Women working on artillery range-finders at the firm of Barr and Stroud, Glasgow, circa 1917.

subject of German birth would be served". In Nottingham a deputation of naturalized Germans called on the Mayor and made a public declaration of loyalty and allegiance to the King. Their

> *sympathies were entirely with this country, for which some of their sons were fighting. They viewed with abhorrence and detestation the cruel and inhuman acts committed by order of the German authorities by land and sea, and devoutly hoped that British arms might prove successful. "It is a most serious calamity for us," said Mr R. F. Stiebel, the spokesman. "Unfortunately it is impossible to select one's place of birth, but we have lived here in peace and happiness."*

Similar demonstrations of loyalty took place in Bradford, Manchester and in nearby Salford where the claims arising out of the riots would eventually cost the ratepayers nearly £1,700. In Gateshead a young man was ordered to pay £8 to cover the cost of a plate-glass window he had smashed. The Mayor told him that "whatever the Germans did we must be law-abiding. There might be murder in the end." Not murder but suicide claimed the life of naturalized British subject 54-year-old baker Frederick William Zohn of Galleywall Road, Bermondsey. He had lived in Britain for nearly 30 years, and killed himself after repeated attacks on his premises. At North London Police Court, the chairman of the bench told rioters: "You are not furthering the interests of your country by behaving in this way. It is not patriotism. It is the very opposite." In March 1916, the *Brighton Gazette*, looking back on the riots, commented:

> *After the sinking of the* Lusitania *there was (and the British Government never sought to deny it) a spontaneous outburst of popular feeling which, especially in the working class quarters of London and Liverpool, led to regrettable manifestations. These manifestations were repressed with the full police force at the disposal of the authorities. No German man, woman or child was seriously injured but in suppressing the disturbances injuries were received by 107 ordinary and special constables and 865 persons were arrested and charged with the offences.*

By the time the *Brighton Gazette* published its commentary on the riots, another atrocity had taken place which rivalled the *Lusitania* sinking in inflaming British public opinion against the "wicked Hun". In his diary Charles Balston recorded how:

... on 19th October (1915) the nation first heard of the execution of Nurse Cavell on the charge of harbouring British, French and Belgian soldiers in Belgium. On the 22nd the papers furnished a report of the arrest, trial, death sentence & shooting of this noble-minded woman.... She was condemned to death at 5 pm on 11th and despite every effort that could be made by the American minister at Brussels, was shot by lantern light at 2 am the next morning in the Prison of St Giles.

The McGuire sisters of Liverpool voiced the outrage felt by most people in Britain when they wrote to their sister in America of "poor Nurse Cavell ... the one the beasts of Germans have just executed in Belgium for assisting Belgians to escape. We imprisoned German women we caught spying + and did not shoot them. She wasn't a spy & had been nursing German wounded. She was brave and collapsed at the last minute, poor thing. It is to be hoped she fainted when they shot her. She has been fairly haunting me all day – fancy meeting your death like that – not a friend or even a woman near you."

Ethel Bilbrough, ultra-patriotic and Hun-hating, shared the outrage. As did Frank Lockwood: "Nothing has so moved the world as the murder of Nurse Cavell.... A sentence of death on a woman – a good woman at that – is terrible, but then, nothing is too bad for the German barbarians."

Some unscrupulous people tried to cash in on the Cavell epic. In June 1917, 19-year-old domestic servant Annie Elizabeth Middleton, who had posed as Nurse Cavell's sister (Edith was 50 when she was executed), was sent to borstal for three years for stealing clothes. Cavell's memory remained potent: in September 1939, at the beginning of a new world war, it was reported that crowded cinema audiences "repeatedly hissed the scenes of German troops marching victoriously through Belgium in the Great War when the film *Nurse Edith Cavell* was given its first presentation in Washington DC".

Only slightly less horror and indignation was felt in Britain at the end of July 1916 when the press reported that Captain Charles Fryatt, "the martyred Captain of the *Brussels*", had been "put to death by the Huns at Bruges on 27th July. His offence consisted in bravely piloting his vessel in defiance of a murderous U boat on March 28th 1915. During a voyage from Amsterdam on 22nd June last, Captain Fryatt, less fortunate, was taken prisoner, with his ship. Tried by mock court-martial, he was executed contrary to the enemy's own law, and before neutral influence could be brought to bear on those responsible." As ever, the Kaiser himself was saddled with the personal responsibility. The captain "was shot by special instructions of the German Emperor", despite the fact that "German naval prize regulations, issued on the eve of war, recognized the perfect legality of Fryatt's act in trying to ram the U boat that was attacking him". As the war approached its end, Charles Balston recorded that hatred of everything German continued to be at boiling point, especially with their conduct of the war at sea:

> *Anything lowdown or cruel done to our ships and our seamen … gives us such a feeling of disgust and anger for the evildoers that if it does not find expression it becomes the more enduring. Thus Mr Balfour when heard of the sinking of the liners* Leinster *and* Hirano Maru *in the Irish Channel in October 1918 in which 878 lives were lost could not contain his indignation and commenting on the news to his audience of American press representatives exclaimed: "Brutes they were when they began the war and brutes they remain at the present moment." Coming as these sinkings did at the end of the war, when the Germans were suing for peace, well did Mr Balfour add that he could not measure their wicked folly and that such crimes could not have gone on for so long if they did not commend themselves to the population which committed them.*

But throughout the war, amidst all the "Hate the Hun" clamour, some voices calling for objectivity and sanity were raised. Even *Punch* wrote in May 1915: "We are sorry to see that it has been suggested that the German eagle on Banbury Cross, placed there to commemorate the marriage of the Kaiser's father with the Princess Royal should be obliterated. It ought not to be forgotten, difficult as it is to realize now, that the Kaiser's parents were gentlefolk." And back in October 1914, Dr Gregory Forster, the Provost of University College, announced that

> *students of German and Austrian nationality at the college, some of whom had remained in this country … had applied for re-admission to the college. They were known and trusted friends of theirs, and they were glad to readmit them. There were also freshmen of German and Austrian nationality. Their admission to the college was only*

*continuation of that policy of freedom and toleration which was a
characteristic of the place.*

The following month, Captain Charles Mowbray, a badly wounded
officer of the Suffolk Regiment, tried to put the record straight when he
addressed the Cambridge Union. *The Cambridge Magazine* reported that:
"nothing could have been more impressive than the generous way in which
the speaker referred to our opponents. 'The Germans', he said, 'have behaved
on the whole pretty well' – and he went out of his way to contradict the
'exaggerations which have been appearing in our press at home on the subject
of their brutalities'." Mowbray went on to say that when the Germans had
shelled hospitals and churches it was "always because the English or French
were using them for avowedly military purposes".

If Mowbray's views, as a serving soldier, were treated with respect, the
same could not be said of the unctuous and priggish Archbishop of York,
Cosmo Gordon Lang. Early in the war Lang had tried to put in a good
word for the Kaiser, saying: "I resent exceedingly the gross and vulgar way
in which the German Emperor has been treated in the newspapers.... I
have a personal memory of the Kaiser very sacred to me." A view which
earned the prelate a singing poetic rebuke from *Punch*:

*His Grace of York maintains the Kaiser's
Merely the dupe of bad advisers
And, simply to avoid a fuss
Reluctantly made war on us.
One marvels what his Grace will say
When, peradventure, some fine day,
Thanks to his German friend, he hears
York Minster crashing round his ears!*

So great was the obloquy showered on the Archbishop that it was
said his hair turned white overnight, and from appearing a youthful
50-year-old he now looked 20 years older. Other divines also got into
trouble because of their apparent leniency towards the enemy. In April
1915, after the Rev. Edward Lyttleton, headmaster of Eton, had called
"for consideration for Germany", he was severely pulled up short by Dr
Wakefield, the Bishop of Birmingham. According to Charles Balston,
Bishop Wakefield "said it was highly dangerous to mislead the Germans
into thinking we wished to be lenient with them & that our first duty
was to bring them to their knees, to show them how unworthy their

STOKING THE HOME FIRES

ideals and conduct of the war was and to prevent them from doing it again". The Primate of Ireland, Dr Crozier, went further, declaring that the personal injunction to "love your enemies" had no application to "the German Emperor and his cruel vassals who were not only the enemies of civilization & of all that was lovely & of good report, but the enemies of our common faith & of Jesus Christ. It was they, he said, who had forced the war & we could never allow ourselves to suffer the fate of unhappy Belgium." Archbishop of Canterbury Randall Davidson in a Day of Intercession address "asked for the blessing of God upon the cause we were defending and maintained that we had a 'clear conscience' as regards the war." A week before, on the steps of St Paul's, the fire-eating Bishop of London, Dr Ingram, preaching to the City Territorials, told them "we were fighting for Christianity against paganism".

Charles Balston thought that "while the Church in 1915 gave a clear lead to the nation in the necessity of fighting for the country's cause & the cause of religious civilization, in 1916 the lead of the church was not so clear". And so he was pleased that on Christmas Day 1916: "The Church again stepped forward in the person of the Dean of Westminster to reprobate President Wilson's pretensions as a peace-maker at a time when there could be no peace and reminded us of only doing that which was honourable in the sight of men. We hardly needed the injunction; but it was right that the Church should voice it."

Ethel Bilbrough had nothing but admiration for her near namesake Dr Bilborough, the Bishop of Dover, and included in her war diary a short newspaper piece on him:

> *The Bishop Stands By: Here is the bomb-defying Bishop, the Bishop of Dover, who, "as an expression of sympathy with the East Coast raid sufferers, has decided to sleep in Ramsgate on moonlight nights and share the anxiety of any possible alarms". Doubtless he had the opportunity for doing a considerable amount of anxiety-sharing in the early hours of yesterday morning. This is the right spirit for the clergy, and if more of them were to show it – well, I leave it at that. Dr Bilborough, the Bishop, held many important appointments in the North of England, and in his youth was a great footballer.*

Christian charity and forgiveness towards the enemy appeared to be sadly lacking in the country as a whole. The Anti-German Union, founded in April 1915, demanded: "We must root out the German canker which has eaten its way deep into our national life. Unless that is done, all the sacrifices made by our soldiers and sailors will have been frustrated; and in the end Germany will gain by peaceful penetration the victory denied to her arms."

A lead to this end was given by the King in July 1917. Two years previously, on 14 May 1915, a week after the sinking of the *Lusitania*, the Garter banners and insignia of the Kaiser, his son the Crown Prince "Little Willie", Austrian Emperor Franz Joseph and four other German sovereigns and princes had been removed and degraded from the choir of St George's Chapel, Windsor. Now, on 18 July 1917, as Charles Balston wrote in his diary, "to the great gratification of the country, a proclamation was published announcing the new name of the Royal Family and renunciation of the use of all German titles and dignities such as Dukes & Duchesses of Saxony and Prince & Princesses of Saxe-Coburg and Gotha." A leading article in that day's *Daily Telegraph* declared: "... public opinion throughout the Empire will applaud the step." *The Times* journalist Michael MacDonagh noted in his diary that the change of the royal family name from "Hanover" to "Windsor" was "The talk of the town ... this means the complete severance of the Royal Family from all association with Germany. It is a matter of national importance and historic interest. This must tend to bind Throne and People in a still closer and more spontaneous fellowship." But the editor of the ultra-conservative *Morning Post,* the self-righteous and self-important H. A. Gywnne, wrote to *eminence grise* Lord Esher: "I think the majority of the people are of the opinion that these changes in names and titles are rather a foolish concession to a few anonymous letter-writers – most of the public really don't care a hang one way or another."

The King himself was in no doubt about what he felt about the Germans. A year later, on 29 July 1918, he gave an audience at Buckingham Palace to the dashing and debonair US Assistant Secretary of the Navy, 36-year-old Franklin D. Roosevelt. In the course of the audience, FDR noted that when the King talked about German atrocities in Belgium "too horrible to include even in the Bryce Report" and "the wanton destruction of property", his jaw "almost snapped". Furthermore, the King told his American visitor, "You know I have a number of relations in Germany, but I can tell you frankly that in all my life I have never seen a German gentleman."

The Royal Family's "complete severance" with all things German seemed to be more than amply justified in the light of the "news" only a few weeks earlier. In mid-April 1917 the papers reported "the loathsome admission that the German armies in the field maintain Corpse Utilization Establishments where soldier dead are 'rendered down' for lubricating oils, fats, and pig food". The "news" of this latest example of "Hun ghoulishness" came as no surprise to Frederic William Wile, pre-war Berlin correspondent of the *Daily Mail*:

> *I am quite sure that I was induced to believe in the Corpse Utilization confession not only by the evidence of my own eyes, but by what everybody who has lived in Germany knows of the everyday attitude of mind there towards such things. I am not generalizing. Not all Germans are thugs and murderers. But the national point of view towards the work of thugs and murderers is such as to make body-boiling and corpse factories not only possible but inevitable.... Germans are born and raised in an atmosphere of cruelty, tyranny and bestiality.*

And in his gold-medal-winning essay for the Royal Colonial Institute, nine-year-old Victor J. Wilmoth of Emanuel Road, Balham wrote, "The South Sea islanders, although they are supposed to be savage could teach the Germans a lesson in kindness."

Such "revelations" as the corpse factory only added to the already almost hysterical anti-German mood of the country. An Englishwoman married to a German was foolish enough to attract attention to herself "by saying in public hearing that 'Count Zeppelin was a gentlemen'". For that and for also not registering as an alien, she received a stiff fine of £25. Even more foolish was Charles Edward Kohler, a 30-year-old electrical engineer working in a Clyde shipyard. In December 1917, he was found guilty of a breach of the peace by shouting out in the street: "I am a German and proud of it. The British are cowards. I would die for Germany," and could count himself lucky to get off with just a fine of £2. Two months later, the Nore Yacht Club passed a resolution declaring that: "... no man of alien enemy birth is eligible for membership, or shall be introduced as a visitor or compete in any club competition. Any member competing against a man of enemy birth in England or elsewhere shall forfeit his membership." At Highgate and Muswell Hill stern notices appeared, stating: "No person of enemy birth or nationality

allowed in the workrooms of the Highgate War Hospital Supply Depot."
In Henley-on-Thames, the wife of a tobacconist serving in the Royal
Navy also put up a notice. It read unequivocally: "I will not knowingly,
now or after the war, serve any enemy alien. Conscientious objectors'
custom not required."

At the annual conference of the Amalgamated Union of Operative
Bakers, Confectioners and Allied Workers of Great Britain and Ireland
there was a heated debate over the proposal from the Newcastle branch
that: "No enemy alien be allowed to join the union for 20 years after
the cessation of the war." The Portsmouth branch suggested reducing
the boycott to five years, but this was rejected. From Sheffield, delegate
Hawksworth strongly objected to the resolution. "There were aliens in the
country," he told the conference, "who were perfectly loyal to the principles
of the union, and this resolution would rule them out." Hawksworth
generously wanted "friendship for all, no matter what colour they were,
white or black or any other colour". In the event, a decision was deferred
and the matter referred to the Baking Trade Joint Industrial Council, "to
see what the employers were going to do".

To show friendship, let alone compassion, to any German in Britain
was asking for trouble. In July 1918, the press reported the case in Banbury
of young Percy Blencowe, who was fined £5 "for interfering with the
administration of a German prisoner camp". In a misplaced act of kindness
Percy had given some tins of cocoa to German prisoners of war, and the
"magistrates expressed the hope that the punishment would be a warning
to others". Similarly, at Leigh in Lancashire, a 16-year-old canal-boat
boy received a month's prison sentence for giving cigarettes to a German
prisoner of war. Less altruistic, one suspects, were the motives behind the
actions of Shrewsbury builder's wife Mary Hayes and her maidservant
Alice France who were fined £10 and £2 respectively for breaches of the
Defence of the Realm Act. The court was told that: "Mrs Hayes's house
and garden face the recreation area of a German prisoners' camp. A letter
box was found hidden outside the barbed-wire barrier of the compound.
Letters from Germans were found in France's box. She stated that the
letters she sent to the prisoners were drafted by her mistress. In one was
the phrase, 'I would fain clasp thee to my bosom.'" The Bench was less
than impressed and thought that the offence would "likely to lead to the
escape of prisoners and characterized Mrs Hayes's conduct in associating
with murderers as disgusting and criminal". A lesser fine of £1 with costs

of £2 2s (two pounds, two shillings) was received by Ethel Walker, the wife of a fruiterer in London's Holloway Road. Her misdemeanour was to send bottles of stout, at 10d (ten pence) a bottle, to Herr Rehttens, the former German consul at Middlesbrough, and now an inmate of an aliens' internment camp.

In June 1918, Eton Rural District Council protested against "British labour being employed to empty cesspools for German prisoners at the Stoke Poges camp, while our prisoners in German camps have to look after their own sanitary arrangements". And the Manchester Board of Guardians likewise protested about German prisoners of war using their "fine hospital at Withington" when "many British wounded have had to go to inferior hospitals". A 53-year-old farmer, Job Usher of Greenhill Farm, near Devizes, suffered a death sentence, albeit not of the judicial kind, when he tried to help German prisoners. Two of them were cleaning a whey tank on the farm when they were overcome by gas fumes. Usher, seeing their plight, rushed to the rescue, but he too was overcome and all three men died. And there was more than a whiff of disapproval when *The Times* reported on 26 June 1917 that: "A bunch of flowers placed on the grave of the crew recently brought down in East Anglia bears the following inscription:- 'These flowers are from an Englishman who understands that each of these souls is somebody's son.'"

Anti-German hysteria reached a crescendo with the Pemberton Billing Trial at the end of May 1918. Noel Pemberton Billing, "a rather flashy young man" and an "unsuccessful aeroplane builder" in Clementine Churchill's forthright opinion, had achieved both national prominence and notoriety in pushing for a more aggressive British air policy. In January 1916, he had been narrowly defeated in a by-election at Mile End. Two months later he tried again, this time in East Hertfordshire. In just under two weeks, wearing his distinctive leather flying coat, monocle and bowler hat, he travelled nearly 1,500 miles (2,400 km) round the constituency in his lemon-coloured motor car, addressing 116 meetings. At one of them he was greeted by six-year-old Baptist minister's son Kenneth Cripps and his chums, who chanted:

Pemberton Billing,
Pemberton Billing,
If we vote for you
Will you give us a shilling?

"PB" won the seat with a handsome majority of nearly a thousand votes – 4,590 to 3,359 – over the Government candidate. Entering Parliament on 14 March 1916, unconventional as ever, he made his maiden speech the same day. This set the pattern for the parliamentary career of the self-styled "Member for Air". His constant interruptions, when he "bounced up and down like a Jack-in-the-Box", coupled with an ill-concealed disdain for House of Commons conventions won him few admirers in Parliament. On 25 July 1917, after one of his interventions of "prodigious length", a fellow MP, Major Archer Shee, accused PB of being "caddish and offensive". Pemberton Billing promptly challenged Archer Shee to repeat these remarks outside the Lobby. The two men later met and fisticuffs ensued as *Punch* reported: "Palace Yard was the scene of the combat, which ended … in ARCHER downing PEMBERTON and BILLING sitting on SHEE. Then the police arrived and swept away the hyphens." The next day PB challenged Archer Shee to a 20-round boxing match at the National Sports Club, the loser to pay £105 to the Red Cross. The Major, wisely no doubt, turned down the offer.

In October 1916 Pemberton Billing had founded his own "independent *viewspaper*, as opposed to *newspaper*", entitled *The Imperialist*. One of its first targets was former war minister and Lord Chancellor Lord Haldane, who had been injudicious enough to describe Germany as his "spiritual home". On the other hand, the new Prime Minister received a verbal bouquet. Lloyd George, PB said, had "brains and bowels, was a glutton for work, possessed wonderful tact, indomitable determination, together with the personal charm of the Celt, which also provided him with that subtle but indispensable faculty for getting the very best out of men he worked with and infusing them with his own enthusiasm." But Pemberton Billing soon became disillusioned, and a year later was writing: "We may yet live to despise and dismiss Mr Lloyd George because he has told us much … that was not true!" The Prime Minister, for his part, was reported as saying that in his opinion the 36-year-old maverick MP was a dangerous man.

Just how dangerous became increasingly clear after the publication of an article by PB entitled "The First 47,000" in the penultimate number of *The Imperialist* before its name was changed to *The Vigilante* on 9 February 1918. Pemberton Billing wrote: "There have been given many reasons why England is prevented from putting her full strength into the War. On several occasions in the columns of *The Imperialist*

I have suggested that Germany is making use of subtle but successful means to nullify our efforts…. Within the past few days the most extraordinary facts have been placed before me which co-ordinate my past information."

These "most extraordinary facts" had been given to PB by his newly appointed American-born assistant editor, Captain Harold Spencer. Spencer told his chief that the Germans had compiled a sensational directory containing the names of 47,000 names of British men and women who, because of their addiction to "the evils which all decent men thought had perished in Sodom and Lesbia", were wide open to blackmail. The book, which Spencer told Pemberton Billing he had seen in the possession of the German Prince William of Wied, pre-1914 King of Albania, included the names of "Privy Councillors, youths of the chorus, wives of Cabinet Ministers, dancing girls, even Cabinet Ministers themselves while diplomats, poets, bankers, editors, newspaper proprietors and members of His Majesty's Household followed each other with no apparent order of precedence".

Unfortunately, PB was unaware that his new assistant editor had been discharged from the British Army suffering from "delusional insanity" and so Spencer's claims were unreliable, to say the very least. Popular romantic novelist and food hoarder Marie Corelli now acted as a catalyst. She sent Pemberton Billing a newspaper clipping drawing his attention to two private performances of Oscar Wilde's *Salome*, to be sponsored by Dutch-born but now naturalized British subject Jakob Thomas Grein and his Independent Theatre Society, with Canadian dancer Maud Allan in the title role. Grein was automatically suspect as he had founded the German Theatre in London, and Maud Allan was widely believed to be a lesbian. The fact that she had been invited to 10 Downing Street during the Asquiths' occupancy led to rumours that the former premier's wife likewise harboured sapphic tendencies. In PB's absence due to ill-health, Spencer published a short paragraph in *The Vigilante* of 16 February 1918:

The Cult of the Clitoris
To be a member of Maud Allen's [sic] private performance in Oscar Wilde's "Salome" one has to apply to a Miss Valetta of 9, Duke Street, Adelphi, W.C. If Scotland Yard were to seize the list of those members I have no doubt they would secure the names of several thousand of the first 47,000.

Immediately sensing that Spencer had overstepped the mark, PB stopped him from publishing any further "revelations". But it was too late, and both Maud Allan and Grein started criminal proceedings for obscene and defamatory libel. After two appearances at Bow Street Police Court and an initial one at the Old Bailey, Pemberton Billing's trial began there on 29 May 1918.

With a renewed German offensive towards Paris and victory seeming to be as far away as ever, the war-weary British public looked forward to finding relief in reading the press coverage "of the high jinks at the Old Bailey, during the six days of what *The Times* later referred to as 'A Scandalous Trial'". They were not to be disappointed. The presiding judge Mr Justice Darling, an old enemy of PB's, played it strictly for laughs and behaved in a generally buffoonish manner. PB was as flamboyant as ever, duelling with Darling and riding roughshod over normal court procedure. Witnesses included Spencer, the King's personal surgeon Sir Alfred Fripp, the fashionable Jesuit priest Father Bernard Vaughan and Oscar Wilde's former lover Lord Alfred Douglas. But Pemberton Billing's star witness was Eileen Villiers-Stuart, a fantasist and conspiracy theorist in the Spencer class and now enjoying a sexual relationship with PB. She claimed to have actually seen the wholly fictitious Black Book, and a high point of drama was reached when PB asked:

"Is Mr Justice Darling's name in the book?"
"It is."
"Is Mrs Asquith's name in the book?"
"It is."
"Is Mr Asquith's name in the book?"
"It is."
"Is Lord Haldane's name in the book?"
"It is."

Such sensational "disclosures" ensured maximum press coverage. On 30 May 1918 the *Daily Mirror* devoted half its front page to the trial while incidentally informing readers that the "French fall back fighting on Soissons". Four days later *The Times* juxtaposed its account of the trial with news of the "Great Battles between the Oise and the Marne", as the Germans made their last desperate lunge towards Paris. In France, Alfred Duff Cooper, a second lieutenant in the Grenadier Guards, wrote to his secret fiancée Lady Diana Manners:

No one here speaks or thinks of anything but the Billing Trial. Even my Commanding Officer – the most regular of regular soldiers – greeted me when I first met him for the first time today not 200 yards from the front-line trenches with – 'What do you think of Fripp's evidence. I should have thought he knew more about clap.' The general feeling is that anybody who is anybody is in the book.... What with Margot [Asquith], Haldane and Mrs Keppel and Neil Primrose I think that we may congratulate ourselves that our friends are well represented.

At 3.15 pm on 4 June, the jury retired to consider their verdict. It took only one hour and 25 minutes to return a verdict of "Not Guilty". The verdict was greeted with cheers and applause both in the court room and outside the Old Bailey, where a large crowd had gathered to acclaim "Good Old Billing". He emerged triumphant along with both his wife Dot, who was, ironically enough, half-German, and his mistress Eileen Villiers-Stuart.

The next morning the leading liberal newspaper the *Manchester Guardian* drew its readers' attention to the fact that: "No one has ever thrown so much dirt on people more respected than himself, and yet come so near to being a popular hero. Few people have made such a miasma and escaped punishment for creating a public nuisance." At the ultra-right-wing *Morning Post*, editor H. A. Gwynne thought that the trial had demonstrated the "very serious indication of a state of feeling in the country which may be quite dangerous, and certainly would have been dangerous if left in the hands of Billing". Furthermore, "A Billing, or a Bottomley, has it now in his power to bring about almost a revolution, for it is well to remember that there is a feeling of profound distrust throughout the country of the politician." At the front, Second Lieutenant Duff Cooper wrote:

"The result of the Billing Case has made me positively angry.... Really I feel that a country is not worth fighting for or preserving in which a Billing is still allowed to libel, a democracy which can produce 12 idiotic jurymen still allowed to rule, and a judge as utterly inept as Darling allowed to administer the law. But I suppose one should be grateful to Billing. He has kept the whole army amused for several days and provided a topic of conversation to officers who can never find one for themselves."

CHAPTER THREE

The inclusion of Margot Asquith's name during the Billing Trial was not the first time during the war that the former Prime Minister's wife had been the subject of rumour or scandal. Duff Cooper's commanding officer for one was convinced that she was a "female bugger" or at the very least a "lesbite". And back in April 1915, the singularly unpleasant *Morning Post* editor H. A. Gwynne was reporting to General Sir Henry Wilson that Mrs Asquith had been "so drunk in a private house … that she was sick in the drawing room and on the stairs going away". A few months later Gwynne was writing that Margot was now going about "talking pro-Germanism". Both the *Daily Mail* and *The Globe* claimed that the Prime Minister's wife had played tennis with German officer prisoners of war at Donnington Hall in Leicestershire and regularly sent them food parcels. Stung by the hate mail sent her, Margot sued *The Globe* and received £1,000 in damages. But Mrs Asquith's "pro-Germanism" was just one of the countless rumours that gained currency in Britain between 1914 and 1918.

One of the first was of a phantom Russian army which had supposedly landed in Scotland. The men were said to have travelled south by rail "with snow on their boots" to get to the Western Front. Vera Brittain was told by her dentist that a hundred thousand Russians had landed and a whole trainful of them had passed through Stoke-on-Trent, while cigarette and chocolate vending machines on station platforms were rumoured to be jammed with Russian kopeck coins. Throughout August and early September the rumour persisted. On 14 September the Press Bureau officially denied that any Russian soldiers were on the Western Front, but the rumours persisted. The London *Evening News* commented:

> *All roads lead to Rome, and the railroad from Archangel led everywhere. The Cossacks were seen – though the blinds were always down – at Peckham, at Chichester, at York, at Bristol, at Ealing, at Darlington, on Ludgate Hill Bridge, Evesham, at Peterborough. A grey cloud of fierce, whiskered men went rolling down to Cheltenham, at Euston their passing closed the station for 36 hours; at Rugby they drank great draughts of coffee. In the East End children playing by the railway embankment were gladdened with showers of Russian money thrown to them from a passing train. Cossacks swarmed at Southampton, and a London milkman, clattering his cans to*

salute the dawn, saw myriads of the north march past him in the silent, awful streets.... Of course, there was always this suspicious circumstance; you never met a man who had seen the Russians. You met a man who knew a man who had seen the Russians; and this should have aroused our suspicions.

It was left to Margot Asquith's kinsman Under Secretary of State for War Harold Tennant officially to deny the rumour in Parliament on 18 November 1914 in response to a back bencher's question: "I am uncertain whether it will gratify or displease my honourable friend to learn that no Russian troops have been conveyed through Great Britain to the Western area of the European War."

Hard on the heels of the Russians appeared the Angels of Mons. In the *Evening News* of 29 September 1914 there had appeared a short story entitled "The Bowmen" by mystic-leaning writer Arthur Machen. It told of how the previous month a British soldier invoked St George to conjure up Henry V's Agincourt archers to come to the aid of Sir John French's desperate British Expeditionary Force. This soon transmogrified into the legend that angels and heavenly bowmen had actually been seen in the ranks of the BEF during their first action at Mons on 23 August 1914. And despite the fact that, as with the Russians with snow on their boots, witnesses to the Angels of Mons were always anonymous and thus untraceable, a number of clergymen, including the Reverend Alexander Boddy of All Saints, Sunderland, were firm believers in the divine intervention at Mons. In Liverpool, the McGuires wrote to their sister in America about the angels: "It seems queer doesn't it? I wonder if it is possible for the spirits of the men who had been killed to help their comrades?" Similar stories persisted throughout the war. In April 1918, at the height of Ludendorff's offensive, heavenly cavalrymen were said to have come to the aid of Sir Douglas Haig's men fighting with their backs to the wall in France, while a polyglot army made up of deserters from all the warring nations was said to inhabit no-man's-land.

In May 1916, a bizarre story began circulating both in Britain and neutral America that Sir Robert Baden-Powell, hero of the siege of Mafeking during the Boer War and founder of the Boy Scout movement, was in the Tower of London charged with espionage. Baden-Powell, who was of the firm opinion that you could always tell a "wrong 'un" if he had a high-pitched voice, wrote to the papers: "I regret the report that I am sojourning in the Tower of London under a charge of espionage cannot be correct, as I was taken out and shot a month ago – according to a Chicago newspaper. I am not clear which country I was spying for, but at the moment I am fairly busy on work for Great Britain." The following month, another hero of the war in South Africa, Lord Kitchener, was drowned on the way to Russia when his ship HMS *Hampshire* struck a mine. Almost immediately the rumours began circulating that Kitchener had not perished. His sister Mrs Frances Parker firmly believed him still to be alive, and it was variously claimed that he was a prisoner in Germany or "deep in enchanted sleep" in an Orkneys cave, "ready and waiting for his country's call". Yet another Boer War hero, Sir Hector "Fighting Mac" Macdonald, was the subject of an equally fanciful rumour. In 1903, he had committed suicide in a Paris hotel over a looming homosexual scandal. But from 1916 onwards there were stories that the suicide had been faked and that the highly successful German Field Marshal August von Mackensen, conqueror of Romania, was in fact Macdonald. Lord Haldane was rumoured not only to be the Kaiser's illegitimate brother but to have a German wife into the bargain. Admiral Sir John Jellicoe, failing to live up to public expectations that he was another Nelson, was rumoured to have been shot in the Tower along with Sir John French.

The press were always eager to report them when genuine, albeit minor, miracles did happen. But not always to everybody's satisfaction. In 1915, a Mrs Maunders of Twickenham, Middlesex, was informed by the War Office that her husband had been killed in action. After a decent interval of mourning, in due course she received and accepted a proposal of marriage. But just a few days before the wedding, a letter came from her supposedly dead husband stating that he had been badly wounded and left for dead. Found by the Germans, he had been nursed back to health and was now in a prisoner-of-war camp. In the same year that Mrs Maunders "lost" her husband, Private A. W. Brace of the Duke of Cornwall's Light Infantry lost the use of his legs and was discharged. But in a taxi accident at Fishponds, near Bristol, the shock he received was such that he immediately recovered the full use of his legs. And in January 1916 it was reported that "while a comic film was being shown at a Norbury cinema theatre Cyclist J. Hopkins of the Army Cyclist Corps suddenly recovered his speech, which he had lost through being 'gassed' at Ypres. He returned to the local war hospital chatting gaily and is now on 10 days' furlough before reporting again for the front." Even more "miraculous" was the case of Corporal Joseph Freckleton of the 7th

Battalion of the King's Liverpool Regiment. He had been rendered deaf, dumb and blind at the fighting at Festubert in 1915. He had gradually recovered his sight and hearing but remained dumb until New Year's Eve that year. Then, during a dance at a wedding at which he was best man, he yawned and recovered his full speech and then "sang a song, to the pleasure of the wedding party".

For the families of those soldiers less fortunate than Freckleton, Maunders, Hopkins and Brace, there was always the hope of contacting them "on the Other Side" through spirit mediums. The American Civil War had seen a boom in attempts to communicate with the dead of Gettysburg and other battles, and it was rumoured that Lincoln himself had taken part in a seance at the White House. In November 1918 *The Graphic* informed its readers that "the ancient interest in Spiritualism is gaining fresh impetus daily through the *psyche* of the multitudinous slain on the battlefields. Oceans of discarnate souls are only a little way off in time and space." Furthermore, "there is comforting reading for those who have lost sons in the war in Sir Oliver Lodge's very intimate Study in Humanity Personality, *Christopher*". Sir Oliver, a world-renowned physicist and Principal of the University of Birmingham, had already published a hugely successful book on the subject. Entitled *Raymond, or Life and Death*, it was described as "a startling vision of the life of dead subalterns on the Other Side". Lodge's son Raymond had been killed in action on 14 September 1915, but only 11 days later, according to Sir Oliver, he had started communicating with his distraught parents through the mediums of Gladys Osborne Leonard and Alfred Vout Peters. *Raymond* was published in the winter of 1916. It was immediately dubbed by the *Daily Mail* "Sir Oliver Lodge's Spook Book; Half a Guinea's Worth of Rubbish", its author described as being "as easily credulous as the sad creatures who fall a willing prey to the soothsayer and fortune teller". But most reviewers were more respectful, if sceptical, and the book proved a terrific bestseller for the remainder of the war.

Sir Arthur Conan Doyle, creator of Sherlock Holmes, was the other famous adherent to wartime Spiritualism, publishing his psychic testament *The New Revelation* two years after *Raymond*. Sir Arthur's son Kingsley, severely weakened by wounds received during the Battle of the Somme, died during the 1918 Spanish Flu pandemic. Sir Arthur sought to contact him on the "Other Side" through the agency of two mediums, Eusepia Palladino and Margery Crandon, both of whom were later to be exposed as frauds. A friend described Sir Arthur: "Among all the notable persons attracted to Spiritualism, he was perhaps the most uncritical. His extreme credulity, indeed, was the despair of his colleagues, all of whom, however held him in the highest respect for his complete honesty. Poor, dear, lovable, credulous Doyle! He was a giant in stature with the heart of a child."

Sadly, there were many like Palladino and Crandon claiming to be in touch with loved ones on the "Other Side" who were only too eager to cash in on the misery and gullibility of relatives of the fallen. The *Daily Mail* was in the vanguard of the popular press set on exposing psychic fraudsters and fortune tellers, with the *Daily Express* not far behind. Prosecutions soon followed. In December 1917, 38-year-old Louise Hutchinson, "who had interested herself in psychic research since childhood", was fined £10 with costs of £10 10s (ten pounds and ten shillings) for "fortune telling" at the Dak Bungalow, part of the Oriental Restaurant off Brompton Road. Three months later, Marie Charles or "Madame Chailer" as she preferred to be known, also of Brompton Road, appeared at Westminster Police Court charged with fortune telling. For lack of any real evidence the magistrate Mr Francis dismissed the case and "when the decision was given there was a bust of cheering and clapping of hands by a number of fashionably dressed women and men".

Mrs Kate Ventnor of St Clement's Mansions, Fulham was not so lucky. A woman police plant told the court that Mrs Ventnor had predicted to her that she would be marrying a tall, fair widower early the next year. "You are very loving," Mrs Ventnor told the plant before charging her 2s 6d (two shillings and sixpence), "but you can hate as well as love." In her defence Mrs Ventnor told the court: "Many scientific men visit me. I have a sympathetic gift and they come to me for advice. I have a very sympathetic nature, and it comforts them." Despite insisting that she was a spiritualist and not a fortune teller "who deceived servant girls", Mrs Ventnor received a fairly stiff fine of £10.

Phoney spiritualism, vice and hatred of the wicked Hun all came together in the person of 71-year-old masseuse and medium Annie Sophia Sharp, alias "Madame Jacques", of Portsdown Road, Edgware. In February 1917, she came up before Marylebone Police Court on the charge of professing to tell fortunes and for harbouring an enemy alien, 40-year-old Dorothea Ludolph of Hamburg. Mrs Julia Mason told the court that she had visited "Madame Jacques" who had said that Mr

Mason was now a prisoner of war. Sadly, though, her husband would soon be passing on to the "Other Side". But happier days would come and Julia would re-marry a friend of her husband's called Harold. In fact Mr Mason was a civilian and relatively safe at home. A younger friend of Mrs Mason's had gone with her to "Madame Jacques". The friend had been told by "Madame" that she would be having a large family, "but need not do so if she went to her", the implication being that an abortion could be arranged. For harbouring Ludolph, Sharp was given a three-month prison sentence and another one to run concurrently for fortune telling. Just over a year later, Sharp was in court again. Among her many other misdemeanours, the court was told that: "For years she had been obtaining large sums of money by crystal gazing and had induced young girls who went to her to have their fortunes told to lead immoral lives. She had a place in Bond-street for her fortune telling and a house in Maida-vale which was used for immorality." But most damning of all, she "had numerous friends in Germany".

SEX, DRUGS, DRINK AND RAGTIME

MR ASQUITH SAYS IN A MANNER SWEET AND CALM:
ANOTHER LITTLE DRINK WON'T DO US ANY HARM
(Song from the 1916 show *The Bing Boys Are Here*.)

On 2 September 1916, Yorkshire lithographic artist Frank Lockwood wrote in his diary with more than a touch of exasperation: "What a time we are living in. England – the land of the free – was never less free than it is today." Nearly half a century later, the iconoclastic and immensely popular historian A. J. P. Taylor was to write: "Until August 1914 a sensible, law-abiding Englishman could pass through life and hardly notice the existence of the state, beyond the post office and the policeman." The First World War was to change all that completely. And never before had the nation's morals and spiritual welfare come under such scrutiny and regulation as they did between 1914 and 1918.

On the outbreak of war, as Charles Balston recorded in his diary, the Government, after "protecting the economic interests of the country set to work to issue regulations for its safety and to enable them to take over such land, buildings and other property as might be needed for purposes of defence, billeting and the manufacture of munitions". This was accomplished on 13 August 1914 with the passing of the first Defence of the Realm Act or DORA as it soon became known. The provisions of the Act and subsequent additions gave the Government unprecedented powers over all aspects of British life. On 20 November 1914 the influential newspaper proprietor Lord Riddell, an intimate of Lloyd George, noted in his diary:

The Defence of the Realm Acts are being consolidated. The drastic and unique provisions of this legislation have not attracted the attention they deserve. The legislation has taken place so rapidly that the measures have not been properly discussed. The press have been singularly ill-informed and lacking in criticism regarding a law which wipes out Magna Carta, the Bill of Rights, etc., in a few lines.

Charles Balston listed just a few of DORA's provisions in his diary:

The clearing of any threatened areas, the extinction of lights and the issue of search warrants & warrants for arrests to punish offences such as suspicious conduct, giving information, the spreading of false reports or inciting to mutiny, sedition or disaffection.... Any British subject or alien could be proceeded against for infringing the act or in any way endangering the state.

The authorities were not slow to enforce the new regulations and throughout the war newspapers were full of reports of prosecutions of citizens who had dared to defy "Dame Dora" as *Punch* had characterized the new Act. In January 1916, no less than 56 offences under the lightning restrictions of DORA were heard by magistrates at Wycombe, Buckinghamshire. The same month, 70 motorists were summoned at Feltham, Middlesex, "under the Defence of the Realm Act for not carrying proper lights on vehicles after dark". Collier John Fisher was fined 12s (twelve shillings) at Leigh, Lancashire, for "a breach of the Lighting Order, by striking a match in the street at night". At Kingston upon Thames, Francis W. Billings, landlord of the North Star pub near Surbiton, was fined £1 for "failing to reduce the intensity of the lights on his premises on 21 October. When a police-sergeant spoke to him about the matter he said, 'What about the moon?'." At Bognor, a council meeting discussing the resort's lighting was told by chairman H. H. King that "the town should not be so conspicuous at night, as in the event of a Zeppelin raid Bognor might be mistaken for Portsmouth". That opinion met with a sarcastic rejoinder from *Punch*: "It would be small consolation to England, if Bognor Cinema Palace fell, that Portsmouth Dockyard had been saved." Even up in Liverpool, relatively safe from air attack, two firms occupying offices in the Royal Liver Building were fined £10 and £5 respectively for "allowing lights in their windows to be visible from the outside".

What in the next war would be described as "spreading alarm and despondency" could also get Britons into trouble. In May 1915 at

Stratford-upon-Avon, chauffeur Albert Henry Brooks received a fine of £5 with the alternative of a month in prison, "on a charge under the Defence of the Realm Acts of spreading false reports as to an alleged disaster to the Warwickshire Yeomanry at the Dardanelles". A £5 fine for breaking DORA regulations was also given to Gertrude Hardman of Great Lever near Bolton two years later. At the Lancaster munitions factory where she worked, Hardman "had made false statements in the presence of a number of new workers regarding the character of their work, which frightened them and made some unwilling to start work". For using insulting and obscene language to a group of wounded soldiers, a grocer's porter from Dublin received a two-month prison sentence "on a charge under the Defence of the Realm Act". For being injudicious in "publishing information calculated to be useful to the enemy", Edgar Allen, the editor of a technical journal, received a fine of £100. And when a Birmingham socialist and gas worker declared in public: "It does not matter to me whether I am under Germans, Russians, or Kaiser Wilhelm, or anyone else," the city's magistrates sentenced him to three months' imprisonment.

Leniency was sometimes shown, as in the case of Ernest Aves, Chairman of Trade Boards. A summons against him had been brought at Berwick-upon-Tweed for taking photographs in a forbidden area. It was dismissed with a payment of 12s (twelve shillings) costs after Aves told the court "that he took the snapshots of the two bridges at Berwick merely on account of their architectural interest and beauty". Holidaying in Dorset in July 1915 at Lulworth Cove, Ethel Bilbrough was "placidly sketching on the cliff [when] a khaki sentinel approached me and calmly demanded my sketchbook, as sketching was forbidden within three miles [4.8 km] of the coast! I had to give it up of course, but relieved myself by saying some *most* unchristian things!" Ethel's sketchbook was returned nearly three months later, and "it amused one to think what a lot of trouble these good people had given themselves over a practically empty and harmless little sixpence sketchbook!"

To treat DORA's regulations flippantly was asking for trouble, as Coldstream Guards Captain George Whitaker discovered in July 1917. On leave and in civilian clothes, he was asked his nationality by a policeman while walking on Ryde pier head. He replied "Chinese", and was detained by the constable, to whom he said, "You civilian police are too officious and ought to be in the trenches. You would then have a sense of humour." Whitaker was fined £1 for "making a false statement to the aliens officer".

Many in Britain, like Mrs Annie Purbrook of Hornchurch, Essex, found the lighting restrictions particularly tiresome: "oh, how dreary the winter world looked; you can't think how depressing it was and somebody was constantly being fined for a forgotten blind or a blazing hall light.... People who neglected their lights were badly thought of as being careless of public safety."

In May 1916 came a piece of legislation that was to prove the most enduring of all passed during the Great War. For some years, the idea of obtaining an hour's more daylight by putting the clocks forward had been advocated, notably by William Willett of Chislehurst, Kent. But few in Britain had given it much thought or support. The coming of war and the urgent necessity of securing as many hours of daylight as possible now gave the idea fresh impetus. Other countries, notably Britain's French ally and her German and Austria-Hungarian enemies, had adopted daylight-saving schemes. Britain followed suit on 8 May 1916 when a resolution of adoption was introduced in the House of Commons by Sir Henry Norman and carried by 170 votes to 2. A short Bill was immediately passed that all clocks were to be put forward by one hour at 2.00 am on Sunday 21 May, and put back an hour at 3.00 am on 1 October. It was estimated that £2.5 million would be saved in gas and electric light bills as well the other more obvious benefits of Daylight Saving. Ethel Bilbrough, conscious and proud of the Chislehurst connection, railed at "our tardy stupid government" for taking so long to introduce the scheme and recorded in her war diary: "We altered all our own timepieces at 9.30 on Sat. evening and then went to bed as we had made it 10.30!! So we got all right without any difficulty, and without any loss of sleep! though there were several dolts in England who 'raised objections'. I believe there are people who will want to argue and make objections when the Last Day comes!!" Reviewing the advantages of the scheme, Ethel thought that "the greatest benefit of all is after dinner, when it is now broad daylight till close on ten! and instead of having to get the gas lit & sit reading in doors, one can just go for a good walk, or do some gardening, or indulge in any other daylight occupation. Taking it all round, everyone has reason to bless the name of Willett!" But not, it would appear, scientist J. H. Willis of Norwich, who in April 1916 wrote to the *Morning Post* condemning daylight saving time, on the grounds that too much sunshine would be enervating and that "life is more virile in Northern latitudes".

There were other patriotic citizens like Isabel Macnamara of Bayswater who made suggestions on how to make the country safer. Anticipating a slogan of the next war, "Careless Talk Cost Lives", in December 1914 she wrote to *The Times* wishing

> *you would draw the attention of the War Office and the Admiralty to the way in which soldiers and sailors talk to strangers and answer all their questions (as far as they can). Only yesterday, at one of the Underground stations, I was horrified to hear a sailor, who had obviously gone through a strenuous time, answering every question put to him by a stranger.... I did all I could short of going up to him and pointing out the folly of allowing himself to be "pumped". I particularly noticed that the stranger attached himself to him in a determined manner, and then I spoke to one of Thos. Cook and Son's men who happened to be on the platform and asked him to put the sailor on his guard. But by then the train had left the station taking him and his new friend.... Surely the authorities should issue a regulation on this vital subject, forbidding men in either service to answer any questions.*

In 1914, and indeed throughout the war, there was a real fear of a German invasion, fuelled perhaps by pre-war novels and plays such as *The Riddle of the Sands* and *An Englishmen's Home*. And so, as Charles Balston recorded:

> *it was arranged by the local and military authorities that in the event of a threatened or actual invasion or landing on the East Coast, the inhabitants of towns & villages in Essex should all retreat by certain specific routes to the interior, even as far as Oxfordshire. Printed instructions were issued to householders telling them how much luggage they could take & by what roads to travel. The prospect however left the people cold. They had too much trust in the navy to fear the Germans.*

Many perceived an even greater threat to Britain than a German invasion. On 28 February 1915, Lloyd George told a Bangor audience: "Drink is doing more damage in the war than all the German submarines put together." A month later he declared to a deputation from the Shipbuilding Employers' Federation: "We are fighting Germans, Austrians and Drink, and so far as I can see the greatest of these deadly foes is Drink." As early as 25 August 1914, steps had been taken in Sheerness to curb excessive drinking, with public houses put out of bounds to soldiers and sailors in the early evening. In Cardiff, a few days later, all pubs were ordered to close at 9.00 pm, and similar earlier closings took place in Clerkenwell, Woolwich and Greenwich. Britain's Russian ally went much further, as Charles Balston noted in his war diary:

> On 21ˢᵗ October we learnt that the Government sale of Vodka or alcohol ... was prohibited; and this self-denying ordinance was followed ... by a further order prohibiting the sale of all alcoholic drinks in Petrograd, including beer, even in first class restaurants and clubs.... We can hardly imagine such an edict in England ... and it has been said that this imperious decree was one of the causes of the Revolution in Russia....

But the following year, with claims that excessive drinking by munitions workers was hampering production and thus impeding progress on the fighting fronts, Balston wrote that: "Lloyd George ... threatened the country that as Russia had prohibited the sale of vodka and France of absinthe, so England would restrict the sale of whiskey. He was as good as his word. The Govt. brought in a bill introducing heavy liquor duties; and later passed an act enforcing shorter hours for the sale of liquor, forbidding 'treating' and reducing the standard strength of beer and spirits." Meeting the Chancellor on 10 April 1915, the King's mother Queen Alexandra said: "Mr Lloyd George, I hear you are wanting to turn us all into teetotallers." By then her son had been brought reluctantly into the controversy over drink. Twenty years later it still rankled with the monarch, as junior Cabinet minister Anthony Eden was to discover during an audience:

> the King told me, with some indignation, how his renunciation of alcoholic drink had come during the war. It seemed that Lloyd George had come to him much troubled about heavy drinking among munition workers, which, he said was having an influence on output. Could not an example be set by His Majesty? The King was reluctant, asked for more information and said he would consider it. Whereupon Lloyd George went out and told everyone that the King had agreed. "A scurvy trick," His Majesty thought.

An announcement was made that from 6 April no alcohol would be consumed by the King or in the Royal residences. In his diary that night the King wrote: "This morning we have all become teetotallers until the end of the war. I have done it as an example, as there is a lot of drinking going on in the country. I hate doing it, but hope it will do good." According to Charles Balston: "Thus did the King, not for the first time, show his appreciation of what the situation demanded & his sincere determination to help the cause."

As it turned out, apart from Lord Kitchener, very few followed the King in taking the Pledge, and certainly not the Prime Minister, whose fondness for the bottle was only too well known. In fact the total sum spent on drink in the first six months of 1915 was £8 million more than for the same period in 1914. A Liquor Traffic Central Control Board, equipped with seemingly far-reaching powers, was set up to regulate the nation's drinking. Brewers were ordered to reduce the strength of their beer, and the pubs were now generally opened only from 12 noon to 2.20pm and again from 6.30 pm to 9.30 pm. The sale of spirits was restricted to weekdays between 12.00 noon and 2.30 pm and there was a ban on "treating" whereby pub customers had to order and pay for their own drinks. In his diary, Frank Lockwood wrote: "It seems very funny to see nearly all the public houses turn out at 9 pm but it must be funnier to see the room [after 9.00] sat round with men all drinking Oxo, lemonade and other non-intoxicating drinks." And rotund music-hall comedian Ernie Mayne bemoaned both the scarcity and quality of wartime ale in his ironic ditty "Lloyd George's Beer".

The police kept a sharp eye out for infringements of the new regulations. In Kingston upon Thames, the constituency of Home Secretary Sir George Cave, the landlord of The Three Fishes pub in the Richmond Road was fined £10 with costs of three guineas (three pounds, fifteen pence) for serving a customer a glass of milk laced with rum out of hours. The customer received a fine of £3 with a week to pay. Fines totalling £12 were also dished out to the landlord, barmaid and two women drinkers at the town's Three Compasses pub in Eden Street for breaking the Non-Treating Order. Pleas of ignorance were no excuse. And at the North London Police Court, Mr Hedderwick, the presiding magistrate, said he could not believe that "both the barmaid and the person charged with treating should be under the impression that port wine was non-alcoholic". The famous music-hall comedian Fred Karno, licensee of the Island Hotel, the "Karsino" at Hampton-on-Thames, was fined £30 for selling whisky over the maximum retail price. Ellen Read

Rogers of "Lindisfarne", Hersham Road, Walton, was sent to a home for 12 months and bound over for the same period for supplying whisky at her home to wounded soldiers. The court heard that Mrs Rogers had previously been convicted for the same offence and fined £20, but in her defence, "it was stated that she had given way to drink".

Some people still thought that not enough was being done to curb the nation's drinking. Sir Frederic Cardew, the 86-year-old former Governor of Sierra Leone, wrote to relatives in Paris from his Oxfordshire home that he found "it is sickening that the Government do not take more drastic measures for the suppression of the drink traffic, but the people themselves are to blame, particularly the middle and upper classes, very few of them followed the lead of their king & Lord Kitchener and banish liquor from their table. It shows a shocking want of loyalty & patriotism." On a visit to London in October 1915, Sir Frederic was appalled that: "The drinking habits of our people are increasing and the habit has extended to the women in a remarkable degree, the night before last passing down Praed St the public houses were full of women, the bars crowded, it was a shocking sight." It was not just the "lower orders" that were being hauled over the coals for excessive drinking. In May 1917 Fleetwood Henry Williams from London appeared before a Scarborough court on a charge of drunkenness. The Chief Constable said that Williams, "described as an Inspector of Foods for Yorkshire, had behaved in an extraordinary manner in various shops", and to one female shop assistant even claimed to be Lord Devonport, the Food Controller. Williams pleaded that he had been working 14 hours daily and "took whiskey on an empty stomach", and was fortunate to receive a comparatively lenient fine of 10s (ten shillings).

During the war many towns and cities were the scenes of what a century later would be called "binge drinking" and subsequent rowdy behaviour. In March 1918, Kingston upon Thames Magistrates' Court heard from a police constable how in the town's London Road, two teenage boys "arm in arm with some girls charged into passengers boarding a tramcar and pushed other people off the footpath. The two boys were shouting 'out of the way you *yobs*'." The last word was an unfamiliar one to the chairman of the bench who was told by the police witness: "It's a slang expression, boy spelt backwards." The constable continued: "It is simply disgusting in Clarence Street on Saturday and Sunday evenings. The youths always create a disturbance directly the blackout time comes and the lights go out." A few months earlier, Kingston's local paper the *Surrey Comet* had reported how at 11.30 pm on a Saturday night, a policeman had heard a noise coming from the town's Apple Market. There he saw three girls, "all in their teens, shouting and singing and one of them was acting in a disgusting manner under a lamppost". Taken into custody, the three girls, Elizabeth, Sophia and Daisy, were each bound over for six months in the sum of £5.

There was drunken, abusive and violent behaviour on public transport too. In Eden Street, a policeman told the court, an intoxicated soldier home on leave had tried

> *to board an omnibus but the Conductor refused to let him on and the bus went off. Another bus came up and the Conductor said "I won't have him on my bus because of bad language." The Conductor got off the bus and the defendant said "I'll fight you" and put himself in a fighting attitude. I got between them and told the Conductor to go on. The defendant continued with bad language and I took him into custody.*

At the police station a doctor certified the soldier, a sergeant in the Imperial Camel Corps, drunk. He was subsequently bound over in the sum of £5 for three months with costs of 10s 6d (ten shillings and sixpence) to cover the doctor's fee. Two other men who were turned off a tram for drunk and disorderly behaviour, and subsequently fined £1 each, gave as their excuse that they had been "seeing a pal off and had a little jollification". To which Kingston Mayor Alderman Charles Burge replied: "What a pity you can't do that without getting drunk." On the brighter side, the press reported that convictions for drunkenness in the City of London had dropped dramatically, and only 12 out of the 36,000 inhabitants of genteel Tunbridge Wells in Kent had been convicted for drunken behaviour during 1915.

The country's temperance movement was not slow to take advantage of the opportunity presented to ram home the message that abstinence from alcohol now equalled patriotism, and also the need for a healthy and sober Britain. The Church of England Temperance Society published a pamphlet, "Alcoholism and the Future", informing readers that: "In 1915 maternal drinking was the curse of Scotland. There was much infant debility and malnutrition, so called, which was really syphilis or alcohol as a rule." In March 1917 another temperance organization, the Strength of Britain Movement, called for total abstinence and warned:

"The coming POTATO FAMINE means a greater need of grain for food. Not an ounce can be spared to be wasted on alcoholic liquor." The Movement was doubtless gratified to learn in November that: "The beer scarcity in the Liverpool district is now greater than at any previous stage. Practically every public house in Widnes was closed during the weekend." The Armistice brought no slackening of effort on the part of the Church of England's Temperance Society:

> It is going to be an extremely trying time to everybody when our lads "from out over there" come back to us. The drunkenness witnessed in our streets when the troops returned from the Boer War is well remembered by most of us. It is unnecessary nonsense to ask if we shall be glad to see the boys back. But is it to be expected that we are going to sit still and do nothing to prevent a recurrence of those awful scenes?

"It is with great regret", wrote Robert P. Moncrieff of Gosforth, Newcastle-upon-Tyne on 17 March 1916, "that I have to announce a considerable increase in the consumption and expenditure of Tobacco during the past year." Moncrieff calculated that the increase in expenditure was "the enormous sum of £4,840,000" and, "When it is considered that no real benefit accrues from the habit of smoking, but that undoubted injuries are inflicted in many ways, it is deplorable that the people of the United Kingdom, at a time like this, when the Nation is in fact, struggling for its very existence, should deliberately waste such an enormous amount on a mere weed which disappears in the air as 'smoke'." Moncrieff reckoned that Britain's total tobacco bill, along with pipes, matches and "Tobacconists sundries", came to a staggering £38,480,910. In "normal times", the increase in duty on tobacco would, Moncrieff wrote, "have caused a 'slump', but the abnormal wages which have been earned by the working classes in munitions, war stores, etc., during 1915, has enabled the workers to snap their fingers at the increase in prices and to buy their 'baccy' as usual."

The Manchester-based British Anti-Tobacco Society naturally enough shared Moncrieff's concerns. Among its publications was the sixpenny pamphlet "The Smoking Craze: An Indictment, with Reasons, and an appeal to Christians" by Frank Ballard DD MA BSc etc. A more detailed condemnation appeared in Herbert H. Tidswell's "The Tobacco Habit" in which "the author's aim is to call attention to the ill-effects of Tobacco on all functions of the body. He seeks to prove by facts and statistics that Tobacco Smoking effects men, women, and children and is race-suicide." The Society also produced an Anti-Smoking Chart that "should be Hung Up in every DAY and SUNDAY SCHOOL". It showed "the Evils of Juvenile Smoking ... and its retarding influence on the healthy mental and physical development of growing boys". One boy who sadly failed to heed its warning was 16-year-old Robert James Victor Blair of Angel Road, Brixton, a clerk at Woolwich Arsenal. On 24 September 1918 at Newington, an inquest heard how Blair, "described as an inveterate smoker of cigarettes ... died suddenly ... and the doctor who made a *post mortem* examination attributed death to syncope [loss of consciousness from a drop in blood pressure] accelerated by his cigarette smoking".

In Woolwich back in 1914 the District Medical Officer of Health, Dr S. Davies, had conducted his own personal investigation into the link between cancer and smoking. Among his findings was that of the 33 patients who had died of cancer of the lips, tongue and jaw, 25 (76 per cent) had smoked excessively. But the scant publicity given to the link between cancer and tobacco did little if anything to curb smoking in wartime Britain. Most smokers would have taken comfort from *The Lancet*, which advised: "The cigarette, in moderation, is a valuable solace in a time of anxiety ... smoking indubitably affords relief and diversion in all nerve-straining tasks". At Easter 1918, so great was the demand for tobacco in Sheffield that "the leading tobacconists were completely sold out of cigarettes and the cheaper brands of pipe tobacco, and queues of as many as a hundred men were seen outside small shops in the industrial parts of the city where 'twist' and 'shag' could still be obtained". Albert Henry Brook, a grocer of Bitterne, Hampshire, was fined a hefty £30 for "doing his bit" to alleviate the tobacco shortage. A Southampton court was told he had "bought cigarette ends picked up in the street at 4s [four shillings] a pound, and added them to tobacco, and sold the mixture as ninepenny shag."

Smoking, which before the war had been regarded very much as a male preserve, was now practised quite openly by women, and not just by "flappers". The *Manchester Guardian* told readers: "There seems to be no doubt that a very large number of even young girls have since the war taken to smoking cigarettes.... Munition girls smoke a good deal, but it seems that the most confirmed smokers are to be found in those Government offices where they are permitted to smoke during office hours." The YWCA was torn as to whether girls should be allowed to smoke on its premises: "… generally speaking, while the habit is never encouraged it is permitted…. The general feeling among the authorities is that it is a pity young girls should smoke, but that it would be extremely difficult to stop them." In Hornchurch, Essex, Annie Purbrook thought it a pity too that her daughters' friends indulged in such "a useless and expensive habit". But in September 1916, a grand juror at the Central Criminal Court was excused attendance because he was busily engaged on a War Office contract to supply 64 million cigarettes.

On 25 September 1914, *The Times* published a highly unusual letter from Guillermo J. Hill of Wrexham Lodge, Hemstal Road, West Hampstead:

> *Sir, I enclose ½oz of dried coca leaves. Coca leaves are got from two South American plants, Erythroxylon coca and Erythroxylon bolivianum, and contain an alkaloid 'cocaine'. The leaves have been used from time immemorial by the South American Indians. Their effect is to dull the mucous surfaces of the mouth and stomach, with which the saliva produced by chewing them comes into contact, thus blunting for long all feeling of hunger. The cocaine being absorbed produces on the central nervous system a stimulating effect, so that all sense of fatigue and breathlessness vanishes for a time. It was by the use of coca that the Indian post runners of South America were able to achieve their extraordinary feats of endurance. I can testify to the great benefit obtained by its use, especially in long rides over arid plains and mountainous districts. I strongly urge on the Government to supply the Expeditionary Forces with say, 1oz for each unit, this being sufficient for 48 hours, at the small cost of twopence.*

Three days later came a stinging rebuttal from C. Streatfield, late District Magistrate, Benares, India. "In your issue of today's date", he wrote, "you have a letter recommending coca leaves. It is well that the public should be warned that cocaine is a most dangerous drug. The cocaine vice has only recently been introduced into India, but it is now in many places recognized that the cocaine habit is a much more serious vice than either opium or hemp. It is therefore most seriously to be hoped that no individual hearing of the marvellous effects of this drug will unwittingly allow himself to become a victim of this vice."

Mr Streatfield's opinion would appear to have been substantiated at the end of November 1914 by the inquest on the body of Mulka Reuti

Gwalin, aged 34, who had died of cocaine and morphine poisoning. At the inquest, civil engineer James Sidney Lee of Redcar, Yorkshire, told the court that he had lived with Gwalin for 18 years after first encountering her in an Assam coal mine. "Like nearly all Indians," Lee said, "Gwalin was in the habit of taking drugs – opium or cocaine." Lee was a user too, and he and Gwalin had come to London earlier in the year and stayed in a boarding house. But the place was "full of Germans on the roof listening and talking", so they moved to a hotel. From there Lee went out and bought some cocaine from a Holborn chemist, without having to sign the Poisons Book. When he returned he found Gwalin on the floor unconscious. She was taken to St Bartholomew's Hospital and there pronounced dead. After hearing that Gwalin took 10 grams ($^1/_3$ oz) of cocaine a day, the jury returned a verdict of Death by Misadventure.

To most Britons at the time, even fans of Sherlock Holmes, the words "drug habit" would have undoubtedly conjured up the image of a Chinese opium den. And throughout the war that image was reinforced by fairly regular prosecutions of men like "Leu Chan, 41, a Chinaman of Limehouse, fined 40/- [forty shillings] at Thames Police Court for having in his possession utensils for smoking opium, and also opium prepared for smoking".

On 3 January 1916 "Quex", the *Evening News* gossip columnist, told readers:

> *I see that other people are turning their attention to the growing craze for opium smoking…. West End Bohemia is hearing some dark stories of what is going on. But still more prevalent is the use of that exciting drug cocaine. It is so easy to take – just snuffed up the nose; and no-one seems to know why the girls who suffer from this body and soul racking habit find the drug so easy to obtain. In the ladies' cloakroom of a certain establishment two bucketfuls of thrown-away small circular cardboard boxes were discovered by the cleaners the other day – discarded cocaine boxes.*

A few weeks later, on 11 February, the papers were reporting the case at Folkestone of Horace Dennis Kingsley and Rose Edwards who were each sentenced to six months' imprisonment with hard labour for selling cocaine to Canadian soldiers. During the trial it came out that there had been 40 cases of the "drug habit" in a nearby camp. The following day, *The Times* medical correspondent commented: "The evidence would seem to show that they acted on their initiative and were actuated only by motives of personal greed. This, if it is a true estimate of the case, is a matter for satisfaction, for cocaine is more deadly than bullets when a man yields to its influence." There followed a longish account of the drug's use in North America and effects on its takers: "Its victim is exalted to heaven and then cast down to hell.... If he goes far enough his sanity may become dependent upon his use of the drug; deprive him of cocaine and you make a lunatic of him." After confirming Streatfield's account of the cocaine habit in India, with the additional neat xenophobic touch that *Austrian* steamers had played a large part in smuggling the drug into the sub-continent, the article concluded: "It will be evident from this that to the soldier subjected to nervous strain and hard work, cocaine once used, must come as a terrible temptation. It will, for an hour, charm away all his troubles, his fatigue, his anxiety; it will give him fictitious strength and vigour. But it will also, in the end render him worthless as a soldier and a man."

To help combat the drug menace, the authorities turned to Britain's newly created women's police service. Mary Allen, pre-war suffragette, pioneer policewoman and future enthusiastic adherent of Sir Oswald Mosley's British Union of Fascists, recalled:

> *In 1916, at the request of the Admiralty, we trained and supplied selected policewomen ... to help tackle the problem of the drug traffic, which was then growing to very dangerous proportions among soldiers back on leave from the Front. Under the ghastly war conditions, dope seemed to some of the soldiers a way of escape of escape from terror. And there were plenty of harpies ready to supply the stuff that would end by robbing the men of decency, self-control and courage.*

One of Allen's subordinates actually "disguised herself as a prostitute, got to know all her supposed colleagues, moved in circles where she was in extreme danger from the drug-runners, and obtained information of a most important kind ... in connection with drug-running ... the main source of drug supply was traced, and the authorities crushed it with a merciless hand, after a lightning raid by combined military and civil police and detectives."

Allen was being more than slightly disingenuous with her recollections. In May 1916, the papers reported the failure to prosecute William Johnson, a denizen of Soho, for trying to sell cocaine at 2s 6d (two shillings and sixpence) per packet to women in Leicester Square. The magistrate, reluctantly dismissing the charge, "sincerely hoped that the result of this case would lead to a speedy and drastic alteration of the law". The suggestion was made that "it would be more expeditious to make some addition to the regulations under the Defence of the Realm Act". Commenting on the case the next day, a correspondent in *The Times* thought that: "Cocaine and opium have far more women victims than is imagined, and the stress and anxiety caused by the war aggravate the evil." It was not cocaine nor opium but morphia that was the favoured drug of society beauty and wartime nurse Lady Diana Manners, daughter of the Duke of Rutland. On 9 January 1916, her ardent but secret suitor, Foreign Office clerk Alfred Duff Cooper, recorded in his diary: "Diana in bed all day – she and Katharine [Asquith, the Prime Minister's daughter-in-law] took morphia last night. I hope she won't become a *morphineuse*. It would spoil her looks." A month later, Duff wrote that Diana was again ill in bed as a result of her experiments with morphia. But on 11 March, he too was persuaded to have one-sixth of a gram of morphia injected and "woke late feeling extraordinarily well". Lady Diana's addiction continued throughout the war and beyond.

Back in 1916, it was felt that stronger regulations rather than gentle chiding words were needed. So, after energetic canvassing by Sir Malcolm Delevingne of the Home Office, Defence of the Realm Regulation 40B came into force on 28 July 1916. From that date, the possession of cocaine or opium – but not yet cannabis or heroin – except by authorized professionals such as doctors, chemists and vets, was a criminal offence. The law might have changed but drug abuse continued to be both a headache for the authorities and good copy for the newspapers. In May 1918, the papers reported the case of 45-year-old nurse Beatrice Wilson, who had resorted to forgery to obtain morphine to feed her addiction, and received a year's imprisonment. But it was the death, through a suspected drug overdose on 27 November 1918, of musical-comedy star and actress Billie Carleton that caused a sensation in immediate post-Armistice Britain. Although Billie was a cocaine user, it was probably a combination of other factors that caused her untimely demise aged just 22. She died during the early hours of the morning following the Victory Ball at the Albert Hall at which Lady Diana Manners had appeared as a triumphant Britannia, and her death was, in the words of *The Sketch*, "regretted by many". None more than her dealer, the highly dubious, epicene and louche Raoul Reginald de Veulle, who was tried and acquitted of her manslaughter. He received an eight-month prison sentence under DORA 40B. In sentencing him on 7 April 1919, Mr Justice Salter remarked that it was "a strange thing to reflect that until quite lately these drugs could be bought by all and sundry like so much grocery".

On 4 December 1916, just as serial adulterer Lloyd George was about to become Prime Minister, the National Council of Public Morals convened a conference at London's Sunderland House. Bishop Russell Wakefield of Birmingham presided, and in his opening address he deplored the fact that: "Every kind of looseness of life, almost, was encouraged by the war conditions". In his own diocese, "they had tens of thousands of young people who had come munition-making from distant towns and villages. Every temptation was put before them...." The Bishop sincerely hoped that the religious leaders present would combine to confront the pressing problem of the nation's morals. The Chief Rabbi agreed that the problem was "so vast that they needed a union of all the forces that could be arrayed against it – they wanted a union of all churches". Delegates came forward with their own experiences and to offer solutions. Leading Baptist Rev. F.B. Meyer said that although they had closed down 2,000 brothels in Lambeth and Southwark during the last 25 years, "the evil today was more rife than when they started. These brothels were frequented by soldiers, and the streets were full of girls of 15 and 16 who were throwing themselves at the feet of soldiers and sailors." Monsignor Canon W. F. Brown thought that it was because "they had kept the priest out of the school, that they were now reaping the reward". Prebendary William Carlile, founder of the Church Army, was of the opinion that "this was a woman's question. The holy influence of a good woman would do more", he was confident, "than any man could do." The conference was told by a Dr Schofield that "the existing cause of all this trouble was the part that alcohol played in encouraging sexual vice". And Dr Mary Scharlieb deplored the situation: "After two years and four months of war we had not yet awakened to a sense of our danger."

But even as Dr Scharlieb spoke, there were those taking active steps to both guard and improve the nation's morals and sexual health. The Somerset Branch of the National Council for Combating Venereal Disease was particularly active. Its members gave over 100 lectures, which, according to their annual report, were much appreciated: "One poor woman who went said, 'I only wish every mother had been present to hear it. I am thankful I was there, I have learnt so many useful things I never knew before, me and my friend each brought different books so that we might exchange them.'" On matters of public propriety in Bournemouth during the summer of 1917, the Beach Committee were much exercised over the vexed question of whether "bathers coming from their apartments in bathing costume covered with a mackintosh or overall, and bathing without the use of a machine" were infringing the by-laws. Eventually it was decided that "an overall used in this way may be regarded as a screen. If, however, the practice is abused they will reconsider the question." Happily, no impropriety would appear to have taken place on the highly successful experimental mixed bathing days at the public baths in Richmond, Surrey. Indeed, the number of bathers of both sexes, it was reported, had increased by over 1,000 compared with other days.

The Young Men's Christian Association was in the forefront in warning of the moral dangers that awaited young soldiers coming to the capital. According to the YMCA pamphlet "Waiting all Night for the Train", "Tens of thousands of soldiers arrive in London every week with time on their hands…. It is hard to believe, but it is literally true, that there are among us numbers of people, working sometimes in groups, whose whole object is to rob and wreck the Tommy passing through the town. They aim particularly at Canadians and Australians, because they have most money. The men in some of these gangs dress themselves in khaki, and boast bogus ribbons, VC and DSO decorations. What wonder that the young Tommy, landing at Waterloo or waiting at Euston, responds to their greeting! They drug drinks, sometimes they apparently use ether. I am not writing melodrama, but sober fact. Hundreds of young fellows have been ruined by these harpies." But help was at hand: "The YMCA in London has had a straight fight with this evil. Every night young men go out from its rooms scouring the streets, picking up the helpless and homeless Tommy, housing him and sending him on the next day in safety."

There was some consolation too in learning from Sir James Crichton-Browne at the annual general meeting of the Sanitary Inspectors' Association that in the opinion of "a well-versed Italian correspondent… the British soldier was undoubtedly the best-fed, the cleanest, and the healthiest in the field". Sir James thought that: "With cleanliness – moral and physical – in their favour, we should have no misgivings as to the final success of our men over the dirty and demoralized, however courageous, millions opposed to them."

The YMCA's sister organization was also alert to the dangers of loose morals in wartime. The YWCA warned that: "Under the pretence of friendship some men and some women wickedly try to get hold of girls. They make fine promises, but these are traps. These false friends sell the girls they have trapped for immoral purposes. For the girls this means dishonour, shame and weakness. For the Nation also it means dishonour, shame and weakness." To prevent this from happening, girls should not "stand giggling at the street corner trying to attract notice from the passers-by. It looks as if you thought you were cheap goods for sale." Neither should they "accept presents from any man who is not a relation, to whom you are not engaged or who is not really a very old and trusted friend". Because: "If you do, he may afterwards demand a recompense at the price of your honour." And, as the ladies of Somerset had been told,

The worst infectious disease is Venereal Disease, commonly called the "bad disorder". This is spread though immoral conduct between men and women and therefore ought not to exist. But also it may sometimes be caught by innocent people, through kissing, through using towels, cups, spoons, etc. that have been infected and not thoroughly washed. Also through dirty seats of lavatories. Let each one of us insist on all lavatories being kept clean and decent, otherwise they are sources of danger. If they are decently used, kept clean and the seat dry, there need be no fear of infection. Never allow more than one person to enter the lavatory at the same time. Anything else is a degrading practice, and a most likely way to catch disease. If you have run the risk of infection of Venereal Disease, early treatment is the only hope of cure, and the hospital will give, free of charge and in confidence, the only treatment that is any good. Never go to quacks, they are worse than useless. Loss of time lessens the chance of cure."

In Blackburn, Lancashire, the fear of contracting VD briefly held back 18-year-old virgin soldier Corporal Fred Airey from embarking on an affair with Maggie, a young widow and friend of his sister Lena. Fred had won the Military Medal in France and was home on 14 days' leave when he met Maggie. She was, in the parlance of the time, "fast", and on their first meeting asked Fred, "You'd like to take me to bed wouldn't you?" Fred told her of his fears about VD but she assured him that he would be her first lover in over a year. Hearing this, Fred found his "defences were crumbling, and my desires were beginning to get the better of my fears". The couple went upstairs and

> *she began to undress. I was quite shaky and wondering if I was doing the right thing. How could I expect to marry a virgin if I went with Maggie? But by this time she was helping me out of my clothes and then we flopped onto the bed. Before I knew it my seed had hit the wall over her head. She thought this quite funny, but told me to relax and lay down beside her, and it would not be long before I could do it again. Sure enough, after a few minutes I got the urge again, and this time we made love. What an experience! 'Boy, you nearly knocked my hat off!' exclaimed Maggie.*

Fred spent the rest of his leave with Maggie, often going dancing and spending a "dirty weekend" at the seaside. Fred recalled: "The affair went on until I had to report back and rejoin my unit in France. All my fears and worries about women just seemed to evaporate, as Maggie broke through my youthful ignorance and confusion. On our last day I asked her to marry me, but she declined, and I am glad she did, in a way. I was still very young, and had much to learn yet…. As it is I have her precious memory to cherish. She certainly made a man of me."

Fred was fortunate in his brief romance with Maggie. Other soldiers were not so lucky with their partners and VD remained a major problem both for the authorities and for the unfortunate sufferers. In March 1917, the City of London Corporation decided to set up, at the cost of £600, a venereal disease centre at the Royal Albert Docks for the treatment of merchant seamen in the Port of London. And to the fury of feminist organizations, Regulation 40D of the Defence of the Realm Act was introduced. It made it "an offence for any woman suffering from venereal disease to solicit or to have sexual intercourse with a member of His Majesty's Forces". Despite strong protestations from the Medical Women's Federation, the newspapers were soon reporting cases like that of Ellen Carter. A married woman with a husband serving in France, at Eastbourne in May 1918 she received a six-month prison sentence "for communicating a venereal disease to two soldiers". But to obtain a prosecution was not always easy. "The difficulty was one of time, namely the lapse of time between the inception of the disease and the examination of the woman," prosecutor Herbert Muskett told Marylebone Police Court on 9 August 1918. Later the same day, at Lambeth Police Court, and for that very reason, a frustrated Muskett failed to get a conviction against 21-year-old prostitute Edith Odell, charged with infecting a Canadian soldier. Mabel Hewlette, a year younger than Odell, was less fortunate. She received five months' hard labour for infecting another Canadian soldier, Private Melville Turnbull, despite her plea that "if she had communicated the disease to the soldier she did not know it, and she was very sorry". Although, as Muskett told the court, "The public would be appalled if they knew the number of young soldiers who were rendered unfit for service through contracting venereal disease," 40D was an early casualty of peace, being revoked on 25 November 1918.

As the YMCA noted, tens of thousands of British and Empire soldiers, like the unfortunate Private Turnbull, were now thronging the capital, and safeguarding their moral welfare became a concern to many. Leading the field was the bachelor Bishop of London, Arthur Winnington-Ingram, whom the *Daily Mail* described as "a man of broad views and generous sympathies with all classes". Those generous sympathies did not extend to the sex industry, as the Bishop made amply clear in June 1917 to a conference of National Vigilance Association and the International Bureau for the Suppression of the White Slave Traffic. He told delegates that they must see that the large number of soldiers from overseas return to their own countries "clean and healthy". The Bishop was of the opinion that there had been a considerable improvement in the morals of London during the past 40 years but much remained to be done. "We must make it much hotter for brothel keepers to carry on their evil trade in London," he continued. "I am all for amusement, for music halls; I am all for giving the boys a good time when they come to the city. I am in favour of getting the girls on the streets placed in suitable homes. The life of a prostitute and the keeper of a brothel should be realized as social crimes." The Bishop's sentiments were greeted by cheers from the Caxton Hall audience, who next heard from Sir Edward Henry, Commissioner of the Metropolitan Police. Sir Edward agreed with the Bishop that "life in London streets was cleaner and better than a few years back", putting this down to the special attention given to notorious areas by his police and the new women patrols. Since the war began, Sir Edward's men had arrested and brought before the magistrates 19,025 girls and women charged with soliciting, 90 per cent of whom had received fines.

Conditions in most of the capital's streets, Sir Edward believed, were "not open to adverse criticism". Unfortunately, the same could not be said of London's open spaces. "I have very detailed information about the condition of things in Hyde Park, Sir Edward told the delegates. "I may say that there, at almost any time during the evening, couples can be seen behaving in a most scandalous manner. To my mind, the evil-doers are persons to whom no consideration should be shown."

On the platform with the Bishop and the Commissioner was Lieutenant-General Sir Francis Lloyd, General Officer Commanding, London District and the man responsible for the conduct of soldiers in the streets of London. Sir Francis refuted the idea that the soldiers were not being adequately looked after. He then told the conference that in mufti [civilian clothes] he had paid visits to the areas of alleged vice and had found the reports of them "grossly inaccurate.... Comparing, say, the Waterloo-road, now with what it was when he was a young Guardsman, the improvement was beyond all recognition." Sir Francis continued: "Today and yesterday I have taken special means of trying to stop the soldiers' part of the vice. I cannot touch the woman. I have special measures to deal with Hyde Park. 1 could do with ten times the number of police I have. I have only 130 policemen for the metropolis. Still, I know I cannot get more; the men are needed at the front."

Despite Sir Francis's assurances, the papers were full of lurid stories about Waterloo Road. It was described variously as "a centre of vice" and "an open sewer", and there were frequent reports of the prosecution of some of its denizens, such as 21-year-old Sylvia Brown, who had "behaved in a disgusting manner outside the Union Jack Club". Also up before the magistrate was 61-year-old Lord Headley, charged with being drunk and disorderly in Waterloo Road. His Lordship told the court that he

> could swear on his honour as a gentleman, an Englishman, and a peer of the realm that he had drunk no more than two bottles of stout ... he had been brought up on stout and should continue to drink it, but his religion forbade excess. He denied that he put his arm round the neck of a woman. He might have so forgotten himself to try and kiss a pretty young woman – he had done it before – but not an old frump.

Lord Headley got off with a fine of 10s (ten shillings) with the option of seven days in jail. A much stiffer sentence of 12 months' hard labour was handed out to 34-year-old Woolwich Arsenal munitions worker Alice Gerdes of Fair Street, Bermondsey. She was found guilty of procuring two girls for immoral purposes and of allowing young children to reside in a disorderly house, where "Colonial soldiers had been taken in a very drunken state". Sentencing her, Judge Rentoul remarked on the difficulties that the authorities were encountering in dealing with the "Waterloo-road scandal … because the girls who frequented it were not common prostitutes but apparently working girls who adopted that mode of life in the evening".

The papers also reported that similar scenes of depravity and "rampant prostitution" were to be found in Horseferry Road near Victoria Station. There Ada Sawiehi, "a smartly dressed girl of 14", and her 18-year-old cousin Vanda, "British subjects but Russian Poles by descent", were arrested for accosting soldiers at 11.00 pm on a Saturday night. Even in ultra-respectable Bath, the Watch Committee was compelled to enforce Section 18 of the 1908 Children's Act to prevent girls under 16 "loitering about the streets", and to instruct the city's police to caution the girls and their parents.

The Great and the Good were quick to pronounce on the nation's morals in wartime. General Sir Horace Smith-Dorrien, "a distinguished soldier who has seen much service" but who had been effectively "bowler-hatted" in April 1915, was of the opinion that the music hall and cinema were to blame. The General asked: "Who can possibly argue that vulgar and suggestive gags, such as some popular actors give vent to, or low-toned revues and cinemas can do anything but lower the morals of the youth of the nation?" This opinion would seem to have been borne out by the prosecution of the North Metropolitan Theatre Company Ltd for "allowing improper conduct at the Rink Cinema Stroud Green-road, Hornsey". A police constable and his female colleague of the Women's Patrol paid a visit to the cinema on 4 February 1918, only to find that "in one part of the house a number of soldiers and girls were reclining in each other's arms, and that several acts of impropriety took place". The company's defence counsel pleaded that: "innocent courtship was often misconstrued by persons out to detect immorality, and so long as there were sexes cuddling would continue in public places, and even on the Embankment in daylight." This cut no ice and the company was fined £20 with £42 costs.

If Sir Horace thought that immorality stemmed from the music hall and cinema, his "Heavenly Twin", as some of the press dubbed him, the

Bishop of London, identified London's night clubs as a principal source of evil. They were, the Bishop wrote, "for the most part the haunts and hunting grounds of sharks and loose women whose business consists of exploiting the follies and weaknesses of those who are induced to visit them, and that the existence of these places in war-time is a danger not only to the individuals who resort to them, but also through them, to the nation". Already the military authorities had attempted to prohibit officers in uniform from visiting nightclubs. Some who had done so, like Lieutenant-Colonel Wilder and Lieutenant High of the Army Service Corps, had even been court-martialled. They had gone on a "beano" to the New Holborn Dancing and Supper Club, and both claimed ignorance of the War Office prohibition. In another case, in which 28-year-old milliner Amy Lewis was charged with robbing Royal Artilleryman Francis John Merritt of £4, the court was told that the couple had gone to a night club at 1.00 am. There, with four others, they had got through several brandies and sodas, four bottles of champagne, more brandies, and a bottle of wine. "A perfect scandal … and a positively disgraceful state of things," was the verdict of Robert Wallace, the chairmen of the bench, "I had no idea such things were going on in London."

In April 1917, during an inquest at Hackney, Coroner Dr Wyn Westcott told the court that "he was afraid that the ancient and honourable custom of marriage was going out of fashion, as every week he had one or two cases of men and women living together unmarried". A view shared a few months later by Mr Justice Lawrence who, in sentencing a young collier to three months' imprisonment at Glamorgan Assizes for bigamy, told the court: "… this crime was absolutely rampant. Respect for the marriage ceremony seemed to be dying out altogether." Both men were being unduly pessimistic, although certainly the number of marriages had declined. In 1914, there had been 352,833 marriages in the United Kingdom. The number shot up to 421,311 in 1915, dropped to 333,570 in 1916, and further decreased in 1917 to 310,410. There was likewise a decline in the birth-rate. In 1914, there were 1,101,551 births, a drop to 1,024,378 in 1915. 1916 saw the number drop still further to 986,892, with an even sharper decline to 852,157 in 1917. The *Daily Mail* pointed out, rather obviously, that: "The acceleration of decline in 1917 is no doubt due to the fact that the application of compulsory service to married men towards the middle of 1916 must have resulted in an increased proportion of married recruits from that time onwards."

The perils of conducting irregular sexual liaisons were brought only too clearly to light in the early morning of 2 November 1917, when asylum attendant Thomas Henry found two parcels near his house in Regent Square. They contained the torso, arms and legs of Emilienne Gerard, a 31-year-old French soldier's wife. On the night of 31 October, 22 Gotha bombers had attacked London, killing ten people, injuring 22 and doing nearly £23,000 worth of damage. When the alert had sounded, Emilienne at first decided to take shelter at Great Portland Street Underground Station which was near to where she lived at 50 Munster Square. She then changed her mind, thinking that it would be safer in the basement of the house of her lover Louis Voisin, a 42-year-old French stableman and former butcher. Arriving at 101 Charlotte Street, Emilienne found that Voisin was not alone. With him was another lady friend and lover, Berthe Roche. A violent altercation took place, with Voisin and Roche repeatedly hitting Emilienne about the head before strangling her with a towel. Voisin, utilizing his skills as a butcher, then cut the body up before going off in horse and trap to dump the torso, arms and legs in Regent Square. In an attempt to make out the killing had been the result of xenophobia, Voisin also left with the remains a scrap of paper on which he had written "blodie Belgium". The police traced Emilienne's address through a laundry mark on the body's clothing. At Munster Square, they came across a note from Voisin which led them to 101 Charlotte Street, where they found Emilienne's head, hands and earring in the coal cellar. There were also bloodstains up to the ceiling of the cellar. Voisin claimed that he had gone to Munster Square to feed Emilienne's cat, and there had found her head and hands which he had brought back to Charlotte Street and hidden in the cellar for fear he would be accused of her murder. When asked to write "bloody Belgium", Voisin again misspelt it "blodie Belgium". Found guilty, he was sentenced to death and hanged at Pentonville Prison on 2 March 1918. Voisin was one of 61 people who were hanged in Britain between 1914 and 1918. His lover Berthe Roche was later tried and found guilty of being an accessory after the fact. She received a seven-year prison sentence, but was soon found to be insane. Committed to an asylum, she died on 22 March 1919.

Sometimes the issue was not immorality but what would now be termed post-traumatic stress. On 9 February 1918, 16-year-old Woolwich Arsenal clerk Nellie Trew was raped and murdered on Eltham Common. A few days later the press published a photograph of a Leicestershire Regiment badge found at the scene of the crime. It was immediately recognized by Ted Farrell of the Hewson Manufacturing Company on Newman Street as belonging to his workmate David Greenwood, as did a button torn from a man's overcoat found by Nellie's side. Greenwood had enlisted in the army underage and at 17 years old had been buried alive by a shell explosion at Ypres. It was argued that shell shock had caused the 21-year-old to act as he did in raping and murdering Nellie as she made her way to Plumstead library from her parents' home at Well Hall. It took the jury three hours to find Greenwood guilty, but the foreman added that "in view of the youth of the prisoner, his service to his country, and his previous good character, they desired to recommend him to mercy". Greenwood was nevertheless sentenced to death, but after "long deliberation" Home Secretary Sir George Cave commuted the sentence to life imprisonment. Greenwood spent the next 15 years in prison before being released in 1933, aged 36.

Naval deserter William Burkitt also escaped the hangman's noose. On 28 August 1915, he had turned up at his mother' house in Gillam Street, Kingston upon Hull, and announced, "I have done Polly in." Polly was Mary Jane Tyler, a married woman living apart from her husband, with whom Burkitt had shacked up after deserting from HM Trawler *Dinas,* having previously absconded from HMS *Hero.* Mrs Burkitt went round to Polly's house in Derwent Avenue and found her lying in a pool of blood. It was later established that she had been stabbed three or four times and that the fatal wound had severed her jugular vein. On 23 November 1915, 28-year-old Burkitt came up before the North and East Riding Assizes at York charged with Polly's murder. In his defence, he said that he and Polly had been arguing over a snapshot that she had found in which he had his arm around another woman. The argument led a fierce struggle during which he had accidentally stabbed her. Evidence was produced that Polly was far from being above reproach when it came to morals, "having been unfaithful to many men". The jury only took an hour to decide that Burkitt was guilty not of murder but of the lesser crime of manslaughter, and he was sentenced to 12 years penal servitude. Released in November 1924, he went on to kill twice more, both his victims being, like Polly, married women living apart from their husbands. In May 1939, as a new world war loomed on the horizon, Burkitt was sentenced to penal servitude for life. He died in prison in 1956.

In other cases, the war may have told unambiguously in a defendant's favour. One such was the case of 34-year-old Lieutenant Douglas Malcolm, whom the *Daily Sketch* described as "a Royal Artillery officer engaged at Divisional Headquarters at the front. A handsome member of a wealthy Scottish family." On 14 August 1917 he had shot dead his wife Dorothy's lover Anton Baumberg in an unprepossessing boarding house at Porchester Place behind Paddington Station. Baumberg, who preferred to be addressed as Count Anthony de Borch, was described in the press as "an adventurer of Russian-Polish and Jewish extraction", and few tears other than Dorothy's were shed at his demise. The fact that he was an Austrian citizen who bore an uncanny resemblance to the new Emperor Karl and that he was Jewish condemned him in many people's eyes. Baumberg was patently not a gentleman and most probably, as rumoured, a German spy. Malcolm was tried at the Old Bailey, defended by former Home Secretary Sir John Simon, whom Asquith had dubbed "The Impeccable" and Lord Beaverbrook considered "the last word in logic". Sir John pulled no punches, describing Baumberg as "one of those pieces of human refuse that are carried along on the tide of great cities".

The two-day trial, which relegated war news to second place in the press, was unique in British legal history as the first case of a *crime passionel* where the guilty party was set free on grounds of self-defence. Sir John's summing up in Malcolm's defence received a three-minute ovation from spectators in the courtroom and it took the jury only 20 minutes to deliver a "Not Guilty" verdict. The *Daily Mirror* reported that: "For quite five minutes pandemonium reigned. Solemn-looking ushers raised their arms and appealed for order in vain. The noise was deafening. The scene resembled the unrestrained jubilation of a pre-war football match – a man seated at the extreme end of the judge's bench cheered and waved a straw hat in a most frantic way." The *Mirror* considered the trial to be "probably the most sensational love tragedy ever unfolded in a criminal court in this country", declaring that "the story of how Lieutenant Malcolm shot the bogus Count in order to save his wife's honour appealed especially to women". But not all women. Nina Boyle, a leading suffragette and Secretary of the Women's Freedom League, regarded "the Malcolm case an insult to every woman in England and a disgrace to the country, the courts, the Bench and the Bar." Malcolm returned to the Western Front almost immediately after the trial. He was awarded the Military Cross for "conspicuous courage and devotion to duty" during the last days of the fighting.

Moral stigmas such as illegitimacy were still very strong. At a meeting of the Alliance of Honour in May 1915, Mrs Bramwell Booth of the Salvation Army told delegates:

Few realized that here were about 37,000 illegitimate children registered annually, and undoubtedly there were numbers not registered. Their existence and treatment was not only an injury to the community, because it involved such tremendous wastage and the withdrawal in numberless instances of the mother from a useful industrious life, but it was a wound in the moral character which must work paralysis and death in the parents, and was a violation of the moral foundations which God designed should build their communities.

In his speech to the Alliance, the Bishop of Chelmsford said that while he thought that "the unmarried mother must be adequately provided for, it was another thing to treat the woman as if she was an honourable married woman. There should be some difference made between that family and the family born in holy wedlock."

In July 1916, a City of London inquest on a newly born male baby found floating in the Thames was told by a policeman that a large number of infants had been similarly found, "about nine months after the beginning of the war". But "owing to the better provision made for children of unmarried girls there were now very few cases". Sadly, the disgrace at the prospect of becoming an unmarried mother drove many young women to desperate measures. In June 1917 at Lambeth Police Court, two nurses, Louisa Davies and Grace Jenkins, were accused of murdering Daisy Armstrong during an abortion that went disastrously wrong. In Lambeth a few months earlier, the inquest on the body of 27-year-old Rose Bullen heard that she died as a result of an abortion or, as the press euphemistically called it, "an illegal operation". And at the Central Criminal Court, a woman was, typically, sentenced to a year's hard labour for performing an abortion.

Bigamy too had its stigma. In July 1916, bigamist Edith Russell tried to commit suicide, which was then still a criminal offence, by throwing herself off Blackfriars Bridge. The court was fairly lenient and she was bound over for £20. Lenience was often shown to bigamous soldiers. In February 1916, Sergeant W. Smith of the East Surreys, who was serving a year's hard labour, was granted the King's Pardon and allowed to rejoin his regiment. Less than ingenious excuses for bigamy were sometimes offered up. Loss of memory was a frequent one, as in the case of Private Charles Bell of the West Yorkshire Regiment. He married war widow Ada Taylor on 20 May 1916, only to be arrested a week later as a deserter. It was subsequently discovered that he was still married to his wife Sarah of Morley, Yorkshire, with whom he had tied the knot back in July 1908. Bell told the bench that he had lost his memory owing to illness and had no idea that he had been married before. The following February at Old Street Police Court, a man accused of bigamy pleaded that when a child he had had a fall, which affected his head. The magistrate told him to go away and tell that story somewhere else.

In the midst of all the moral outrage and soul-searching, a judicious warning note was struck by no less a figure than James Marchant, the Director of the National Council of Public Morals, who wrote in August 1916:

While I whole-heartedly support all wise movements to mitigate evils as exist in our music-halls and elsewhere – whose entertainments are often more inane than immoral – I am most anxious at the present time that we should not hold London before the eyes of our enemies as an immoral city. It is indeed infinitely better than Berlin, and I feel it savours of unpatriotism to make a public sensation of the evils we all deplore. The whole tone of the nation is undergoing deep improvement, and it seems to me to be un-English and unjust to choose this moment to cry aloud from the rooftops that London is a sinkhole of iniquity. Amateur detective spying on our morals at this time is to be deprecated.

Such "amateur detective spying" as often as not led to the unpleasant crime of blackmail. In April 1917, for instance, two absent-without-leave army privates, Robert Smith of the East Surreys and Frederick Carter of the London Regiment, were charged with attempting to blackmail Captain H. E. V. Huggett of the Royal Fusiliers. The court heard that Huggett, in an act of "grave impropriety", had invited the two soldiers back to a friend's flat in St Andrew's Mansions, Dorset Street. There, the soldiers demanded money from Huggett, threatening "that if the Captain did not comply with the request they would charge him with indecency". Huggett strenuously denied that any indecency had taken place. But his case was hardly helped by the fact that the friend he had approached to obtain money to buy off Smith and Carter had reportedly said, "I suppose you have been up to your games again."

The 1885 Criminal Law Amendment Act, which was to remain on the statute book until 1967, made illegal all homosexual acts between males, consenting or otherwise. Oscar Wilde's trials and imprisonment had taken place only 20 years or so before and his shadow still loomed large. Indeed, in October 1914, two of the playwright's former lovers, Lord Alfred Douglas, the infamous "Bosie", and Robbie Ross were locked in a well-publicized legal battle over libel. A few months later, 20-year-old Charles Garrett was arrested for importuning in Leicester Square by two CID detectives. The court was told that Garrett had been "partly in clerical attire and wore two crucifixes on his breast". But, more damning still, "in his possession were found two books by Oscar Wilde". In a letter read out in court, Garrett claimed to be doing "rescue work among soldiers … picking up drunken soldiers between midnight and 2 am. It was his own idea. He saw it wanted doing and came forward to do it." With two previous convictions for similar offences, Garrett was found guilty and sentenced to a year's imprisonment with hard labour and 25 strokes of the birch.

In March 1918, Christopher Millard, Wilde's bibliographer and the model for Mr Deacon in Anthony Powell's *A Dance to the Music of Time*, received a year's imprisonment for an act of gross indecency that had taken place on 18 December 1915. Millard, who in the early Twenties was to casually remark to the teenage Powell, "You know, you're a great temptation," had already served three months' hard labour for a similar offence back in 1906. Prosecuting counsel and stern moral crusader Sir Archibald Bodkin described Millard as "a civilian who had something to do with literature", and told the court that, "In December 1915, the condition of things in certain busy parts of the West-end of London was a scandal to civilization." The *Recorder* agreed: "… in 1915 such conduct was rife in London…. The conditions of things at that time were truly appalling, and in many cases the persons involved were educated men." The law came down very heavily on them and on others who were, in the coded expressions of the day, "So" or "Musical". In April 1917, 25-year-old Robert Trevelyan was sentenced to 21 months' hard labour and 15 lashes of the "cat" (a rope whip of nine knotted thongs) for soliciting in Oxford Street while, "masquerading in feminine attire". The unfortunate Trevelyan had already received 25 strokes with the birch for a previous similar offence. A few weeks after the Armistice,

40-year-old vocalist and "professional impersonator of women" Arthur
Grayson of Stockwell Green got a comparatively lighter sentence of six
months' hard labour for "importuning male persons in the Strand". For
a similar offence in November 1918 at Bedfordbury, Belgian refugee
Joseph Marie Adolf Troupin received six months' imprisonment and a
deportation order.

King George V was famously heard to remark of homosexuals, "Why,
I thought people like that always shot themselves." And that was indeed
the sad fate of Private William Mason of the King's Liverpool Regiment,
who on 16 July 1916 while "undergoing detention for masquerading as
a woman ... shot himself at Aldershot". At his inquest, "it was stated
that he was a good soldier, but had been 'ragged' for effeminacy." A
verdict of "Suicide during temporary insanity" was returned. In those
days homosexuality in men was invariably equated with effeminacy.
And so when the court heard that Kenneth Stewart, charged with Ernest
Crosby for improper conduct off Waterloo Road in April 1918, had
in his possession a pot of face cream and powder puff, his "guilt" was
automatically assumed. And the fact that Frederick Leslie Allbeury had
"already undergone a sentence as a rogue and vagabond for importuning
male persons" guaranteed a sentence of six months' hard labour for
wearing a uniform to which he was not entitled.

Because it was said that the King's grandmother Queen Victoria could
not comprehend it, lesbianism was not illegal. Yet although music-hall
stars like Vesta Tilley and Ella Shields nearly always wore men's clothes
or military uniforms on stage, any other woman caught doing so could
find herself open to prosecution. In January 1917 at Chatham, Mrs
Jane Macgregor was fined 13s for unlawfully wearing the uniform of an
officer of the Royal Engineers. Mrs Macgregor "admitted that she went
into public houses wearing the uniform, which had been lent to her,
and pleaded that she had only done it as a joke". Six months later, in
Liverpool, Gertrude Macdonald got a much stiffer sentence of 14 days'
imprisonment "for wearing His Majesty's uniform without permission".
But when 21-year-old Mabel Joyce appeared in a Newcastle court
dressed as a cowboy she was perhaps unsurprisingly merely remanded
for medical observation.

Looking back on the last months of the war, Collie Knox, then a
personable 20-year-old homosexual army officer serving in the London
Aircraft Defence Area, wrote how:

London at that time had taken on a curious, spurious gaiety. The gaiety of a people who had supped so full of the horrors for so many years that they now cared little what happened. Many of my friends had cast what morals they had ever had to the winds and there were parties night after night where revellers tried to forget the daily casualty lists and the growing conviction that we were caught up in a madness which would never cease.

Collie, who in the Thirties went on to become the most influential of Fleet Street radio critics, had invitations showered on him: "Flattered, I accepted and night after night I went out and met a few decent people and a great many worthless ones."

Annie Purbrook, on hearing of the death of her soldier nephew Charlie at this time, reflected in her diary:

Why, oh why, if humanity was in control and care of a mighty loving kindness, why should trouble fall so heavily on some, while others went scot-free? No! There was no justice; things happened just anyhow, no beneficent plan, no wise control; the truly wise were those who got all they could from life and pushed their way through, taking all the satisfaction and pleasure they could.... I had thought that horrible, but why should they not?

But this was by no means the general view. Throughout the war there had been constant criticism of those "worthless ones" who appeared to be "enjoying the war" and not pulling their weight in the nation's war effort. In May 1917, as the U-boat offensive was still biting hard, a correspondent wrote to *The Times* how he had visited a small village in Rutland and found that the school had been taken over for a wedding feast: "I looked in and saw the tables loaded with food of all kinds, including a three tier wedding cake. As I left the village I met a taxi-cab with six or seven young men of military age going to the wedding...." It transpired that the local vicar had remonstrated with the groom about the ostentatious display of the wedding feast and the use of the school in term time, but to no avail. The correspondent concluded in disgust: "These facts speak for themselves, and show how little our remote villages realize the position of the nation to-day. I was also told – this, of course, is hearsay – that the bridegroom had boasted of his prosperity during the war and expressed the hope that it may last a good while." In a nicely juxtaposed piece on the same page, the paper reported how arrangements were being made to distribute 3,000 lbs (1,400 kg) of cooking potatoes to the poor of Holborn.

Three months earlier, in an account of the recent "crop of dances" ("extremely smart and in all respects well up to pre-war conditions") and the ensuing criticism, *The Times* had commented

> *that there are whole circles in society, both in London and elsewhere, in which the spirit of sacrifice is utterly unknown, and "pre-war conditions" still flourish without the smallest regard for the exhortations of the Prime Minister and the Food Controller. The more exalted the position of the offenders, the greater the difficulty in instilling economy into those well-paid industrial communities which are said to be "enjoying the war". But it is a matter of nothing less than life and death to this country and there should be no exceptions to the rigorous self-denial which has been willingly undertaken by the great mass of our people. If nothing but the pillory will bring these thoughtless spendthrifts into line, then the pillory it must be. We shall not hesitate to expose them wherever the facts are beyond dispute."*

The Times was as good as its word and among those pilloried was the famous and popular actor Fred Terry, "of the well known theatrical family", who while appearing in *Nell Of Old Drury* in Cardiff had illegally used his car and received a fine of £5. Sir Henry Robertson, chairman of the Merionethshire War Agricultural Committee, was luckier. He was fined only 10s (ten shillings) by Llangollen magistrates for using his motor to go salmon fishing without a permit. A stiffer fine went to thoughtless Ethel Bryan of Kensington Gardens Square, Bayswater, who left her car in the street thus "bringing tramway car traffic to a standstill while she was in a tea house".

Throughout 1917, *The Times* and other papers continued to rail against those "people who still regard the war less as a struggle in which they have any part than as a rather remote spectacle in which they may if they choose display a detached interest". Typical of this attitude, it was claimed, was a party of horsewomen who in late April had deliberately ridden across a number of small allotments in southwest London. "The actual damage done may not have been great, but that is not the real measure of the outrage. Every man who is trying to grow food on those plots would tell you that the utter callousness of the act, not the extent of the damage, was the thing that revolted him."

It was not just the upper classes that were at fault: "The middle classes, which are often inclined to be the most self-complacent, are by no means blameless. Among them, it is true, are many households which have found it hard to adapt to a fixed income, or a reduced income, to soaring prices; and no class has made more ungrudging sacrifices." That said, "There are middle-class families to whom the war has meant gain, and gaining luxuries unattainable before." In support of this argument, the Spring 1917 Number of the *Draper's Record* was quoted on the subject of nightdresses and similar apparel. "Most retailers have been experiencing exceptional demands on their stocks", the trade paper noted, "by those who have hitherto only been able to cast longing eyes on fascinating garments beyond their purchasing power." *The Times* sadly concluded that:

Beyond all question, there are many who if they could vote by ballot would be greatly tempted to vote for the war's indefinite continuance; not because they would deliberately prolong the misfortune of others, but because they have a deeper sense of their own benefits than of other people's losses. For them it is easy, because human nature impels that way, to be resolute for a fight to the finish.

To the Armistice and beyond, the moral health and spiritual welfare of the nation was a constant theme in public, pulpit, Parliament and press. One of the country's leading judges, Mr Justice Darling, considered that "the harm that the war had done to the morals of the people of this country was far beyond any material damage that had been caused". And in March 1919, as the peacemakers conferred in Paris, Sir Dyce Duckworth, pillar of the Church Army, told an Aeolian Hall audience how much he deplored the

many signs of decay of religious feeling and carelessness of morality. When they heard of wild dances – amid noises only fit for West African savages – held in London drawing rooms, when they observed the hideous characteristics of dress among young people, the want of discipline among children, and among all classes desecration of the Lord's Day, these were palpable indications that the morals of old England had become degraded.

CHAPTER FIVE

ANYTHING A MAN CAN DO...

SISTER SUSIE'S SEWING SHIRTS FOR SOLDIERS
(Title of a 1914 song.)

In March 1917, writing a letter which paid scant attention to either punctuation or grammar, Joe Hollister of New Cross reflected how:

> *It's extraordinary the amount of female labour employed in the City now; in the trains of a morning of ten passengers in a compartment there is generally an average of eight females, the Bank of England employ over 400, there was a flutter of excitement in Gracechurch St. the other day at two girls with trouser overalls cleaning the windows of shops, the Railway Companys [sic] have employed them of course for a long time while tramcars, omnibuses, mail-van motor cars, Carter Paterson vans, all the Caterers, newsvendors, bootblacks, lamplighters, latherers in barbers shops, in fact in almost sphere of activity, when "Tommy" comes home, he will be keeping house & minding the kids while the missus earns the pieces.*

In 1914, the female population of the United Kingdom stood at 23.7 million, of whom 5.9 million (including girls over the age of ten) were, in the parlance of the day, "gainfully employed". Another 12.9 million were "not occupied" and 4.8 million were children under the age of ten. Just over 2 million women worked in industry, mainly in the clothing and textile trades, and 1.5 million were employed in domestic service. By 1918, the number of women "gainfully employed" had risen to 7.3 million and the Government's listing of "Processes in which Women are successful" required "*twenty-six* tightly published foolscap pages" to record all the jobs that British women and girls were now engaged in for the war effort.

By the time of the Armistice 220,000 women and girls were working in Government offices, an increase of 175,000 since August 1914. At the same time, 117,200 women were employed in transport compared to just 18,200 in 1914. Before the war 61,000 women were employed by the Post Office, mainly in clerical jobs and cleaning duties. Their male colleagues numbered approximately 189,000 and they were mainly engaged on postal deliveries, sorting and telephones. By 1918, the number of men had dropped by 80,000 while the number of women employed, and now in a much wider range of jobs, had increased by 60,000. Women employed in commerce and businesses rose from 505,200 in 1914 to 934,500 by the end of the war.

Back on 19 March 1915, Charles Balston had recorded in his war diary how

> the papers announced that the Government had taken the important step of calling upon women to register themselves for paid employment in the nation's service to fill the vacancies where labour was insufficient or to release more men for the fighting line. It was expected that they would be of use in farm and dairy work, in leather stitching, brush making, in clothing machinery and light machinery for munitions.

A couple of months later Balston noted that the Prime Minister had "appealed to employers to release more men and to employ more women, declaring that their work had been found most satisfactory". The same month, "women were asked to carry home their own shopping parcels, a practice already largely in force, and it was affirmed that they had been found most useful in tending lifts, driving motors, acting as commissionaires and taking the part of policemen. Already 11,000 were enrolled & doing a score of things that would formerly have been considered scandalous for them to perform."

Right from the start of the war, British women had been eager to come forward to "do their bit". The lead came right from the top. On 20 August 1914, Queen Mary, in what only three weeks before would have been considered an unthinkable collaboration, had with the aid of Mary Macarthur, Secretary of the Women's Trade Union League, launched The Queen's Work for Women Fund. It was done in "the firm belief that the prevention of distress is better than its relief, and employment is better than charity". A day later, it was announced that the Ladies Guild of Charing Cross Hospital, "working day and night for a fortnight", had finished a complete outfit of garments for 32 beds at the hospital "which will be available for British wounded". In Hornchurch, Essex, Annie Purbrook wrote:

> *Our Parish lost no time in organizing a Women's Association for help in time of War. Twenty-four of us each took a district and canvassed it to obtain money for the purchase of materials and promises of help in making them up into shirts and socks for soldiers, bandages and comfortable garments for the wounded ... we met weekly to carry on this work ... we all felt so glad to be doing something to help.*

And the Mayoress of Wandsworth was photographed "sitting all day long in the street knitting for soldiers and collecting for the War Fund".

On a more elevated social plane, Viscountess Parker appealed in the papers for "contributions for the 5th Dragoon Guards of cigarettes tobacco, chocolate, shirts, socks, warm scarves, and mittens, or for money to buy them". *The Graphic* told its readers that "Lady Lytton has been indefatigable in organizing a fund and personally giving her services for the care of wounded soldiers now quartered at All Saints Hospital, Vauxhall Bridge Road". Meanwhile the National Union of Women's Suffrage Societies made the decision to suspend political suffrage agitation in order to concentrate on the war effort. And the Forward Cymric Suffrage Union, although continuing its crusading, opted also to raise funds with a sale of work organized on 23 October 1914, the proceeds of which went to the relief of Welsh families rendered destitute through the war.

Suggestions on how women could contribute to the war effort flowed in. "Is it too much to ask", enquired an anonymous correspondent to *The Times*, "that when there is a need for all available young manhood of the country our leading clubs and hotels should substitute waitresses for waiters?... the change from waiters to waitresses would have the double effect of providing men for the Army and work for a class of women who will be neglected by the relief funds." At the same time, Margaret Taylor was worried about the effect of the demon drink on the moral health of servicemen's wives, who were

> *now better off than they have ever been before. Yet I am sure that many workers of the Soldiers' and Sailors' Families Association would bear me out when I say that day after day women come to us assuring us they*

and their children are starving, they have no soles to their boots, and pleading for larger grants from the society. And all the time puffing in our faces fumes of whisky, gin, and the like. Soon these women are to have more money. Cannot the same power that is making our soldiers teetotal make their wives teetotal too?... The money would soon be spent on the children. The bootmakers would be busy. Many trades would flourish. And what a different home-coming would await our Army. Then indeed, we might hope to see a sobered, stronger, brighter England rise from the horrors of this ghastly war.

The early weeks of the war saw a proliferation of new women's organizations that included the Women's Defence Relief Corps, the Almeric Paget Military Massage Corps and the Women's Emergency Corps. The latter, *The Gentlewomen* informed readers on 29 August 1914,

had a twofold object in view. First to find a suitable outlet for the many offers of help from women of all classes in the present crisis, and secondly to provide employment for the many women workers who are thrown out of work owing to the general depression in trade.... All offers of help are warmly welcomed and work will be found for all comers. There are openings for women to help in numerous directions: dispensing, sick nursing, cooking, catering, riding, driving, care of horses, motor-car driving and cycling for distribution work. Funds are badly needed to carry out this enterprise, which is daily growing wider in scope.

A keen member of the new corps was Pamela McKenna, the 27-year-old attractive and vivacious wife of the "tightly-buttoned and over-diligent" Home Secretary. The *Daily Mail* noted: "It is not often that a Cabinet Minister's wife can be seen at a shooting gallery, but yesterday Mrs McKenna ... appeared in the smart uniform of the Women's Emergency Corps and lifted the rifle to her shoulder with the air of a crack shot. Her aim, in fact, was remarkably true."

But all was not plain sailing and the *Evening News* reported in September that: "Charges made against the Women's Emergency Corps of employing 'sweated' labour were emphatically denied by Miss Lena Ashwell at a meeting in the Queen's Theatre." At the same meeting, Lady Aberconway said she was "informed that a million pounds' worth of ready-made clothing was imported from Germany and Austria into this country every year. That enormous shortage must be made up and there ought to be work for every woman who could hold a needle." This suggestion was quickly taken up and the *Morning Post* reported that women of the WEC were

> *engaged in making mine-sweepers' coats of dark wind-proof cloth, lined with warm material. Khaki flannel shirts are also being made, all with linen buttons, as experience has shown that if a bullet hits a china or bone button splinters are an added danger. A waterproof waistcoat with sleeves, properly ventilated, guaranteed to keep its wearer dry as well as warm, is another garment which is being produced.*

Age was no bar to the women's effort and in Kingston upon Thames, Surrey, it was reported that "one of the most active workers at the Mayor of Kingston Ladies' Guild, engaged on making comforts for the East Surreys, is an old lady aged 86".

A few months later, on 9 June 1915, Charles Balston noted how that morning's *Daily Telegraph* had extolled the role of women in the nation's war effort, calling it "a miracle of war". Balston himself wrote admiringly:

> *Young women had realized their opportunities & the daughters of the cultured & leisurely homes were responding to the call of service and sacrifice with enthusiasm. Gone ... are the young ladies of Fanny Burney, Jane Austen, Thackeray & Dickens and the ladies of Cranford would have been scandalized if asked to do the things their descendants cheerfully performed. They had learned the luxury of doing good in the hospitals of France, Gibraltar, Malta & in Serbia – where typhus was raging – hundreds of British women were performing heroic duties and thousands of more were seeking all manner of employment.*

While the popular press might concentrate on the war work of "society beauties" like Lady Diana Manners, the Duke of Rutland's daughter, who was a volunteer nurse at Guy's Hospital, "it was not only the cultured and leisured classes who gave their help. All classes of women did the same. They made shells, became outdoor postmen and messengers; worked in Banks & Railway Stations, Trams & Omnibuses; and served as waiters in large restaurants and in West-End clubs where no petticoat other than a charwoman's had ever been employed."

The press found yet another positive side: "Some ladies, with a knowledge of first-aid treatment, who volunteered for service as Red Cross nurses, were surprised by the number of ordinary household duties they had to study. They found they were mainly required to be domestic servants to the Army. When peace comes they will be better able to look after their own homes." The Shell Crisis of May 1915 and its political fallout "presented a splendid opportunity for the assertion of women's rights with the Government, industry and trade unions". Lloyd George, newly appointed Minister of Munitions in the Coalition Government and in dire need of labour for his factories, saw his opportunity. He enlisted the aid of his old foe Emmeline Pankhurst to front a propaganda campaign to convince both women and employers of the need for female labour on a scale hitherto unimaginable. Charles Balston recorded in his war diary:

> In July Mrs Pankhurst – the leader of the suffragette movement – employed the Women's Social and Political Union to form a procession in London on the (Saturday) 17th of women eager to give their services to their country and announced that Mr Lloyd George would receive a deputation of them.... In bad weather she led the procession of 40,000 women through London preparatory to meting him at the Ministry of Munitions on the Thames Embankment.

To help ensure the occasion's success, Lloyd George had obtained a grant of £3,000 from Ministry funds. The marchers set off in pouring rain with banners that proclaimed "The Situation is Serious. Women Must Help To Save It" and "Women Demand the Right to Serve" to the accompaniment of no less than 90 bands playing suitably martial music.

The Daily Chronicle told readers: "There was something soft and subdued about Mrs Pankhurst when, with her little band of delegates, she entered the big room at the Ministry of Munitions where Mr Lloyd George was waiting. She looked frail, a little tired, as if the solemnity and importance of the occasion were weighing her down. And then the sun suddenly shone through the window, and Mr Lloyd George grasped her hand warmly and smiled." For the occasion the "Welsh Wizard" pulled out all his tricks. "Little Megan Lloyd George sat quietly with big wondering eyes on a couch near the window; opposite at the far end of the room, one of her soldier brothers was waiting to hear what his father had to say. And this intimate personal note relieved the proceedings of formality." Mrs

Pankhurst "put her case clearly and concisely. And her words came from her heart…. 'We want to make no bargain to serve our country,'" she told the minister, who "showed his sympathy in his very opening words, and when he finished one could see that Mrs Pankhurst was deeply touched and completely satisfied." By 6.00 pm when Mrs Pankhurst and Lloyd George emerged from "Munitions House" the crowd was estimated to be 60,000 strong. The Minister of Munitions told the crowd: "The women of this country can help and help enormously. I believe they can help us through to victory. Without them victory will tarry, and victory which tarries means victory whose footprints are the footprints of blood." "Only once", the *Chronicle* reported, "was there an echo of the old pre-war days of the suffragist agitation. 'What about the vote?' a woman demanded shrilly during a lull in the cheering. The Munitions Minister could not forbear a smile. 'We will get her into a shell factory first!' he retorted genially, at which there was much laughter."

Looking back on the demonstration, Charles Balston, with pardonable hyperbole, recorded: "In that moment the Suffragette movement achieved success. The women rushed to work all over the country and having proved quality gained the franchise. A country which contained women like that could not but emancipate them and give them the right to vote for members of Parliament & go there themselves." A few months after the great march, Balston noted how visiting New Zealand Prime Minister William Massey in a *Daily Telegraph* article had drawn attention to the part women were taking in munitions work:

> *A war munitions factory was … the most inspiring sight in Great Britain. The supply of female labour was magnificent in volume and efficiency. In Birmingham, Leeds, Newcastle & Glasgow British women were a priceless aid in the hours of stress and without their help the force our troops would be able to supply in the future would lack sustained power. Where women were employed the output was consistently increasing and there was not the slightest sign that enthusiasm was abating. There is not a slacker among them … and women form the happiest band of workers imaginable.*

But not always. As with the men who joined Kitchener's New Armies before conscription was introduced, women went into munitions for a variety of reasons, of which patriotism was just one, albeit an important one. "I saw the paper asking for people to go and do their bit in the war, so of course I eventually thought I was young, I ought to go. I'd got brothers in the Army so I went," recalled one munitions worker 60 years later. In Leeds, young mother Caroline Webb "never thought about my wage. I went to the shell factory with the idea of helping the country." But money was a powerful incentive too, although young workers under 21 earned lower wages, and female workers in any case received less pay than their male workmates. Lily Godber recalled: "I went because I wanted to save up and get married. They were advertising for munitions workers, good money, and I was only earning five shillings a week." Jane Cox made no bones about why she was in munitions: "I was only working to earn money. The war effort never entered my head. The tragedies that went on during the war never affected me at all." And when Pope Benedict XV made his appeal for peace, the Reverend Reginald Campbell of Birmingham heard

> *a good story in Glasgow ... which shows that some of the commonly accounted gentler sex are militant for other than patriotic reasons.... A lady munitions worker, somewhat addicted to strong waters and stronger language, was exulting to a friend about the augmented income the war had brought her. "I ha' made twa pun fifteen this week," said she, "and twa pun ten the week before – and that auld deevil of a Pope wantin' peace!"*

Elsie Bateson's 45-year-old mother worked in one factory's TNT gangs: "Even hard as it was, it was better than charring." This was a view shared by many women and girls who had been in domestic service and had resented "the indignities of never being thanked, or addressed or acknowledged at all ... and of mistresses who would prefer food to be burnt or thrown away" rather than let their servants have it. In a far cry from the paternal benevolence shown by the aristocrats of TV's *Downton Abbey* to their servants, one pre-1914 housemaid's employer used to check her work by weighing the contents of her vacuum cleaner, only being satisfied if a cup and a half of dirt was obtained. The housemaid went into a munitions factory and the feeling of relief was "like being let out of a cage".

Munitions factories were often huge concerns. At Hayes, Middlesex, the factory consisted of 397 buildings with a total floor area of 14 acres (6 hectares). The factory itself covered nearly 200 acres (80 hectares), and a walk round the boundary fence was almost 5 miles (8 km). This allowed for a regular spacing of the factory "shops" with a distance of at least 75 feet (23 metres) between each, designed to give the workers sufficient light and air and a very necessary safety zone in case of accidents. At Hayes there was a military guard of a colonel, a captain, three second lieutenants and 190 NCOs and men. In addition there were 40 civilian night watchmen and a factory fire brigade "manned" by 60 women fire fighters. The men and women workers were on eight-hour shifts, day and night, and on arrival each passed through a barrier and was given a pass by a "recognizer". These were given up to a policeman a little further on, and no unrecognized worker was supposed to be allowed in under any circumstances. There was a Shifting House where the workers left their outdoor clothes and which could accommodate 7,500 on one shift. Hayes employed 10,000 women and over 2,000 men on the actual making of munitions and there were also several hundred cleaners, carpenters and other ancillary staff.

Like Kitchener's recruits, the new "munitionettes", as they were dubbed by the press, were required to give their ages as this affected their eligibility both for dangerous work and for higher pay. But, as with the case of underage boy soldiers, years were added on without too much enquiry or detection. Just as in the army, there were regular medical inspections. Lily Godber remembered: "We all had to strip off, but keep the skirt on, and then all stand in cubicles, and she'd [the female doctor] stand and view you and then she used to say 'drop skirts' so you were naked and she'd come along and examine." Amy May believed: "You had an inspection by the doctor to make sure you wasn't a man dodging the column." Many women found the new world of munitions frightening. Elsa Thomas, a cartridge-filling section forewoman, encountered an initial degree of both veiled and unveiled hostility from her male colleagues: "They didn't want to show us their livelihood; they knew it was their livelihood. Women were coming in. They were going to cut the wages.... They didn't say it to me, but you had that feeling you were going to take a man's wage from him."

This attitude was not confined to munitions factories. In December 1915 at a meeting in Swansea, the Anthracite Miners' Association strongly protested against the employment of women in any capacity. And as late as May 1918, the South Eastern and Chatham railwaymen passed a resolution "emphatically protesting against the introduction of women to work passenger trains, and pledging themselves to do all in their power to prevent it, in the interests of public safety, and women's safety, and because such work is entirely unsuited to women." There was indeed danger. In May 1916, tram conductor 24-year-old Marjorie Ruby Field from Chislehurst, Kent, died at Charing Cross Hospital after receiving multiple injuries when crushed between two tram cars during shunting operations in the tramway depot at Bexley Heath.

But in the munitions factories there were very stringent safety checks, as Elsie McIntyre recalled:

> *As you walked into the building there were two women, quite severe, searching you, every hairpin out of your head. Then they'd give you a cap with string on. You'd get all your hair under cover – it was long hair then – all scraped in, no hair showing. If you were married at the time you just took your ring off and put it round your neck on a piece of string. And they searched your pockets. You couldn't take a pin or needle or anything at all … that could go up in smoke or catch anything.*

Elsa Bonser remembered: "You take your shoes off. You don't wear any corsets nor rings, nor braces, so that if there's an explosion these things don't get embedded in you." Infringements of these safety regulations were punished very severely In August 1917, at Flintshire Police Court, Eleanor McLennnan, described as "an aged munition worker", was fined £2 for taking a twist of tobacco into an explosive factory. Three months later, two of her co-workers, one a deaf-mute and another aged 67, were sent to prison for a month, while another was given a month's hard labour for taking "gaspers", as cigarettes were nicknamed, into the factory.

Munitions factories issued uniforms to their women workers. At first these consisted of just long overalls worn over the women's usual angle-length dresses. Then trouser and tunic outfits were introduced, to a mixed reception. Crane driver Dorothy Henderson recalled her new uniform as being like "riding breeches … [with] long stockings and shoes and a light fawn hat that you could pull down over your hair, and a khaki coat…. You had another light coat underneath that, for when you were up in the crane…. [The uniform] was more for safety than anything." Dorothy was embarrassed by her new uniform: "I didn't like people to see me in the trousers. I wouldn't come home through the streets like that. No, I used to wear a long overcoat to see it covered." Caroline Webb, a munitions worker at Woolwich Arsenal, had no such aversion: "We used to like the [air raid] warnings go off before ten at night because Beresford Square used to be full of soldiers; we used to have a good old time. Of course us in khaki, we were the centre of attraction. They'd say, 'Come on kids, let's have a look at your new trousers.' We used to toss our heads and think we were the cat's whiskers."

Munitions work was both hazardous and hard, as Mabel Lethbridge discovered when she volunteered to work in the "danger zone" of the factory at Hayes. Mabel had worked as a nurse in Bradford before becoming a munitionette in the autumn of 1917. She and other volunteers found themselves in the

Amatol Section, and this was unlike any other part of the factory in appearance. The shops were larger and farther apart, and here the work of filling shells with amatol soda and T.N.T. was carried out.... I was detailed to No. 22 shed, and here an overlooker showed us round. On a raised platform at the left-hand side were four cauldrons containing the "filling mixture". Each was fitted with an enormous automatic stirrer. Immediately below this platform was a long table, at which twelve girls were working. Four girls stood at the cauldrons ladling the mixture into scoops. The contents of each scoop were weighed, then tipped into an empty 18-pounder shell.... Stacked on the floor were hundreds of empties. I was appointed carrier, and had to carry the filled shells to the machines where they were "stemmed" [the term for pressing the amatol firmly down inside the shell to make room for the fuses].

Mabel's fellow carrier Louie explained the workings of the so-called "monkey machines" used for stemming, to which they had to carry the filled shells, a journey of 50 yards/metres. It was tough physical work and to make it more bearable the girls sang popular tunes: "Hour after hour went by and I felt as though my arms were being pulled out of their sockets and that my back must surely crack beneath the weight. I had no breath to sing and my throat felt hard and dry." Then, "At three o'clock I heard the singing cease and saw the girls rushing to the door. 'What's the matter?' I shouted, thinking perhaps there was a fire or explosion." But a fellow worker told her, "Come on, kid, it's the milk." At the door the women were each given a free pint of cold milk, to neutralize the effects of the poisonous explosives they were using; "twice a day thereafter we had this issue, and very welcome it was". Resuming work, Mabel went:

"To and fro ... carrying each time two shells ... two for the machine and two finished from the machine. My head ached, my shoulders swelled, and the muscles in my calves felt lacerated. On and on till, unable to bear it any longer, I leant, utterly exhausted, against a pile of boxes.... 'Gawd!' said Louie, 'You ain't half soft.'"

Depending on shift arrangements, munitions workers had meal breaks of about an hour or an hour and a half during the working day. Workers brought in sandwiches or pasties, but they could also get a fairly cheap meal in the works canteen. At the Woolwich Arsenal they could bring in cold pies or stews that would be warmed up for them while they worked. To relieve the monotony of the work, as Mabel had found at Hayes, there were sing-songs on the factory floor, concerts in the works canteens and at the huge munitions works at Gretna open-air dancing.

At first little or no provision was made for those married women with young children who wanted "to do their bit" in munitions. Elsa Thomas in Leeds with a five-year-old son was asked by her employer: "'Can you start tonight?' I said, 'Oh no, I've my little boy.' He said, 'Oh any lady'll take him. Arrange to come back at six tonight.' I said, 'Really I can't come back.' He said, 'Our men are called up....' So of course I agreed." Eventually Elsa's mother, sister-in-law and a local shopkeeper took it in turns to look after her son. Dorothy Haigh had a baby daughter and "when it was time to feed the baby it used to upset me. I used to come home mealtimes to feed her. The night time I used to borrow a bike and I used to bike home at midnight when we had our break to feed her then – otherwise I was in agony with pain." Crèches for children of munitions workers were gradually introduced. Stoke Newington claimed to have provided the first municipal crèche for the children of women munitions workers, and in January 1917 it was announced that another in London had just opened. The Ministry of Munitions undertook to provide 75 per cent of the capital cost of £250 and a similar proportion of the annual rent of £60, together with a daily allowance of 7d per child.

Another innovation was the introduction of welfare officers and supervisors. The most renowned among this new breed was Woolwich Arsenal's Lilian Baker, who went on to have a distinguished and enlightened career in the prison service. Caroline Webb recalled: "She was strict but she was good. Of course there were a lot of girls pregnant there – the Arsenal was a massive great place.... She was ever so good to them and I remember she sent round word to our factory to ask us if we'd all give a shilling and we refused because we thought it was disgusting for girls to be pregnant. So she stopped our sugar ration." One of Caroline's fellow workers remembered that the women workers were examined every two weeks: "Well, the girls that got in trouble they found out when they were medically examined. So then you had to go to report to her [Lilian Baker] and she kept you at work seven months.... She had a home which she called the Sunshine Home for babies. But you only could do it once, she let you off, but the second time you arrived there you were told definitely the way you should tread." Not all stories ended happily. Just after the Armistice, 21-year-old munitions worker Lily Dunnigan was tried at Leeds Assizes for the murder of her illegitimate baby boy and sentenced to death by the less-than-sympathetic Mr Justice Darling. But "a jury of matrons was then empanelled, and on finding the prisoner pregnant, execution of the sentence was stayed".

Most of the women munitions workers had husbands, brothers, sons and other loved ones in the army, and Elsa Thomas recalled that they would bring to work letters from them to be read out during breaks. Bonds were cemented in various ways. In October 1915, the *Daily Express* reported on a new phenomenon: "The military and naval fondness for tattooing has spread to many young women in London, who are having the name and often the regimental badge of their swains indelibly marked on their arms." And often, in identifying with soldiers out in France using the ammunition or equipment they had produced, munitions workers personalized their work. Amy May

had two or three letters from the soldiers we packed munitions for. I had one come down to visit me. Oh goodness! What am I going to do with him? I'd put a little note inside the wire coils. He sent me one of those silk cords. What do you think happened? Mother took him out for a drink! Oh, there was always somebody putting notes in – "Hope this finds you well" and so on. If you're lonely you don't mind writing.

Some letters from unknown soldiers led to romance: while serving in France, where he had landed with the original British Expeditionary Force in August 1914, Gunner W. Jones of the Royal Field Artillery entered into correspondence with a young woman whose name had been given to him by a comrade. In June 1916 he came home on leave, and only three days after he first saw his correspondent Gertrude Henly they were married by special licence.

In March 1915, the *Daily Express* had claimed to have found "the loneliest man at the front", Private A. C. White of the 1st Battalion, The Rifle Brigade. White, a comrade reported, was an orphan who had lied about his age to join up, but having no family he had not "received a letter or a parcel since he has been out here; nor is he likely to in the future, for he has no friends". Private White tried to put a brave face on things: "I don't mind as a rule, but when I see the other chaps with their letters an' parcels full o' things to eat, I feel…" "The break in his voice", thought Private Dowdall, White's comrade, "belied his words." Hospitalized with "nerves and general weakness", White was being cured with pills but what he really needed was "a little human sympathy". It was not long in coming. Within two days White had received 470 letters and 200 parcels, and after just a week had got presents, according to the *Express*, "almost enough to set him up for life as a grocer, confectioner, and newsagent!" The bounty received by White included 15 tins each of sardines and herrings in tomato and a like number of jars of Bovril and, very practically, tin-openers. The generosity of the British public to Private White's sad plight had united the Home Front with the Western Front, the *Express* claimed, and was thus a valuable contribution to the nation's war effort.

Soon most of the popular dailies, as well as specialist magazines like the *Link* and *T. P.'s Weekly*, were featuring advertisements such as: "Lonely Young Officer, up to his neck in Flanders mud, would like to correspond with young lady (age 18–20), cheery and good looking". And another soldier, "somewhere on active service", wrote in to *T. P.'s Weekly* welcoming "correspondents, opposite sex, in an exchange of opinions, other than war topics". In the same issue, "Two Solitary Sister Susies, tired of sewing shirts for soldiers", aged 25 and 29, advertised that they "would like to correspond with two lonely Colonial officers or gentleman rankers". Both women, future correspondents were assured, had a fondness for "music, country life and sport". A month later *The Times* informed its readers of "a girl in Stockbridge (Hants), who is interesting herself in writing cheery letters to lonely soldiers, has 38 regular correspondents, distributed as follows:- Five in India, five in Egypt, one in Mesopotamia, one in Salonika, 12 in France, six in England, and eight sailors. She has received over 150 letters from abroad, besides many field service cards." Eventually, worries over clogging up the already stretched army postal service and fears that military secrets might be divulged prompted the Government to issue a D-notice to the newspapers. They were warned "to refrain from publishing letters and advertisements inviting officers and men in the field to communicate with strangers".

When the Zeppelin raids started, munitions workers, no less than ordinary civilians, were in the front line at home. Gladys Kaye was a principal overseer at Woolwich Arsenal in charge of 400 women and girls in three workshops:

> *I used to feel very proud of their wonderful pluck when all our lights were put out when the Zeppelins used to come over ... not only were all the lights put out but all the doors and windows fastened* from the outside *so that we could not possibly get out. There was such a great outcry from the women that after a short time all the doors and windows were left open so that we could escape if a bomb did hit us.*

Caroline Webb remembered: "We had a big air raid one day and our manager came flying in: 'Run for your lives, girls.' Well, there was ninety tons of TNT stored there. So they grabbed us kids and they ran us – of course it was all green fields – they ran us out as far as they could and they tore our aprons off of us and they made us lie on our faces...." Although air-raid casualties among the munitions workers were mercifully small, production fell as a result of the raids. At Woolwich Arsenal on 24 September 1917, when Gotha bombers attacked the capital, the normal output of .303 ammunition by the night shift decreased from 850,000 rounds to 740,000.

The real danger still came from industrial accidents. Caroline Rennles recalled how "a girl that went out left all the powder in the oven and Cissie Peters went on night duty. Of course she opened the oven door and it blew both her eyes out. Of course we got a big collection for her...." Lilian Miles was "soldering a bullet and it sort of went bang". Lilian had three of her fingers broken and "they put my arm in a sling. I had to go to work every day or they wouldn't pay me. They wouldn't let me stay at home." And exposure to TNT led to a jaundiced yellowing of the skin, which the munitions girls were unable to wash out and which was impossible to hide. Caroline Rennies recalled how: "We had bright yellow faces, because we had no masks ... and our front hair was bright ginger. They used to call us canaries...." They had their own "Canaries' Song":

Same as the lads
Across the sea,
If it wasn't for the ammunition girls
Where would the Empire be?

On one occasion the charismatic Prince of Wales, still chafing at not being allowed in the front line, came to Woolwich Arsenal on a morale-boosting visit: "He was the only one that had the pluck to put his feet in danger buildings, inside a powder shop. There were plenty that used to visit the factory but they never put their head inside a powder shop. And he went up and spoke to the girls."

Despite all the precautions, accidents, sometimes on a spectacular scale, continued to take place. On 5 December 1916 at the Barnbow munitions factory at Crossgates, Leeds, which employed 16,000 workers, there was a large explosion in which 35 women and girls, including 17-year-old Edith Sykes, were killed. Believing that Edith's death was as much in her country's cause as those of men killed on the battlefield, her brother obtained a gun carriage from the local barracks to transport her coffin for the funeral.

At Hayes on the afternoon of 23 October 1917, Mabel Lethbridge was working as usual in the "danger zones" despite some concerns over the reliability of the "monkey machines". Suddenly, there was "a dull flash; a sharp deafening roar" and Mabel felt was hurled through the air, "falling down, down, down into the darkness...". She found herself lying quietly on her side before "a blinding flash and I felt my body being torn asunder. Darkness, that terrifying darkness, and the agonized cries of the workers pierced my consciousness." Mabel struggled to get up and found that her workmates' cries "were drowned in a dull roar ... but now the screams held a new note of terror.... Fire, fire ... there was a crazy rush for the doors; the shed became a blazing furnace." And now

swiftly and surely the flames crept nearer ... was something lying
across my legs that I could not rise? I tried desperately to free them,
tugging at the left one, which appeared buried in a mass of blood
and earth. It lifted easily, so easily, so light. Can anyone imagine the
anguish and terror I experienced when I realized that my leg had

154

been blown off, and I held in my tortured hands the dripping thigh and knee?

Mabel, in her agony continually calling out for her mother, had the presence of mind to tear the string from her "magazine" cap and apply as it as a tourniquet. There were more explosions, but "suddenly we became aware of the great noise outside and renewed our cries for help. After what seemed an eternity, Mabel saw in the light of the flames "a long row of ladders show over the top of the walls where the roof had been. Up came the fire-girls, flinging themselves bravely into the furnace, dragging their hose pipes ... the sound of cheering reached me faintly ... through the cries of the wounded ... the flames came nearer, nearer; water poured over my mutilated body ... then a long silence as I passed into a blessed oblivion." For her sublime "courage and high example" that day, Mabel was appointed an Officer of the newly created Order of the British Empire.

The following year, 13 OBEs went to workers for their "extraordinary courage" at the huge munitions factory at Chilwell, near Nottingham. On 1 July 1918, a disastrous explosion rocked the factory (which turned out over 19 million shells during the war), killing 134 and injuring many more. The death toll at Chilwell was nearly double that of the much more famous Silvertown explosion of 19 January 1917. That evening, down in Chislehurst, Kent, Ethel Bilbrough thought instantly that "it was a German bomb that had been intended for Woolwich, but had dropped short and fallen on our lawn instead! The house shook, windows rattled and so deafening and alarming was it that I sat rooted to my chair, breathlessly awaiting the next shock which one felt sure would happen." As nothing happened, Ethel "tore upstairs to look out one of our upper windows which faces the direction of Woolwich, and sure enough the sky was all red and lurid and *vibrating*, then I felt sure the arsenal was blown up and whole of Woolwich in flames!!"

In fact it was an explosion caused by a fire at the Brunner Mond Ltd munitions factory at Silvertown, Poplar. According to Fireman Betts, who was quickly on the scene of the conflagration, in the ensuing explosion "every building in London was shaken. Half a million windows in shops and houses across the river a mile away at Charlton and South Woolwich were broken. The explosion was heard in districts as far apart as Salisbury and King's Lynn." Betts, his wife Polly and their 12-year-old son lived in quarters behind Silvertown Fire Station and his first priority was to get them out before he and his colleagues tore across the road into Brunner Mond's yard. There they were met by the factory's timekeeper, a Scot. "Run for it mon, we'll be gone in a minute!" he yelled out, staggering past Betts, "hatless, distraught, his face distorted by a terrible fear. They were his last words. Then it was though heaven had giddily plunged to meet the earth in a shattering upheaval. In one second the whole world seemed to have crumbled." Betts came to lying on his back on a piece of waste ground 200 feet (60 metres) from where he and his colleagues had been fixing a hose ready to douse the flames.

Soon every available fire engine was converging on Silvertown and, for three or four hours after the explosion, the whole of London was lit by the flames. The local paper, the *Stratford Express*, reported how "The whole heavens were lit in awful splendour. A fiery glow seemed to have come over the dark and miserable January evening." To Betts, "The fire area itself was an astonishing spectacle. Imagine an arc of towering flat-faced factories, with many rows of windows. At that moment they were as if they had been filled with burning coal. Every window opening glared like an iron furnace when the doors are opened ...." Betts wrote admiringly of "one brave girl Norah Griffiths, who helped to hold up a roof that would have otherwise have fallen and crushed to death a number of young children attending a Band of Hope meeting at a local mission hall".

The doctors and nurses at the London Hospital worked with their customary devotion to duty. The hospital's log recorded the explosion at 6.50 pm: "The hospital distinctly moved – a rocking movement. 231 windows broken. Somebody screamed, otherwise no alarm." Poplar Hospital telephoned to ask for help and so did the police: "reported enormous explosion: short of doctors; could we send any? Got five men and three lady doctors: cab of dressings; instruments; morphia; chloroform, &c. One cabman refused to go; abusive; was not going for anybody. Porter took his number. Gentleman in car, although ten miles [16 km] out of London, drove to hospital at once and picked up dressers and dressings, gave him some petrol." The log noted the first injured arrived in "motor-lorries, butchers' carts – all sorts of vehicles": 60 people, some brought in on makeshift stretchers of doors and window shutters, were treated at once but four died during the night. There were many pathetic sights that night at the hospital: "Children were brought up not always injured but dazed. One child of eight with baby in arms and leading a child of four. Couldn't find mother. Kindly driver had picked them up in destroyed streets and brought them up with a load of wounded in motor-lorry.... Admitted woman badly injured – her seven children killed.... Little dog came up with one fearfully injured woman. It wouldn't leave her. We let it go into the ward with her."

Altogether, almost 17 acres of Silvertown were laid waste that night including hundreds of workers' dwellings. The death toll of around 70, including one woman worker, Catherine Hodge, was mercifully small, given the size of the explosion and fire, but nearly a thousand more were injured, including Polly Betts who was "rendered stone deaf". Joe Hollister was not alone when he wrote: "... it seems almost criminal that a high explosives factory should be allowed to be situated in a densely-populated residential district like that when there are vacant spaces lying idle four or five miles [6–8 km] further out." But the country's pet lovers were heartened by the news that "36 cats have been rescued from the ruins of the East London explosion by the London Institution for Lost Cats and Dogs".

A fortnight after the Silverton explosion, Cicely Hamilton, "the recognized authority on feminist topics", told readers of The War Illustrated: "Physically, the nation should benefit by the fact that the number of women working at open-air callings has increased during the war. The field-working, the horse-minding, van-driving girl will tend to belong to a hardy race with an open-air outlook on life." Back in July 1911 it was estimated that the total number of women working on the land was 70,000. Seven years later, that figure had grown to around 250,000, which included not only "village women and girls" but members of the wartime Women's Land Army. In May 1916, a call had gone out for women agricultural workers and "the rush of women for farm work has begun in Sheffield, and the farmers are delighted with the tactful way they go about their duties. Since Lady Mabel Smith, sister of Lord Fitzwilliam, led the way many others have entered the field. A woman with a team of horses is daily following the plough. Others are planting potatoes with convalescent soldiers to help them." By September, down in Surrey, 1,858 women had registered for farm work and about half were already working on the land. A year later, the Food Production Department was advised that "women are being trained as rabbit catchers on various estates in the country, notably at Belsay Castle, where the head keeper reports most favourably on them."

The demand for more "Daughters of Eve" continued, and in January 1917 the Board of Agriculture, under its go-ahead new President, Rowland Prothero, formally established a Women's Branch, which two months later was transferred to the Food Production Department. Its function was to organize women's labour on the land, including the recruitment of a Land Army of women and girls who would undertake full-time service on Britain's farms and go wherever they were needed. Recruitment began in February 1917. The terms on offer to recruits included a month's free training at one of 600 centres set up on farms where there was sufficient accommodation. They were to receive a free uniform and a minimum wage of 18s (eighteen shillings) a week (the pre-war average weekly wage for male workers on the land was 14s/ fourteen shillings). Lloyd George himself wrote: "It was of course very important that the new Land Army should create a good impression in the early days, to counteract the general hostility and distrust of the farming community; and the first recruits were most carefully selected. Out of 47,000 applicants who turned up in the first rush, only 7,000 were accepted." The lucky ones were issued with the Women's Land Army Handbook, which warned them: "You are doing a man's work and so you're dressed like a man, but remember just because you wear a smock and breeches you should take care to behave like a British girl who expects chivalry and respect from everyone she meets." "Work on the land," the *Daily News* confessed, "is not popular among those best fitted to do it. No woman can be expected to enjoy milking cows at four on a winter morning or spreading manure, or cleaning a pigsty. It is frankly admitted indeed, that much of the most necessary work is hard and unpleasant, and by no means extravagantly paid. That is why the appeal is made exclusively to the patriotism of women."

One who responded to the appeal was City worker 20-year-old M. Britton. After passing her medical in London, she was told to report to Wicks Farm at Old Basing, near Basingstoke, Hampshire. Her uniform and those of her companions were sent by post and had to be collected from the village post office: "We did not all have the same size … there was quite a tussle & some of the smaller sizes were snatched & we weaker ones had to accept what was left. However, the quality was quite good, mackintosh, oilskin coat & twill breeches, pullover & smock, & gaiters. We received another set of brown velvet breeches later." The girls were billeted in an old cottage, "very nice & clean…. A sort of dormitory upstairs with single iron beds (very clean, scrubbed boards on the floor) a large table downstairs & a woman from the village came & cooked our meals, butter etc. from the farm." When her boots gave her blisters, the farmer's sister gave her Vaseline and bandages. There was little or nothing in the way of social activities, but she was sometimes able to take weekend leave, and most weeks she sent home her washing by post.

After some weeks learning how to weed, the girls were issued rail tickets to go to Somerset for more intensive work. They were there, under canvas, for several weeks: "six to a tent, all feet to the pole, sack filled with clean straw to lie on". Each morning they were driven in an army lorry "to fields to pull flax for aeroplane wings & linseed oil. Lined across the fields we pulled it up and laid it down as we went. It came out easy from the red soil." One day a farmer kindly gave them a flagon of cider to drink, but generally "our meals in the big marquee were poor, cold ham, green in parts, uneatable". From Somerset she was sent to West Malling in Kent to do tree banding in the fruit orchards before finally being ordered to Meopham. There, in "nice digs" and with convivial company, she worked on the threshing machine for the rest of the war: "... when the Armistice came I asked to leave & get back to a City job – My resignation was received with thanks & told I could retain my uniform."

Under the auspices of the Board of Trade was the Women's Forestry Corps, an enthusiastic member of which was a Miss B. Bennett, who was sent to work at Chilgrove Camp "miles from anywhere, absolutely isolated". The morning after her arrival, "the snow was too thick to work so we carried wood from the piling stations and sawed it up for indoor use in case we should get snowed up. We have breakfast at 6.30 and another at 9.30 – After lunch (enamel plates and mugs and tin knives and forks), we went to the woods and started our new work. It is great, axing at great trees. We were given a bill hook, an axe, a saw and a cord measure." The next day was "grand. Very cold but the work is fine. It is great to see a grand old tree crash to the earth and feel that you did it alone – Life is just what I have always longed for. After dinner tonight we had some music. It was strange to see the girls dancing, breeches and jerseys, in a log hut with a stove in the middle. It will be glorious here in the spring." It was not just youngsters who were helping out on the land. In November 1916 at Williton, Somerset, three women aged 84, 83 and 82 were all awarded prizes for their wartime farm work.

But not every woman was quite as enthusiastic or committed. In June 1918, it was reported that Grace Smith, "a native of Bristol, and belonging to the Women's Army Forage Department, was at Gloucester ... sent to prison for fourteen days' hard labour for being absent from work without leave". A few weeks before, Sarah Hopkins of Cwm, Monmouthshire, had received a two-month prison sentence for continuing to draw her husband's separation allowance to the tune of £94 after his discharge from the army. Her excuse being that his beer was costing her 15s (fifteen shillings) a week. And 32-year-old Ellen Pinkard of Northampton was hardly a shining example of Britain's womanhood at war either. She was a soldier's widow, receiving £1 a week from the state, but the court was told "she had pawned practically all the bed clothing". Her three children, "hungry and dirty", were found locked in the house one Saturday night and "Mrs Pinkard was later discovered in a public house with a soldier's arm round her neck." Pinkard was sentenced to four months' imprisonment with hard labour for neglecting the children.

Throughout the war, the press was assiduous in telling readers of the "unusual" jobs, or at least those which had previously been male preserves, that British women were now taking on. On 15 December 1915, the Mayor of Chester announced that the next day women would start work as lamp-lighters. In the town for some time already women had been employed delivering letters in place of postmen who were now in the forces. Glasgow Tramways Department was the first to employ women on its vehicles and by September 1915 there were 800 female conductors, or conductresses as they were called. In May 1916, Glasgow also started employing women as Sub-Station attendants at 35s 6d (thirty-five shillings and sixpence) for a 42-hour week. The London General Omnibus Company got off to a slower start: it was only in February 1916 that it started to recruit women as conductresses. The first hundred started work the following month and a year later there were over 2,500 conductresses on London's buses.

Around this time, Shanklin on the Isle of Wight appointed its first woman rate collector and Birmingham licensed women taxi drivers, the first city to do so. In Ealing, the council started employing women park keepers, and "wives of lodge-keepers now on active service are permitted to remain in possession so long as they perform their husband's duties". In Norfolk, 15-year-old Miss Clarke of Thetford was appointed Town Crier and official bill poster while her father served in the army. She made her first "cry" on 14 August 1916, "the object being the recovery of a lost railway ticket". The month before, Bethnal Green Borough Council approved the appointment of a woman doctor as Assistant Borough Medical Officer of Health with an annual salary of £350, and Wycombe saw the first woman band sawyer employed in the town's furniture industry. That same month there were no less than 69 applications for the position of London County Council woman inspector of massage establishments and employment agencies. The job, which paid an annual salary of £120, went to Mrs Kate Isobel Hoole. And when the caretaker of Avery Hill Training College was killed on active service, the LCC gave the job to his widow.

The next year St Pancras Borough Council elected two women, Florence Anderson and Annie Hunter, as health visitors, to be paid £100 per annum. In April 1917, it was announced that women were now acting as bell-ringers at the parish church at Beaumaris on the Isle of Anglesey. A few weeks later, the Vicar of Epping announced that he too was seeking women bell-ringers. In that month also, *The Times* reported that "Women are beginning to do the work of chimney sweeps called to the war". And Miss Violet Pope, newly employed as a "ferryman" at Kingston, Surrey, received the Royal Humane Society's certificate for rescuing a drowning boy from the Thames. Six housemaids employed by Lambeth Guardians left to become bus conductresses, and in April 1916, the Western Ambulance Section of Metropolitan Asylums Board found it necessary to employ women drivers "owing to the further depletion of the motor driving staff by the calling up of men to join the forces". Willesden Council started employing women refuse collectors in January 1917, "the work to be carried out on Sundays as well as week days". As the war entered its fourth year, it was reported that "though 62 years of age, Mrs Taylor, wife of Mr Harry Taylor, of Ringmer, Sussex, is working as a road sweeper tarring the thoroughfares. Her husband, who is just on 70 years of age, brings her home from work each evening on a tandem bicycle."

Despite a claim by a no less than a personage than Mr Hubert Hall, the Assistant Keeper of Public Records, that women could undertake clerical tasks more "neatly and effectively" than men, occasionally mistakes were made. In March 1917, Frederick Ward, Southwark's deputy mayor, told how when one of the borough's leading employers put himself down under the National Service Scheme as an "organizer" he was sent to the docks to unload ships. When he protested, "it was found that the girl clerk who had dealt with his application form had entered him in the records as 'organ grinder'". And some professions still continued to be male preserves. On 20 July 1916, "a woman wearing a barrister's wig and gown, tried to enter the Law Courts ... in the King's Bench Division, but was refused admission". In Belfast a month later, the Corporation refused, by 23 votes to 17, to co-opt Mrs McMordie, a former Lady Mayoress, as a councillor, on the grounds that "electors had not given a mandate for the admission of women to the corporation".

There were some women, like pre-war suffragette Sylvia Pankhurst, who, unlike her mother Emmeline and sister Christabel, passionately opposed the war. She called it "a war of iniquity falsely extolled as the war to end war". At her many wartime meetings she not only continued to call on the Government to introduce a Bill to enfranchise every adult man and woman, but also implored it to stop the war. Her views on the war were endorsed by the Women's Peace Negotiations Crusade, which in July 1916 held a rally in Glasgow demanding an end to the conflict. But the demonstration turned out literally to be a damp squib as it was forced to end prematurely when an exceptionally violent thunderstorm, lasting two hours, hit the city.

Britain's younger citizens too rallied to their nation's cause. A month after war was declared, the headmistress of a London school sent the *Daily Mirror* some of her children's thoughts on the conflict. One nine-year-old boy wrote, "Boys and girls can help their country by asking boys of nineteen years of age to go to the war." He had already been frightened when "out in the street there was a great bang and everyone thought it was some Germans that had dropped a bomb. But it was not. It was only a bladder burst in the wheel of a 'bus." Another boy noted: "The Kaiser said he is not going to give in until there is not another horse and man left. The Kaiser is silly, because he ought to give in as there are a lot of Germans dead and wounded on the battlefield. If I saw a German I would scoot for my life and if he fired at me I would lie down in a moment." Another had worked out what he would do "if the Kaiser was to come into my classroom. I would sit still. If he was to shoot at me I would dodge under the desk." Moreover, "everyone thinks that the German Emperor has gone mad, and so do I, the way he is carrying on". A girl pupil wrote, "I hear Lord Kitchener is leading us in war. He is a very kind-hearted man and brave." Sadly, "... mother thinks that this is a fatal war and she keeps crying every time she thinks of it." And one boy had his own radical solution to end the conflict: "I think the men who started the war ought to lead their Army and get shot."

More practical assistance from Britain's boys and girls was not slow in coming. In the vanguard was the Boy Scouts' Association headed by Chief Scout Sir Robert Baden-Powell, Boer War hero of the siege of Mafeking. Just before the war, "BP" had told an audience of City bankers that his hobby was "to get hold of the lads of the next generation, and make them a credit to their country". He was as good as his word and in London on the outbreak of war 25,000 Boy Scouts were immediately organized "for civic duties which consisted in helping various Government departments, municipal authorities, guarding electricity stations, and acting as messengers etc.". Baden-Powell issued an appeal to boys to come and join the 152,333 Scouts already in the movement: "Boys of Britain! Don't go about waving flags and shouting because there is a war. Any ass can do that. And don't stay idle doing nothing – that is almost worse. Come and do something for your country. She needs help. The Boy Scouts are now a service in all parts of the Kingdom. Come and join the nearest troop in your own district, and do duty like a man." Soon, along the East Coast there were 1,200 Scouts on watch with coastguardsmen for the anticipated German invasion. In Kent, Surrey and Sussex, 5,000 Scouts were on duty guarding bridges, culverts, telephone and telegraph lines, railway stations and reservoirs. The older-established Boys' Brigade rallied round too, and so did the Church Lads' Brigade, which like the Scouts provided cadets to guard waterworks and tunnels and act as messengers. As soon as war broke out, the Jewish Lads' Brigade also placed its entire organization at the Government's disposal "for any duties that might be assigned it".

With the coming of air raids, the Scouts expanded their "excellent skill and usefulness". Baden-Powell believed that the air raids had "come as a godsend to Scouts as it gave such a point to their training. They went rushing into the streets and brought in persons with slight wounds. The raids gave a tremendous impulse to the training in first aid." BP told "how during a daylight raid on London a bomb was dropped on the train in which he was going to address a meeting. He went to one poor fellow, who had his thigh badly cut, but someone got there before him. 'Can I be of any help?' he asked. The other man looked up and made the Scouts' sign. He was a Scout already on the spot."

From the end of October 1917, several hundred Boy Scouts were on regular air-raid duty blowing bugles to sound the all-clear. A not very charitable Home Office disowned any responsibility for "Boy Scout buglers who may be injured while on air raid duty". A business firm promptly offered to pay for a Lloyd's policy to cover "350 of the lads". This would ensure that the parents of any "little patriot killed by bombs or shrapnel" would receive an indemnity of £50. In case of injury, half that sum was to be made payable for medical expenses. Other Scouts were trained in fire fighting, but all of them, BP told an Oxford audience in August 1917, "were trained for discipline, smartness, alertness and using their wits, but chiefly for playing the game for their team and not for themselves." Lloyd George was more generous than the Home Office, at least in words of praise, when he said: "The young boyhood of our country, represented by the Boy Scouts' Association, shares the laurels for having been prepared with the old and trusted and tried British Army and Navy." Scout Leslie Pike of Thatcham, Berkshire, certainly lived up to the Scouts' motto "Be Prepared". He was on patrol when "he saw three men hiding in a hay rick, and asked them what they were doing. Their statements aroused his suspicion and he informed the police, who found the men to be German prisoners missing from their camp." Leslie's feat was matched by the cadets of the Erith Company of the Church Lads' Brigade who captured a German spy, while their comrades in Birmingham were on duty guarding the entire system of the city's water works "which cover seventy miles [112 km], and necessitate both day and night guards".

"Be Prepared" was also the motto of the Scouts' sister organization the Girl Guides, headed by BP's sister Agnes. A 1918 resumé of their work noted: "The girls are encouraged in every way to retain their womanliness, so that they may be good mothers and good Guides to the next generation." That year the movement numbered 50,000 Girl Guides and 2,500 younger Brownies, and their wartime activities included: "provision and maintenance of a recreation hut for soldiers in France, in which Guides are serving, and the equipment of hostels and first-aid dressing stations at different centres for dealing with injuries received through air raids or accidents; assisting as orderlies at Red Cross hospitals, Government offices, munitions works. They also supply comforts to men at the front ... and during the past year many could be seen in London streets trundling little handcarts, collecting waste paper."

Britain's schoolchildren also did their bit. Just days after the Germans launched their gas attack at Ypres on 22 April 1915, Churchill's wife Clementine made an appeal for young volunteers to make respirators for the troops. "There was", the *Evening Standard* told its readers on 29 April, *a rush of workers to save our soldiers, and children are eager to begin too. The explicit instructions from the War Office show how simple the work is, and the young people who were not quite able to help in "sewing shirts for soldiers" have now their opportunity. The London County Council yesterday arranged that respirators should be made by the elder children of the elementary schools.*

In Bedford, local schoolchildren helped turn out 20,000 masks needed for the men of the Highland Division. Aged 15, Annie May Roberts went to work at Hepburn and Gale's gas mask factory at Grange Road at 12s (twelve shillings) a week, but, unlike many others, she was not guided by patriotism. Sixty years later she recalled: "No, I wasn't proud to think I was making gas masks for soldiers, oh no, no, it was just another job."

At Churchill's Alma Mater, Harrow, the boys made splints and crutches for the wounded in the school workshop. And after the summer holidays of 1916 they were each asked to bring back two books to be sent to soldiers at the front. On a lower social scale, the children at the Willesden Poor Law Home at Neasden each week sacrificed their weekly cake allowance, sending it to the local military hospital. Schoolboy Arthur Westcott of Kew Gardens sent a parcel of comforts to Admiral Sir John Jellicoe's flagship HMS *Iron Duke*. They had been bought with the proceeds of the sale of Arthur's hand-painted postcards. Sir John was suitably grateful: "It is very nice for us in the Grand Fleet to know that dear little people like you at home are thinking of us and praying for us and working for us, and we are very grateful to you." Also sent "to Admiral Jellicoe's boys away in the North Sea" were "two or three or sometimes even four cwt. of vegetables and fruit", collected by the girl pupils of Bromley Road School, Beckenham. One of their teachers told *Home Chat* magazine: "I only have to ask the children 'Would anyone like to help such and such a fund?' and up goes every hand in the room. And every one of them – even the babies – will bring pennies for the fund in question. Pennies that used to be spent on sweeties and cinemas are saved willingly and gladly for the soldiers." The pupils raised enough money to endow a bed at the local Red Cross hospital. *Home Chat* reported, "… they now look upon that bed as their own personal property – and the patient as well – inasmuch as the boys have promised to keep him supplied with cigarettes and the girls with chocolate. Rather sweet idea, isn't it? And, I am told, entirely the children's own." Their efforts were not confined to Britain, for some of the girls had "made a quilt to be sent with a parcel of warm things for the poor Serbian peasants". At St Mary's Sunday School, East Molesey, Surrey, the children collected money to buy specially made sets of chessmen and draughts for the blind servicemen at St Dunstan's. And in just one month at the beginning of 1917, schoolchildren in Ramsgate contributed £300 to war savings. At the country's leading girls' public school, the *Daily Graphic* reported, "during their spare hours the pupils at Roedean College, Brighton, are making furniture to be sold in aid of the Garrett-Anderson Hospital Funds. They have themselves purchased the necessary material and their work is excellently done." In Leeds at Christmas 1915 it was reported that, "owing to the scarcity of both male and female labour, 100 schoolboys are to be employed at Leeds Post Office". Two years later, the country's schoolchildren were mobilized by the Food Production Department (*see* Chapter 6) to collect blackberries to be made into jam for the troops. Pupils from Hornsey schools went to work as fruit pickers on the estates of jam manufacturers Chivers and Sons at Histon near Cambridge. There "the boys and girls have combined business with pleasure in a very happy manner, proving highly successful as pickers and spending an enjoyable holiday amid the healthiest surroundings. Paid at the ordinary rates, they have earned excellent wages. They have slept in well-equipped, hygienic dormitories, each with a bathroom attached, and spent their spare time in the attractive recreation rooms provided."

That summer, Alleyn's Boys' Secondary School at Dulwich dispatched a large party of pupils to work on the land, and boys from Marlborough College helped out on local farms, donating their wages, which totalled £43 7s 6d (43 pounds, seven shillings and sixpence), to Savernake Hospital. The previous year at Rugby, Headmaster Dr David announced "that so far as the employment on the land of boys from Rugby School was concerned, they had already had many more applications than they could possibly meet". At the beginning of November 1917 it was announced that the children of Potters Bar had collected a ton and a half of chestnuts for use in the manufacture of explosives.

When war broke out, the future actor-manager 12-year-old Donald Woolfitt was a pupil at Magnus Grammar School, Newark. The school formed a cadet corps and four times each week Donald went to school in khaki, learning drill and how to handle a rifle. Each summer the corps joined hundreds of other boys for two weeks training at a camp in Leicestershire, where they went on the rifle range and night manoeuvres.

In the summer, too, Donald went to work on a large farm at Long Bennington. There he learned how to handle horses and to cut and stack corn, working each day from 5 am till dark. Back home, with his passion for the stage, he would regularly entertain wounded soldiers at Newark General Hospital and take part in war-charity concerts at the town hall.

Not every British boy, or girl, lived up to Donald's high standard. In 1917, the Howard Association reported: "Figures issued by the Home Office show that during the war there has occurred a grave increase of juvenile offenders, and especially juvenile thieves ... the increase in juvenile offences is 34%, and the increase in thefts nearly 50%. The situation is not confined to any one area. Juvenile lawlessness has spread through the country like a plague." At least 12,500 more children than in peacetime, the majority boys, had come before the courts. The Recorder at the Central Criminal Court deplored the fact that "there had been a great epidemic of crime among children since the war. All discipline seemed to have disappeared. The old-time remedy of birching boys had quite gone out of fashion, but it was the proper remedy." It certainly was administered to four young Jewish boys, each aged 13. They described themselves as members of the "Black Button Gang" and admitted to stealing a box of sprats from a fishmonger's window. A 10-year-old from Enfield got six strokes of the birch for stealing £29 from his munitions-worker mother before absconding from home. After sleeping in fields and barns, he was finally caught by the police; he was carrying a gun, sword and pistol. Thomas Wilson from Liverpool was sent to borstal for three years. He had broken into shops and stolen £305. With the money he travelled to London, "and was seen distributing money on the Thames Embankment and afterwards, under the influence of drink, in the company with two girls in Trafalgar Square". At Norbiton station, four schoolboys aged 10 and 12 were caught throwing stones at trains, thereby "endangering the safety of the passengers". The boys received fines of 15s (fifteen shillings) and 7s 6d (seven shillings and sixpence) and a stiff telling-off from the magistrate.

The causes of this rise in juvenile delinquency were not difficult to determine. They were, according to a wartime survey of the problem, "chiefly to be found in the withdrawal from child-life of adult personal influence, and in the curtailment of those social and educational agencies that hitherto have occupied so large a part of a child's life, and on which those responsible for him had come to rely". An inquiry into 400 cases of juvenile delinquency showed that in two instances out of five, the father was in the forces. One typical case found: "Father in the Army. Mother not short of money, and home well cared for. Two well grown boys 12 and 14, both out of control. Mother's attempts at correction met by threats of assault. 'Two better boys couldn't be found when their father was home, yet he never raised his hand to one of them.' Mother complains of the lads' bad companions, and of late hours. One has been arrested for gambling and the other for theft." Even if the father was at home, he was usually engaged for long hours on war work: "Father a munition worker, much night work and overtime; an hour and ten minutes' walk to the factory, no tram, and cannot get a house nearer; mother at home. One lad, 14, whom mother cannot control – 'and his father might as well be in France for what good he is: he's never here when he's wanted'. Lad arrested for theft." Another family had a 14-year-old daughter, previously a punctilious attendant at chapel and Sunday school. But with her father out in France, she had become uncontrollable and "has been recently arrested for loitering on a railway station with soldiers".

There was, of course, considerable soul-searching as to what was to be done. The Reverend J. Glass, Vicar of St Paul's, Leamington, thought that the two chief things in a boy's life should be "to say his prayers and wash the back of his neck; the one would remind him he had a soul to save, the other the reality of the unseen". Edmund Spender wrote that: "Juvenile crime is largely due to the misplacement of surplus energy. Our towns have for the most part been built with haphazard disregard for the national need to make some adequate provision for the recreation of children, and often the only spaces available are bolted and barred by official Bumbledon...." Thus, after school hours classrooms, playgrounds and playing fields should be thrown open "so long as proper control is exercised".

The resourceful Chief Scout came up with his own solution. Baden-Powell proposed that each Scout should take "at least one street boy under his charge" and introduce him to the character- building activities of the movement. "We find", wrote BP, "that the worst hooligan soon makes the best Scout: he only needs direction for his adventurous energy and attractive pursuits to fill a void." By following that plan, not only would juvenile delinquency decrease, but it would lead to "increasing future efficient citizenship for the State".

CHAPTER SIX

DIGGING FOR VICTORY

NEVER MIND THE FOOD CONTROLLER,
WE'LL LIVE ON LOVE
(Title of a 1917 song, sung by Florrie Ford.)

On 12 October 1942, Sir Henry and Lady Hoare entertained James Lees-Milne of the National Trust to dinner at their stately home Stourhead in Wiltshire. During the meal of soup, whiting, pheasant, apple pie and dessert, washed down with Rhine wine and port, Lady Hoare asked their visitor: "Don't you find the food better in this war than in the last?" Lees-Milne, born in 1908, replied that he was rather young during the First World War, but certainly remembered the rancid margarine at his preparatory school. "Oh you were lucky. We were reduced to eating rats," replied Lady Hoare, much to Lees-Milne's surprise. "No, no, Alda," Sir Henry intervened, "You keep getting your wars wrong. That was when you were in Paris during the Commune." And although the British people were never reduced to eating rats, there were times during 1917–18 when the nation's food supplies were perilously low. Sir Arthur Lee, Director of Food Production, wrote dramatically: "This was the deadliest secret of the war at that stage, and to the very few of us in the know it was as ceaseless and nerve-racking an anxiety as the powers of hell could devise."

During the war's first days, the panicky run on food stores greatly offended, among others, J. C. Ker Fox, Brevet Major, Lieutenant-Colonel, National Reserve, who wrote in much indignation on 5 August 1914 to *The Times*: "When I went to the Army and Navy Stores yesterday I was disgusted to see hundreds of people whom one cannot dignify by calling them men and women, laying in tons of provisions. It is a

169

time of war, and we are fighting for our existence as a nation. Surely the Government ought to confiscate these private stores, and fine and imprison the selfish brutes who are hoarding them." In a forlorn attempt to appease Major Ker Fox, the Stores' Mr Gascoigne wrote that there had been "no disposition by the management to fulfil orders of exceptional magnitude". But this attempt at appeasement failed and on 8 August the Major promptly counter-attacked:

> *I accuse the Army and Navy Stores of nothing. But I accuse a great number of their customers of laying in large hoards of groceries and provisions during the last 10 days and I say it is a grossly selfish and unpatriotic proceeding.... What is the reason that my 7s [seven shilling] order from their provision department on the 4th inst. was only delivered last night, and a 4s [four shilling] order from their grocery department has not reached me at the time of writing?... Perhaps the "gentleman" who was standing next to me and wanted 10cwt [10 hundredweight, or 508 kg] of flour could tell Mr Gascoigne the reason.*

In August 1914, despite the Major's patriotic indignation, "All English housewives immediately thought of food; fathers too for that matter," according to 49-year-old housewife and mother of five, Annie Purbrook of Hornchurch, Essex. In her war diary she recorded how her husband Charles had told her "to send a larger order for groceries and to pay no ready money. I confess I did not understand why, but, however, after the third bank holiday, paper money for one pound and ten shillings was circulated and large amounts of silver were disgorged; all the gold was called in." As it turned out, the provisions the Purbrooks eventually ordered were not much more than their usual order, and Annie was glad "because we read in the newspapers that the fact of numbers of people trying to obtain large supplies of food was selfish and unpatriotic and likely to create panic". But, like Major Ker Fox, the Purbrooks had to wait for their provisions, since "the government had commandeered many of the horses of the firm with which I dealt and indeed everywhere the same thing happened, there were very few horses to be seen anywhere".

On the outbreak of war the National Food Fund was established with the aim of "feeding those who had become destitute through the war". This was because, according to a 1916 survey of the Fund, "it was thought at the time that there would be a considerable amount of distress among British poor, but happily this has not turned out to be the case". The main beneficiaries of the Fund were Belgian refugees fleeing the German invasion of their country. By May 1916, the survey found that although over 125,000 refugees from Belgium had become self-supporting, the Fund was still feeding each day in the capital 4,596 Belgian refugees, 21 from Serbia and 1,776 destitute Londoners. The previous Christmas, the Fund had received as gifts no less than 970 lb (440 kg) of fish from Billingsgate, 2,373 lb (1,076 kg) of meat from Smithfield, 2,167 lb (983 kg) of groceries, 3,696lb (1,676 kg) of potatoes, 92 turkeys, pheasants and geese and 1,135 loaves of bread together with a "great number of plum puddings".

Some relief on the nation's food front was afforded by the Empire. On 21 August 1914 *The Times* reported that:

> *Messrs Price and Co., Lilford Road Bakery, Coldharbour-Lane, Camberwell, offer to bake into bread enough of the Canadian gift of 1,000,000 bags of flour to the Motherland to make one quarter of a million pounds of bread, spread over deliveries approximately 10,000 weekly, free of all cost in the manufacture and delivery to any authorized depot in the neighbourhood of their bakeries in suburban London.*

Nonetheless, it was not long before Annie Purbrook noticed that prices began rise sharply. Sugar nearly trebled, and "bacon, usually 10d [ten pence] or less, was difficult to buy at double the price; eggs were the most scarce and rose from 1d [one penny] to 5d [five pence]; meat was also scarce and dear, and bread and flour rose more slowly in price but none the less surely, and I wondered what the really poor would do". In common with most British middle-class homes, the Purbrooks were soon adopting household economies. Annie recorded that: "The children were old enough to understand when I told them we must cut off some of the unnecessary extras such as jam and breakfast relishes. They were most good about it and I can remember no complaints either then or at any time, and their absolute content and cheerfulness made the food privations rather a pleasure than otherwise." At teatime, Annie wrote, "we had plates of bread and butter and others of plain bread upon which jam was allowed. Also we agreed to go without sugar in our tea. Some of us did not like this; I for one found it very unpalatable." But tea itself soon rose in price and Annie recorded: "We hear to-day that tea, which was 1/6 [one shilling and sixpence] and 2/6 [two shillings and sixpence] per lb is now 5/- [five shillings] and butter hardly procurable."

By December 1916, lithographic artist Frank Lockwood of Linthwaite, Yorkshire, was complaining in his diary: "Since the war the price of foodstuffs has increased 78 per cent. Sugar is very difficult to get hold of & the housewife must spend 5/- [five shillings] before she is entitled to 1lb [450 g] of sugar. We are able to have what they call 'standard flour' in the New Year." A fortnight later, while awaiting his call-up, Frank was writing: "For more than a week we have had no sugar & we have been drinking tea without it & coffee & cocoa with treacle in its place. We have tested rice pudding sweetened with the same sticky substance. The result was quite passable but there is nothing like the right stuff in the right place."

A year later, tea itself was in short supply, and Mr M. Grieve of The Whins, Chalfont St Peter, Buckinghamshire, wrote to the *Daily Mail* suggesting that herbal teas be used to meet the shortage, "as being far the most healthful substitutes". Moreover, Mr Grieve wrote, "they can also be blended and arranged to suit the gastric idiosyncrasies of the individual consumer. A few of them are agrimony, comfrey, dandelion, camomile, woodruff, marjoram, hyssop, sage, horehound, tansy, rosemary, stinging-nettle and raspberry." A suggestion which brought from *Punch* a poetic rejoinder:

But oh, it wrings the teardrop from my eye
To think of Polly putting on the kettle
To brew my daily dose of stinging nettle.

By the time Frank Lockwood was sipping his sugarless tea, the Government had finally created a Ministry of Food Control. At the beginning of the war, a Cabinet Committee on Food Supplies had been set up, a Royal Sugar Commission established, and the Board of Trade given control of the supply of milk. The export of food, except by licence, was forbidden and the Board of Agriculture appointed a consultative committee to help stimulate production. The German submarine campaign which began in February 1915, if not galvanizing the Government into direct action on the food front, led to the formation of the Ship Requisitioning Committee which worked with the Ship Licensing Committee on the best way to utilize shipping tonnage.

Charles Balston wrote in his diary that because of the U-boat sinking of food ships: "The Government was soon confronted by the necessity for provisioning the country and they started by encouraging agriculture and buying up food stocks with State Funds." On 15 June

1915 arch-Imperialist grandee Lord Milner was appointed chairman of the Food Supply in War Time Committee, and two months later Lord Crawford, President of the Board of Agriculture, promising state aid, urged Britain's farmers to increase domestic food production. On 6 September, Balston noted in his diary that "enormous grain stocks were being collected in London warehouses". He later heard that: "The Government were secretly buying wheat and sugar all over the world to keep prices down and that they had got hold of the refrigeration and so prevented a heavy increase in the price of American frozen meat."

In the New Year, Balston wrote how sugar imports were being cut by a quarter, with new restrictions on the import of fruit and tobacco. "After the shipping problem", he noted in March, "came that of high prices & food supplies.... There was a shortage of milk owing to a shortage of labour and a scarcity of butter." By October, the retail price of milk in Balston's London suburb of Dulwich had risen to 6d (sixpence) a quart, and in nearby Lambeth "in view of the increased price of milk the Guardians have arranged to use more condensed milk and have ordered 37,500 tins" for the workhouse inmates. A month earlier Poplar Town Council had petitioned the Government "to assume control of the food supplies of the nation". President of the Board of Trade Walter Runciman "pointed out that the Government had already obtained control of the sources and supply of the sugar, wheat and meat but could not altogether restrict prices as it was a world problem affected by foreign competition, but that the Govt was giving unremitting attention to the whole subject". Runciman added that it would be injurious to the nation's morale if the British "were to regard themselves as a blockaded people, scrambling for bread tickets and meat coupons" like the Germans.

But the nation's morale was already being dented by the food problem. High prices and profiteering were the subjects of the most frequent complaints, as in Sheffield where grocers were said to be charging for paper bags for food. Back in February, the papers had already reported that: "Fine Cheshire cheese has never been so scarce or dear as now. At Chester … farmers brought in 22 tons, which were sold immediately, one special lot going for 120s per cwt [six pounds per hundredweight/ 50 kg]." Food crime, too, if not rampant, was on the increase. That same month at Thames Police Court, a labourer was remanded for stealing tea from the docks in a specially made bag hidden under his shirt. The Court heard that "he had another bag fixed to the waistband of his trousers, and more tea was found in cloths round his legs". And a market meat porter, sentenced six weeks later at the Guildhall for stealing mutton, asked the Aldermen to treat it as a first offence "as he was the father of 22 children, and had some at the front".

At Easter, the Birmingham Master Bakers' Association decided that the delivery of Good Friday hot cross buns should be curtailed as much as possible, and that all buns should be sold for one penny with no special offers or discounts. There was bad news too in October for the inmates of the Walsall workhouse: the Board of Guardians, by a majority of one, decided to substitute suet puddings and treacle for plum puddings at the Christmas dinner. Already the St Pancras Board of Guardians were saving £600 a year by using margarine instead of butter in their workhouses. A more Christian attitude was displayed by the Belfast Board of Guardians who refused to substitute margarine for butter in the diet of their workhouse inmates – this despite the Local Government Board inspector's advice that the use of margarine "would have the effect a saving of £1,040 per annum". In West Ham it was reported that "Nurses have offered to go without cake if the Guardians will substitute butter for margarine".

In the month before Christmas 1916, Charles Balston recorded that:

having dealt with milk and flour, steps were taken to obtain a return to potatoes & to interview the Managers of the principal hotels and restaurants with a view to restricting courses at meals and economizing [on] food. The next step was to institute by law the observance of meatless days. It was clear that the exigencies of war transport & the activities of the enemy submarine were beginning to put us, like the Germans, on short commons.

To preside over the nation's efforts, the new Prime Minister appointed Lord Devonport as Britain's first Food Controller. Lloyd George was under the misapprehension that Devonport's notorious brusque and high-handed manner was a sign of strength of character. At the age of 20, after working for Tetley & Sons, he had started his own tea-importing company and then went into the retail trade, founding the International Stores, which by 1890 had 200 branches. Elected to Parliament in 1892 as the Liberal member for Devonport, he played an important part in setting up the Port of London Authority, of which he acted as unpaid chairman from 1909 to 1925. But there, "although his dock reorganization and investment programme were constructive achievements, he became notorious as an exponent of the invincibility of employers". During the 1912 Dock Strike, his inflexible stance and contemptuous attitude had prompted dockers' leader Ben Tillett to shout at a meeting, "May God strike Lord Devonport dead!" At this the men chanted: "He shall die, he shall die."

Now, with Christmas 1916 approaching, he took office just as food was about to become a major obsession with the people of Britain. The Christmases of 1914 and 1915 had been almost indistinguishable from pre-war celebrations, although they had both seen some "patriotic" economies. On 12 November 1914 the press had reported that "The Lambeth Guardians yesterday decided that in order that the Poor Law schoolchildren may have an opportunity of appreciating the position of national affairs the usual practice of allowing each child an egg for breakfast on Christmas morning be suspended this year". *Punch* commented ironically: "If this doesn't learn them to love their country, it ought, at any rate, to encourage them to honour and respect the patriotic Lambeth Guardians." The same day it was also reported that:

> *At a meeting of the Metropolitan Asylums Board a proposal to reduce, in view of the war, the allowances and usual Christmas fare of the patients in the Board's hospitals was strongly deprecated by Father Higley, who said that instead of making the coming Christmas a sad one people ought to rejoice because of the righteousness of the war which this country and her brave Allies were waging. Ultimately, it was decided that the usual Christmas extras be allowed.*

But the war and its far-reaching effects on the Christmas culinary front could not be ignored, as *The Graphic* recognized in an article "Shopping with Santa Claus" on 5 December 1914:

> *With the strain of war-time affecting practically everybody, happy is the family where the housewife is a clever 'manager'. A very good aid to real food economy is HP Sauce, for it is wonderful what it will do in transforming cold meat, the remainder of the joint, or what not, into a dainty entrée; or just as a relish, in making a cold repast appetising. These few examples demonstrate what may well be termed "enjoyable economy".*

The next year, things were much the same, although in November the National Union of Women's Suffrage Societies organized a Patriotic

Housekeeping Exhibition in London. Among the exhibits were: "Pre-war Meals and War Meals, revealing where thought can save money" and "Pulses: The Poor Man's Beef". Visitors were informed that both cheese and nuts were "more concentrated food and more nutritious than meat" and the "fallacy of Jelly" was revealed. The exhibition organizers were confident that if the public followed their advice and economized wisely, no less than £20 million a year could saved. As Christmas approached, the papers reported that tons of turkeys from the Tiverton and South Molton districts of Devon were readily available in the shops. But in Liverpool "in view of the absence of distress in the city", the Liverpool 'Hotpot' Fund Committee decided to dispense with the distribution of Christmas hotpots. Christmas Day 1915 in Bedford was observed as "Serbian Day", with households urged "to do without a traditional Yuletide tasty morsel" and contribute the balance to the Serbian Relief Fund. In Kingston upon Thames it was reported that: "… three large cakes, weighing about 150lb, made by the girls who are learning cooking in the elementary schools at Kingston, will form part of the Christmas 'treat' for the wounded 'Anzacs' and other soldiers at the Red Cross Hospital at New Malden."

But Christmas 1916 was different. The day before Christmas Eve, Lord Northcliffe publicly renewed his call for rationing. "A year ago," he wrote,

> when I advocated this, and started the Home-Grown Food Exhibition, I was derided as an alarmist, stigmatized in certain quarters with a variety of uncomplimentary epithets, among them "lunatic" and "advertiser", while sneers as to my earlier efforts in the matter of "standard bread", aeroplanes and shells were not lacking. Today, who shall deny the necessity for the most instant and effective organisation of our food supplies? The only way in which the poor can be protected from the wealthy bourgeoisie is by the issuing of meat, bread, and sugar tickets, so that the industrial labouring classes, on whom the high food prices press so much more heavily than on the wealthy, may have an opportunity of getting their share in some equality with the rich.

That same day Grace Curnock wrote in *The War Illustrated*:

> If the Food Controller by any chance comes to dine in my house on Christmas Day I do not think that he will have to cavil at the extravagance of my Christmas fare: he will not even be able to blame

me for "Christmas dinner as usual". Frankly I cannot afford to pay the greatly increased price for the time-honoured ingredients for the menu even if the country could afford to let me have not only the food but the freightage and labour involved in its arrival at my door. Christmas dinners if up to tradition must be left this year to such profiteers who, while making money out of their country's need, will certainly refrain from economising for their country's need.

Before the war a typical Christmas-dinner menu for Grace's family and visitors, totalling four adults, three children and three servants, would have comprised of:

Clear Soup
Dover Sole in White Wine
Roast Turkey, sausages
Chestnut Stuffing, Bread Sauce
(or Roast Beef, or Goose)
Brussels Sprouts, Potatoes
Christmas Pudding, Mince Pies
Stilton Cheese, Celery
Oranges, Apples, Almonds and Raisins, Candied Fruits, Chocolates,
Nuts and Crackers
Champagne, Port, Madeira, Liqueurs, Whisky, Brandy, Soda Water,
Lemonade, Ginger Wine.

"From to-day's point of view," Grace wrote, "it looks an impossibly heavy and extravagant dinner, doesn't it? Yet we 'sat down' to it in 1913, even in 1914; a few people cut down some items in 1915, but this year such a menu should exist in no house." To emphasize her point Grace went on to record the increase in prices. The price of the soup had gone up 50 per cent; the Dover Sole had nearly tripled. Turkey had gone up from 1s 3d (one shilling and threepence) a pound/450 g to 2s (two shillings) and the prices of sausages from 10d (ten pence) a pound to 1s 3d (one shilling and threepence). Brussels sprouts had doubled from 2d (twopence) a pound to 4d (four pence) and potatoes, which cost less than a penny a pound in 1913, were now two pence halfpenny. The family's Christmas pudding, which had cost 7s (seven shillings) before the war, was now priced at just under 12s (twelve shillings), and the Stilton had gone up from 1s 3d (one shillings and threepence) to 2s (two shillings). Alternatives to the Christmas turkey had also risen sharply in price. Goose, which could be got for under a shilling a pound in 1913, now cost as much as 1s 8d (one shilling and eight pence), although the rise in sirloin of beef was not so marked, going up only 4d (four pence) a pound from 1s 3d (one shilling and threepence) to 1s 7d (one shilling and sevenpence). And while Grace noted "the increase in the price of meat is relatively lower than in any other items", prime back bacon had gone up nearly 6d (sixpence) a pound, fresh Devonshire butter from 1s 7d (one shilling and seven pence) to 2s 3d (two shillings and threepence) a pound and English cheddar cheese from 11d (eleven pence) to 1s 6d (one shilling and sixpence). The price of a pound box of Digestive biscuits had risen from 2s 2d (two shillings and two pence) to 3s 6d (three shillings and sixpence), and three pounds of beef dripping from 1s 9d (one shilling and nine pence) to 3s 6d (three shillings and sixpence).

These increases all conspired to make it a less than Merry Christmas. In Hornchurch, Annie Purbrook counted herself lucky that, with lard at 2s 4d (two shillings and four pence) per pound and almost impossible to get hold of, "a friend gave me at Christmas two half pounds of lard, and a Major's wife one day brought me a most acceptable present of a pound of dripping. Strange gifts were they not?"

Summing up, Grace Curnock told her readers:

My children will keep the season as a Church festival, and I shall try and make it as bright as possible for them, but as far as extra food is concerned they most certainly will get nothing more than a slightly richer pudding than on usual days with "a fire round it", but I am afraid that there will be no crackers and no snapdragon [a game involving raisins and flaming brandy]. The bread and the cakes will be made of war flour, and baking powder and egg substitutes will take the place of eggs in the cakes; almonds and raisins and chocolates and sugar icing will be things of memory only, though I do think we may manage a few chestnuts and oranges.

And she concluded her article with a warning: "The one great thing for everyone to remember this Christmas is that there is a *world's food shortage*, and that to fail to economize in food consumption is tantamount to putting a brake on our endeavours to beat the Hun."

Many in Britain, like Annie Purbrook, identified enemies closer to home, "greedy monsters to be found almost everywhere who sought to make a profit by holding up supplies and only letting food dribble out at huge prices so that they might line their pockets ... the despised war-profiteers or the *nouveau riche....*" *Punch* agreed and in November 1916 published a cartoon set in "The Dim Future" with the son of a War Profiteer asking his parent: "Father, who did you do in the Great War?"

Annie looked to the Government to step in and to control matters "by issuing food coupons and to see that as far as possible they were justly and conscientiously used". Devonport's appointment seemed a tentative step in the right direction. But a month into 1917, Germany began her campaign of unrestricted submarine warfare. On 4 February, Ethel Bilbrough recorded in her diary: "Germany is now desperate, and thinks by stopping all our imported foodstuffs, to starve us out. The war is coming very near home...." The day before, writing of the voluntary rationing scheme suggested by Devonport, Georgina Lee recorded:

Today we are rationed for the first time! The rationing will affect only 3 comestibles so far:
Meat 2½lbs weekly per head
Bread 4lbs weekly per head
Sugar ¾lbs weekly per head
We do not exceed this liberal allowance already, at least we have not lately. We are seven in the house, I reckon we can have weekly:
13 loaves of 2lbs each with 1½lb Flour for puddings etc.
½lb Flour for cake
As for sugar, for weeks past I had imposed a limit of 5lbs for the household. Now I see I can use another ¼lb, if I can get it! It has been very difficult to procure sugar at all, most grocers absolutely refusing to supply any. But my dear Army and Navy Stores allow a certain fixed proportion on grocery orders. The meat will be more difficult as the 2½lbs include bone. It includes bacon for breakfast and ham so it will mean a great deal of goodwill and patriotic loyalty on the part of the women, because these rations are at present left to honour to enforce. There is to be no system of tickets as yet, as in Germany. But the Government will resort to compulsion if the country does not respond.

Not everyone was quite that ready to respond. A few weeks later Ethel Bilbrough was writing:

Food is getting distinctly scarce and one begins to feel as if one were living in the days of the French Revolution! But a great deal of nonsense is written by people saying we must not think of giving even our crumbs to the poor birds. Because we are fighting against brutes must we ourselves become brutes? Feeling strongly on the matter I wrote to the Mirror *... though from its extremely flippant tone, I never expected to see it in print.*

But Ethel's letter *was* printed:

I cannot agree with "H.H.S." as regards "Birds and Bread". In theory it is excellent to say that "not a crust should be wasted" but as a matter of fact in every well-to-do house stale remnants of bread are treated very much as they always have been treated, so why disappoint our little feathered friends who brighten this sombre world with their music, and at the same time free our precious crops from insect pests?

Ethel's concerns were not just for her "little feathered friends": "We are not allowed to feed our horses on corn any longer and the poor dears are growing dull and slack on hay! And dog biscuits can no longer be got for love or money which is serious!" But that month, with the sinking by U-boats of 886,610 tons of British, Allied and neutral shipping, the authorities were not inclined to be lenient with those thought to be wasting Britain's food supplies. Charles Angus of Abercynon, South Wales was fined £10 for feeding fowl on wheat, and so too, with £20 special costs, was Charles Norton Manning of Valley Farm, Leckhampstead, Buckinghamshire. At Highgate Police Court, William Cordwell Bibby was fined £2 for feeding a horse, "kept for pleasure", on oats. And in Carmarthen, Evodia Hughes was summoned for buying 102 lb (46 kg) of meat in ten days. Her excuse was that the meat was for her "St Bernard dog which had a weak heart and required careful feeding". Food for Britain's pets did indeed seem to be under threat. A crisis meeting was held at Hove in June 1917 to protest against "the proposed destruction of dogs by crushing taxation". Lady Warwick, presiding, told the gathering: "… all they asked for was to keep the present stock of animals as best they could. Even though their own food should fall short, they would willingly share it with their pets."

That spring, as the losses of food ships mounted, the public were constantly reminded that: "Bread is now precious and every crumb should be eaten." In April 1917 *The Times* reported that in five streets in the Summer Lane district of Birmingham, "22 pieces of bread were picked up in one day, 33 on another, and 27 on a third". The pieces were all "substantial in size". So, to drive home the message, the King called on his people to eat less bread. His appeal, given on 2 May 1917, was couched in much the same language as a similar one made by King George III in 1800 during the Napoleonic Wars:

We, being persuaded that the abstention from all unnecessary consumption of grain will furnish the surest and most effectual means of defeating the devices of our enemies … earnestly exhort all those of Our loving subjects, the men and women of Our realm who have the means of procuring articles of food other than wheaten corn, as they tender their immediate interest and feel for the want of others, especially to practise the greatest economy and frugality in the use of every species of grain: And We do for this purpose more particularly exhort and charge all heads of household to reduce the consumption of bread in their respective families by at least one-fourth of the quantity consumed in ordinary times, to abstain from the use of flour in pastry and moreover carefully to restrict or wherever possible to abandon the use thereof in all other articles than bread.

The proclamation was read in churches and chapels nationwide on the next four Sundays and the Lees family heard it at St Peter's, Cranley Gardens, Chelsea, on 27 May. But munitions worker Mabel Hilton of Waltham Cross either failed to hear the appeal or chose to ignore it, and was fined £10 for throwing away 4 lb 11 oz (2.2 kg) of bread into a dustbin. Another woman was overheard to say: "In my own household we hardly eat any bread at all. We practically live on toast."

On 29 May, Lord Devonport added his exhortation to the King's:

By a strict care of our daily bread we can best help the men who are gallantly fighting on sea and land to achieve victory, and so share with them the joys of the peace which will follow. No true citizen, no patriotic man or woman will fail the country in this hour of need. I ask all the members of your household to pledge themselves to respond to the King's recent Appeal for economy and frugality and to wear the purple ribbon as a token.

But despite these brave words, the very next day Devonport resigned "for reasons of health". His six months' tenure of the Ministry had been far from happy or successful. *Punch* had attacked his dilatoriness in a cartoon entitled "Alimentary Intelligence" published on 11 April. At the Ministry of Food Control, Mr Punch asks Devonport, in the guise of a commissionaire: "Do you control food here?" He receives the reply: "Well, sir, 'control' is perhaps rather a strong word. We give hints to householders, and we issue 'grave warnings'." In his diary Charles Balston summed up Devonport's time at the Ministry: "… he started by putting the country on rations and on its honour not to exceed them. Sugar, potatoes, bread & meat were rationed. In the case of bread, no loaves under 12 hours could be sold by bakers and the flour was mixed with husks. We were enjoined to eat less of it and to help us in doing so the price of bread was increased to a shilling a quartern loaf. The manufacture and sale of pastry was also restricted, lest we should adopt Queen Marie Antoinette's suggestion to substitute cakes for bread."

Furthermore, Balston noted, "The sale of paste for putting up wallpaper and of starch for stiffening linen was prohibited. Racing was restricted to reduce the consumption of oats." All these restrictions "had an inevitable effect on the health of the nation, especially as the quality of the standard flour issued by millers varied and some bakers were not so skilful or scrupulous as others in making palatable bread and this was shewn in the loss of fat and reduction in weight and also in skin-troubles and ill health."

Lloyd George now looked round for a new Food Controller. The post was seen as a poisoned chalice, but eventually Lloyd George persuaded his old political foe Welsh industrialist and "Coal King" David Alfred Thomas, Baron Rhondda, to take on the job. It proved an inspired appointment. Rhondda, or "DA" as he was generally known, had survived the sinking of the *Lusitania* and had been much amused by a poster for the *Cardiff Evening Express* the following day which ran:

GREAT NATIONAL DISASTER
'D.A.' SAVED

He had joined Lloyd George's government in December 1916 as President of the Local Government Board, having already worked for the Ministry of Munitions in arranging supplies from the United States. At the Local Government Board he had been frustrated in his main aim of establishing a Ministry of Health, and only took on Food Control with the greatest reluctance. On taking office he made two prophecies to Professor Edward Gonner, his Director of Statistics. He said he knew the work would kill him and that he would soon be the most unpopular man in Government. Sadly, "The first came true. The second was certainly false, for before he died in July 1918, he had won the unstinted confidence and regard of the nation."

Rhondda's appointment was announced on 15 June 1917. A paragraph on the new Food Controller soon appeared in the *Sunday Herald*:

> *Lord Rhondda doesn't seem to believe in the cold shouldering of women that is reported from some of the services. There are to be four women on the Food Consumers' Council, and he wants every local food committee to have at least one woman member. I have heard this week that his work in combating the food havoc of the U-boats is done with particular intensity, because Lord Rhondda was aboard the* Lusitania *on her last voyage, and is not likely to forget what U-boats can do. How much more like a bishop than a business man he looks!*

Charles Balston wrote approvingly of how Rhondda "immediately declared war on high prices and blackmailers and asked for and obtained ample powers to deal with both…. The price of the quartern loaf was to be reduced to 9d [nine pence]; prime joints were to be 6d [sixpence] cheaper, sugar cards were to come into operation & local authorities were to have drastic powers for better distribution…." But all this was to take time, and though the introduction of the convoy system had reduced sinkings by U-boats, the public were still enduring severe shortages. Florrie Ford sang of their plight in a popular song "Never Mind the Food Controller":

> *Never mind the Food Controller*
> *We'll live on love*
> *Just one kiss and a squeeze*
> *Will be better than bread and cheese*
> *Never mind my sugar ration*
> *For your lips*
> *I've got a passion*
> *They're so sweet*
> *They'll sweeten all my tea and coffee*
> *They're as sweet as any toffee*
> *Never mind the Food Controller*
> *My turtle dove*
> *For at breakfast and dinner*

CHAPTER SIX

We can have a little a cup of love, sweet love
And you can warm it up for supper
Never mind the Food Controller
We'll live on love.

An ex-officer recalled too that soldiers home on leave "adored hearing Heather Thatcher sing 'Coupons for Kisses'".

At the time Florrie Forde recorded her song, in the spring of 1917, the country was suffering from a severe potato shortage. Charles Balston first noted a scarcity in January; then in March: "It was stated that the country did not have enough for another month. In some places they were not for sale at all and the newspapers recommended us to eat dried-peas, haricot beans, swedes, parsnips, salsify and beetroot instead." Things had improved somewhat by 5 May, when it was reported in *The Times*: "A large number of women were attracted to Kingston upon Thames yesterday by the announcement that a local firm of drapers, Bentalls, were disposing of potatoes in lots of 6 lb each. The line of waiting women was over a half a mile [800 m] long." Among them was Ellen Sophia Charman (whose husband George was in France with the Royal Fusiliers), together with her six-year-old son Cyril. Ellen, whose eldest son 15-year-old Edward was now the Charman family's principal breadwinner, and the other women were admitted 20 at a time to Bentalls, where they were served their potatoes by the store's women assistants.

One of the war's casualties on the home front was the old adage "The customer is always right". In Chislehurst, Ethel Bilbrough fumed: "Prices of course are awful…. Yesterday, I wanted to buy a small tinned tongue which formerly cost about 2/- [two shillings] to my consternation the man demanded 4s 6d [four shillings and sixpence]!! I walked straight out of the shop with *no* tongue beyond what nature has blessed me with gratuitously & I used it freely!" Annie Purbrook was more sympathetic to shop workers: "We can now buy no sugar, butter, margarine or meat without presenting coupons. It is often quite confusing and I often feel sorry for the shop people, for some of them look terribly worried." Food control was imposed across institutions. It was reported that the Camberwell Guardians "as a war economy have revised the dietary for the healthy inmates of the East Dulwich Workhouse. Butcher meat is to be withdrawn except on Sunday, and on Tuesday and Friday the dinner is to consist simply of bread, cheese, and rice." And the pupils of a Chertsey secondary school were denied their lunch when burglars broke in and "took all the food possible, including a joint for the scholars' mid-day meal".

All over the country, advice was being freely offered, and stratagems, palatable and otherwise, experimented with to eke out the nation's larder. In Hackney, bakers using 114 tons of potatoes to bake bread saved enough flour for 146,832 loaves of 2lb (900g) each. In Hastington, Derbyshire, an experimental supper was held with a menu which "consisted of roast hedgehog (baked a la Romany) and stewed 'hotchi-witchu' (Romany for hedgehog), with new potatoes and vegetables". In Devon, tramps admitted to the casual wards of the county's workhouses had their bread allowance cut from 8oz (225g) to 4oz (112g). An appeal was made by Freemason "P.M. and P.Z." to his brethren requesting them to suspend Masonic lodge dinners and to "practise self-denial for the sake of the nation". The Government was petitioned to assure the public that "while they go short voluntarily the German prisoners and interned aliens are not enjoying full rations". From Harrow, a teetotal correspondent wrote to the Ministry of Food Control suggesting that the bread ration of beer drinkers should be reduced 1oz (450g) for every pint of beer. But despite the situation, the City of London Piscatorial Society, meeting in March 1917, decided to enter a protest against the sale for human consumption of fish from the lakes of London's public parks, waterways and reservoirs.

There was pride in undercutting recommendations. A Manchester man told the papers that back in 1897 he had begun to experiment by eating half as much as he usually ate, "and now at 70 I am uncommonly fit, and I am quite sure that many others would derive equal benefit from following this advice". A "Dorset Rector" proudly claimed that his household, which included three servants, had already been living for nearly a year on a diet comprising less bread, less meat (including bacon) and less sugar than the quantities recommended by the Food Controller. And a solicitor declared: "By recent experiment I find that a sedentary worker can well live on half the ration suggested … I will therefore now live on half my ration, releasing the other half for a munition worker, whose active life requires a larger amount." But H. V. Plum, master at Kelly College, Tavistock, considered the meat allowance "insufficient for healthy growing boys in a boarding school". Thus he hesitated to cut down the meat ration until he was certain that the Ministry of Food Control "demands it in the interest of the country. As far as I can judge at present we can avoid stinting the boys on the allowance of sugar and on flour also, I think; but I do believe we require another ¼lb [115 g] of meat per head."

Britain's traditional sweet tooth was much exercised by the shortage of sugar. In February 1917, Dr George Coates had written to *The Times* from the Athenaeum Club to enter a plea for sugar cards.

> *Either, he says, there is not enough sugar to go round, or some selfish people are securing far more than their share. He points out that his household, consisting of seven people, has not for months been able to procure ¾ lb [350 g] of sugar per head per week. Yesterday he spent over 30s [thirty shillings] on various groceries at five large shops and could secure only 1 lb [450 g] of lump sugar and a promise that he might have 2 lb [900 g] of granulated and sifted sugar in three or four days. Yet, he adds, I could have bought any amount of sweets or chocolates.*

On the same day, another correspondent, calling herself "House-keeper", expressed amusement at the suggestion that people should limit themselves to ¾lb [350 g] of sugar per head per week: "I consider myself lucky if I am able to obtain 1½lb [675 g] of sugar per week for my household of five people."

The month before, *The Times* had reported:

> *There is a new restriction in certain tea-shops which, having raised the price of their tea and coffee, now limit the use of lump sugar. It is alleged that customers helped themselves too freely in some cases, and it is suspected that they sometimes abstracted a few lumps for home use. To cope with these supposed depredations the sugar bowl is now produced only for a few moments when the waitress asks whether one lump or two is needed.*

Sugar was in such short supply and so highly prized that when William L. Fairbrother, a grocer from Moira, Leicestershire, was pulled up for not having proper lights on his motor cycle, he unsuccessfully tried to bribe the policeman who had stopped him with 2½ lb (1 kg) of sugar. And on the agenda of the annual London district Synod of the primitive Methodist Church at High Wycombe there appeared a notice that visitors would be welcome but "they should bring their own provisions, including sugar".

Ice cream was a casualty of the war, but the ice lolly one of its "inventions". The manufacture of ice cream was stopped in January 1918. Two months later Lord Rhondda met a deputation from the London and South of England Ice Cream Manufacturers' Association. They petitioned him to give their members a small allowance of sugar and to remove the ban on making ice cream so that traders could use up their existing stocks. Because the ban "would have inflicted grave hardship on a number of innocent persons, including many of the allied Italian nation", it was eventually modified in June. By then Achille Pompa, the association secretary, already had some good news for his members. He had "received letters from various local food committees stating that they have no objections to fruit cordials being frozen in water and sold as a summer delicacy provided that no sugar is used. This is considered a satisfactory substitute for ice-cream and is absolutely pure."

Britain's youngsters played their part in the nation's battle against the U-boat for food. Lectures on food economy were given to London schoolchildren, who were then asked to write up their own thoughts. A nine-year-old boy wrote: "If I here [sic] of any people grumbling about not enough food I shall tell them not to be grumbling about not enough food.... Many people have to eat less than you." A little girl wrote: "The besieging of Paris [in 1870–71] was far worse than we are now. Why! They would think it a treat to get a mouse, and that cost 1/9½d [one shilling and nine-and-a-half pence]." Another girl recognized that: "Food is so scarce because the subermarines [sic] sink our food vessels and because all ships are scarce, so if you give your baby in the pram a piece of bread see that it do not throw it in the gutter to waist [sic]." A boy sympathized with the Food Controller: "Lord Rhondda's position is no enviable one; his work is most difficult, for he has to provide for rich as well as poor, and some peace fads poison his ideas and tasks in abundance." A sentiment echoed by an 11-year-old girl: "Bravo for Lord Rhondda's care of the nation's food. I am one who will volunteer to win the war by saving food." Children helped in practical ways too. The boys of Eton dug potatoes, and in Kent 832 boys were released from the county's elementary schools to work on the land. In Buckinghamshire children collected 70 tons of blackberries for jam, in Gloucestershire 80 tons, and 41 tons each in Oxfordshire and Northamptonshire. And during the summer holidays the headmaster, his wife, staff and the all the older boys of Mayford School, Woking, "trekked" out to do agricultural work.

If Britain's children were doing their bit, quite a few adults were not, andfood hoarders came in for short shrift. Popular novelist Marie Corelli was fined £50 for hoarding tea and sugar at her Stratford-upon-Avon home, and in January 1918 the same fine, with costs of five guineas (five pounds and five shillings) was imposed on Hilton George Tyson of Hollybush Lodge, Southgate. Some thought he got off lightly, for he was found with no less than 115 tins of fish, 187 lb (85 kg) of biscuits, 65 lb (29 kg)) of tea, 106 lb (81 kg) of sugar, 56 lb (25 kg) of lard and 57 lb (26 kg) of bacon in his possession. Eliza Drake of Duckett Street, Stepney was more modest in her hoarding. She was found in illegal possession of "only" 9 lb (5 kg) of tea, 20 lb (10 kg) of sugar and 3½ lb (1.5 kg) of coffee. For which she was fined £30 with the alternative of 60 days' imprisonment.

Throughout 1917 and 1918, those breaking some of the other aspects of the increasingly stringent food regulations felt the full force of the law too. At Croydon Magistrates' Court, grocers Meller and Robinson of London Road, Mitcham, were fined £40 for selling butter at excessive prices, while in Hastings grocer Alderman Jabez Stace received a fine of £20 for selling margarine as butter. In late October 1917, fines totalling £200 were imposed on 13 Liverpool shopkeepers for selling butter "at prices exceeding the sum fixed by the Food Controller". And a confectioner in the city was fined 50s (fifty shillings) for selling chocolates at over 3d (threepence) an ounce "without the consent of the Food Controller". The previous month, Marlborough Street Police Court had fined Emile J. Monico of the Café Monico, Piccadilly, £7 with £3 costs "for permitting excessive consumption" in his restaurant. When the police raided Samuel Gold's bakery in Stepney they found he had illegally baked 214 white loaves; the magistrate at Old Street Police Court ordered them to be sent to the London Hospital and fined Gold £50. At Willesden Police Court seven bakers were each fined £2 for selling short-weight bread. The same day at Bow Street, fruiterer Israel Cohen of St Martin's Lane and costermonger David Stevens were each fined £3 for selling strawberries at a price exceeding the controlled one of 9d (nine pence) per lb. In rural Spalding on 15 May 1917, farmer George Henry Goose of Whaplode Drove was fined £100 for selling his potatoes above the maximum price.

The press, especially Lord Northcliffe's papers, were tirelessly on the alert for "food hogs". In February 1917, the *Daily Mail* located one in a City restaurant where he consumed what only three years earlier would have been considered quite a modest luncheon of "half a dozen oysters, three slices of roast beef with Yorkshire pudding, two vegetables and a roll". The *Mail's* stable mate *The Evening News* found another in a London restaurant who guzzled "a large portion of beef, baked potatoes, Brussels sprouts, two big platefuls of bread, apple tart, a portion of cheese, a couple of pats of butter and a bottle of wine. We understand that he would have ordered the last item on the menu but for the fact that the band was playing it." The same week, the papers contained both a report that the Food Controller was about to forbid the throwing of rice at weddings, and also invaluable advice that when having "Sparrows as food, the feathers are most quickly got rid of by removing them with the skin".

In January 1918, Mary Graham of Newton Abbot, Devon, wrote to a family friend serving in Mesopotamia (present-day Iraq):

There is only one subject of conversation in this country, and that is the wait for food. No one has had any cheese for a long time, butter is very hard to get and even margarine is not to be had. A small grocer's shop here was "rushed" a few days ago – I found a huge crowd when I passed – the women and children were packed in a tight mass right out into the road.... I asked a woman what was going on? "Oh! Margarine!" said she. When I came back about half an hour later, the police were there, just finished turning the people out. I heard later, that the shop was regularly looted ... all the dry fish was stolen, and a quantity of jam and biscuits and other things. He shut his shop up for the rest of the day. It appears that someone reported that he had margarine, and the whole contents of the Newton slums etc. ran for supplies. He said he had none, and they would not believe him, and one woman slapped his face!!!

On occasion the public took the law into their own hands. On 27 February 1918 *Punch* featured a cartoon entitled "Everyone a Food Controller":

First Lady (in tramcar after two hours in the queue): "Did yer see that food 'og in the check coat and skirt wiv 'alf pound of margarine in each pocket?"
Second Lady: "Why, yes – I pinched one."
First Lady: "So did I!"

The Ministry of Food Control under both Devonport and Rhondda continuously bombarded the public with advice on how to make the best of their rations and other foodstuffs available. A Food Economy Campaign was launched under the direction of Kennedy Jones MP, one of Lord Northcliffe's pushy young men. He was a tremendous drinker: Lloyd George saw him polish off a whole bottle of green Chartreuse in one evening. But drink did not impair his capacity for work and he set about the new task with enthusiasm and energy. Jones wrote to all his fellow MPs "so that the urgency of the problem to be solved may be put prominently before your constituents". And he told the public:

> *The frontiers of this war are not only in France and Belgium, in the Balkans and in Mesopotamia. They are nearer home. Our household tables are the battle-line and Hindenburg is waging his real warfare there ... the wasteful bread-knife is a weapon given into the hands of the enemy.... Bread is life, and if Germany can rob us of our bread by preventing it from reaching our shores ... then she will have deprived us of our power to strike a fatal blow.... Eat one pound of bread less per week and begin at once. That's a plain downright way of helping to win the war.*

Leicester responded to Jones's appeal. In the first report on the food economy campaign to the National War Savings Committee, the town claimed to have voluntarily reduced its consumption of bread and flour by 23 per cent. To help things along, the National Food Economy League produced a series of instructive booklets, titles of which included "Patriotic Food Economy for the Well-To-Do" and "War-Time Recipes for Households where Servants are Employed".

Jones pressed popular entertainers like Harry Lauder into service. On 26 March 1917, the "Scottish Minstrel" was among those who addressed a meeting of 2,000 domestic servants "from most of the big households in London, as well as many from the country" at the Theatre Royal, Drury Lane. Lauder, "alluding to the presence of black hats and black dresses as symbols of sacrifice", told the audience: "Do not fail to make further sacrifices now, because the lad in the trenches never hesitated when the call came." Amid the ensuing cheers, he went on to say it was vulgar to overeat and: "Incidentally, he told the audience that by economizing he had in two weeks saved 15 pieces of sugar. If in the next fortnight all those present would do likewise they would save between two and three tons." The meeting ended with a resolution being passed that pledged "those present to cooperate with employers in carrying out the regulations of Lord Devonport and the authorities on the question of rations to households generally".

On the platform with Lauder that day was Constance Peel, a pre-war journalist and writer on household management. Now 49 years old, Constance had organized a Soldiers' and Sailors' Wives Club in Lambeth and worked for the National War Savings Organization before she was asked at the beginning of March 1917 to join the Ministry of Food Control. There, along with Maud Pember Reeves, she was co-director of the Ministry's Women's Service. During her year at the Ministry, Constance addressed no less than 176 meetings on the economical use of food. Her advice and that of her colleagues was not always well received: "When at a cookery demonstration a bean dish was suggested as a substitute for meat which it was so difficult to obtain, a good lady laughed ironically. 'Give me 'usbin' that muck? Yes, I don't think!' Whilst another added, 'Give 'im beans, an' get a black eye for me pains!'" Even fish in some homes was not considered "proper food". Constance recalled: "I have seen a long line of women waiting outside a butcher's shop when the next door shop, a fishmonger's, was full of fish and empty of customers. 'Why wait hours to get meat', I asked a woman once,' when you could get fish without waiting?' 'My 'usbin' 'e wouldn't eat fish for 'is *dinner*,' was the reply made in a tone which would have surprised me had I suggested a diet of rattlesnake." And *Punch* ran a cartoon of a decidedly Semitic-looking *nouveau riche* profiteer's wife asking a fishmonger: "Er – can you tell me if – er – really nice people eat herrings?"

Constance wrote that when she joined the Ministry the situation on Britain's food front looked so serious that: "… it was thought wise to prepare for a time when, in order to secure the utmost economy in food and fuel, to free women to do the work of men and to ensure that children should not suffer more from malnutrition that might be inevitable owing to the scarcity, national kitchens would be required." Already the Salvation Army had shown the way and opened public kitchens in Nottingham, the birthplace of the Army's founder William Booth, and Leeds. Constance told readers of *Reynolds Weekly*:

> *I am confident that after Westminster Bridge-road kitchen, which is to be opened by the Queen next Monday, has been in operation for but a very little while, the old style unimaginative Sunday dinner will have lost much of its popularity in that district. At this kitchen … one of our chief aims will be to give Carlton cooking* [Carlton was a quality London restaurant] *to the people at prices within the reach of the*

poorest. Nevertheless, the kitchen is not for one class alone. There is nothing of charity to the scheme – only an attempt to save waste and to help the food supplies of the nation to go further.

Accompanied by her daughter Princess Mary and a posse of notables that included Constance, Lord and Lady Devonport, Lady Rhondda and Mrs Kennedy Jones, Queen Mary duly opened the first National Kitchen on 21 May 1917. A gushing *Evening Standard* reporter wrote rhapsodically of the occasion:

War conditions and fairy tales seem about as far distant as East from West, but there is something quite like the charming once-upon-a-time tales of our youth in the picture of a Queen and a Princess really and truly helping children of their subjects to rice pudding and boiled onions! Yesterday afternoon I elbowed my way through a crowd of women, children and soldiers in the Westminster Bridge-road, and heard voices remarking, "Er Majesty will 'and out the food an' the Princess dish it up," and just as things happen in Fairyland this prediction came true. Standing in the crowd gave one a vision of the people's loyalty, and "lidies" took off their hats in order not to intercept the view of other "lidies" as Queen Mary, in a grey coat and skirt and pretty pink be-plumed hat, accompanied by the Princess, in a coat and skirt and a sailor hat with a wreath of spring flowers, stepped into the New Kitchen for All. Crowds of children and their parents, each armed with a mug, jug or plate, swarmed into the "food bar," where Queen Mary stood for a long time serving rice pudding, while Princess Mary piled up generous penny platefuls of onions. For an hour and a quarter the royal ladies remained in the kitchen, and the Queen was delighted that so many of the orders were for so wholesome a dish as milk pudding.... The war certainly brings new experiences to everyone, and although, if you live in Lambeth, it must be exciting to be served by the Greatest Lady in the Land, I daresay it is quite interesting for a royal lady to wait on her subjects.

Although they received the royal seal of approval, National Kitchens came in for much initial criticism and Lord Rhondda said in public that he was "rather disappointed at their slow progress". But they had a powerful advocate in best-selling novelist and temporary civil servant at the Ministry of Information Arnold Bennett, who wrote in the *Daily*

News: "National kitchens ought to be encouraged and patronized and cried aloud for." That may have been the case, but as a Roman Catholic priest in Barrow-in-Furness pointed out: "… the working-man would have his meals at home as long as he could, and would not take his family out to an 'eating house' except as a last resort … the fried fish shop he knew, the cold supper bar where he could buy tripe or 'trotters' he was acquainted with, but a restaurant was not in his line." Nonetheless, 169 National Kitchens, as well as many other public restaurants, were in operation by the time of the Armistice. In Birmingham, there was even a National Kitchen tram which offered half a pint of soup for 1d (one penny), vegetable pie for 4d (four pence) with dumplings and potatoes at 1d (one penny) a portion, and rice or ginger pudding at 1d (one penny) a time. During the September 1918 Trades Union Congress, delegates and their wives, together with visiting American labour leader Samuel Gompers, visited the National Kitchen at Derby. There, merchant seamen's union leader Joseph Havelock Wilson was challenged to make a Yorkshire pudding. This he accomplished successfully and the finished pudding was dispatched to the local military hospital. Many National Kitchens, like those at Sheffield and York, had started life as municipal "communal kitchens". But, as Arnold Bennett pointed out: "The popular antagonism to word 'communal' should be noted, for it is significant. Britons are too individualistic and independent to like anything communal." An attitude well understood by Churchill, who in the next war rejected *his* Ministry of Food's term "Communal Feeding Centre" for the more homely "British Restaurant".

As well as the National Kitchens, the war saw a number of other cheap eating places spring up. For the many women and girls now working in the City, in January 1917 the Girls' Friendly Society opened the City Women Workers' Rest and Refreshment Rooms at Ludgate Hill. Light luncheons "at moderate prices" were served daily day except Saturdays. Another innovation was "The Cafeteria" at 52 Marsham Street, Westminster, described as "an attempt on a small scale to organize a quick service system to meet the needs of those people – women war workers in particular – to whom economy of time is important". Prospective customers in Whitehall were told that it is "on the lines of the Cafeteria so well-known in Canada, where a help-yourself system has long been common, owing to the shortage of waitresses", but "it is only since the War that this problem has become acute in England".

By this time it was evident that Kennedy Jones's Food Economy campaign had not been a success. So, a second attempt was mounted, this time under the direction of Sir Arthur Yapp, a pillar of the Young Men's Christian Association. Sir Arthur, whom Constance Peel described as "a tall, large man who wears eye-glasses and always appears placid and good-tempered and sometimes very absent-minded", had served the YMCA for 30 years and had raised £1 million for its war work. He now set about trying to tackle Britain's food problem, and *Punch* recognized his efforts in a limerick:

> *There was a stout fellow called Yapp*
> *A great Red Triangular chap*
> *And now he's working still harder*
> *To stock the State larder,*
> *And never has time for a nap.*

To this end he created the League of National Safety, which immediately launched a huge publicity campaign. The League's posters were found everywhere:

> *THINK!!*
> *FOR EVERY 100,000 TONS OF WHEAT*
> *SAVED BY ECONOMY*
> *28,000 TROOPS*
> *CAN BE RATIONED*
> *AND TRANSPORTED*
> *FROM AMERICA*
> *Eat one loaf a week less*
>
> *CARRY HOME YOUR OWN PARCELS*
> *MOTORS, PETROL &*
> *HORSES ARE URGENTLY*
> *WANTED AT THE FRONT*
> *Join the League of National Safety*
>
> *TO-DAY,*
> *FOOD COSTS THE*
> *LIVES OF BRAVE MEN.*
> *AN AVERAGE CARGO OF*

MEAT WILL FEED ONE
MILLION PEOPLE FOR
TWO WEEKS.
Economy saves lives

On a more practical basis, the League issued, under the slogan "Waste Not, Want Not, Economy Will Win the War", a series of recipes leaflets which included "Eighteen Very Cheap Dishes", "Delicious Stews" and "Thirty-Four Ways of Using Potatoes". It also sent out speakers to spread the word, although they were warned to be on their guard, because: "Some districts and some industries such as the cotton industry, are undergoing severe restrictions. It would be unwise to lecture cotton operatives on the need for economy or to accuse them of wasting food." On the other hand, there was no harm in informing audiences that when it came to potatoes: "Irishmen live on potatoes with a bit of fat bacon, and the Irish peasant has the greatest strength of any people in these islands."

Sir Arthur targeted Britain's young citizens too. Every head teacher was written to and asked to form a School Legion of the Junior League of Safety: "… the token of the Adult League, the anchor, could be worn by the children who joined the League." Those who did pledged:

I believe that I can help my country in all the following ways:-
By eating enough – in order that I may grow up strong.
By not eating more than enough and by eating very slowly.
By wasting nothing and damaging nothing; neither food nor any
other material.
By being cheerful.
By signing this form and by wearing the anchor.

But despite Sir Arthur's best efforts his scheme was destined to flop. Constance Peel believed that: "Had this League of National Safety been started in the early days of the Food Economy it might have met with success, but it came too late." Besides, Sir Arthur and his prissy, preachy manner "did not find favour with the London Press". Nor did it help that there were persistent and malicious rumours that he himself was a food hoarder and "that while preaching economy he had obtained two sides of bacon for his private consumption". Lord Rhondda too was accused of hoarding; tea in his case. But the tea in question was actually for the military hospital housed at his Welsh home.

Christmas 1917 was the bleakest of the war. As it approached, Rhondda's ministry planned a "patriotic" Christmas dinner consisting of French rice soup, filleted haddock, roast fowl and vegetables, plum pudding and caramel custard. The Ministry calculated that this would cost 10s 2d (ten shillings and two pence) for four people, a statement that Constance Peel found hard to believe as a single fowl was now fetching 10s (ten shillings) in most towns. She noted too that once again it was the near-destitute who were going to suffer most: "The poor souls in Maidstone workhouse were ordered cornflour instead of Christmas pudding, but at Epsom the more kindly authorities added a trifle to the Christmas dietary." Constance also recorded that the children's traditional Christmas stocking orange was now retailing at 6d (sixpence) each. Four years before, at Christmas 1913, Whiteley's was selling a box of 200 Jamaican oranges – "the sweetest obtainable at this time of the year" – for 10s 3d (ten shillings and threepence).

Much more successful than the League of National Safety was the appeal made to the public by Rowland Prothero, the extremely able and energetic President of the Board of Agriculture, to grow their own fruit and vegetables. Setting an example, the King and Queen Mary dug potatoes at Windsor, and Lloyd George grew them in his kitchen garden at Walton Heath. In his war diary, Charles Balston wrote: "Those who had no gardens were granted allotments on unoccupied lands & in public parks and we had the novel sight of vegetables growing in Kensington Gardens just south of Kensington Palace. Everybody turned gardener who was able to dig and eventually we had potatoes enough and to spare." Among those answering the call were the Kersey sisters. They were photographed by the *Daily Mail* tending their allotment, one of half a million by July 1917, on the site of a demolished building between Fleet Street and Fetter Lane in the City. And on "what was doubtless the inner-most allotment in London" the Misses Kersey were able to grow cabbages, cauliflowers, beetroots, tomatoes and marrows. Elsewhere in Britain, Sittingbourne Council was not alone when in November 1917 it announced that its recreation area was going to be converted into free allotments. A year later, just before the Armistice, the papers were reporting that there were now over 1.4 million allotment holders in England and Wales. Sadly, disaster sometimes struck. In September 1917 practically all the war allotments at Plough Lane, Wimbledon, were flooded and their produce destroyed when the River Wandle overflowed its banks. Deliberate damage was not unknown either. In November 1917, at Liverpool Assizes, farm labourer Samuel Woods was sentenced to three years' penal servitude for setting fire to and destroying food produce to the value of £2,500. Woods, whose defence that he was mentally deficient, had quarrelled with the farmer and in setting the produce alight had exclaimed: "There go your ******* profits!"

Another couple who responded to Rowland Prothero's appeal to what, in the next war, would be called "Dig for Victory" were Annie Purbrook and her husband Charles. In their garden in Parkstone Avenue, Hornchurch, Essex, "… kind Mother Nature has given us a good store of her fruits for the present, for our garden is yielding generously of apples, pears, potatoes (many people are digging up their lawns to grow potatoes), greens, marrows, and beans." Annie's speciality was marrows, which

have been really quite amusing this year. We had often tried to grow them but seldom had any real success. This year I tried my hand at vegetable growing and I put some marrow seed in quite early. Soon it was up and truly it flourished like a green bay tree. I suppose the weather suited them for in a few weeks there was quite a tangled forest of marrow growth. I expected the family to expostulate at the continuous appearance of marrow on the table for breakfast, lunch and dinner; day after day it appeared in some form, we had it boiled, fried, baked, mashed, cooked with tomatoes, and stuffed; but good temper prevailed, and before the frost came we brought in about forty weighing on average ten lbs [4.5 kg] each. Some we gave away and the rest we stored, hanging them up in the pantry and on the landing upstairs. Never was there such an unforgettable supply of marrows. They lasted until well over Xmas and were most useful during this difficult and rationed food time.

Scholars from King Henry VIII School, Coventry, who back in March 1912 had debated on the possibility of war a with Germany, did their bit and at their harvest camp in 1917 picked beans and no less than 25,000lb (11,400kg) of apples.

Assistance, albeit reluctant, in growing Britain's food to try and offset the damage done by U-boats was provided by German prisoners of war. Back in June 1915, Colonel W. H. Walker, Conservative MP for Widness, had asked the Board of Agriculture if it "would communicate with county councils of districts where German prisoners are interned with the object of making arrangements for employment of prisoners for haymaking and other harvest help". This was duly done and it was reported that Boreham Woods Council in Hertfordshire had been asked to find accommodation for 75 German POWs to be employed on the land. Not all were anxious to help the British war effort, quite the reverse, as retired Colonel Sir Percival Marling VC noted in his diary when several escaped from the camp at Beechley, Gloucestershire: "Our old keeper dug three of them out of a hay-stack on my property.... They had stolen bacon and other food out of a farmhouse the previous night, and I had the pleasure of trying them at Lydney Petty Sessions, and sentencing them to six months' imprisonment in Gloucester jail."

Down in Chislehurst, Kent, at the start of 1918 Ethel Bilbrough recorded, "… meat is getting scarce and we have had no butter or margarine for a fortnight!" Perversely, she felt

> *rather glad, because when we are struggling with a slice of horrid dry toast that rebels against going down one really feels that one is last taking part in the war!!*

And

> *how* poor *people live is a mystery! For fish is ruinous, and in a little Kentish village at Xmas rabbits were being sold at 6/- [six shillings] and 10/- [ten shillings] apiece!! And now this week one reads in the paper of fowl going for 15/- [fifteen shillings]!! Worst of all, the English-man's standby – bacon – is unprocurable!"*

Putting things in perspective, Ethel reflected: "… all this is vastly insignificant in comparison to air raids, which everyone lives in terror of when the moon gets full!"

Even in parts of the country unthreatened by Gotha bomber raids, the mood over the food situation was turning sour. In Newcastle, Methodist minister James Mackay noticed: "Long queues of women waiting for tea, sugar, butter in the cold wet streets every day. It does not keep the will to victory. Distribution must be improved. The men in these government offices do not understand the people." In Manchester, Henry Clemesha, the Deputy Commissioner for the Food for the North-West of England, noted how January 1918 saw "the first indisputable evidence that the shortage of food, which had been talked about so much and so long, was actually upon us. Queues had begun to form in the streets of towns, and customers to go from shop to shop in the endeavour to satisfy their needs." Clemesha was dismissive of Sir Arthur Yapp and his League of National Safety:

> At a time when persons were often unable to obtain sufficient supplies of certain foodstuffs it would have been a mockery to have continued to preach the virtues of doing with less. So the literature, the leaflets, the memoranda, the instructions, the pledges, the certificates and the blue anchors – which together must have cost many thousands of pounds – were suffered to lie about until they got fly-blown and dusty; Sir Arthur Yapp disappeared and the Executive Officer was free to get on with the real work of the Ministry, which was the rationing of the people.

It could not come a moment too soon for the *Daily Mail*. Its readers were reminded that:

> It is not a little pathetic to observe that a year ago, and even two years ago, the Daily Mail was urging the Government then in power to introduce compulsory rations. Thus on 13 November 1916, we said: "Ministers should at once prepare the organization for a system of bread tickets. It took the diligent Germans six months to get their system in action, and it will take our officials quite as long. They ought to be getting to work on it now, not putting it off."

Yapp had maintained that: "As long as we are not rationed Germany knows that her submarine campaign has been a failure," and the imposition of rationing did not come without a great deal of soul-searching at the Ministry. There, one evening in January 1918, its Parliamentary Secretary J. R. Clynes, whose own constituency was North-East Manchester, asked Lord Rhondda: "Will the country stand for wholesale rationing?" The dramatic reply was: "Without rationing we're done. It might well be, Clynes, that you and I at this moment are all that stands between this country and revolution."

Compulsory rationing of meat, butter and margarine finally began on 25 February 1918 in London and the Home Counties. Ten days before, the Lees household in Chelsea were "all in the throes of filling in our registration cards for butter or margarine and meat. The meat allowance per head per week is very small, one shilling and 3 pence worth of butcher's meat (three coupons of 5d [five shillings] each), and 5 ounces [140 g] of bacon (uncooked), or ham or poultry…. We can only have 4 ounces [115 g] of butter or any kind of fat." The Lees' four-year-old son Harry and all children under 10 were allowed half the adult ration: 7½d (seven pence, ha'penny) worth of meat and 2½ ounces (70 g) of bacon etc.

One dramatic result of the introduction of rationing was the spectacular fall in the numbers of those queuing outside food stores in the capital. During the week of 28 January to 2 February, a month before rationing began, the Metropolitan Police calculated that the total number of people queuing was 1,521,294. The highest daily total was on Saturday 2 February when a staggering 566,657 would-be shoppers were counted. The first full week of rationing saw the total drop to 208,115, the next to 60,150, and by the beginning of May only 4,225 people were counted in food queues.

While food queues dwindled, the Ministry continued vigorously to prosecute and publicize those contravening the ever-more-stringent food regulations. During 1918 throughout Great Britain, there were 28,657 prosecutions for food offences, with fines averaging £4 7s 2d (four pounds, seven shillings and two pence). The highest number of prosecutions – 24,296 – was in England, but Ireland, with a population of only 4.4 million, recorded 13,870 offences. And what was more, the *National Food Journal* noted with disgust that "Outside the Dublin Metropolitan Area, the fines imposed are trifling. In the majority of cases they range between 1d [one penny] and 5s [five shillings]." Back in England, in Smethwick hefty fines of £50 and £25 were given to a man and his wife who "had 'invented' a third person and drawn rations in excess of the amount they were entitled to". The same court fined two butchers £10 for not detaching the requisite coupons.

Reviewing 1918 in his diary, Charles Balston acknowledged the achievements of Ministry of Food Control under Rhondda, including the great leap forward in "collective feeding". But as a pensioner, he also noted with some feeling that: "… this did not ameliorate conditions in homes where the rush for war work and for service in the various restaurants caused a servant problem and obliged people to either do their own housework or give up their houses and go into boarding-houses, private hotels or apartments. It was a great hardship for the old and helpless who found themselves driven out of house and home and for those who had little time for household work." But during 1918, Balston thought there had been a distinct change for the better from the previous year in the nation's morale. "Instead of depression, " he wrote, "a feeling of camaraderie grew up in the country as the old class distinctions weakened and everyone began to mix and work together in a new spirit of equality and friendliness. Rationing taught us to bear each other's burdens and to share and share alike. From the King and Queen to the humblest individual there was only one aim – 'To win the war'."

On 3 July 1918, at the age of 62, "the man who had effected this great change and who earned himself the reputation of being the most successful Food Controller any belligerent country had produced" died of heart disease and rheumatic fever at his home at Llan-wern in Monmouthshire. The next day the *Daily Mail* eulogized the dead minister:

> *Lord Rhondda's death will be mourned in every British home. The public work of no other Minister of State has ever so intimately affected domestic hearths as the great work of the food Minister, to whose courage, devotion and administrative genius millions of homes owe their present assurance of daily bread.... Lord Rhondda spent himself mercilessly. He has died for his country as truly as any soldier on the field of battle.*

Forgetting how she had castigated Rhondda back in January, Ethel Bilbrough now paid him a generous tribute. "Lord Rhonda [*sic*], the great Food Controller has just died," she wrote.

> *Poor man. He had rationed himself too severely, and when he got ill with pleurisy or something, he had no strength left to fight against it. But he will be much missed for he worked out the appalling problem of placing England under food rations with amazing skill and foresight. It was he who introduced the ration cards which every soul has had: no one could get any meat or butter or bacon or poultry without presenting in exchange an absurd little paper coupon.... In years to come people will hardly believe that such things really <u>were</u>, and yet they not only exist at the present day, but the whole scheme has worked wonderfully well, in spite of the stupendous difficulties that had to be overcome.*

CHAPTER SEVEN

BRITAIN'S FIRST BLITZ

TEN LITTLE ZEPPELINS ... WHAT A TREAT FOR ENGLAND SAID THE KAISER WITH A LAUGH
(From the song "Ten Little Zeppelins".)

On the night of 19 January 1915, German navy Zeppelins L-3 and L-4 raided Britain's east coast, the first of many forays by the "Hun aerial baby-killers". According to *The War Illustrated*:

A thrill – not of horror nor of dismay, but of disgust – went through all Britain on the morning of 20 January, with the news that on the previous night, between the hours of eight o'clock and midnight, Yarmouth, King's Lynn and two or three smaller towns in the north-east of Norfolk had been visited by German airships and subjected to cowardly bombardment. The amount of damage done was small – no more than has happened often in a gas explosion – the loss of life slight; but the loathsome blood-mad fiends who could do this foul work and rejoice stirred every Briton's heart to sterner resolve to crush that degraded nation whose war methods are more savage than those lowest races known to anthropology.

That night, Yarmouth residents Martha Taylor and Samuel Smith had the unhappy distinction of being the first British civilians to be killed in an attack from the air.

Nearly 30 years later, in February 1944, George Bernard Shaw remembered how, at the beginning of the earlier war, he had written "a letter to *The Times* urging that air-raid shelters be provided for children". However, "*The Times* refused to publish it because the editor was shocked by the implied suggestion that the enemy could, or would bomb schoolchildren." Sadly, that did indeed prove to be the case, and between January 1915 and August 1918, 252 British children were killed and 542 seriously injured by German bombs.

The Graphic featured the first raid in its 23 January issue, with the headline "An Airquake in the time of War", and modestly boasted how the paper had anticipated such an attack as far back as May 1909, "though the present raid was made more fearsome by explosive bombs which killed four peaceful people". And, being in ignorance of a ruling by the Kaiser that the bombing of royal residences was strictly forbidden, the paper also reported that "several bombs fell near Sandringham, and it is not improbable that the Royal estate was the objective of the airmen".

The raid, while unwelcome, was not unexpected. As early as 6 August 1914 the German military airship Z-VI had bombed the Belgian city of Liege, and a few weeks later her sister ship the Z-XII had bombed Antwerp, causing death, destruction and injury among the great port's civilian population. And, as *The Graphic* pointed out, the threat from German airships was not new. In Britain from 1909 onwards there had been numerous "airship scares", uncannily similar to UFO sightings in more recent times. The *Norfolk News* of 25 January 1913 had reported how, the day before: "Between midnight and 1 am, an airship or aeroplane was seen overhead by several residents … it passed very quickly and then returned three or four minutes later." On 8 February, the *News* told how: "Multiple witnesses, including two women and a former army officer using binoculars, saw three mystery aircraft heading west at 6 pm, one flashing a red light. At midnight a man heard an aircraft overhead."

Four years previously, in May 1909, at the height of an earlier wave of "airship sightings", the *Observer* had approached the craft's inventor, Count Zeppelin himself, for an opinion. The Count's forthright response came in a telegram from the airship works at Friedrichshafen: "I don't believe in ghosts." But in the late summer and early autumn of 1914, what many in Britain had previously regarded as something out of an H. G. Wells novel, or newspaper silly season fodder, had become a distinct and unpleasant reality. To counter the threat, that same Friedrichshafen factory was bombed by the Royal Naval Air Service on 21 November 1914, and other raids were mounted on Zeppelin sheds at Dusseldorf and Cuxhaven.

At home, lighting restrictions in London were announced on 17 September 1914. Illuminated signs were prohibited and street and shop lights were partially obscured. In December the lights were further dimmed and shop and street lights smeared with black or dark blue paint. On London's buses and trams there was only just enough light to collect fares. Most of these measures were taken up by other British towns and cities, especially after air raids began in earnest. Later, in October 1916, came an order "for the sake of economy and safety" for shops to close early. In Dulwich, Charles Balston, retired from the Indian civil service, wrote of how all the restrictions "made London and other towns very gloomy; but we went to bed and got up earlier and the public generally accepted the regulations with serenity and the shop assistants with gladness. The darkened trains were trying, but when lighted they served as guiding beacons to air raiders."

The partial blackout brought with it both hazards and brushes with the law. On 12 October 1914 the press reported: "At an inquest on Saturday on the body of a middle-aged, unknown woman who was run over and fatally injured by a motor-bus in Whitehall on Thursday night, the driver of the omnibus stated that he did not see her until he was within a few feet of her, owing to the lights being subdued." The Coroner Mr Ingleby Oddie, *The Times* reported, "expressed the hope that those responsible would issue instructions that drivers of motor-omnibuses should reduce speed after dark." That same day, 46-year-old Edward J. Nash, "described as a beer house keeper of 232 High Road, Chiswick", appeared at Acton Police Court. The court heard how on Saturday 10 October "there were three lamps with three incandescent burners in the defendant's bar, which threw light across the footway and halfway across the road". Two police constables asked Nash to reduce the light, but he refused so they entered the bar and turned out two of the lights. Nash "got in a rage and said 'Are you the ******* German Kaiser?' and tried to relight the lamps. The police prevented him and took him into custody." Nash was fined £5 with costs for obstructing the police in the course of their duties.

Another precaution taken in the capital was the draining of the lake in St James's Park to prevent it from becoming a bomb-marker for Whitehall. But Zeppelins, as yet untried over Britain, remained a source of humour. *Punch* in its issue of 23 September 1914 featured a cartoon entitled "A Use for Zeppelins" showing a "belated Citizen (who has been lamenting the loss of his latch key all the way home)" arriving at his bombed house: "Hello! Here's a bit of luck!" And much hilarity was caused by a German plane attacking Dover on Christmas Eve. A single bomb landed in Thomas A. Terson's garden, wrecking the cabbage patch and knocking his gardener James Banks out of the tree he was pruning.

But the "futile Zeppelin savagery on the Norfolk coast" of 19 January 1915 amply demonstrated that the threat from the air was no joke. Ten days before the east-coast raid, the Kaiser had, with the utmost reluctance, given his assent to raids on London, but he stipulated that only military objectives should be attacked, and not the residential areas of the capital. A later Imperial ordinance sanctioned the bombing of docks and factories as far west as the Tower of London. But before the capital came under attack, further raids were mounted on east-coast targets. During one of them, the *Lancet* reported,

> *a well-known surgeon was performing the operation of tracheotomy at a nursing home when German aircraft came over the place at night. The town electric current was at once cut off. All the lights went out suddenly, and this, too, at the very moment when the surgeon in question was opening the windpipe. Fortunately, it was not the first attack delivered against this place, a fishing and sea-bathing resort. Taught by experience, the operator made it a habit to warn his nurses and other assistants that lamps should be kept ready for use during all operations which had to be undertaken at night. This precaution may have saved the small patient's life. With but a trifling delay the tracheotomy was completed and the child, we are glad to report, is now doing well.*

Lord Kitchener and his cabinet colleagues were not short of advice from the public on how to deal the "Zeppelin menace". T. H. Morgan of Torquay penned a letter to *The Times*:

> *As to air raids, what I am about to suggest is, I am quite aware, unnecessary in experienced quarters. It is this. When a long rise in the barometer, occupying many days, takes place to some high position above 30 inches* [76 cm] *(as just happened) it means for a time a most probable stable condition of the air, and just the one that would be seized by the enemy's airmen for a quiet and safe flight to our coasts. Let me therefore recommend all coast towns to be on guard on such occasions; for we may be sure they will be the ones that will be watched by our enemies.*

From Brooks's Club, Henry A. Blake warned:

We have endeavoured to conceal vulnerable points of attack by night by extinguishing all lights but no systematic attempt has been made to control the movements of motor-cars that may be used to assist the movements of hostile aircraft, with the exception of control barriers round London. At such a time with the country demonstrably open to attack, all roads should be blocked at intervals and the movement of motor cars controlled.

Author Sir Henry Rider Haggard, describing himself as "a dweller in a happy hunting ground of Zeppelins, against which I have been obliged to insure stock and crop and everything else at considerable expense", came up with one idea of how to deal with the air raiders. "Why cannot we meet Zeppelins with Zeppelins?" he asked: "… airships of the right sort could rise when warned of the approach of Zeppelins and wait aloft to attack them when they came."

A practical suggestion regarding both the danger in air raids to valuable stained-glass windows and that of flying glass came from John Furley, based on his own experience during the 1870–71 Siege of Paris and the Commune: "One thing I noticed at that time was the manner in which windows generally had been criss-crossed with strips of paper stuck upon glass. This method undoubtedly saved much destruction of glass from concussion, which often affects a large area, although it is no defence against projectiles."

Advertisers quickly cashed in on the threat from the air. "Better for the folks at home than thinking about Zeppelins" read an advertisement for the Orchestrelle Company's Pianola Piano: "Any distraction that will divert your family's thoughts from such morbid things as air raids is worth consideration just now, for whilst the man of the world accepts these 'gas bags' at their true valuation, they often represent a very real menace to nervous children and imaginative women." "Hall's Wine – the Supreme Nerve Restorative" was not slow either in publishing a testimonial from a Southend resident:

During the recent Air raid over this town, Hall's Wine proved a great help to us, as I happened to have a bottle by me. It worked wonders when administered to the ladies, and prevented the nervous collapse of several when the bombs were dropping and the strain on

the nerves was at its worst. I have used Hall's Wine with great benefit
on various occasions, but have greater faith in it now than ever.

The manufacturers of "Kyl-Fyre" fire extinguishers advised that in "Zeppelin air raids, incendiary bombs will cause many fires which in incipient stages can be easily extinguished" by their product (price 5/6d [five shillings and six pence]). The public were further warned: "Be prepared. The Fire Brigades cannot be in all parts at the same time. N.B. In the recent air raid on Southend there were more Fires than FIRE ENGINES." Their competitors Minimax Fire Extinguishers went one better and proudly announced:

AIR RAIDS. Read what the well-known MINIMAX Fire
Extinguisher can do. A fire occurred at 11 pm on May 26th 1915. It
was caused by <u>incendiary bomb</u> from hostile aircraft. Both the bomb
and the material it set fire to were <u>extinguished</u> by one MINIMAX
Fire Extinguisher. For obvious reasons we cannot mention the place
[Southend], name of user, but we have in our possession a signed
document giving above particulars. MINIMAX was also used at a
previous fire caused by hostile Aircraft with effective results.

Citizens with valuables to protect were urged to "Use Chubb's Safes to Resist Bombs and Explosives". And the General Accident, Fire, Life, Assurance Corporation Ltd assured the public: "It is not too late to insure against Death or Personal Injuries by Aircraft – hostile or otherwise." Newspapers vied with each other to offer their readers insurance against air raids. The *Sunday Herald* offered its readers £25,000 free air-raid insurance – "the largest sum any newspaper has ever insured its readers for" – to cover "Injuries or Death through AIR-RAIDS, NAVAL BOMBARDMENTS, and the EFFECT OF OUR OWN ANTI-AIRCRAFT GUNS".

Throughout February 1915, London's museums were reported to be "steadily perfecting their arrangements for dealing with any outbreak of fire that might occur as a result of air raids". At the British Museum the Elgin Marbles were consigned to the basement and "from almost every gallery some object or group has been removed to safer quarters and, in the near future, the greater part of the Assyrian Collection will be placed in one of the more spacious underground galleries". The rooms of the National Gallery were being made, as far as possible, fire-proof and "in almost every corner are large bins of sand. Scores of pictures have been removed from the walls and taken below ground." At the London Museum similar air-raid precautions were taking place, while in South Kensington "perhaps the best-known of all the wonderful birds, beasts and fishes in the Natural History Museum is the Great Auk, and now this ancient bird, with her egg, has been placed in the basement with other rare specimens of the world's fauna".

On 9 February 1915, the Home Office issued a public-warning poster about detecting German aircraft. Its appearance outside *The Times* office "attracted widespread attention … and rapidly drew a large crowd" who read that:

> *The public are advised to familiarize themselves with the appearance of British and German airships and aeroplanes, so they might not be alarmed by British aircraft, and may take shelter if German aircraft appear. Should hostile aircraft be seen, take shelter immediately in the nearest available house, preferably in the basement, and remain there until the aircraft have left the vicinity: do not stand about in crowds and do not touch unexploded bombs. In the event of hostile aircraft being seen in country districts, the nearest naval, military, or police authorities should, if possible, be advised immediately by telephone of the time of appearance, the direction of flight, and whether the aircraft is an airship or an aeroplane.*

Throughout the late spring of 1915, the Zeppelin raids were edging nearer London. Ipswich and Bury St Edmunds were raided on 29/30 April, and on 10 May the German army Zeppelin LZ-38 commanded by Captain Erich Linnarz attacked Southend. One of her bombs, which fell in Rayleigh Avenue, had a placard attached to it with the inscription: "You English. We have come, and will come again soon. Kill or cure. German." At 120 North Road an incendiary bomb went through the roof, killing Mrs Agnes Whitwell as she lay in bed and seriously injuring her husband. After the raid, which came only three days after the *Lusitania* sinking, there were anti-German riots in the town. Five shops in the High Street and Queens Road, rumoured to be German or Austrian owned, were attacked and wrecked, and 250 soldiers had to be called out to restore order.

Linnarz returned to bomb Southend on 26 May and now felt confident to take on London. And so on the evening of 31 May, the LZ-38 set off to raid the "Fortress of London". Linnarz appeared over Stoke Newington at 11.20 pm, and steered southwards along Kingsland

Road dropping 30 high-explosive and 90 incendiary bombs as he went. Fortunately, the LZ-38 was flying at such a great height that her aim was bad, with, it was reported, "the bombs nearly all falling into gardens". Nonetheless seven people were killed and 35 seriously injured.

Georgina Lee, middle-aged and upper-middle-class, living in Chelsea with her solicitor husband Charles, recorded in her diary on 2 June: "The Zeppelins came to London last night!! But no one was aware of it until we opened our papers at breakfast. Not a word has leaked out as to the parts of London they passed over. But I was having tea with Mrs de la Rue just now. Her sister told us she had heard, while slum-visiting in the north-east that they had been over the City Road, the Angel Islington, and at Shoreditch."

Pre-war suffragette, dedicated pacifist, socialist and social worker Sylvia Pankhurst had been only too aware of the raid. She was writing at her home in Old Ford Road, London E3, when:

> on the silence arose an ominous grinding ... growing in volume ... throbbing, pulsating ... filling the air with its sound ... then huge reports smote the ear, shattering, deafening, and the roar of falling masonry ... the angry grinding still pulsated above us. Again that terrific burst of noise; those awful bangs, the roar of falling buildings, the rattle of shrapnel.... The thought of the bombs crashing down on the densely populated city was appalling.... More crashes! More crashes!... Again more crashes!... and each more monstrous ... what a burst of sound, tremendous; the very earth shook with it!... More crashes ... again ... again ... again.... At last it was over. Next morning there were pieces of shell on our flat roof. Swarms of children were out in the road picking up shrapnel, prising up with impromptu tools the bits of metal which had embedded themselves in the road.

The next day Sylvia encountered a new phenomenon, that of "air raid tourism": "To see the devastation wrought by last night's raid unaccustomed visitors came flocking to the East End – well-dressed people in motors, journalists, photographers, high military officials, Red Cross nurses, policewomen, travellers from all over the world. Impatient passengers on tops of buses were asking before they had yet passed Bishopsgate: 'Is this the East End?'" At Shoreditch Church, rumoured to have been hit by bombs, Sylvia came across prurient sightseers, their "chins uncomfortably upstretched, arguing whether the thin shadow cast by the lighting conductor might really be a crack". For most of the day there was a constant parade of the curious passing the churchyard, with "a cluster always gathering round the ancient stocks, because some lingered to look at them from interest, and others craned over their shoulders to see if those who paused were looking at a bomb". Soon, disappointed at the lack of obvious bomb damage, most of the sightseers gave up the search and returned home.

Throughout the rest of 1915, London continued to come under attack. On 20 July the Kaiser raised his embargo on unrestricted raids on the capital but with the proviso that historic and cultural buildings should be spared. A bizarre touch was added on 8 September when a large ham-bone bearing a caricature of Sir Edward Grey on one side and the message "A memento from starving Germany" on the other was dropped from the Zeppelin L-13. Just over a month later the biggest raid of 1915 on London took place and, despite the Kaiser's proviso, Lincoln's Inn Chapel was damaged. There were 17 people killed and 21 injured when a bomb fell in front of the Lyceum Theatre in the Strand. James Wickham, a call boy at another theatre, the Gaiety, wrote of the atmosphere in the capital that night:

London was rather "on edge". Yet, true to the "carry on" policy of the British nation, the West End, it seemed, did not lack gaiety on that October night ... restaurants were crowded. From behind the heavily curtained windows of the big hotels ... The popping of champagne corks. The pulse of dance music. Heady laughter. There were toasts, farewells, tears, promises, kisses. War! Tonight – Blighty. Tomorrow – who cared?... Theatres were flourishing.... At the Gaiety we had been playing 'Tonight's the Night' to packed houses."

And 18-year-old James thought it

almost impossible amid all this light-hearted gaiety to realize horrors being enacted a hundred miles distant. Had it not been for the ubiquitous khaki – in stalls, in pit, in gallery – the war would have seemed even more remote.

At 9.00 pm, with 20 minutes to go before the interval, James was sent out with his friend Billy, a 15-year-old theatre pageboy, to catch the last post. Stopping to light a cigarette, he remarked to Billy: "They say the Zepps are on the way, the swine." No sooner had he had he spoken than *there was the sudden crackle of anti-aircraft gunfire, and simultaneously a dreadful sound that London knew only too well – a sound like no other on earth. It was the mournful wail created by the velocity of a descending bomb. In one brief terrible moment before the impact I instinctively knew it was coming directly where we stood. I was not wrong. It exploded three yards from where we were standing. It flung me against the wall next to the pit entrance to the Strand Theatre. It sucked me back in again. It dashed me to the ground. Masonry fell. Glass rained. I felt unhurt; only dazed. Yet I had twenty-two lumps of shrapnel embedded in me.*

James was carried downstairs to the Strand Theatre bar, where he asked about Billy and was told that his friend had been blown to pieces. James could still hear the "dull vibrant thud of more bombs" as other casualties were brought in, carried on theatre boards: "… some were moaning, some calling for missing friends and relatives. Someone rushed in and said a London General omnibus had been blown to bits in Aldwych, opposite the Waldorf."

Every one of the five theatres in the vicinity was used as an emergency first-aid post: "Here, where suddenly tragedy had taken the place of earlier hilarity, doctors attended to the wounds." James was struck by the irony of "the shrapnel-riddled boards that hung forlornly outside the Gaiety proclaiming 'Tonight's the Night'." But one of the show's stars was the hero of the night:

Mr Leslie Henson worked valiantly to calm the audience when the terrific din occurred outside the theatre. Many rose in alarm. Chorus girls stood transfixed on the stage. Some were on the point of running into the street in their flimsy attire. Mr Henson saw all the dangers. He ordered the orchestra to strike up a rollicking tune; he led the girls in a lively dance, he cracked jokes and struck comical gestures. The situation was saved.

The Bishop of London would have approved. In a letter to his diocese that month, he wrote: "There must be a kind of glorying in London at being allowed to take our little share of the danger in the Zeppelin raids. Cowardly and brutal as they are, and carried out contrary to all international law, they have this advantage." He went on to quote "a gallant old clergyman" who had voiced the same sentiment:

Above: "Without rationing we're done." A food queue in Reading, Berkshire, 1917.

Above: "Suburban man was setting an example to his betters." A demonstration by allotment holders and others at Friern Barnet, spring 1918.

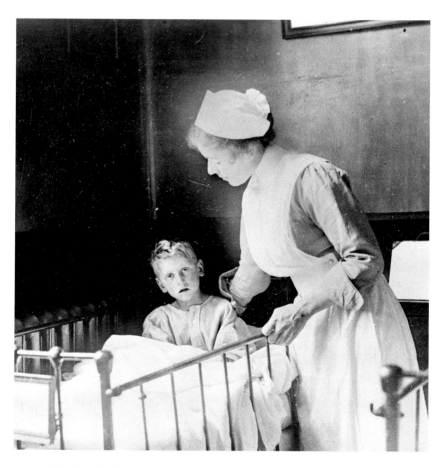

Above: "It is hard to believe that such things could be done in these days of civilisation and Christianity. I hope God would forgive the authors, for our people never could": Tommy Grant, one of the victims of the Gotha raid on Southend, Sunday 12 August 1917. Tommy's brother James was killed and another brother and sister badly injured in the attack.

Above: "It had been arranged that hostilities should cease at 11.00am and the street clock stands at 11.40am." The scene in Winchester's main thoroughfare, Monday 11 November 1918.

Above: "I stood aside from the delirious throng, silent, alone, ravaged by memories."
The crowds outside Buckingham Palace, 11 November 1918.

The Zeppelin passed right over our house and was there spotted by the aircraft. One of their fuses, weighing 1 lb 5 oz [600 g], fell 6 ft [1.8 m] from my front door, just where I stood, and it was hot when I carried it in. It was a terrific but very splendid sight, and it has had for me something exhilarating in it; for like most old men, I have felt so selfish in being comfortably at home out of danger, and now, at any rate, one is allowed to feel that we may take our share a bit after all."

Not everybody was quite so eager to take their share of danger, and in the press there very soon began to appear advertisements aimed at the well-heeled faint-hearted:

AIR RAIDS
To enjoy immunity from the dangers of Hostile Aircraft <u>and</u> the worries of housekeeping visit
The EMPIRE HOTEL, BUXTON,
OR
The EMPIRE HOTEL, BATH.
In both of these Establishments the acme of luxurious comfort may be obtained.

But most Londoners, including the capital's children, had no option but to remain. A survey of youngsters' attitudes to the Zeppelin raids was undertaken by Dr Charles Kimmins, the LCC's Chief Inspector of Schools. From five schools, 945 children, aged 8–13, wrote a 15-minute essay on their experiences of the September and October raids. As many as 96 per cent had experienced one or both raids. Dr Kimmins found that at eight years of age the gunfire "bulked very largely" in the essays, but no personal feelings were expressed and there was no evidence of fear. Even at that age the girls looked after their younger siblings. At nine the boys "thoroughly enjoyed the raid", and spent as much time as possible in the streets, but amongst the girls occasionally "great fear was expressed". At ten, boys tended to be very talkative and for the first time there was distinct evidence of fear, though not nearly as marked as with the girls. At that age boys too began to look after their younger brothers and sisters. One wrote: "A picture over mother's bed fell on her head and on the baby. The baby went unconscious, and my mother shook her, and then she was alright." At ten, girls tended to be much frightened but also bellicose, "making vigorous protests against German spies; they go to bed in their clothes lest the Zeppelins should return". One girl recounted how: "People were running about like mad bulls and the windows were falling out like rain."

At 11 years of age, boys now showed no sign of fear at all: "My cousin pointed to a star and said she thought it was a Zeppelin. 'Fathead,' said I, politely. 'It cannot be a Zeppelin. It does not move.'" The girls now also seemed to be less fearful: "Mother said she did not want to see the Zeppelins again. I do…. I knew what our brave soldiers and sailors have had to go through day after day. This kind of thing makes one realize what war is; and yet dropping bombs on harmless people is not war. That night I felt bitter towards the Germans. I felt I could fly to Germany and do the same thing to them." The 12-year-olds, both boys and girls, still showed no sign of fear, and the boys had become keen souvenir hunters: "The bomb did not go off, so I went to get it, but burned my fingers. A copper came running round the corner and he took it." The 13-year-olds tended to be more thoughtful. "I was cleaning the stove", one boy wrote, "when the room was lighted by a lurid glow, followed by a bang. 'Zeppelins!' I exclaimed, and straightway rushed into the street. The air raid was a failure, the idea being to frighten the people of London. It did not succeed, the feeling being one of curiosity." "I was a bit frightened when the bomb burst, but we have only to die once," wrote another. "I could have seen the Zeppelins, but I thought, 'If I do I shall always see them when I look up into the sky,' so I would not look at them."

Dr Kimmins found that there was not only little evidence in the essays of fear but much mothering by young girls "towards those more helpless". He was struck by one nine-year-old who rushed home and got her teddy bear to take down to the cellar. He also noted how small a part the father appeared to play in the family during the raids. In 95 per cent of the essays no reference was made to him, and when it was, it tended to be far from flattering: "My father was frightened during the raid and he ran into a beer shop and got under the counter and stayed there until it was all over." Apart from policemen, firemen and soldiers, men in general were often the subject of uncomplimentary remarks: "A man came into the public house and said 'Give me half a pint. If I am going to die I will die drunk.'"

The most graphic accounts of the raids were written by the older children:

My mother rushed into my room and carried me bodily into the kitchen, where I was among friends. I said, "Why all this excitement?" They said, "the Zeppelins have come," and I said, "Good gracious! You don't say so."

Suddenly a piercing beam of white light short across the sky. Guns spat viciously out of the darkness at a cigar-shaped body far up in the clouds.

I was coming out of a cinema with my uncle and I noticed people were rushing to and fro in the streets. I went up to a policeman and said to him, "What does all this mean?" He replied gravely, "The Zeppelins have come." "What?" I said, "Do you mean to tell me that these terrible monsters have come at last?" And he replied, briefly, "They have."

It was not just to London that the "terrible monsters" came. Towns all over Britain were bombed, often by mistake due to navigational errors. On 31 January 1916, Wednesbury in Shropshire was bombed by the Zeppelin L-21 in the mistaken belief that it was Manchester. Just as the audience at King's Music Hall in Earp Street were settling down to the second half of the melodrama *The Faithful Wedding*, bombs began to fall in the area of King's Street. Mrs Smith, who lived on the street, went out to see what was happening, and returned to find her house bombed and her husband Joseph, daughter Nellie (aged 13) and son Thomas (11) all dead. At the music hall most of the audience ran out into the street and then to the comparative safety of the cellars of a local pub and the church. A fortnight after the raid the *Shropshire Chronicle* gave its readers "a few useful hints for personal safety when the Zeppelins come"; advice that was now being given all the country:

Get indoors as soon as you hear the first bomb fall or the first gun fire and stay there until the firing is over.

Find the best cover you can. Go down to the lowest floor cellar, if you have one. Keep away from the window. Flying splinters of glass are highly dangerous.

Make sure of a plentiful supply of water to put out fires due to incendiary bombs. Dry fine sand and dry fine soil are useful for putting a fire out, but water is the easiest and best safeguard.

Never touch an unexploded bomb or shell. If you are in the street when a bombardment begins keep cool and make for the best cover you can find. Excitement and thoughtfulness are as bad as fright. If no shelter be available and bombs are dropping near you, throw yourself down on your face. You thereby reduce the mark for rising splinters, and you have a better chance of saving your face.

Do not be in a hurry to come out of your shelter. Remember that even when the Zeppelin has passed over you a shell aimed at her miles away may conceivably drop missiles in your street.

A few days before this excellent advice was published, the Town Council of Wallasey in Cheshire thought it prudent to insure their new town hall for £40,000 against air raids. And Captain Harold Wilberforce-Bell, on leave from France, noted how: "In many houses, beside each bed are a gas-mask, mouth-pad, and a bottle of solution, designed to give protection from the gas fumes of incendiary bombs."

Edinburgh was raided on 2–3 April, a bright moonlit night. One bomb hit a warehouse filled with £44,000 worth of whisky and the ensuing blaze lit up the whole city. Visiting trade union leader David Kirkwood heard "a terrifying explosion. Windows rattled, the ground quivered, pictures swung. We all gasped. I ran to the window and saw Vesuvius in eruption…. I opened the window. A great flash greeted me from Castle and then, above the roaring, I heard the most dreadful screeching and shouting. The inmates of Morningside Asylum had started the pandemonium."

In less dramatic language a detailed report of the raid was made by Detective Inspector Peter McAusland. He recorded that the first bombs were dropped on Leith at 11.50 pm, that the raid lasted until 12.25 am the next morning. A bomb fell in the playground of George Watson's College, Archibald Place, wrecking the classrooms on the ground and first floors, to the delight of at least one pupil who wrote in his diary: "On my road into school this morning I met several joyous persons who informed me that Easter holidays had begun – compulsorily – there were some compensating features even about an air raid."

Bolton, Lancashire, was bombed on 25 September 1916, and the following morning at 8.30 am Thomas Sanderson, the verger of Holy Trinity Church, Trinity Street arrived at the church to find a hole in the roof and, scattered about on the floor, a bomb that had broken up on impact but had failed to explode. As in London after its first raid, Bolton became the scene of "air-raid tourism", with people coming from as far afield as Liverpool to view the damage. The local newspaper reported that: "In the roads and streets leading to the unfortunate south central area there were literally thousands of people … it was almost impossible to get near the scene where the greatest damage had been done: the streets were choked to overflowing."

That same night Sheffield was raided. This was the city's fourteenth alert, and the warning, given by electric buzzers, was sounded just before 11.00 pm. The first bombs did not begin to drop until 12.25 am, when two incendiaries landed in Burngreave Cemetery. A high-explosive bomb fell in Danville Street killing 49-year-old Frederick Stratford who had opted to stay in bed. The final official tally of the dead was 28, the majority being killed in Cossey and Corby Streets. The Zeppelin's youngest victim was one-year-old Horace William Hames and the oldest 76-year-old Ann Coogan. There were 89 houses seriously damaged in the raid, while 150 suffered minor damage.

Similar sights and scenes came to Nottingham early next morning when it was raided for the first and only time. The raid lasted for just 15 minutes, but three people were killed and eight injured. In Broad Marsh, labourer Harold Renshaw was in bed with his wife when the first bombs fell just after 1 am. One of them crashed through the Renshaws' ceiling, setting fire to their bedding and night clothes. Harold suffered severe burns and died later in hospital, but although severely traumatized, his wife was physically unharmed. In Newthorpe Street 44-year-old tailor's cutter Alfred Taylor Rogers and his wife Rosanna were also in bed when a stick of bombs fell on their house and surrounding properties. Alfred was killed in bed, but Rosanna's body was found in the street, blown there by bomb blast. An inquest ruled that they "had been murdered by person or persons unknown, through the explosion of bombs dropped from an airship". But the jury added a rider to the verdict: "… the town was exposed to the risk of attack by airships entirely by the action of the railway companies." This was because the Midland Railway Company had refused to turn out its lights even after the air-raid warning had been given. A storm of protest ensued and a deputation of 25 mayors petitioned home defence supremo Lord French to demand the complete cessation of railway traffic at night. But they were told, as had been an earlier deputation from Sheffield, that "the complete stoppage was the enemy's object; to give way to such a desire would be playing into his hand, while it might cause the Army in France to become short of essential munitions."

The Zeppelins' victims were not just to be found in large industrial towns. In the early of morning of 3 September 1916, the L-16 Zeppelin, in order to speed its flight back to base, jettisoned bombs on the small Hertfordshire village of Essendon. The bombs mortally wounded Frances and Eleanor Bamford, aged 26 and 12, the daughters of the village blacksmith. In the early evening of Saturday 2 September, 12 naval Zeppelins and four military airships had set out on their most ambitious raid yet on London. Extra bombs were loaded, a total of 260 high explosives and 200 incendiaries. But the raid ended in almost total failure. One of the army airships, the SL-11, after crossing Essex, had made a rapid sweep to the north-west of the capital in order to approach London from its supposedly most vulnerable side. She then turned south, bombing the suburbs at 1.00 am, but was soon detected by the searchlights and "was beautifully held, to the great benefit of the guns. Wriggling like an eel, so it seemed, to avoid the lights, she turned off towards Edmonton." And there she was met by Lieutenant William Leefe Robinson of the Royal Flying Corps flying an obsolescent Be2c biplane fighter. Robinson went straight into the attack: "I flew about 800 feet [244 m] below it from bow to stern.... I then got behind it.... I was then at a height of 11,500 feet [3,505 m].... I had hardly finished the drum [of Lewis machine gun incendiary bullets] before I saw the part fired at glowing. In a few seconds the whole rear part was blazing."

Seen by thousands of Londoners, the flaming SL-11 fell like a stone, burning furiously for two hours on the ground. Her demise was also seen by all the other raiders within 50 miles (80 km) and that effectively killed the raid. They turned tail and made for home.

Awarded an immediate Victoria Cross for his exploit, the dashing and debonair Leefe Robinson was the hero of the hour and the idol of the public and illustrated papers such as *The War Illustrated*: "Lieut. Robinson, with his handsome features, boyish laugh, modest courage, and infallible skill approximates to the ideal hero of the air...."

"I hardly know how I felt," wrote Robinson to his parents, "as I watched the huge mass gradually turn on end, and – as it seemed to me – slowly sink, one glowing, blazing mass – I gradually realized what I had done and grew wild with excitement. When I cooled down a bit,

I did what I don't think many people would think I would do, and that was I thanked God with all my heart." He could scarcely believe his ears as London reacted to his magnificent feat:

> *It swelled and sank, first one quarter of London, then another. Thousands, one might say* millions *of throats giving vent to thousands of feelings.... All the sirens, hooters and whistles of steam engines, boats on the river, and munition and other works all joined in and literally filled the air – and the cause of it all – little me sitting in my little aeroplane above 13,000 feet* [3,962 m] *of darkness!! – It's wonderful!*

Robinson's victory did not come alone. Three weeks later the L-32 was shot down and fell, a blazing wreck, near Billericay. Then on 2 October, Germany's leading Zeppelin ace Heinrich Mathy in the L-31 was brought down over Potters Bar. As it fell in flames "roaring like a furnace" the crew were seen "leaping vainly for their lives, and in the glare presented a hideous sight as they fell and were broken horribly upon the meadows. Meanwhile the watching crowds, exultant, roared out the National Anthem."

The exploits of Robinson and his fellow Royal Flying Corps pilots were celebrated in song when comedian Henry Bluff recorded "Ten Little Zeppelins" for Winner Records in February 1917. Britain's naval airmen shared the triumph. Over Yarmouth as dawn was breaking on 28 November, the L-22, which had bombed Chesterton and Trentham, was engaged by Royal Naval Air Service pilots. They included Flight Lieutenant Egbert Cadbury, scion of the Quaker chocolate family, and Charterhouse public schoolboy Gerard Fane who had volunteered under-age and had only just turned 18. Their colleague Sub-Lieutenant Edward Pulling delivered the *coup de grace* just after 6.00 am, and the L-22 fell, burning furiously, into the sea, leaving only a patch of oil on the water.

Despite the hopes of Munich newspaper *Neueste Nachrichten* that "attacks will be more frequent in future", the Zeppelin menace was now a bugbear in eclipse. But a new and more deadly threat to London was about to appear. In his 1925 account of Germany's air offensive against Britain, Captain Joseph Morris was to write: "When the War shall be but a faded memory, the Zeppelin will be long remembered, but the Gotha will be forgotten. The German airship was a symbol of terror, yet it fascinated the public. The Gotha made no such popular appeal.

Nevertheless, so far as air raiding is concerned, the Gotha proved the more sinister and deadly weapon."

The statistics bear out Captain Morris. There were 52 effective attacks on Britain by Gothas and the huge Giant bombers between 25 May 1917 and 19 May 1918. They dropped a total of 231,000 lb (105,000 kg) of high-explosive bombs and 14,300 lb (6,500 kg) of incendiaries which killed 282 civilian men, 238 servicemen, 195 women and 142 children and seriously injured 741 male civilians, 585 women, 400 soldiers and sailors and 324 children. The monetary value of the damage done by the Gothas was estimated at £1,418,272. And by the time of their last raid, the threat they posed had forced the Government to have ready to defend London and southern England no less than 469 anti-aircraft guns, 622 searchlights, 258 height-finders, 10 sound-locators; 376 aircraft, manned or serviced by 600 officers and 4,000 other ranks, were on hand to tackle the raiders, and a further 82 officers and 2,573 men maintained the balloon barrage. But of the 60 Gothas lost during the year of Britain's "First Blitz", only a third succumbed to home defences. Eight were shot down by fighters and 12 by anti-aircraft fire. The rest were lost in crashes, most often at their bases in occupied Belgium. After apparent defeat of the Zeppelin in the autumn of 1916 there had been a slackening of defence measures, and at one stage there was a possibility that the lighting restrictions would even be relaxed. But the Coal Controller stepped in and demanded, for reasons of national economy, an even greater reduction of public lighting, and so in February 1917, out of a total of 12,000 street lamps in Sheffield only 45 were lit.

Three months later, at 5.00 pm on Friday 25 May, the first mass daylight aeroplane raid on Britain was made by 21 bombers. The Gotha air offensive began with an attack on Folkestone and the nearby Shorncliffe army camp, where 17 Canadian soldiers were killed and 93 injured. In Folkestone itself the toll was much higher: 16 men, 31 women and 25 children were killed and 31 men, 48 women and 12 children seriously injured. The majority of casualties were suffered in Tontine Street, crowded with Friday-afternoon shoppers queuing outside Stokes grocery store. The Chief Constable Harry Reeve described the scene: "I saw an appalling sight I shall never forget. Dead and injured persons were lying on the ground. A few horses were also lying dead between the shafts of vehicles, and fire had broken out in front of premises that had been demolished." Ten-year-old Win Reynolds heard one of the horses screaming before it died; it was "a horrifying, uncanny sound", and when 14-year-old tobacconist's assistant John Pannett rushed to the scene he saw "dead animals and people lying everywhere, a terrible sight … it was too much to take in … there were horses there with all their insides running out. The scene was too awful and I ran back the way I came as fast as I could."

Among the dead in the Tontine Street carnage were sisters Gertrude and Mabel Borthwick, aged 12 and nine, and three members of the family of William Norris: his wife Florence and their two-year-old daughter and baby son just ten months old. A fresh wave of anger swept Britain, and only minor satisfaction was derived from the steadfast behaviour of the town's Girl Guides at a school service during the raid when, according to a eyewitness writing in *The War Illustrated*, "a terrific explosion seemed to make the building rock … the headmistress entered … and told us that an air raid was in progress; we must remain where we were. We did; and I want to say that as long as life lasts I shall remember with admiration and pride the perfect self-control and cheerfulness of those eighty daughters of England."

On 5 June, Shoeburyness and Sheerness were the Gothas' next targets. They saw 13 dead, 34 injured and £5,003 worth of damage done, but there was some small consolation in that a Gotha was brought down by anti-aircraft fire. The same day Lord French warned the Army Council that the "means placed at my disposal for aeroplane defence are now inadequate and that a continuance of the present policy may have disastrous results". How disastrous was shown only eight days later when, on Wednesday 13 June, the Gothas launched their first daylight raid on London. Francis Perrot was the *Manchester Guardian's* London correspondent. Looking up into the sky, Francis thought that the Gotha formation "… Looked like a huge swarm of gnats on a summer evening. They seemed to be moving from the north due south, sending out a faint droning hum as they went. They were dead black against a grey filmy sky." The anti-aircraft guns – "archies", as the troops in France had nicknamed them after the George Robey music-hall song "Archibald, Certainly Not" – were "thundering away all the time" but "the effect was far less terrifying in the bright morning than it used to be in the ominous fire-shattered darkness of Zeppelin nights. Finally, the whole swarm rose higher and disappeared from our sight behind a black bank of cloud." Meanwhile people were out in their gardens "watching this astonishing spectacle which they could do in comparative safety, for the aeroplanes were not directly overhead.

There was a great deal of excitement, even exhilaration, and very little fear, but everyone was running risks from falling shrapnel, which was brought home to us in our suburb later on when residents taking their walks … picked up ugly lumps of metal in the street."

Soon the Gothas passed over and "swooped on, pursued, harried, but not seriously disturbed, down upon the Metropolitan area". There "all the guns in Central London spoke out with a tremendous rumbling noise, and mixed with it came in a minute or two the unmistakable shattering roar of bomb explosions. Bombs were dropped very quickly, and for two or three minutes they seemed to fall at the rate of one every two or three seconds."

Railway engineer Cecil Allen was at Liverpool Street station that morning when

> suddenly telephone messages began to come into the General Manager's office that German planes had crossed the coast; in rapid succession we heard that they were passing Shenfield, Romford, Ilford, Stratford and the time now had undoubtedly come to make a hasty exit. So I dashed down the stairs of the hotel bridge and along No 9 platform to the subway, and had just got to the bottom when there followed the roar of bombs exploding at the outer end of the station.

Almost immediately following the raid, bizarre rumours started to circulate. One man claimed to have seen two of the raiders brought down in Hyde Park, another at Moorgate. Many parts of London, it was claimed, were littered with the corpses of German airmen. St Paul's was said to be in ruins and Guy's Hospital razed to the ground by incendiaries. But most people behaved sensibly and large numbers had taken shelter. The military correspondent of the *Morning Post* Colonel Repington was not the only one to note that there had been no panic. Some Londoners had even been unaware that a raid had taken place. In Chelsea, Harry Lee's nanny rushed in "white and scared", and asked his mother Georgina, "Didn't you hear the bombs, Madam, and the guns?" But all Georgina had heard were two faint booms and one aeroplane droning in the sky. Thinking the guns were practising, she had not paid the slightest attention, writing how "it shows how little one can be aware in London of what goes on only a mile or two away".

Francis Perrot was told how

the working girls of London behaved splendidly. The telephone girls at the exchanges, with bombs bursting round them, went on dealing with a host of calls, even treating politely subscribers who complained that they had been kept waiting some minutes. Women tramcar and omnibus conductors stuck to their job. In some factories the girls refused to take cover and gathered in joking groups on the roofs. All over London women and children were being guided to shelter in the Tube railways and so on.

And wounded Tommies back from France and caught out in the open were invited to shelter in private houses. "Oh it's all right," one of them replied, "this is only a fleabite to what we get out there every day."

Despite this attitude, which in the next war would be expressed in the defiant slogan "London Can Take It!", the capital's citizens were angry, for as Francis concluded his dispatch:

... you cannot convince Londoners after yesterday's experience that the City's defences are adequate to the new warfare. The raiders came at their leisure ... they bombarded London with sufficient leisure to be able to discriminate with a fair amount of accuracy, forming at the same time a target that one would think no guns could miss; and they got away from England without losing a man. London now wants to know the reason why.

Despite the bland official assurance that "happily the loss of life and damage was small", in fact the raid was the most deadly of the war: 162 people were killed, 462 seriously injured and £129,498 worth of damage done. Among the dead were 18 children from Upper North Street Schools, Poplar, killed when a 110-lb (50-kg) bomb blasted a class of infants. Only two of the dead were over five years old. One of 30 injured survivors was Rose Moorhouse, who recalled:

We didn't hear anything, no noise, no bomb falling. Next thing I remember was that I felt heavy, I could scarcely breathe. I kept falling into unconsciousness, then waking up and going to sleep again, then waking up to hear the sound of myself moaning. I couldn't speak and I couldn't move. I had bits of debris in my mouth. Things come into your mind, and all I wanted was my mum.

After three days and nights buried in the rubble, Rose was rescued due to the persistence of her older brother Jimmy who refused to give up the search for her: "I remember them taking me out of the ground and they got this stretcher. I remember I felt the fresh air when they got me into the open. Then I was placed in an ambulance and taken to Poplar Hospital."

Charles Balston was full of admiration for the stoicism of the survivors: "There were distressing scenes but the unhurt children behaved as true Britishers and obeyed the orders of their teachers." Rose's classmates were buried a week later. Many of the floral tributes bore the same message: "To our children murdered by German aircraft." And when the Prime Minister toured the bombed districts, he was greeted by cries of "Don't forget the reprisals!".

The call for reprisals became even more strident after the next raid on London. Saturday 7 July was a fine morning, with a rising easterly wind, the sun obscured by mist and drifting clouds, when 22 Gothas attacked the capital. From Dulwich, Charles Balston thought that they "looked like a large flock of vultures circling and hovering over their prey in the city. It seemed that the most fearful destruction and loss of life must result for the noise of bombs, of shells bursting in the air and of machine and defence guns firing was tremendous." In fact, the raiders dropped 9,845 lb (4,475 kg) of bombs, killing 57, wounding 193 and doing £205,622 worth of damage. It was, the *Daily Mail* raged, the greatest humiliation and disgrace since the Dutch fleet ravaged the Medway back in 1667. But the majority of Londoners appeared to take the raid in their stride: "The omnibuses continued on their routes and comparatively few persons appeared to run for shelter, and the inevitable errand boy walked by whistling and quite unconcerned at the height of the racket."

Writing to relatives in Ealing, a London office female clerk told her how: "… the stairs were thronged with a perfectly quiet calm crowd of people going down (to the basement) in order with no scrambling or pushing – and in less than 3 minutes nearly a thousand people were congregated in the passages & rooms of the basement. There was no panic or screaming or fainting." To keep their spirits up, her fellow shelterers sang popular tunes like "The Long, Long, Trial": "I never shall forget the sound of those girls singing in the cellar room of a London office while the Germans flew over us & death dealing shells were bursting all around." She herself "never thought of death or injury" but rather of "what silly things one thinks & worries about instead of big things in times of danger. It never bothered me a bit that the whole room might be totally wrecked, but I was *terribly* worried because I'd left my pince-nez in my table drawer & so my glasses would run the risk of being broken going home loose in my bag!!!"

But there *were* some ugly scenes of panic, as *The Times* journalist Michael MacDonagh witnessed at Blackfriars Underground station. There, as people rushed to shelter "a second terrific explosion … added swiftness to our feet. The girls of the Lyons and ABC tea shops at the station were in our wake, some of them being helped down, screaming hysterically."

In the aftermath, the general mood became ugly, as Lloyd George found out when again he toured the bombed districts. Women were especially vocal in their demands for reprisals, shrieking out: "Let us pay those German devils for killing our children. If this Government won't do it, we will." And that night anti-German riots broke out at London Fields "where a large body of men and women, the latter forming the majority, paraded the Broadway and attacked the premises of several butchers and pork butchers. The shop fronts were demolished, and in two instances the premises were entered and thrown into the street." What so annoyed and frustrated Londoners was the seemingly insouciant attitude of the raiders. But London had been raided by daylight for the last time. However, only a week later the Gothas returned, their target Southend. The seaside town's ordeal began just before 6 pm on 12 August when the town was still full of Sunday trippers. The raiders dropped over 4,400 lb (2,000 kg) of bombs, killing 32 people and seriously injuring 43. The youngest victim was Lena Golding, aged seven, and the oldest 70-year-old Charles Humphries. Among the day trippers killed that evening in Victoria Avenue on their way to the station were Mrs Jessie Orton and her six-year-old daughter, also Jessie, of Bethnal Green. After the raid the town's post office was inundated with enquiries from anxious relatives, an official there telling the local paper: "We have never been so over-burdened with telegrams and as for telephoning you cannot hope to get through to London in less than three hours." The paper also published an account of the experiences of a local resident:

The greater part of somebody's allotment was transferred into my back bedroom. When the raid was over, and I emerged from my shelter under the stairs, I found every window in my house broken, all the doors blown open, and vegetables scattered all over my back rooms, by a bomb dropped 50 yards away. The place was full of suffocating sulphurous smoke. The noise was terrifying, and yet my little son slept through it all.

In the aftermath of the raid there was great indignation that, despite the fact that the streets were full of holiday-makers (an estimated 50,000 that day) and people going to church, no general warning had been given. The police and fire brigade had been alerted at 5.22 pm, but all the townspeople had received was "verbal advice from policemen to take cover". The indignation was not confined to Southend. The whole issue of warning the public of air raids had proved both controversial and unresolved ever since the first Zeppelin attack in January 1915. But now the situation had become acute, especially as there were rumours circulating that the Germans would soon be dropping poison-gas bombs on London. Fearing that public warnings might lead to what in the next war would be called a "deep shelter mentality", and that production would be seriously affected, the Government, according to Fredette's *The First Battle of Britain*, "only gave in gradually and reluctantly". From July 1917, in London a system was introduced under the control of the Metropolitan Police Commissioner. Warning was to be given partly by maroons (sound bombs), fired into the air, and partly by the police on foot, on bicycles or in cars carrying "Take Cover" placards. In December, night warnings were introduced, but only within strict time limits, and it was not until 12 March 1918 that authorization was given to use maroons at any time day or night.

Although Churchill had minuted as far back as September 1914 the need for some sort of passive defence apparatus, in 1914–18 there was nothing comparable to the Air Raid Precautions and Civil Defence organization of the Second World War. But throughout the country there were approximately 30,000 Special Constables on hand for air-raid work. In both London Gotha daylight raids, over a thousand Specials had been on duty, and beginning in October with the Specials of "E" Division, they began to receive steel helmets and gas masks for their air-raid tasks. By then the Germans had switched their tactics and the Gothas were now raiding the capital by night, a campaign that would continue in varying intensity until May 1918.

The first night raid took place on 4–5 September 1917 and lasted for two hours; 57 bombs were dropped, killing 16 Londoners and seriously wounding 56. Three of those killed, including the conductor, were on a passing tram when a bomb dropped on the road opposite Cleopatra's

Needle on the Victoria Embankment. A gas main was ruptured and the Tube line had to be closed for 24 hours because of escaping gas. For three weeks the capital enjoyed a breather, but on 24 September the Gothas returned and "for over a week at the end of September 1917, a handful of German airmen held sway over millions of Londoners".

There was no talk now of any amelioration of the lighting restrictions, as author Douglas Sladen found to his cost. On 11 October he was fined £1, or in default seven days' imprisonment, for "allowing a bright light to shine from a window of his house at Richmond Green during a recent air raid". Sladen offered the court the feeble excuse that "the light was left burning by his sister, who had come up from the country and did not know the regulations". Even in faraway Lincolnshire, Canon Sutton, rector of Brant-Broughton, was fined a hefty £5 for failing to screen the lights in his church. In the blacked-out streets, fatal accidents were occurring much more often. Gunner William James Palmer of the Royal Garrison Artillery was knocked down by a motor ambulance in Stamford Street, near Waterloo Station, during a raid on 31 October 1917. But he was not to die of his injuries until over a year later, in November 1918, two weeks after the Armistice.

As the raids increased, a new Defence of the Realm regulation was put into effect, stipulating that: "The occupier of any premises must allow them to be used by the public as a shelter against hostile attack by air if he is requested to do so by the police." More public buildings now opened their doors for Londoners to shelter in. Up in Hampstead the municipal authorities issued a list of such buildings, and announced that, "in addition to the Town Hall, a number of private buildings, Chalk Farm, Belsize Park and Hampstead Tube stations, the authorities have had placed at their disposal, the newly completed but unopened tunnel on the London and North-Western Railway from Loudon-road to Chalk Farm. It is nearly a mile long, is perfectly bomb-proof, and would accommodate many thousands of people." The crypts of some churches provided shelter too, and during the raid on Sunday 30 September 1917, the organist at Kensington's St Mary's Abbot kept up the shelterers' morale by playing hymns for over two hours.

The iconic image of the 1940–41 Blitz is that of Londoners sheltering from Luftwaffe bombs in the Tube, and at the end of September 1940 it was estimated that 177,000 were regularly using the Underground as a shelter. But in 1917–18 more than the double that number were taking refuge there. In May 1918, the Royal Academy displayed Walter Bayes's "Under World", which depicted a scene in a Tube during a raid. *The Times* wrote:

> *A few years ago so large a picture, painted and conceived thus, would have been impossible in the Academy; and now it makes all the other pictures in the room look like chromolithographs. And why? Because, though it has its obvious faults, it is something really conceived and really painted. The figures are drawn, in paint, not to look like people as one sees them in a tube when one is bored with mankind, but to express the strangeness of the event, the malaise, the strained nerves, the queer contrasts. It will tell posterity, not how one particular tube looked at a particular moment during an air raid to a commonplace observer, but how people's minds were affected by it.*

The reality of conditions and facilities in the Tube for shelterers was hardly ideal. At King's Cross, Lady Morrison-Bell was appalled to see "crowds & crowds of poor people from the slums all around Kings X had assembled & brought their beds & furniture & babies". She heard a women describe the Tube during the night raids: "She says the appalling state of them when thousands of people with babies etc., have been standing for hours there, with no lavatories or anything, is indescribable & the tube stations have to be *disinfected!!* after the crowds leave."

On a visit to London from Norfolk, 17-year-old Bruce Belfrage of Gresham's School, Holt, "had just left the platform at Baker Street tube station and was making my way up to the street. Suddenly there was a wild stampede as hundreds of people terrified by one of the raids on London, came pouring down the emergency stairs and on to the platform. It was a real panic and many people were crushed, or fell and were trampled underfoot. Two were pushed on to the live rail." Bruce managed to save himself by getting up on to one of the platform seats, but it took him an hour to get to the surface. The experience left him with a lifelong distaste for travel by Tube.

Distasteful too were the many stories of "aliens" panicking during the raids and of their bomb dodging down to Brighton and Maidenhead. During the raid on 29 January 1918 there was a panic, and among the dead were 75-year-old Isidore Schagrin and Louis Belitsky aged five. At their inquest the Coroner delivered that:

the deaths appeared to have been due to panic almost entirely on the part of persons who might be called foreigners or who were of foreign extraction. One would have hoped that people living in London would by this time have regained their powers of self-confidence and control – qualities which would have enabled them to act very differently and not in a way unworthy of men and more approaching the ways of the lower animal.

The court was told by a police superintendent that in the shelter he had been "amazed at the number of strong, able-bodied young men, nearly all aliens or of alien type, and it was these people who were largely responsible for the trouble". But, he continued, "I am proud to say that we have not had the slightest trouble with the English people." *Punch* featured a "witty news item": "The rumour that in consequence of the recent invasion of a popular sea-coast resort by denizens of the East End, the local authorities have decided to change its name to 'Brightchapel' is at present without foundation."

Punch also featured anti-Semitic cartoons that would not have looked out place in Julius Streicher's *Der Stuermer* during the Third Reich. One entitled "Our Maidenhead Bomb-Dodgers", in the issue of 17 April 1918, depicted one "indignant alien" saying to another: "Here's a nice trick to play! Ten guineas [ten pounds and ten shillings] for two rooms in this miserable hole haf I all through this last moon paid – a beautiful moon, mark you, and not von air-raid on London – the dirty Huns!" And in its 5 June 1918 issue the magazine ran a "humorous" story entitled "A Little Retreat". In it "Isidore Steinwicz" attempts to seek safety from the bombs because "the next raid ... on London will be more terrible than ever.... If things get much worse our beloved Galicia would be a safer place than England to live in."

Although the Underground and Government-building basements offered shelter to over a million Londoners, local authorities continued to look to their own air-raid defences. In Southwark, 25,000 sandbags were filled by the staff of the borough council and distributed to local air-raid shelters. In nearby Bermondsey, provision was made for 97,000 shelterers, and in 18 places electric red "Warning" and green "All Clear" signals were installed. The raids caused businesses to adjust their hours of opening. On 3 October 1917, Derry & Toms of High Street Kensington informed prospective customers that "their Establishment will close for the present at 5 o'clock, to enable their staff to reach home earlier under existing circumstances. Early shopping is therefore advisable." Leading actress Gladys Cooper wrote to her husband: "We had a packed house this afternoon, but of course these beastly raids starting again have upset the business tonight."

"Lady Di" in her column in *The Sunday Evening Telegram* thought that:

This recurrence of night raids has made the business brisk in lingerie salons, especially among flatland dwellers, for it's quite the thing now to have coffee and cake parties after a raid, with brandy neat in liqueur glasses for those whose nerves have been shaken. And such parties do give chances for the exhibition of those dainty garments that usually you have to admire all by yourself. Which reminds me. Don't forget an anklet and a wristlet of black velvet – the wristlet on the right and the anklet on the left!

Punch commented sourly that "Lady Di"'s advice was "hardly a clarion call to efficiency".

For those Londoners wishing "to avoid Air Risks" altogether, there were always places like the Royal Beach Hotel at Southsea. It advised potential patrons that it had: "Perfect immunity from air raids with Naval and Military protection day and night". And in *The Times* advertising columns there appeared tempting offers for those seeking a safe "Funk-hole" from the Gothas: "AIR RAIDS. – Peaceful country rectory, Hampshire, well out of danger zone, can receive three or four paying guests. Large garden, beautiful scenery, high, bracing. Simple life. £10 each weekly."

But most "stuck it" and perhaps took heed of a piece of advice in the *Daily Mail:* "Paradoxical though it may seem, to keep cool in an air raid your body must be warm. There are sound physiological reasons for this. On receiving warning, everyone, even if indoors, should at one put on an extra wrap – say, cloak or overcoat. A hot drink from time to time, such as milk, or cocoa, also helps." And the Feline Defence League advised pet lovers that for their safety "cats should be brought inside the house during air raids".

In 1914–18, there was no official Government Evacuation Scheme of children on the lines of "Operation Pied Piper" in September 1939. Some children, like Georgina Lee's son Harry, were privately evacuated;

in Harry's case to his grandfather's house in Wales. But, as an official survey proudly noted, the majority stayed:

> *eager to do their bit by helping to "keep the flag flying" at home or in school. So when London was put to its severest test by a prolonged series of air raids, the schools stood their ground. The blows that were intended to terrorize London failed in their purpose; for, whatever else the bombs may have achieved, they failed to shake the nerve of the London child. There were a few scenes of horror and there were many anxious hours, but the schools "carried on" through it all, and on the unanimous testimony of their teachers, the children "were splendid".*

According to a report by the School Medical Officer: "Contrary to the view expressed by some to the effect that air raids would be found to increase generally the incidence upon school children of nervous complaints, there is no evidence at all in the results of the age group examinations that there has been any general strain arising from this cause upon the mass of children." Gladys Cooper wrote to her husband Buck in France how their daughter Joan aged seven and two-year-old son John were coping with the night raids:

> *We had a raid last night which started just after twelve and went on till 3 am. We took the children down to the sitting-room. John only woke for a moment and said, "I want to go back to my little bed." Joan was awake most of the time and was very amused. She said the singing noise that the shell makes as it leaves the gun was the funniest noise she'd ever heard.... John wanted to know who made the air raids. He also called them "Hunderstorms" which seems to me a remarkably good name for them.*

Not all children took the raids with such sang-froid, however. *Punch* informed readers in January 1918:

> *Mr Punch ventures to plead on behalf of the pitiful case of those poor children who are suffering from air-raid shock. For every child that has been wantonly killed by the Huns, many score have suffered terrible injury to their minds and nerves. For these innocent victims of cruelty a home has been opened at Chailey, in the lovely Sussex Weald. In fine weather they learn gardening and nature study, and*

indoors they sing and dance and have stories told to them. Mr Punch is confident that many of his readers, if only out of gratitude for the greater safety which their own children enjoy, as compared with poorer ones in humble and more exposed conditions, will generously respond to his appeal.

The Lord Mayor set up an air-raid relief fund and, from faraway but loyal New Zealand, Wellington schoolchildren raised and cabled £500 for child sufferers in the London raids.

The impact on adult minds was also evident. On 23 March 1918, there was an inquest on the body of 46-year-old Dr Robert Trevor, a pathologist at St George's Hospital. He had died of morphine poisoning. The jury heard how Trevor had been desperately overworked both at the hospital and as a Special Constable during the air raids. Mrs Trevor told the court that the raids had had "a very bad effect" on her husband, making him "very depressed". A verdict of "suicide during temporary insanity" was returned. Air-raid shock was the excuse given at the Mansion House a month later when 57-year-old George Thomas Verney was sentenced to two months' imprisonment for stealing £8 from his employers, the Forest Gate Estates Ltd. The court heard how his company had entrusted Verney with 10s (ten shillings) weekly to pay the mother of "a lad at the front … but it was alleged that instead of handing over the money Verney spent £8 of it in drink, his excuse being that, owing to air raids, his nerves had become upset that he had been driven to drink and he did not know what he was doing". "A mean and contemptible fraud" was the Lord Mayor's damning verdict. And after a raid in October, a gang that included 15-year-old munitions worker Elizabeth Lucas of Church Lane, Islington and her labourer father Frederick came before the magistrate accused of looting a bombed drapers shop and stealing clothes worth £10 7s 6d (ten pounds, seven shillings and sixpence).

Spreading "alarm and despondency" about air raids could also land the rumour-monger in jail, as Michel Flaum found to his cost. On 12 October 1917, Thames Police Court sentenced him to six months' hard labour and a fine of £40 for "spreading false reports about an air raid". On the other hand virtue brought its rewards. For bravery in rescuing people from bombed houses after an October raid, Sub-Divisional Inspector Frederick Wright was presented with a cheque for £15, and £12 each went to Constables Robert Melton and Jesse Christmas.

The funerals of those killed in the night air raids were often elaborate affairs. One such was held on 26 October when eight victims, including four children, were buried. Following a church service which ended with the congregation singing "Abide with me", the coffins were borne out of the church and placed on a gun carriage and seven funeral cars. In the procession to the cemetery there were contingents of the Royal Naval Volunteer Reserve, the Salvation Army, the divisional and Special Constabulary, the mayor and corporation, 20 clergymen and a representative of the district recruiting staff. Six bands marched in the procession playing solemn music, and the streets were lined with thousands of people. At the cemetery buglers sounded "The Last Post" and a naval firing party fired several volleys over the graves.

Although the Coroner had said: "I am afraid we shall have to grin and bear it and keep our peckers up, and trust to our own aeroplanes and guns to do their best," such occasions only brought more calls for reprisals. Charles Balston wrote that after a royal visit to bombed areas, the King himself was heard to remark: "I wish some of the people who preach against retaliation could see some of this." Another morale-boosting visit by the King and Queen took place after the penultimate raid on London. On 7–8 March 1918, a single bomb, weighing one ton, fell on Warrington Crescent, Maida Vale, and "the street, one of fading Victorian elegance with its four-storey brick houses, was devastated". Ethel Bilbrough's brother, living in nearby Randolph Crescent, gave his sister a vivid account of the raid:

> Thank God we are all alive! But it has been a near thing. We got the "warning" at 11.20 and went down into the basement; the guns had just started when there was a most appalling crash that it is possible to describe. Lilian was hit on the head by a bit of plaster but mercifully it was nothing serious, and they were all very brave. The houses struck (just the other side of the gardens) are gone, and every home in the crescent is wrecked. After the "all clear" had gone I recollect forcing back the billiard room door (smashed off its hinges & piled with debris) and then we saw that awful sight of the houses across the garden all one fire and reduced to ruins, many poor imprisoned people being below and powerless to get out, and I shall never forget their heart-rending screams to my dying day. All night long hundreds of rescuers were working furiously, but it was over 15 hours before many bodies could be recovered. Our vicar worked magnificently

and so did a local doctor who managed to pump oxygen down a pipe to those who were being suffocated by the heaps of debris beneath which they were buried.…

"To come very near death, teaches one to value life," was Ethel's comment on her brother's account. London's ordeal was nearly over. On 19–20 May 1918, the capital was raided for the last time. It was the largest attack mounted, and 49 people were killed, 177 seriously injured and £177,317 worth of damage done. Special Constable Hubert Ord was on duty at Goodge Street Underground station that night. He found that "the stench was the worst feature, which the confined precincts of a tube station with no ventilating apparatus did not improve". The all-clear was sounded at around 3.30 am, and for 20 minutes or so, while having a rest, Ord and two other Specials found themselves the only occupants of the entire station "with its paraphernalia of debris". Then suddenly a man appeared running down the platform shouting out "They're coming back, they're all coming back!". And it was not long before Ord and his colleagues saw pouring through the arched entrances "a motley human torrent with their burdens of baskets, beds and babies, to pitch once more on Goodge Street asphalt strand. However, on this occasion the pilgrimage was of short duration, as the air raiders only returned for a skirmish and in half an hour the all clear was again given."

Just as his son and daughter-in-law would do in 1940–41, after the raid the King with Queen Mary again dutifully visited the bombed districts. Michael MacDonagh came across them talking to some bombed-out survivors near the Bricklayer's Arms on Old Kent Road. "They talked to us", one woman told MacDonagh, "as though they were one of ourselves." And at the height of the raids, Edinburgh-born John Hammerton, in words that would find an echo in 1940–41, paid tribute to the citizens of his adopted city:

There is one compensation for enemy air-raids. They have served to make us realize more than ever the common bonds of humanity, and called into dramatic action that innate sense of duty that has been ever a British asset in the hour of trial. One only has to instance the many acts of devotion in humble life in the midst of unparalleled peril, or to point to the quiet and efficient way in which all ranks of public servants have been tried and not found wanting – the police and the "Specials", tram and bus employees, men and women alike, railway workers of all grades, and many others who if they had failed to "carry on" would have added greatly to the disturbing effect of the raids. Even the panic of the alien poor was handled with tact and sympathy and understanding. The misunderstanding was on the part of the Hun.

KEEPING BRITAIN'S SPIRITS UP

BUT ARE WE DOWNHEARTED? NO!
(From the title of a First World War song.)

Looking back on the contribution to the nation's war effort made by the British entertainment industry between 1914 and 1918, *The Stage Year Book* was in no doubt that: "To the task before it, our stage in all its branches applied itself with an energy and in a spirit of both self-preservation and self denial that the historian will not fail to record. In such anxious days it was for the stage to play a tonic part – to help and divert, cheer, and brace the hearts and minds of the people." A view shared by the King himself, who told theatrical impresario Oswald Stoll, "I felt anxious to show my personal appreciation of the handsome way in which a popular entertainment industry has helped in the war with great sums of money, untiring service, and many sad sacrifices."

War, or rather rumours of war, had been a feature of the British stage for some years before 1914, most famously with the production at the end of January 1909 of *An Englishman's Home*, a melodrama in three acts. Written by "A Patriot" and produced by Frank Curzon at Wyndham's Theatre, it depicted "the impact on a comfortable but spineless lower-middle-class family in Essex of a foreign invasion". The first night caused a sensation, and it soon became known that the playwright was Major Guy du Maurier of the Royal Fusiliers, whose brother Gerald was a renowned actor-manager. The play received the royal seal of approval on 11 February 1909, when the then Prince and Princess of Wales, the future King George V and Queen Mary, attended a performance. Aged 12, Anthony Eden saw it more than once and believed himself "sufficiently sophisticated to be sceptical whether a mixed bag of British soldiers and sailors could really have arrived in time for that rescue in the last act". To reinforce the play's "message", the programme contained an advertisement for a serial "The Invaders" in the magazine *Answers,* and announcements of miniature rifle clubs, the City of London Territorial Association, the London Rifle Brigade and other national-service associations. The *National Review* reported that recruiting for war minister Richard Haldane's new Territorial Army had risen sharply due to the play's success. It congratulated du Maurier, who was to die in action in March 1915, for "accomplishing what others have vainly tried to do by more humdrum methods". A less reverent but wittier tribute was contained in "The Englishman's Home", one of Harry Graham's "Ruthless Rhymes for Heartless Homes":

I was playing golf the day
That the Germans landed;
And all our troops had run away,
All our ships were stranded
And the thought of England's shame
Very nearly spoilt my game.

Spurred on by du Maurier's success, Bernard Townroe, a Territorial Army officer in the South Lancashire Regiment, wrote *A Nation in Arms,* which was produced in September 1909 at Warrington with a stirring commendation from "Bobs" – Field Marshal Lord Roberts VC – himself. *The Times* thought that Townroe's play, which contained the deathless line "Battleships cannot climb hills", would not have been staged had it not been for the success of *An Englishman's Home.* From the Warrington audience, it received "a cordial reception. There was a large house, which included a representative attendance of officers and men from the local barracks and of Territorials in uniform." It failed, however, to obtain a West End run; du Maurier's play's success, too, was short-lived: "For six months Wyndham's Theatre was crowded. Then *An Englishman's Home* flopped. Either it had exhausted its public, or the public mood had veered."

By 1911, in a musical riposte to the threatening attitude displayed by Germany during that summer's Agadir Crisis, the Drury Lane Theatre show *Hop o' My Thumb* featured the song "The Bulldog's Bark" with its defiant refrain "We mean to be top-dog yet, bow wow!":

There are enemies around us who are jealous of our fame,
We have a might Empire, and they'd like to do the same.

And they think the way to do it is to catch us as we nap,
While they push our friends and neighbours from their places on the
  map.
But if upon our property they'd trespass in the dark,
They'll find a good old watch-dog that can bite as well as bark.

As the song was sung, a gigantic Union Jack unfurled on stage, and
the entire cast and chorus roared out a resounding "Bow-Wow". The song
was the show's big success, although one critic rather sourly commented,
"One sees in a flash the whole complicated fabric of international
relationships reduced to the level of a dog-fight."

In August 1914, with that "complicated fabric" in tatters, Britain's
entertainment profession, in the main traditionally conservative and
ultra-patriotic, rose, if somewhat unsteadily, to the occasion. In its
10 October 1914 issue, *The Graphic* included a photograph from the
London Opera House's production of *England Expects* by Seymour Hicks
and Edward Knoblauch. It depicted a battle scene more reminiscent of
Waterloo than Mons, and doubtless prompted the plaintive editorial
query: "One wonders whether the war will produce a great melodrama,
as the American Civil War has done, notably in Mr (William) Gillette's
fine plays, *Held by the Enemy* and *Secret Service*. Our own efforts in this
direction are terribly amateur home-made productions, suitable only for
sixpenny galleries. Why?"

That autumn, no less than 24 patriotic plays, similar to *England
Expects*, and with equally inspiring titles such as *Call to Arms*, *God Save
the Empire* and *Soldiers' Honour*, ran in London's theatres, where now
after each performance the National Anthem was played. At the Empire,
a spectacular entitled *Europe* was staged. *The Graphic* pronounced it
"excellent, especially the manipulation of the map of the Continent as
background, the combatants emerging from little doors in their respective
countries. The Heights of Dover, with Britannia surrounded by her
children, gives one quite a thrill." But in January 1915, *The Graphic*,
in reviewing the 14-year-old but updated play *On His Majesty's Service*,
which now included German spies as well as "British pluck", was still
wondering "whether the war will produce a really intelligent play".

One fairly successful stab in that direction was *The Man Who Stayed
at Home* by Lechmere Worrall and J. E. Harold Terry that opened at
the Royalty Theatre on 11 December 1914. Its hero Christopher Brent,
played by Dennis Eadie, was thought to be a "slacker" who had failed to

enlist: "His sweetheart was very vexed with him about it, and another damsel even offered him a white feather." But in reality he was

> *on the track of German spies, who appeared to have learned the tricks of their business from the "spy stories" in the English newspapers. Not a trick did they omit, from the concealed wireless ... the carrier pigeon (with all the proper maps properly tied to its leg) to the bomb timed to go off at midnight and set the house on fire (as the most convenient signal the spies could think of for submarine U-11 in the offing).*

The play was well received and "the spectacle of the triumphant spy catcher embracing his sweetheart (with her hair down) to the accompaniment of guns outside putting an end to submarine U-11 afforded that combination of patriotism and domestic affections which all honest British playgoers find irresistible". So irresistible, in fact, that the following year it was made into a film by the London Film Company with Eadie and other members of the cast reprising their stage roles.

It was reckoned that no less than 50 espionage dramas were performed during the first two years of the war alone, and as late as August 1918 *The Freedom of the Seas* opened at the Haymarket "with the thrilling spectacle of villains sending wireless messages to U-boats". Once again they were outwitted and unmasked by Dennis Eadie, this time in the guise of a former solicitor and now sub-lieutenant in the Royal Naval Volunteer Reserve. The female lead, played by Billie Carleton, initially rejects the Eadie character as being a weakling. But Eadie becomes a hero by engineering the sinking of a U-boat, and as the curtain falls he "sweeps Billie into his arms and they kiss".

The exploits of real-life naval hero teenager Jack Cornwell VC, whose gallantry in remaining at his post aboard HMS *Chester* during the Battle of Jutland had captured the public's imagination, also featured on the stage. His brother George, who had already doubled for Jack in a photograph for the *Daily Sketch,* appeared as him again in the unlikely setting of the musical farce *Where's the Chicken?* and later in another musical, *Jolly Jack Tar*, which ran for a disappointing 67 performances at the Prince's Theatre at the end of 1918.

While George Bernard Shaw, whose *Pygmalion* had shocked and secretly thrilled audiences in 1913 when its heroine had used the swear word "bloody", was undoubtedly right when he said the wartime public preferred "silly jokes, dances, brainlessly sensuous exhibitions of pretty girls", war plays continued to attract audiences. One such was Stephen Phillips's experimental *Armageddon*, produced in June 1915. It consisted of a series of *tableaux parlants* which started and finished in Hell, and featured, among other scenes, the German bombardment of Rheims, the Kaiser's press bureau and a rather premature Allied occupation of Cologne. A critic wrote, "Imagination, you will gather, is brought into perilously sharp contrast with the realities of today." But the grim reality of war, just over a month after the first gas attack at Ypres, did feature in the play. The same critic, tongue in cheek, wrote,

> *I cannot close without warning my friends to take their respirators with them when they go to view Armageddon for there is an asphyxiating shell (three inch and French) which penetrates the German headquarters and reduces its occupants to a condition of permanent coma (painless you will be glad to hear) … and its fumes achieve the object of all dramatic art, which is to get across the footlights.*

War's realities had already been brought forcibly home to London's theatre land at the end of the previous month with the first Zeppelin raid on the capital. Later, in October, Lena Ashwell, indefatigable organizer of troop concerts, and May Witty, future Dame of the British Empire and "Miss Foy" in Hitchcock's *The Lady Vanishes*, opened in an escapist melodrama, *Iris Intervenes* by John Hastings Turner. "It is most regrettable," wrote *Punch* editor and theatre critic Owen Seaman, "that his first production should have collided with the Zeppelin season. It was no fault of his or of the players that the audience was so small. For myself, I took comfort in the thought that the moon was nearing her full cycle; that Artemis, in fact, as well as her sister Olympian Iris, was "intervening".

Before 1914, an evening at a West End theatre was very much a social event. And while it was not expected of those in the pit and the gallery to don evening dress, it was *de rigueur* for patrons in the stalls and dress circle. But in 1915, signs started appearing in theatres in London and elsewhere, stating "Evening dress optional, but unfashionable", with the strong implication that it was unpatriotic too. Now khaki, if not predominating, was to be seen everywhere in theatres, both in the audience and on the stage. Horace Vachell's *Searchlights*, which starred Sir Henry Irving's son Harry, even featured a shell-shocked officer played by juvenile lead Reginald Owen. Captain Bruce Bairnsfather's cartoon character, the archetypal British Tommy "Old Bill", was brought to the stage in 1917 by impresario Charles B. Cochran in *The Better 'Ole*. It starred Arthur Bourchier as Old Bill, and – with realistic scenery, catchy tunes and witty lines like: "Where were you eddicated, Eton or Harrods?" – proved a great success, running for 811 performances. One critic wrote: "It is a tribute to the essential truthfulness of Captain Bairnsfather's conception and Mr Bourchier's acting that one comes away from *The Better 'Ole* feeling that there must be thousands of "old Bills" at the Front fighting for our freedom." Soldiers on leave especially enjoyed the ditty about the seemingly never-ending supply at the front of Tickler's plum and apple jam:

> *Plum and apple, apple and plum…*
> *We've all had some!*

and "roared at that well-worn joke with hearty appreciation".

Besides the war itself, other topical social issues provided the stage with both subjects and backdrops for drama. In 1917, Mrs Patrick Campbell, the leading actress of the day, appeared in *The Thirteenth Chair*, a murder mystery set during a spiritualist seance. Lady Cynthia Asquith, the former Prime Minister's daughter-in-law, thought it "a really admirable exciting play – we enjoyed it immensely. Mrs Campbell was excellent as the medium." The aliens question was tackled, none too successfully, in *The Prime Minister*, a 1918 pot-boiler by popular dramatist Hall Caine, which had as its basis the rumours still circulating about the supposed pro-German sympathies of the Asquiths, and the pre-war employment of Frau Anna Heinius as governess to their son Anthony. The "ever fresh subject" of the Honours System provided the theme of *The Title* by Arnold Bennett. It starred future knight and Hollywood stalwart C. Aubrey Smith, and in the cast was a young Leslie Howard, just invalided out of the army, who played his part "with great freshness". C. Aubrey Smith also starred in *The Knife*, an American "crook" play that opened at the Comedy Theatre in April 1918, on the very day Sir Douglas Haig was penning his "Backs to the Wall" order of the day in France. According to *The Times* theatre critic: "The tremendous question tackled and triumphantly overcome in *The Knife* … is the man of science, capable of great discoveries for the benefit of suffering humanity if he can only get hold of one or two individuals to vivisect, is this potential benefactor of the race justified in abducting and vivisecting members of the criminal population for this great purpose?" The play caused a minor sensation and on 16 July 1918, Lady Cynthia Asquith noted in her diary: "We went to 'London's greatest thrill' – 'The Knife' – a really good flesh-creeper with clever acting by Kyrlie Bellew in the part of the drugged girl." Drugs also featured prominently in *Anthony in Wonderland*, starring Charles Hawtrey, theatrical mentor to the young Noël Coward, and in *The Hawk* in which the ubiquitous Dennis Eadie played a Hungarian morphine addict. The fraught subject of anti-Semitism in Britain's faltering Russian ally provided the plot for *The Yellow Ticket* which opened in September 1917 and starred Gladys Cooper, very much a "Forces' Sweetheart":

I'm a trooper, I'm a trooper
They call me Gladys Cooper

On 9 November, only two days after Lenin's coup in Petrograd, Lady Cynthia Asquith and the newly commissioned Second Lieutenant Duff Cooper went to see it. Lady Cynthia had

> *seldom enjoyed a play as much ... a real, satisfactory melodrama, with enough to make one laugh too. I rocked when the villain suddenly opened the folding doors and reveals a large double bed to the terrified gaze of his victim. I was amazed by Gladys Cooper – she looked too lovely, and acted very, very well. The play seemed very tactless towards the Russians – I don't suppose it would have been allowed before the rebellion.*

It was soon recognized that "after strenuous months in the trenches, few men will waste precious leave upon plays of ideas or propaganda", and the most popular stage entertainment during the war took the form of light-hearted revues and musical comedies. The most popular of them all was *Chu Chin Chow*, written and produced by and starring Australian-born Oscar Asche, who reputedly devised it one rainy afternoon while waiting to play golf. It opened at His Majesty's Theatre on 31 August 1916, ran for 2,238 performances and was seen by 2,800,000 people, one of whom was stage-struck teenager Donald Wolfit who pronounced it "... A wonderful show – simply splendid". The initial cost was £5,356 17s 9d (£5,356, seventeen shillings and nine pence), which included £1,858 15s 5d (£1,858, fifteen shillings and five pence) for the costumes and £235 16s 9d (£235, sixteen shillings and sixpence) for the orchestra. By the time the show's run ended in 1921, it had brought in £700,000, of which Asche received well over £100,000, most of which he gambled away. Asche, who had previously produced *Kismet*, described his new extravaganza as "an Eastern revue", but *The Times* theatre critic thought, "It is, in fact, everything by turns and nothing long – a kaleidoscope series of scenes now romantic, now realistic, now Futurist or Vorticist, but always beautiful, with action passing from the sentimental to the droll and from the droll to the grim, and yet with the unity of a familiar tale, the old *Arabian Nights'* tale of the Forty Thieves … an overwhelming entertainment … an immense success." The music, "always rhythmical and rather sugary", was by Frederic Norton and the most famous number in the show was his "Cobbler's Song", sung by the tenor Courtice Pounds. *Punch's* theatre critic was as enthusiastic as his colleague on *The Times* in dishing out the superlatives: "a splendid spectacle … full of excellent fun … a very considerable artistic achievement". And despite "a highly immoral ending … I would like to assure the Commander-in-Chief that the entertainment would not disturb the most sensitive subaltern or confuse his maiden aunt". But Lord Chamberlain, the theatre censor of the time, on seeing the play, did object to "this naughtiness" of scantily dressed slave girls, and for a time they were obliged to dress with a little more decorum. In 1940 during the next war the show was revived and, although interrupted by the Blitz, ran for a creditable 238 performances.

Hardly less popular with wartime audiences was the *The Maid of the Mountains*, a Ruritanian musical comedy, also produced by Oscar Asche and starring Jose Collins, whose pin-up graced many a dug-out in France. Set in a brigands' mountainous encampment, the show first opened at Manchester's Prince's Theatre on 23 February 1916. It was then substantially rewritten and re-opened on 10 February 1917 at Daly's Theatre in London where it ran for 1,352 performances. Its hit songs included "Love Will Find a Way" and, in those more innocent days, "A Bachelor Gay". When the *Maid* opened, 24-year-old Jose Collins was paid a not inconsiderable £50 a week, but when "it was plain that Daly's had found a goldmine", her salary shot up to £300, and soon she was receiving a weekly £800, including the income from her gramophone records of the show's tunes. At the same time Lloyd George's prime ministerial salary was £5,000 a year.

In April 1916, the "Prime Minister of Mirth" George Robey, Britain's leading music-hall comedian, had been offered the then record salary of

£500 a week to appear at the failing Alhambra Theatre in a new revue *The Bing Boys Are Here*. Described as "a picture of London life in a prologue and six panels", it was to become, along with *Chu Chin Chow* and *The Maid of the Mountains*, one of the greatest wartime stage successes. "It will always be linked", wrote theatre critic A. E. Wilson,

> *with the cheerfulness that enlivened the leaves of thousands of gallant young men … for long The Bing Boys was the show that simply had to be seen. Night after night the house would be packed with khaki. Young subalterns on leave invariably made their way to the Alhambra…. No production ever was so well timed and so adapted to the mood of the moment. It was staged at the period of … the long battle of the Somme, and it seemed miraculously designed as a tonic for the young men who had endured, or were about to endure, the squalor and hardships of trench warfare.*

Of its star, author Max Pemberton wrote:

> *We at home will never understand what the name of George Robey means to them out there. His jests are repeated in the silence of No Man's Land. The night winds carry the echo of his laughter to the German trenches. In darkness and despair weary men will see visions of the great lighted house and figures of pretty women and flowers from the gardens of England – and upon this scene comes a modest, retiring fellow who has but to look at them to banish their ills. Shall we wonder that their personal affection for him surpasses anything known in the history of the theatre?*

The Bing Boys opened on 19 April 1916, ran for 378 performances and was seen by 600,000 people, before being replaced (without Robey) by *The Bing Boys Are There* on 24 February 1917. A year later its title changed once again, this time to *The Bing Boys on Broadway* with Robey returning to the cast. In the original production Robey's co-players were the lugubrious comedian Alfred Lester and the rising star Violet Loraine. With her he sang the show's biggest and most enduring hit song, the duet "If You Were the Only Girl in the World and I Were the Only Boy":

> *If you were the only girl in the world*
> *And I were the only boy,*
> *Nothing else would matter in the world to-day,*

We could go on loving in the same old way.
A Garden of Eden just made for two,
With nothing to mar our joy;
I would say such wonderful things to you,
There would be such wonderful things to do,
If you were the only girl in the world
And I were the only boy.

Written by American-born Nat D. Ayer, the song was inevitably soon parodied by the troops in France:

If you were the only Boche in the trench
And I had the only bomb
Nothing else would matter in the world that day
I would blow you up to eternity....

At the altogether Dickensian preparatory school St Cyprian's at Eastbourne, stage-struck 12-year-old Cecil Beaton *en travestie* as Violet Loraine performed the song for staff and his fellow pupils, who included future secular saint George Orwell and literary entrepreneur Cyril Connolly. So powerful was Cecil's rendition that Connolly recalled:

The eighty-odd [pupils] *felt there could be no other boy in the world for them, the beetling chaplain forgot hell-fire and masturbation, the Irish drill sergeant his bayonet practice, the staff refrained from disapproving and for a moment the whole structure of character and duty tottered and even the principles of hanging on, muddling through, and building empires was called into question.*

In 1936, looking back on the song, an ex-soldier believed:

It is not possible that anyone who was of military age during the Four Years can ever forget George Robey and Violet Loraine singing in The Bing Boys 'If You Were the Only Girl In the World'. The success of that song does not seek explanation in the circumstances of the time. It had a good tune, and two great artists were on the top of their form in the rendering of it. But it has a place in memory above and beyond that to which its merits entitle it. So many of those who were delighted by it went away when the curtain had fallen to encounter no pleasure ever again. The delight of so many more was sharpened by the knowledge that that might be their fate.

In another song from the show, "Dear Old Shepherd's Bush", Alfred Lester performed a parody of the one of glut of American "down home" songs, telling the audience: "I've just been told to sing an American ragtime song. I've never done one before, but I'll have a try at it. You've got to keep on counting four and taking breaths in between the lines":

I'm on my way back home to dear old Shepherd's Bush
That's the spot where I was born.
Can't you hear the porter calling?
"Queen's Road, Piccadilly, Marble Arch, and Bond Street"
Oh, I'll not wait,
I mean to reach that gate
Through the crowd I mean to push
Find me a seat just anywhere,
Tram, tube, train, bus, I don't care
'Cos mother and daddy are waiting there
In dear old Shepherd's Bush

Lester, Loraine and Robey also sang the other popular hit "Another Little Drink Won't Do Us Any Harm" which included a sly allusion to the Prime Minister's fondness for the bottle:

Mr Asquith says in a manner sweet and calm
Another little drink won't do us any harm

The show proved a smash hit right from the start, and writing in *The Play Pictorial,* B. W. Findon commented: "I do not think I have ever seen either Mr George Robey or Mr Alfred Lester to better advantage, while Miss Violet Loraine has absolutely topped her high professional reputation. The cast is full of clever people, and at the risk of being invidious, I must pay tribute to the delightful dancing of Miss Phyllis Monkman."

Phyllis, another "Forces' Favourite", featured that summer in a bizarre publicity stunt staged by *Pearson's Weekly.* In its issue of 8 July 1916, the magazine asked "Who Will Marry Phyllis Monkman?" and went on to announce a competition in which the prize was a series of dates with Phyllis which might lead eventually to wedding bells. The competition was to be in four stages. The first required the hopeful Tommy, or indeed young male civilian, to fill in a form describing himself. Phyllis would pick 50 to correspond with and from those, six would be chosen for a personal introduction. From one of those six, the "charming actress and dancer in search of her Ideal Man" would select the man who most approximated her ideal. And if he matched up, she would then marry him. The idea was a runaway success, and in the next fortnight the magazine received thousands of entries, many coming from "our fine fellows who are fighting out in France and hoping they'll be the lucky ones". Phyllis replied to them in a weekly column. She promised that she was thinking of all lonely sailors and soldiers, but especially those men who had been wounded on the Somme and were now "resting in Blighty, getting fit to go back and punish the Huns some more". But at this stage, the military authorities, already exasperated and disturbed by the huge volume of lonely soldiers' correspondence, stepped in and stopped the competition. And Phyllis went on to become the *chère amie* of Prince Albert, the future King George VI, before marrying fellow entertainer Laddie Cliff.

The Bing Boys had been co-written by theatrical polymath George Grossmith Jnr, who was responsible for producing a number of other wartime stage successes, as well as serving in the Royal Naval Air Service. His London production of *Tonight's the Night* opened at the Gaiety Theatre on 18 April 1915, and ran for 460 performances. Based on a French farce, *Les Dominos Roses*, it starred Grossmith with Haidee de Rance as his leading lady. But the show's undoubted success was juvenile lead Leslie Henson, not least when a Zeppelin bombed London's theatre land on 30 October 1915 (*see also* Chapter 7). Leslie remembered that there was nearly a panic in the theatre that night:

> *I was "on" in the first act at the time, and while feeling the shock of the explosion and a bit panic-stricken, too, I became aware of the stalls rising like a field of waving corn. I saw our musical director jump up in his seat and whip up the orchestra into one of the liveliest numbers, so I leapt on to the couch (specially fitted with strong springs) and proceeded to jump up and down on it in time to the music. That brought laughter, and gradually the audience recovered and took their seats again.*

Henson's fellow actor James Blakeley was unwell that night, "and the tension this raid produced made him worse. We sat with him in his dressing-room to keep him company while we awaited the return of the Zepp – not feeling any too good, for outside the Lyceum a gas main had been hit and the gas was alight, presenting a wonderful target." But Leslie recalled that even in his misery and suspense Jimmie Blakeley retained a sense of humour. "Oh, this is awful!" he groaned. "Why doesn't the King send the Kaiser a telegram, saying, 'Listen Bill, this is really going too far!'"

Grossmith's next production at the Gaiety was *Theodore & Co.*, also based on a French farce, which opened on 19 September 1916 and ran for 503 performances. The *Daily Mail* wrote: "Only the war economy of words precludes a string of laudatory superlatives. Enough to say that *Theodore and Co.* made a thumping success." After a few months, the *Sunday Herald* believed that: "*Theodore & Co.* seems to be on for the duration. The soldiers, from [Prince of Wales] Edward P. to the gallery private, who go at least once every time they are on leave, would miss it horribly if anything happened to it." It too starred Grossmith and Henson, with Peggy Kurton providing glamour as "Fudge Robinson of the Crimson Comics". Monocled Davy Burnaby made a splendid Bompas, 24th Duke of Shetland, and his rousing number "What a Duke Should Be" brought the house down each performance:

Oh! If you wonder what a duke should be
Just you take another look me
I'm doughty, I'm gouty
I'm wonderful to see
All my people, I own it's true
Looked on Noah as a parvenu
By gad, you can search your family tree
But you'll never find a duke like me.

The lyrics of Burnaby's song were written by Clifford Grey and the music by theatrical wunderkind 23-year-old Ivor Novello. Ivor, gay in every sense of the word, was at the time combining a none-too-successful career as a Royal Naval Air Service pilot with that of composer. In the latter role he had hit the jackpot with his song "Till the Boys Come Home", much better known as "Keep the Home Fires Burning". A year or so after its first appearance, the *Daily Mail* wrote on 1 December 1915: "By 1915 a change came over the songs of the British soldiers. They began to sing a new and haunting melody, the first of all songs specially written for the war to gain universal popularity. Composed by a brilliant young man, Ivor Novello, this song, 'Keep the Home Fires Burning', has become the Battle Hymn of the Great War." Most of the song's lyrics were written by American poetess Lena Guilbert Ford, a friend of Ivor's redoubtable mother Madame Clara Novello Davies, but he came up with the title and opening line:

Keep the home fires burning,
While your hearts are yearning,
Though your lads are far away they dream of home;
There's a silver lining through the dark cloud shining:
Turn the dark cloud inside out,
Till the boys come home.

It was first performed in public at the Alhambra Theatre in the late autumn of 1914 by Sybil Vane, one of the members of Madame Clara's Royal Welsh Ladies' Choir. It took off immediately and the next day musical publishers Ascherberg, Hopwood and Crewe were inundated with requests for copies of the sheet music. A few weeks later, as a member of actress Lena Ashwell's concert party, Ivor performed it for the troops. They gave it an equally enthusiastic reception, and within a few weeks Ivor was writing to a friend: "'Till the Boys Come Home' is now heard everywhere, I am glad to say. One hears it whistled in the streets all the time, in all the restaurants, between the acts in theatres, and even on barrel organs." Sales of sheet music and gramophone records brought him an estimated £18,000 in royalties during the war alone. At Christmas 1915, "indicative of its popularity with the English people was that … no less than twenty-four famous pantomime principal boys made it the theme song of their shows.

Lady Beerbohm Tree, wife of one of the country's leading actors, wrote to Ivor: "It must be a great pride to you to see the soldiers delight in your music. That half glad, wistful song haunts one wherever one goes, and it will echo all over the world." It certainly did. The following year it was sung and played during the screening of British war films all over the USA, and the claim was seriously made that "the stirring melody, plus the impact of those flickering newsreels taken on the war fronts, was, to a remarkable extent, responsible for the wave of pro-Allied feeling which swept the USA and eventually led to its entry into the war".

Just two years later, on 8 March 1918, a one-ton bomb dropped by a German Giant bomber fell on Warrington Crescent, Maida Vale. Among the 23 dead were Lena Guilbert Ford and her son.

It was not long before Novello's title became both a catchphrase and slogan. "Cigarette smoking among women has increased during the War," reported *The Star*, "It is the way they Keep the Home Fires Burning." And *The Evening News* headlined: "To Keep the Home Fires Burning. Proposals for Coal Economy to be considered." It was seized on too by advertisers: "Keep the Home Fires Burning, but let the copper fire go out and stay out, for it never need be lighted again if you use RINSO, the cold water washer. When the Boys Come Home, they will find wives and sweethearts smiling and happy on wash-day." In the next war, at the height of the Blitz, Churchill was to quip, "I must get Ivor to write a new song, 'Stop the Home Fires Burning'".

In between his none-too-arduous Royal Naval Air Service duties, Novello continued to compose and the *Daily Mail* was soon reporting: "Ivor Novello has followed up his phenomenally successful song 'Till The Boys Come Home' with another find effort entitled 'Laddie in Khaki', the lyric, in this case, written by himself, being set to a forceful march theme with so arresting a refrain – 'Laddie in Khaki, I'm waiting for you' – that is certain to bring it into as great a public favour as the former." Although it, and his other war-themed songs, "The Girl Who Waits at Home", "Just a Jack or Tommy" and "When the Great Day Comes", did enjoy considerable sales, none matched the success of "Home Fires". That would have only one real rival.

"Tipperary" was written by Jack Judge and Henry James Williams and first performed by Judge at the Grand Theatre, Stalybridge, Cheshire, on 31 January 1912. That summer on the Isle of Man it was part of the repertoire of Florrie Forde, but only enjoyed a moderate success. But on 18 August 1914 it gained immortality. Four days before, *Daily Mail* correspondent Charles Curnock was at Boulogne watching men of the British Expeditionary Force disembark. As the troops marched through the streets they sang songs from the Boer War, "Soldiers of the Queen" and "Goodbye Dolly Gray". But then a company of the 2nd Battalion Connaught Rangers passed Curnock "singing, with a note of strange pathos in their rich Irish voices, a song I had never heard before". An elderly French lady asked Curnock what the men were singing and "again I listened as another company of the Connaught Rangers passed us, still singing their plaintive ballad.... 'They sing', I said, 'It's a long way to Tipperary, It's a long way to go....'" Having lived through the 1870–71 Franco–Prussian War, she was overcome with emotion and told Curnock: "It makes me sick at heart to see so many fine men marching to war. They are so full of life. Never have I seen such splendid men. Oh, but they are brave – to go laughing." Back in his hotel that afternoon, Curnock wrote an account of the disembarkation for his paper. "I set aside", he recalled, "the old songs and named only the one sung by the Connaught Rangers. To me it seemed to fill and complete the picture as no other song could do." When Curnock's dispatch arrived at the Press Bureau the censor cut it to pieces but "allowed this story of 'Tipperary' to pass. The *Daily Mail* printed it on 18 August and gave 'Tipperary' in a few hours world-wide fame."

Writing in 1930, Great War veteran and author John Brophy was dismissive of the song: "It symbolized the bland, confident and sentimental ignorance with which England entered the war. Before the end of 1914, although civilians retained their affection for it, the New Armies were nauseated. Attempts to start it were often howled and whistled down." Be that as it may, no less an authority than Dame Ethel Smyth, Britain's most eminent woman composer, asserted that it was more than just a good tune to march to. It was, Dame Ethel avowed, "good music wherever and however it was played". Appropriately enough, it was recorded by Irish tenor Count John McCormack, and the recording made on 15 September 1914 in New York by Billy Murray and the American Quartet soon become a Number One hit in the States. With little persuasion, Jack Judge recorded his own version in July 1915. Judge died in July 1938, 14 years after the death of his fellow composer Henry James Williams. Williams died in Coventry and his gravestone there was inscribed:

AUTHOR OF "IT'S A LONG WAY TO TIPPERARY".
Give me the making of the songs of a nation,
And let who will make its laws.

"Tipperary"'s runaway success spurred on the tunesmiths of Tin Pan Alley to try and emulate Judge and Williams's totally unexpected hit. Already in the musical revue *The Passing Show* at the Palace, where her co-star Basil Hallam had a huge hit with "Gilbert the Filbert", Gwendoline Brogan was singing "I'll Make a Man of You". It had been written by the decidedly Teutonic-sounding Herman Finck five months before the war, but now it turned out to be the show's biggest success:

On Sunday I walk out with a soldier,
On Monday I'm taken by a Tar.

On Tuesday I'm out with a baby Boy Scout,
On Wednesday an Hussar.
On Thursday I gang up wi' a Scottie,
On Friday, the captain of the crew –
And I'm Saturday I'm willing,
If you'll only take the shilling,
To make a man of every one of you.

Both Basil and Gwendoline recorded their songs for the Gramophone Company's His Master Voice label. The Company had produced the first gramophone record in Britain on 2 August 1898, and now in 1914 their average two-sided ten-inch (25-cm) 78rpm records retailed at 3s 6d (three shillings and sixpence) a time, with 12-inch (30-cm) ones costing 2s (two shillings) more. Although the sale of records was on the increase, they were dwarfed by those of sheet music, copies of which could be got for as little as 6d (sixpence), but usually averaged 1s 6d (one shilling and sixpence). In 1914, to have a piano in the parlour was a must for many middle- and upper-working-class homes, implying as it did both respectability and gentility. And as the war continued came the stern reminder that "Simpler Amusements Are the Order of the Day" and that they should as far as possible be enjoyed "quietly and unostentatiously at home, without incurring undue expense and without withdrawing labour from the market for the purpose". In 1917 HMV was advising the public that:

In the terrible times through which we are passing recreation of some sort is a necessity. For one's health sake it is necessary to ward off depression and over-worry. On 'His Majesty's Voice' the World's greatest singers and the World's greatest musicians will give you their best in the quiet of your own home. There is no less expensive or more enjoyable method of spending a happy evening.

To hear those singers and musicians, HMV hornless gramophones cost around £5, with a box of 200 needles retailing at 3s 6d (three shillings and sixpence). The company's first wartime catalogue featured a new recording by the Metropolitan Orchestra of Haydn's "Military Symphony", and advised prospective buyers: "At a time when war is the one topic of conversation among European peoples this double-sided record should be very acceptable." Music lovers were also told about tenor Hubert Eisdell's "My Memories" with its "sweet lyric which will leave the most fragrant memories with all happy enough to hear the record…. By-the-by, this popular singer is an officer in the Royal Naval Reserve, and is now serving with our gallant fleet."

Not surprisingly "at a time when patriotism is welling up in the breast of every British-born citizen", HMV issued a new recording of Sir Edward Elgar's "Pomp and Circumstance March introducing 'Land of Hope and Glory'". HMV were confident that: "No one can listen without experiencing feelings of noble patriotism such is the nature of its immediate appeal. Every Britisher should possess this unique record." In HMV's March 1915 catalogue, the recording of Elgar's musical homage to Belgium "Carrillon" was given place of honour. "Celebrated actor" Henry Ainley recited Emile Cammaerts's patriotic poem "Sing, Belgians, Sing" accompanied by the Symphony Orchestra "under the guiding hand of the Maestro himself". "The whole performance," gushed the catalogue, "is uplifting in its strength, it sincerity, its majesty sweep. We have indeed achieved an artistic triumph that will serve to carry the noble voice of outraged Belgium to every corner of the globe." "Outraged Belgium" was also celebrated in popular ditties. Violet Loraine called for "Three Cheers for Little Belgium", Harry Fay sang "Bravo Little Belgium", while Mark Sheridan sung of how Belgium had put the khibosh on the Kaiser.

The same catalogue that featured Elgar's "Carillon" also contained news of a recording of the *Daily Telegraph's* recruiting song "Courage", performed by "lady tenor Miss Ruby Helder". It was only one of a glut of such songs in the early war period, of which "I'll Make a Man of You" was the most successful, with Paul Rubens's "Your King and Country Want You" – "We don't want to lose you, But we think you ought to go" – as its nearest rival. In December 1915 as conscription loomed, Marie Lloyd, the reigning queen of Britain's declining music hall, did her bit for recruiting and recorded "Now You've Got Yer Khaki On":

Now, I do feel so proud of you, I do honour bright!
I'm going to give you an extra cuddle tonight.
I didn't like yer much before yer join'd the army, John,
But I do like yer, cocky, now you've got yer khaki on.

But it was her fellow artiste, 50-year-old Vesta Tilley, born Matilda Alice Powles, who rivalled both Kitchener and Horatio Bottomley as "England's Greatest Recruiting Sergeant". Her speciality on stage was as a male impersonator "although her basic femininity avoided an excessively masculine performance". Dressed in military uniform, Vesta had a repertoire of recruiting songs that included "Jolly Good Luck to the Girl Who Loves a Soldier", "It's a Fine Time for a Soldier" and the most famous of them all, "The Army of Today's Alright":

I'll show the Germans how to fight.
I joined the army yesterday,
So the army of today's alright.

One of the men that Vesta recruited for the army was 24-year-old painter Percy Morter. He and his wife Kitty went to a performance at the Palace Theatre, Manchester, where, as Kitty recalled nearly half a century later,

> *during the interval they had this recruiting campaign. Vesta Tilley was there and all the band on the stage, recruiting officers with sashes and what have you, and she came out into the audience, walked down either side, the men were getting up out of their seats following her. She had a big Union Jack wrapped around her and she introduced that song "We Don't Want to Lose You But We Think You Ought to Go", and we sat at the front and she walked down and she hesitated a bit and put her hand on my husband's shoulder ... and he got up and followed her too.... We came home that night and I was terribly upset and I said I didn't want him to go and be a soldier, I didn't want to lose him, I didn't want him to go at all but he said, "We have to go... There has to be men to go and fight for the women, otherwise where should we be," and he eventually persuaded me that it was all for the best.*

Percy left next day to join the Loyal North Lancashire Regiment. He was killed in action during the Battle of the Somme on 7 July 1916, ten days before his twenty-fifth birthday.

While Vesta drummed up recruits for Kitchener's New Armies, other entertainers threw themselves wholeheartedly into the nation's war effort. Aged 45, George Robey tried to join up, was rejected and instead became a Special Constable before joining the Volunteer Motor Transport Corps. He organized concerts for numerous institutions such as St Dunstan's hostel for blind ex-servicemen and the Roehampton Hospital for limbless soldiers. Robey raised an estimated £500,000 for wartime charities, including £22,000 for the Merchant Seamen's League and £14,000 for the French Red Cross. His efforts were rewarded with a telegram of thanks from Queen Alexandra, the French *Legion d'Honneur* and a CBE in the January 1919 Honours List. Scottish all-round entertainer Harry Lauder was also decorated for his tireless voluntary wartime work, receiving a knighthood. He organized his own pipe-and-drum band to tour Scotland on a recruiting drive and later wrote, "They tell me that I and my band together influenced more than twelve thousand men to join the Colours; they give me credit for that number, in one way or another I am proud of that." In August 1917, following the death in action of his only son John, he launched a fund for maimed Scottish soldiers and sailors. The same month he recorded an emotional appeal on an HMV gramophone record, addressed "to the English-speaking world", for £1,000,000 needed for the fund.

Earlier in the war, Lauder had written and recorded "The Laddies Who Fought and Won", which proved to be a hit and which he sang both at home and at troop concerts in France. But by 1916, among the soldiers especially but also among many civilians, there was little enthusiasm for war songs, be they patriotic appeals or denunciations of the enemy. Soldiers on leave were not at all keen on being reminded of the trenches, and increasingly war-weary civilians, suffering food shortages and air raids, were unlikely to be much amused by such ditties as Ernie Mayne's "My Meatless Day" or Harry Bluff's "Ten Little Zeppelins". But Alfred Lester did have an undoubted success with his decidedly camp rendition of "A Conscientious Objector" from another Alhambra revue, *Round the Map*. Lester sang of how he "did not object to fighting Huns, but would hate them fighting me", and advised the War Office to:

> *Send out the army and the navy,*
> *Sent out the rank and file,*
> *Send out the brave old Territorials,*
> *They'll face the danger with a smile.*
> *Send out the boys of the Old Brigade*
> *Who made old England free.*
> *Send out the bakers*
> *And the blooming profit makers,*
> *But for Gawd's sake*
> *Don't send me.*

A mock plaintive plea which brought the house down, performance after performance. But escapism was the musical order of the day. "My

Little Grey Home in the West" was a particular favourite of 15-year-old Elizabeth Bowes-Lyon (who would grow up to be the wife of King George VI) as she helped nurse convalescent officers at the family seat, Glamis Castle.

A more robust "home" song was "Take Me Back to Dear Old Blighty", belted out by Florrie Forde and a great favourite at troop concerts. Songs from numerous London revues such as *Zig Zag*, *Bubbly* and *Bran Pie* were popular with both servicemen and civilians. Beatrice Lillie, aged 18, sang of "Little Cinderella, sweet seventeen and never kissed a fella", and her contemporary Gertrude Lawrence had a late wartime success with "Winnie the Window Cleaner", with its topical references to women taking over men's jobs for the duration. Teddy Gerard, a great favourite with the men home on leave and star of yet another revue, *Bric a Brac*, had a hit with her topical song that alluded to the recently named London telephone exchanges:

> *Everybody calls me Teddy*
> *T E double-D Y*
> *Naughty, sporty, never, never haughty*
> *With an RSVP eye*
> *All day long the telephone*
> *Keeps on ringing hard*
> *Are you there, Little Teddy bear,*
> *Naughty, Naughty one Gerrard*

As an ex-officer was to recall, no subaltern worth his salt would return to the front without having in his kit "a record of 'Everybody calls me Teddy' or some other foolish song … [which] he insisted on playing so often that his friends became weary of it and him".

No wartime song, sentimental, risqué, topical, patriotic or escapist, was safe from parody. "Hold Your Hand Out Naughty Boy" became "Keep Your Head Down Fritzy Boy":

> *Keep your head down Fritzy boy,*
> *Keep your head down Fritzy boy,*
> *Last night in no-man's-land*
> *We saw you, we saw you.*
> *You were out there cutting wire,*
> *When we gave you rapid fire.*

If you want to see your father in the Fatherland again,
Keep your head down Fritzy boy.

The typically British characteristic of making light of adversity was amply displayed in a parody of "Chinatown", sung after the four-month-long Battle of the Somme in which a total of a million men, British, French and German, had become casualties:

River Somme, my River Somme
Where the Boche lies low,
Happy land, where all the day
Rum jars come and go.
Trench to trench attacks we make
With a nice aplomb.
How we pray that we shall stay
On the dear old River Somme.

To which the soldier audiences invariably responded: "I *don't* think!!"

They also sang a mocking and ironic accusation of the "shirkers" on the home front. One of those "a-slacking", far away in neutral America, was former British music-hall comic and now cinema superstar Charlie Chaplin. In 1915, he too became the subject of a song parody, first sung by London schoolchildren:

Oh, the moon shines bright on Charlie Chaplin
His boots are cracking
For want of blacking,
And his little baggy trousers
They want mending,
Before we send him
To the Dardanelles.

When war broke out in 1914, it was estimated that the number of cinemas, or "picture palaces", in Britain totalled well over 4,000, with some "super cinemas" like the Majestic at Clapham able to seat 3,000 at a time. Most admission charges ranged from 3d (threepence) to 1s (one shilling) and, although there were fears that when the Entertainment Tax was imposed in 1916 attendances would decline, it was calculated that there were 1,075,875,000 admissions that year, or 20 million a week. The usual programme consisted of one long feature film, a slightly shorter one and then a short. There were also serial films like *The Perils of Pauline* which had arrived from America just before the war and had proved immensely popular with British audiences. Performances were either continuous or, in most suburban cinemas, twice-nightly shows. In 1915, the average length of a film shown in Britain was 1.65 reels, but five-reel films, running for 90 minutes, were not unknown. In Britain, the most successful films during the war were Chaplin's slapstick comedies and five-reel epics like D. W. Griffith's *Intolerance* and his American-Civil-War-era spectacular *Birth of a Nation*.

When the latter was shown at Drury Lane, *The Times* critic was full of enthusiasm. The film was, he wrote, "... an extraordinary fine achievement, instructive, thrilling, amusing, pathetic. It has grandeur." Full of admiration for the battle scenes, he thought though that for British filmgoers "the most interesting and informative part, historically considered, will be the exhibition of the events that happened after the war was over; the incredible sufferings of the whites at the hands of the liberated and deluded blacks." On 21 April 1917, Lady Cynthia Asquith went to see Griffith's other epic, *Intolerance*: "... which as the papers say, 'leaves the spectators gasping'. It is an incredible thing – such a *melange* – great stories each seen in snippets, now a glimpse of the Crucifixion, then a man being hung in America, alternating with scenes from Babylon and the Massacre of St Bartholomew. The Babylon pictures were spectacular, marvellous.... I enjoyed it very much...."

Lady Cynthia was at first less enthusiastic about Chaplin. In April 1916 she was at a party where "... There was a Charlie Chaplin film – a disgusting dentist scene – I scarcely smiled." But soon she was writing of "how good Charlie was". In February 1918, she braved the Gothas and the packed Tube to see him at the New Gallery cinema. He was "excellent" but the accompanying "very long drama, 'The Life of Rasputin' – rather disappointing considering its possibilities". Another Chaplin fan was lithographic artist Frank Lockwood, who recorded in his diary a visit to the Spa Hall, Slaithwaite, on 14 April 1915 to see "... A screaming Keystone comic ... called 'The New Janitor' & it featured Chas. Chaplin, absolutely the funniest & most original comic actor on the films. His very appearance makes you smile, while his actions, well you are bound to laugh." A younger and even more ardent fan was ten-year-old Sid Field of Sparkbrook, Birmingham. A visit one Saturday afternoon to the local Waldorf Cinema changed his life for ever because he "saw on the screen Charlie Chaplin, the little man with the shorn moustache, the shrunken bowler hat, the baggy trousers and sea-lion walk". Sid persuaded his mother to make him a Chaplin outfit and his father a cane, and soon the boy who was to become one of the country's greatest comedians in the next war was performing before his first audience. Tommy Handley and Arthur Askey, two other boys also destined to become top comics in the war against Hitler, cut their entertainment teeth in the one against the Kaiser. Askey recalled:

> *When war broke out, I was frequently asked if I would sing to the wounded soldiers – as if they hadn't suffered enough!... One of my fellow performers was Tommy Handley ... he would sing "The Road to Mandalay" during which I warbled "Roses of Picardy", and then we combined to sing "The Two Gendarmes", in which we thought we were both hysterically funny.*

There were those who worried about Chaplin's influence on British children. In April 1917, a social worker noted how at a cinema benefit performance at Woolwich "a film showed Charlie Chaplin pilfering, and ... that spoilt the programme. The children were all nice and quiet until the Charlie Chaplin film was presented, when they received it with shrieks of delight." As a consequence, "the Child's Care Committee of Woolwich had written to Charlie Chaplin in California asking him to modify some of these things". Earlier in the war, the secretary of the Board of Film Censors had likewise written to the great little man "with the result that there had been a great improvement in his films".

Towards the end of the war, social scientist Dr Charles Kimmins undertook a survey of young people's cinematic preferences. From 6,517 essays submitted, he found that 15 per cent preferred Chaplin's films, a similar percentage cowboy adventures and 25 per cent "domestic stories". War films were preferred by 11 per cent and "crook" films garnered 7 per cent, as did serials, love films 3 per cent and educational ones a disappointing but not unexpected 2 per cent. Eight per cent of the children never went to the cinema at all; the rest went to the cinema more or less frequently. Love films "seemed to be very popular among girls, and purely love stories started with them at the age of about 11". Among those who shunned picture palaces, a nine-year-old girl wrote, "My reasons for not going to cinema are because it gives me a headache. I found that the germs like the dark and therefore cinemas are unhealthy." Health considerations also stopped a ten-year-old boy from going: "I have never been to cinemas. Last year my two sisters went and in two or three days one had scarlet fever and the other measles, so that mother would not let me go as she thought I might get it." And a sensible 13-year-old girl explained: "I don't go to the pictures because of these reasons (1) I save money by stopping at home; (2) it does not do your eyes any good."

Sadly, not all British children lived up to such high standards when it came to the "pictures", and a goodly part of the increase in juvenile crime during the war was laid at the door of cinema. In June 1916 at a meeting of the St Giles Christian Mission, James Gracie told his audience that: "Cinemas showed every sign of becoming a worse peril than 'penny dreadfuls' … children were familiarized with scenes of murder and robbery. What wonder if their impressionable imaginations caught fire, and offences were committed which would not have been committed but for the baleful influence of the picture palaces." Sir Francis Fox JP backed up Mr Gracie's thesis, telling the meeting that some time before he had had a boy up before him for setting fire to a church. The boy had given the excuse that he "had seen it on the cinematograph". In Kingston upon Thames, magistrates showed a degree of leniency to a young thief "led away by the picture palaces". He was bound over for six months on "condition that for that time he should abstain from going to cinemas".

It was not just children, some moralists believed, upon whom the cinema had a detrimental effect. An anonymous killjoy correspondent to *The Times* in February 1917 bemoaned the fact that in his large Yorkshire mining village, with "our three local picture palaces … crowded nightly", local people were "enjoying the war" too much. And the following December another correspondent wrote to complain how he and his wife, in dispatching medical supplies to London hospitals, found their "work much impeded by the large traffic in films, marked 'Very Urgent' … on certain days of the week the approaches to the dispatching offices are choked by film vans and film taxis, mostly with engines left running consuming much needed petrol. We leave it to you to decide, which is the more urgent type of goods – 'Charlie Chaplin' or hospital stores?"

To "eliminate the glorification of crime and vice" on the screen, in May 1916 Carmarthenshire County Council undertook to attach certain safeguards before cinema licences would be granted. A year earlier a concerned "Black Country Vicar" had written to *The Times* suggesting the radical step that if the War Loan just launched "is to have any chance with the 'working class', at least in the Midlands, the compulsory closing of picture palaces will become an absolute necessity. They are probably a more serious menace to the nation now than even drink." But H. W. Ledger, writing from the Royal Picture House, Egremont, Cheshire, reassured him that films had "proved a rich ground for recruiting, and with our 'war topicals' have stimulated many a dull imagination". Bishop Welldon, Dean of Manchester, agreed: "… Whatever faults there might be in cinema shows, they were better than the public house and formed an excellent relaxation of the monotony of industrial life. The serious increase of juvenile crime was due more to the lack of parental control than to the cinema." Moreover, the Belgian Red Cross Society was using the film *War is Hell* to help raise funds for its work and the new Ministry of Munitions "has now approached the Exhibitors Association and asked its help to advertise the call for workers to enrol for the production of munitions of war".

In January 1917, those munitions workers employed by Vickers at their Sheffield works were able to see what was undoubtedly the most famous and successful of all British films of the war, when one of the works' shops was turned over to a screening of *The Battle of the Somme*. The film had opened in London the previous August, while the battle was still waging, and within a few weeks it was claimed that over 20 million people had seen it. Lady Cynthia Asquith went to view it at the Scala Theatre on 9 September, just ten days before she was to receive news of her brother-in-law Raymond's death in the battle. Lady Cynthia thought the film "…Very thrilling and moving, and in my opinion *not* an error of taste, except perhaps the dressing of wounds. Curious to think it will be given hundreds of years hence…." Lucy Clifford of Waltham Cross saw it at the Pavilion cinema at Marble Arch the day after it opened. The first item that afternoon was:

> … *a short and excellent film, also of war actualities. Then, when the band had played "Land of Hope and Glory", came the Somme pictures. The effect was wonderful. You could feel that the immense audience understood, as it had never done before, all that was being risked and suffered for us, and that its heart went out in gratitude and admiration. In the marching and lighter scenes there were vigorous cheers, at the end of more and more cheers; the National Anthem followed, and at the first notes we sprang to our feet, not only in honour of the King, but of the courage, the magnificence, of*

*the men to whom we had suddenly felt so near. As for being painful
– are we afraid of knowing, of seeing, what they are not afraid of
doing for every one of us?*

After "God Save the King" another film was shown, "a long, extremely
well-done film of a celebrated play, with a popular actor and beautiful
actress in the chief parts". Lucy thought that at any other time the film
would have had an enthusiastic audience, but the "Somme pictures
killed it".

Henley Henson, the Dean of Durham, had previously written
protesting about the proposed of showing the Somme film, calling it
"an entertainment which wounds the heart and violates the very sanctity
of bereavement". And at Hammersmith a picture palace proprietor had
refused to screen the film, putting up a notice outside that read: "WE
ARE NOT SHOWING THE BATTLE OF THE SOMME. THIS IS A
PLACE OF AMUSEMENT, NOT A CHAMBER OF HORRORS."

But Lucy Clifford was in no doubt that the film should be shown:
"No, the Somme film is not too painful. It indicates pain and suffering
as the outcome, as well as success, of what is being done; and a good
thing too. Thousands of ease-loving people sitting at home and taking
their pleasure (pleasure – good God!) have deliberately shut their eyes to
it. In showing this film the picture palaces have justified their existence."
A view shared by the highest in the land. The King went on record as
declaring "the public should see these pictures", while Lloyd George was
even more enthusiastic: "Be up and doing! See that this picture, which
is in itself an epic of self-sacrifice and gallantry, reaches everyone." His
secretary and mistress Frances Stevenson, whose brother Paul had died
of wounds in May 1915, saw the film and was glad she had. It gave her
both comfort and a measure of closure.

Despite the Somme film's amazing success and record audiences, it
remained true that "the majority of us turn into the cinema for relaxation
after the toil of the day. We go there to try and forget war and its horrors."
And the public were prepared to pay their film stars well. In March 1916,
the papers reported that Charlie Chaplin, a British subject of military
age but still in Hollywood despite protestations that he wished to be
with the "boys at the front", was to receive an annual salary of £127,000.
The news brought a stingingly sardonic response from an anonymous
"English Cinema Actor". "With great satisfaction", he wrote,

did I read the very patriotic messages Charlie Chaplin recently sent to his comrades and compatriots at the front. Therein the most famous film actor in the world declared that his heart was with the boys, though owing to professional engagements he was unable to join them in the fighting line. He is willing, however, to do his bit in other ways, and has the power if "so disposed" as he doubtless will be, to make it a really big bit. It has been stated that Mr Chaplin's income for the next year will be somewhere in the region of £127,000, rather more than one-fortieth of the estimated daily cost of this war. Should he therefore be content with say, the odd £27,000, think what he could do with the balance for the boys to whom his heart goes out in their time of stress.

Other young male actors nearer home such as rising stars Jack Buchanan and Jack Hulbert also came in for occasional criticism for not being in uniform. But an officer on leave wrote that he "did not, as many civilians did, glower at young or young-looking actors and denounce them as slackers. If they amused him, if they made a joke he could repeat, or sang a song he could hum when he went back, they were, so far as he was concerned, doing a useful job."

A similar degree of forbearance was rarely shown to Britain's young professional sportsmen. In August 1914, British sports enthusiasts, participants and spectators appeared to rally *en masse* to their country's call. All Rugby Union clubs were sent a message that: "The Rugby Union are glad to know that a large number of their players have already volunteered for service. They express a hope that all Rugby players will join some force in their own town or country." That same week it was announced that Lady Wilton had accepted the presidency of a war fund to be organized by women golfers of the Empire. And while the committee of Scarborough Cricket Club had decided to go ahead and hold their annual festival as usual, half the profits would be going to the Prince of Wales's Fund and the other half to various war charities. It was also reported that the entire staff of the Berkhamsted Golf Club, with only two exceptions, had offered themselves for war service, and in future club members themselves would keep the course in good condition. At Chingford Golf Club, 20 caddies were offered a day's pay and the railway fare to go to London and enlist. All took up the offer and 18 of them were accepted for military service. Moved by their patriotism, a club member presented each man with a sovereign. Before departing for the army, the men "all announced they would spend on visiting other local golf courses in order to persuade their caddies to join up". In Scotland, the Honourable Company of Edinburgh Golfers decided that due to the war they would abandon all club competitions. The following May, a proposed trip by British golfers, including champions Ted Ray and Harry Vardon, to take part in the US Open was "severely criticised, particularly by officers at the front, who expressed the view the view that the tour would be inopportune at this time". In the event, it was the sinking of the *Lusitania* that same week, rather than the severe criticism, which decided the golfers to cancel their tour.

With the outbreak of war, most cricket and rugby competitions were scrapped and on 5 August the Oval was taken over by the War Office. The Derbyshire, Lancashire and Nottinghamshire cricket pavilions became military hospitals, the latter two treating nearly 5,000 patients. But the Football League, amidst a great deal of criticism, decided to continue with the 1914–15 season. A month after war was declared, Sir Arthur Conan Doyle made an appeal to both cricketers and footballers to do their bit. Most professional football players were tied to their clubs on one-year renewable contracts, and could only join up if those contracts were cancelled, but Sherlock Holmes's creator told them: "There was a time for all things in the world. There was a time for games ... but there is only time for one thing now, and that thing is war. If the cricketer had a straight eye let him look along the barrel of a rifle. If a footballer had strength of limb let him serve and march in the field of battle."

The 68-year-old Dean of Lincoln, Thomas Charles Fry – soon to become, despite his age, an army chaplain – called for the abolition of professional football, the annulment of all players' contracts and the banning of any man below the age of 40 from attending matches. The Bishop of Chelmsford added his moral authority. "He could not understand men who had any feeling, any respect for their country, men in the prime of life, taking large salaries at a time like this for kicking a ball about. It seemed to him something incongruous and unworthy."

But another churchman obviously thought differently and in February 1915 was well and truly pilloried in *Punch*:

> *In these days, when we have to be thankful that our country has not, like Belgium and France, been overrun by savages, the greater mercies we receive are apt to obscure the less. But Swansea does not forget the smaller mercies. According to a recent issue of The South*

Wales Daily Post, "The Swansea Town FC are coming for the second time to St Nicholas's Church, Gloucester Place, Swansea, on Sunday evening next, at 6.30, when the directors, committee and two full teams have promised to attend the service, that, in the words of Rev. Percy Weston, will be in the nature of a thanksgiving service for their good fortune against Newcastle United." Our compliments to the Rev. Percy Weston, pastor of this pious and patriotic flock.

The previous October, *Punch* had published a cartoon, soon to appear as a poster, by Leonard Raven Hill entitled "The Greater Game". In it Mr Punch sternly admonishes a professional footballer about to play: "No doubt you can make money in this field, my friend, but there's only one field to-day where you can get honour." In angry response, the *Athletic News* rose to the defence:

The whole agitation is nothing less than an attempt by the ruling classes to stop the recreation on one day in the week of the masses.... What do they care for the poor man's sport? The poor are giving their lives for this country in thousands. In many cases they have nothing else.... These should, according to a small clique of virulent snobs, be deprived of the one distraction that they have had for over thirty years.

That attitude cut no ice with A. F. Pollard, whose letter to *The Times* was published on 7 November 1914. "Every club", Pollard wrote indignantly, "who employs a professional player is bribing a needed recruit to refrain from enlistment, and every spectator who pays his gate money is contributing so much towards a German victory." Eventually, under intense pressure from all sides, the Football Association was forced to call on clubs to release unmarried professional footballers in order that they might join up. The FA also agreed to work in conjunction with the military authorities so that recruiting drives could take place at matches, as in music halls and theatres.

Even before then, many footballers had answered their country's call. Every man in Scotland's premier team, Hearts, joined up on 26 November 1914, and the following month the super-patriot MP William Joynson Hicks formed the 17th Service (Football) Battalion of the Middlesex Regiment with, it was claimed, England international centre-half Frank Buckley as his first recruit. Buckley, who rose to the rank of major, later estimated that over 500 men out of the battalion's original strength of 600 were either killed in action or died of wounds. In all, it was reckoned that of Britain's 5,000 pre-war professional footballers, 2,000 joined up. Walter Tull, who had played for Northampton Town, was one of them, and after fighting on the Somme he received a commission in May 1917, becoming the first-ever black officer in the British Army. He was killed in action during the German March 1918 offensive. Willie Angus, a Celtic player during the 1912–13 and 1913–14 seasons, became the first Scottish Territorial to win the VC. At Givenchy in June 1915, despite the loss of an eye, a badly damaged leg and 40 other minor wounds, he went out into no-man's-land and rescued injured Lieutenant James Martin who came from his hometown of Carluke. Seven of Willie's Celtic teammates were killed during the war. The six players from Leicester City who joined up were more fortunate and all survived the Western Front, but 11 former members of Tottenham Hotspur who enlisted were either killed or died of their wounds.

Edwin Latheron of Blackburn Rovers was probably the most famous British footballer to be killed in the war. In eight years he had scored 94 goals in 258 matches and helped his club achieve First Division league titles in the two seasons before the war. He was killed serving with the Royal Field Artillery during the Third Battle of Ypres in October 1917. Only slightly less famous was Sandy Turnbull who had played for both Manchester City and United, and scored the winning goal against Bristol City in the 1909 Cup Final. He joined the Footballers' Battalion and was killed at Arras in May 1917. Two of his former teammates from Manchester United died on active service. Right-back Oscar Linkson was killed on the Somme in August 1916, and amateur reserve player Patrick McGuire lost his life the same year.

The war took a heavy toll of Britain's other sportsmen. Ronnie Poulton-Palmer, the captain of England's rugby team who had been capped 17 times, was killed at Ploegsteert, Belgium, on 7 May 1915. Two days later, Wimbledon singles tennis champion New Zealand-born Anthony "Tony" Wilding died near Neuve Chapelle while serving with the Royal Naval Armoured Car Division. Wilding, aged 31 when he died, had won Wimbledon for four consecutive years from 1910, as well as garnering many other trophies including a bronze medal at the 1912 Stockholm Olympics. Hurdler Gerrard Anderson, who had broken the 440-yards hurdles record, also competed at Stockholm, but due to a freak accident failed to gain a medal there. He was killed at Hooge on the Western Front in November 1914 while serving with the Cheshire

Regiment. A more successful Olympian, rower Frederick S. Kelly, had been in the crew that won a gold medal at the London Olympics in 1908 as well winning the Diamond Sculls at Henley in 1902, 1903 and 1905. Serving with the Royal Naval Division at Gallipoli in 1915, he was awarded the Distinguished Service Cross, but was killed in action the following year on the Western Front. Percy Jeeves was one of the 34 pre-war county cricketers to lose his life. An all-rounder for Warwickshire, Jeeves was killed on the Somme in July 1916. But he achieved immortality when cricket fan and author P. G. Wodehouse, himself safely ensconced in America for the entire war, gave his name to Bertie Wooster's impeccable manservant. Yorkshire's Major Booth, a subaltern in the 15th Battalion West Yorkshire Regiment, was killed on the opening day of the Somme battle, and Kent professional Colin Blythe, who had taken 100 wickets for England in 19 Tests, was killed near Passchendaele in November the following year.

An indirect casualty of the war was W. G. Grace, the most famous cricketer of them all. His death on 23 October 1915 was caused by a stroke, the effects of which were worsened by the Zeppelin raid ten days before. Another great cricketer and a future knight, Jack Hobbs, a member of the Surrey XI that had won the 1914 County Championship, was much criticized for not joining up straightaway. He later explained that he had failed to do so because he was 32, married with four children and had a widowed mother to support. Moreover his financial position was far from munificent, but "I do not wish to make excuses, I merely explain my circumstances. I joined up in 1916, previous to which I had spent my time working on munitions in a factory." Manchester City's Horace Barnes was also a munitions worker, but he was fined £2 in October 1915 for absenting himself from work so that he could play for City against Stockport. While individual sportsmen came under fire for failing to do their bit, the continuation of horse racing was a target for sniping throughout the war. At Cheltenham in March 1915 it was reported that convalescing soldiers domiciled in the National Hunt Committee rooms were going to be turned out to make room for lunch parties of race goers. The Committee soon backtracked, and tried to make amends by offering free entry for soldiers to National Hunt meetings, but the damage was done. The Railway Board of Control withdrew all cheap fares and excursions to race meetings and the press was increasingly on the lookout for those wasting petrol "joy riding" to the races. With much disgust and a great deal of disapproval, it was reported that on 28 July 1916 no less than 531 motorcars and 16 motorcycles had been counted at Windsor racecourse. A similar number were found at Gatwick the following May when the first "War National" was run. A conservative estimate put the petrol consumption that day at over 2,500 gallons (11,250 litres), and the Post Office was criticized too for allowing its services to be used for publishing betting news at taxpayers' expense.

An officer writing to *The Times* felt "sick at heart" when he read reports of crowded race meetings and it was "without any enthusiasm that I and my men have got to go and fight for such people, and perhaps die for them". He was shocked too at the abundance of field glasses carried by race goers when such glasses were "worth their weight in gold in France". Although he had relatives who were members of the Jockey Club, the anonymous officer "blushed for shame" when he read of the Club's debate over the pros and cons of continuing racing in wartime. These people may have been "one's own class and breed", but "with such a lead footballers, dockyard slackers and other 'pleasure as usual' people may well be excused". *The Times* could not have agreed more. Eventually a typically British compromise was reached, as the *Daily Mail* put it in 1918: "there seemed to be a consensus of opinion that … games are absolutely necessary, if only for the sake of the health of the rising generation." And, as the Reverend Everard Digby "speaking in khaki" argued, "It would be a terrible disappointment to the boys at the front – fighting for England as they knew it before the war – to come home and find the country in the hands of killjoys and faddists."

CHAPTER NINE

VICTORY AT LAST

GOODBYE OLD THING, CHEERIO, CHIN CHIN, NAPOO,
TOODLE-OO, GOODBYEEE

(From the song "Goodbyeee".)

Sunday 4 August 1918, the fourth anniversary of Britain's declaration of war against Germany, was, as Ethel Bilbrough wrote in her war diary,

> *a lovely day ... which was fortunate ... as ... a special form of service has been drawn up to be held throughout the land, and ours took place in the old cockpit on the common!! Truly the war has worked wonders! and conventionalities are no longer regarded as they were. The service was held by the Rector, the Vicar and the Wesleyan minister who wisely forgot their doctrinal differences....*
> *It was a very impressive service held under the blue sky of heaven.*

Just a few days before, after recording that "the poor dethroned Tzar of Russia has just been shot, and all Russia is in a state of frenzied revolution and disorder", Ethel had noted: "Things begin to look ever so much brighter than they did, and everyone is going about with a much lighter step and a much lighter heart."

Only a few months earlier, the war situation had been very different. At the beginning of the year, as Charles Balston recalled in his diary:

> *Germany's armies were stronger than ever and ready for their great final effort in France. They had been victorious in Russia, Roumania and Italy. There only remained France and England and far-away America to deal with and their leaders assured them of an early victory. There was no lack of men, the army on the Western Front was larger ever and once the Allies were broken the rest would be easy.*

271

Indeed the outlook appeared bleak for Britain and the Allied cause as 1918 dawned; 1917 had brought considerable disappointment, disillusionment and frustration that not even the taking of Jerusalem in December had dispelled. In Newcastle, Reverend James Mackay had recorded the Holy City's capture in his diary: "11 December 1917: News in this morning's *Guardian* of the fall of Jerusalem. What a strange thrill to read such news. Surely it must mean something. 'When ye see Jerusalem compassed about with armies then!' (Luke, 21:20) What then? God grant it may be the coming of the end." But Mackay was far from optimistic about a victorious end to the conflict: "Everybody is heartily tired of the war. Many are reconciling themselves to a patch-up peace. We must get peace soon somehow or trouble will come.... I do not believe in war. Yet I do not believe in peace at any price. War is hell, a certain kind of peace may be hell too. I honestly believe that I am ready to die were I sure it was the will of God." In Hornchurch, Essex, Annie Purbrook noted the debilitating effect of the war on her 56-year-old husband Charles: "Dad has been feeling very greatly the severe strain of business difficulties – loss of men, shortage of material and three hundred per cent increase of prices, so his doctor has ordered him to take at least a month's rest. We have arranged to go West away from air raids which are so nerve wracking."

As 1917 ended – "a great and terrible year in the history of the world culminating in the Russian revolution and the invasion of Italy, and the entrance of America into the war" – Lloyd George sent a New Year message to the British people. Charles Balston wrote that the Prime Minister "urged every man, woman and child physically fit to do men's work in the factory and field and release men for the army". "We must go on or go under," was the premier's stern rallying cry for 1918. Sir Auckland Geddes, Minister for National Service, seconded the Prime Minster and told how

> *the Russian defection had released 1,600,000 German troops from the Eastern Front and that 450,000 men were wanted for our army, navy and munitions; and that those in civil employ were required to replace the severely wounded and those who had been retired sick. There were, he said, great numbers of young men in the essential industries particularly in engineering trades, for whom substitutes could be found and he asked them to come forward.*

But, Balston noted with some disgust: "… it was these very men who were reluctant to leave safe lucrative work and risk their lives with their comrades across the Channel." Seven of them came up before the Mayor of Bedford for playing football on the public highway. In fining them, His Worship asked with a great deal of exasperation "whether they had read the daily papers. Sir A. Geddes … was asking for 450,000 men, and they were the men he was asking for."

As Balston recorded with even greater disgust, "there was a wave of unrest in consequence of the revolution in Russia". The Bolshevik ambassador in London Maxim Litvinov addressed a Labour conference in Nottingham on 23 January and "met with an enthusiastic reception and Bolshevik agitators on the Clyde were daily reviling the cause of the Union Jack and inciting workmen to down tools". But, Balston wrote with relief, "fortunately the pacifists did not predominate and they were countered by Mr W. F. Purdey, the President of the Labour Conference at Newcastle upon Tyne. 'We must fight on,' he said, 'so long as Germany and her allies refused the principles of peace laid down by the Prime Minister and President Wilson' and the loud cheers of his audience showed that they were at one with him in the matter." At Newcastle, resolutions were passed condemning the "down tools" and strike policy of the Clyde and Glasgow workers. The Amalgamated Society of Engineers was also condemned for its refusal to allow its members to be conscripted.

Events on the Western Front came to a head on 21 March 1918. Three days earlier, Balston noted that war correspondent Philip Gibbs had given the public

> *warning that the attack was at hand … the enemy was massing troops and had been for some time past training picked men as storm troops to lead the way when the attack was made. He however reassuringly said that our defences were strong and our men confident of success and the public look forward with calm for the coming of the great assault…. Then suddenly … the storm broke on the 50-mile [80-km] front between Arras and La Fere and a breakthrough at the weak point south of St Quentin was effected.*

Ethel Bilbrough recorded her reaction to what the Germans had dubbed the Kaiser's Battle, although in reality it was the brainchild of the brilliant but unstable Erich Ludendorff, Germany's virtual dictator since the autumn of 1916. "The 'great push' by the Germans on the Western Front," she wrote *which everyone has been feverishly waiting for has commenced at last, and the Huns in appalling numbers are hurling themselves on our lines, mad to break through. Never has there been a more anxious or critical time in the whole war, and we daily hold our breath for news. Our poor brave boys are far outweighed in numbers by the Germans who have endless fresh divisions always coming up, and it is three to one. Already they have forced us back, but the allies are making a fine stand in spite of the heavy odds against them.*

On Good Friday, 29 March, Ethel fulminated that: "… the last ghastly and inhuman act the Germans have perpetrated has been the shelling of a Church in Paris … which was filled with people taking part in the most sacred and the most solemn service of the year. The Huns have just introduced a new abomination in the shape of a long range gun … and if they got to Calais they would turn it on London." That same day *The Times* announced: "In normal circumstances *The Times* would not have been published today; but, in view of the extreme gravity of the situation on the Western Front, we think it right to continue publication without interval."

Annie Holbrook wrote of the battle in apocalyptic terms:

The great German offensive is now on and this spring of 1918 is such a time of bloodshed as the world has never seen. I read that nearly three and a half millions of Germans had been killed in a less number of months and how many allies we do not know. Sometimes I wonder if the great ruler of the Universe will not with one stroke wipe out these evil days and purge the world as in the beginning of history the Flood came and cleansed the earth, or so we had been taught. Surely there never was a more terrible time. It often strikes me as amazing that we carry on, rising, talking, meals, work, pleasure and rest, just as usual, though never a day passes but we hear of some fresh horror.

Charles Balston thought that although the initial German breakthrough was

our greatest defeat in history … the extraordinary thing about this momentous period in our history was England's calm. Not since the coming of the Spanish Armada, not even in the time of Napoleon, had the country been in such peril; yet though statesmen may have

been alarmed at the result of their mistakes and generals fearful
of the destruction of their armies, still the people went about their
business confident that however heavy the odds against them they
would still come through a winner … the nation remained more
calmly confident than ever.

By August, after a few very anxious months when "our men were fighting as they had never been called upon to fight before", the battle finally decisively turned in the Allies' favour, and Charles Balston could record: "We had no fears of the result and were more sure than ever that we were never likely to become slaves of Prussian junkers and German capitalists; or a breed that would never submit to a degradation such as that to which the Bolshevik Soviets were reducing the Russian people through anarchy & chaos." It had been a near-run thing, but on the home front, spurred on by the rhetoric and example of Minister of Munitions Winston Churchill, the country's war workers had risen to the occasion. A feat even acknowledged by his most bitter critic H. A. Gwynne, editor of the *Morning Post*: "I loathe and distrust Churchill but after the great loss in guns and ammunition in March … he made a prodigious effort and within 6 weeks all the losses were made good and a bit over."

The British people had also dug deep in their pockets. Just before the German attack, a "Tank Week" had taken place in London for sale of War Bonds. In places such as Trafalgar Square, Westminster, Holborn, tanks were sited, each with a sales kiosk to sell War Bonds. Popular entertainers and other celebrities were on hand to sell the bonds and business was brisk as Charles Balston recorded:

… by the end of the week a sum of more £112,000,000 had been
collected and the Chancellor of the Exchequer Mr Bonar Law …
hoped to raise money continuously in this way. His hope was fulfilled
for in August he announced the great triumph of the War Bond
Scheme which by then had collected over 1,000 millions. There could
be no doubt that the public would not allow the war to languish for
want of funds.

All sorts of stunts were employed to raise money for the scheme. From the steps of Marlborough House, Queen Alexandra released a pigeon. It carried an application for £500 War Bonds, subscribed for her by the League for the Treloar Cripples' Hospital, and arrived safely at the Tank Pigeon Loft in Trafalgar Square. Tank No. 113 trundled through

London streets to Holborn, where it collected the Prudential Assurance Company's investment of £628,000, and a Royal Naval airship flew over the capital dropping leaflets which "were eagerly scrambled for that they might be kept as souvenirs". The scheme was replicated, with variations, throughout the country, creating "extraordinary interest, and at the same time a certain healthy rivalry". It was calculated that at West Hartlepool £36 per head of population was contributed, Dundee stumped up £25 per head, followed by York and Sunderland with £18 and £15 respectively. At the beginning of June, it was reported that the "Merthyr tank on the first three days of this week collected £1,026,661, an average of £13 per head of the population, a 'record' for Wales". In Wigan, the tank bank took £103,347 on the day it opened while in the Medway boroughs £42,000 was invested in the first five minutes. Tank "Egbert" made a three-day visit to Durham and raised £234,000. In Glasgow, from where 200,000 men had joined the forces, over £14 million was raised in one week. In Scarborough, "unable to get a submarine moored in their harbour as a 'Bank' during 'Business Men's Week' for investing in War Bonds, the people ... fitted up a tramcar as a tolerable imitation of the underwater craft". In February Acton's War Bond Week began with special church services but "in the absence of a 'Tank' a fire engine is to be used". In April, Colne in Lancashire held an "Aeroplane Week" and raised £150,000 in War Loan stock and War Savings Certificates which "represented nearly £6 per head of the population, and which will purchase 60 aeroplanes".

In 1916, a National War Savings Committee had been established with the "small investor" as its principal target. It proved a great success and a year later there were no less than 26,500 War Savings Associations throughout the country. They had over two million members, "drawn probably in the main from among those who had not previously saved, and who had been induced to do so by a system of collective saving". The Associations were formed "in connection with social groups, such as churches, schools, friendly societies, and among the employees of mines, railways, munitions works, factories, warehouses and shops of all descriptions". There were also Associations in the armed forces, and membership ranged from as little as ten to over 10,000. In schools, it was said that "... teachers were among the most zealous and successful of the preachers of the new gospel of economy, in which very often the parent received instruction from the child". In January 1918 the Associations' magazine *War Savings* gave an account of how in Walsall, with 17,000 children, there were 37 school Associations which, with a membership of 6,397, had subscribed £15,035. A single school in Nuneaton had passed the £1,000 mark, and was well on the way to £2,000. A school in Wigan had raised a similar amount, and in Ashford another "had a thermometer to record progress, the various class-rooms competing for first place". A village school in Hampshire, "away from the high wages of munitions areas", raised over £400 in a year. Six-month-old Edward Hinton, the son of a Royal Marine, was probably the youngest recipient of a War Savings Certificate when he won the champion prize at Deal's first baby show in August 1918, beating 174 other entries.

Throughout the war the traditional generosity of the British people manifested itself by their response to the multiplicity of flag days which, as the *Daily Mail* told its readers, "are now quite a national institution, and have proved a popular method of raising funds". The paper calculated that in 1917 alone over £4,000,000 had been raised by the Flag Day Movement. Ethel Bilbrough noted in her war diary: "It's marvellous what a lot of money is raised for the fund (whatever it may be) by the sale of these little flags which generally go for a penny each, or at most threepence. Yet some people having the cause very much at heart have been known to give a hundred guineas for one!"

In 1917, the first flag day of the year in London was Egg Day on 14 February, which was organized by the National Egg Collection for the wounded and raised £3,865 10s 8d. Among the collection's celebrity backers were George Robey, Lena Ashwell, Sir Arthur Conan Doyle and Horatio Bottomley, who wrote, "Hearty congrats. I saw something of your splendid work when visiting the Base Hospitals. Wish I were a Hen!" The end of February saw Women's Day, organized by the YWCA in aid of women war workers, which raised over £8000. St David's Day saw Welsh Flag Day in aid of the National Fund for Welsh troops. Welsh flags were sold as well as daffodils and leeks as emblems and the Prime Minister's wife Margaret took a leading part as one of the collectors in Whitehall. St Patrick's Day was commemorated with a collection organized by the Irish Women's Association in aid of soldiers and prisoners of war from Ireland. On 13 April Mesopotamia Day took place in aid of the Mesopotamia Comforts Fund. The day's honourable organizer was Miss Stella Maude, "the daughter of the victor of Baghdad", and over £16,000 was realized after all expenses had been paid. Lifeboat Day followed on

1 May, and then on 11 May came Lamp Day, in aid of the London Units of the Scottish Women's Hospitals, during the course of which Florence Nightingale's statue in Waterloo Place was decorated. Four days later, on 15 May, there was Russian Flag Day in aid of Petrograd's Anglo-Russian Hospital which had been patronized by the now deposed Tsar's wife and daughters. £25,000 was collected on 23 May for the YMCA and at the end of the month the Smokers' Fund organized a flag day "to provide tobacco for wounded sailors and soldiers in home and foreign hospitals", with Lady Roberston, the wife of the Chief of the Imperial General Staff, having "charge of arrangements in Whitehall". The Salvation Army held its very first flag day on 9 June and collected over £26,000, and four days later came Armenia Day "to help people of this unhappy nation in their misfortunes". The Women's Auxiliary Force organized Vegetable Day on 11 July "to secure fresh vegetables for wounded soldiers and sailors in winter". A "magnificent total" of £100,381 was raised on 14 July, France's Day, organized by the London Committee of the French Red Cross. There was then a hiatus until 4 October when £32,000 was raised on Sailors' Day which was followed on 15 by Our Day, "the most popular flag day of the year in aid of the British Red Cross Society and the Order of St John". Organized by Miss C. May Beeman from West Bolton Gardens, £1,209,180 16s 1d (£1,209,180, sixteen shillings and one penny) was collected, made up of donations that included £5,000 from the King and collections at home and overseas, with £40,000 raised by street sales in London. A flag day in aid of the National Rumanian Relief Fund was held on 26 October, and on 7 November came Roll of Honour Day in aid of the Lord Kitchener National Memorial Fund, with the flag bearing a portrait of "K of K" enclosed in a wreath, with the motto "Deeds not Words". The last flag day of the year came on 14 December, Italy's Day. Following the disaster of Caporetto, Londoners gave generously to their ally and £11,210 17s 11d (£11,210, seventeen shillings and eleven pence) was raised for the Italian Red Cross and other charities.

Refugees from Britain's Belgian ally had been recipients of much generosity, time and money ever since August 1914. The first appeals for the Belgian Relief Fund had appeared in the press as early as 13 August, and a fortnight later the *Daily Telegraph* was reporting the mass arrivals of Belgian refugees at Folkestone and other ports. Prodigious efforts were made on behalf of those refugees, notably by Campbell Gibson, head of the shipping firm George Gibson & Co of Leith, who was also honorary Belgian Consul there. In just over a year, before his untimely death at the age of 50 in December 1915, he organized the raising of nearly £48,000 and the collection of hundreds of tons of food and clothing for Belgian refugees. His example was followed all over Britain. In Scotland, under the auspices of the Belgian Refugee Committee and Glasgow Corporation, some 140 Belgian families were given shelter in Strathaven. At Bowdon, near Altrincham, Cheshire, the Ladies' Guild met on 27 October 1914 to discuss how best the parish could help refugees from Belgium. In time-honoured British fashion, a committee was formed, and the decision was made to rent a house to accommodate a Belgian family. "Since then," the parish magazine reported, "everything has progressed most happily. In fact from the initial suggestion at the meeting of the Ladies' Guild until the present time the scheme has met on all sides with the kindest and most favourable receptions; everyone connected with the necessary decorating and repairs, the collecting of furniture, and the arranging of it when collected, has vied with the other in his or her expenditure of time, thought and labour." The ladies gained an aristocratic patroness when the Countess of Stamford "very kindly sent a donation, and when the house was ready, paid a visit of inspection, with which she declared herself well pleased". On 10 December 1914, "a family of Belgian refugees from Antwerp, consisting of Monsieur Wante, a well-known Belgian artist, his wife and eight children arrived and took possession". The Wantes, the parish magazine reported at the year's end, "seem likely to settle down happily and comfortably among us for what, though we welcome them heartily, we must hope will not be a long exile, notwithstanding that we already feel that we have increased by them our circle of friends, and hope that this friendship will remain long after the present unhappy conditions of affairs has passed away".

Just before Christmas 1914, the *Daily Express* had made an emotional appeal on behalf of Belgian children:

HAVE YOU A CHILD? IF SO, WILL YOU HELP SOME LITTLE BELGIAN CHILD TO FOOD AND WARMTH AND SHELTER?
There are children in Belgium who have lost father and mother ere they have learned to lisp their parents' names. Children shelterless, children lost, children almost foodless and wholly comfortless. Children whose little brothers and sisters – oh, the pity of it! – have proved "food for

*shot" or bombs. Children shaken by the terror of it all, who may die
unless tender care and proper food are swiftly forthcoming.
While your own children are playing and romping in security this
Christmastide – thanks largely to the Belgian army – will you not
help that other army of defenceless Belgian children who cannot help
themselves? See to it there is some brightness in <u>their</u> Christmas.
WILL YOU GIVE A SHILLING OR AS MUCH MORE AS
YOUR MEANS MAKE POSSIBLE, FOR EVERY YEAR EACH
OF YOUR CHILDREN HAS LIVED IN SHELTER AND
HAPPINESS?*

A more modest plea on behalf of Belgians appeared a few months
later in *The Local*, a monthly newspaper which circulated in London's
Stamford Hill, Stoke Newington, Upper Clapton and Tottenham:

*SMOKERS. Save the Lead wrappers from your Tobacco
Mr Frost (Junior) of 50, Lansdowne Road, will be glad to receive
any lead tobacco wrappers or he will call or send for same. The whole
of the proceeds from the sale of the lead will be given to the Belgian
Relief Fund. While you enjoy your smoke think and do something for
the brave Belgian people.*

In the same issue, *The Local's* unctuous editor Charles Bailey
interviewed Mr Frost's parents, Councillor and Mrs Frost, on their work
on behalf of Belgian refugees. On arrival they offered him tea and "I
thanked them, but having only just partaken of the cup that cheers
without inebriating effects, I declined their kind offer...." The Frosts
had received financial assistance to the tune of the handsome sum of
£105 from Mr Goodwin, "the well known proprietor of the Canadian
Rink Picture Palace". He had also given out complimentary tickets for
the refugees to visit the cinema twice a week "thus enabling them to have
some very interesting evenings". Mrs Percy Alden MD "had been most
generous in gifts of clothing" when the "first batch of refugees arrived
[and] appeared in very scanty attire, having only what they stood up
in having had to make a quick exit from Antwerp owing to the terrific
bombardment". Bailey took great comfort from the fact that he "was
assured that the refugees were all of the better class, one being a large
oil-cake manufacturer, another being a master printer, whose business
was worth £5,000 at Antwerp, others being tradesmen of good standing
with their families". Of the refugees, 15 were in residence at "The

Chestnuts" where, "thanks to our own Council the rooms have been made very comfortable. Furniture has been given by Messrs H. Lebus and the linoleum by Goodwin's, the house furnishers, of Tottenham High Road. Councillor Rowley also supplied the bedsteads; whilst Captain Prescot RE supplied the mattresses etc."

Chislehurst, Kent, also had its share of Belgians, and Ethel Bilbrough found them "nice and refined, not a bit vulgar or common". The "poor outcasts" were received with "ever hospitable arms" and some were accommodated in

> *two beautiful houses on the common, prepared and furnished entirely for them, even down to pianos! Many people took three or four refugees into their own homes for months at a time, a most Christian thing to do! Because it is a terrible thing to part with the peace & privacy of one's own four walls.... Chislehurst has certainly nothing to reproach itself with, for* how *these Belgians ... were cared for and looked after!*

In all, nearly a quarter of million Belgians found refuge in Britain. King Albert's heir Prince Leopold, who was to receive much opprobrium in May 1940 when, unlike his father in 1914, he surrendered to the Germans, together with 20 other young Belgians became scholars at Eton. Some 3,000 of their compatriots worked for Vickers at Barrow-in-Furness, and 2,000 more at the National Projectile Factory at Birtley, Durham. Industrialist Charles Pelabon employed 6,000 Belgians manufacturing shells in an unfinished skating rink at Twickenham, Middlesex. Nearby Richmond, where many of them were lodged, took on the appearance of a Belgian town with plates of *moules frites* freely available. There were fears that with the flood of Belgian refugees, British jobs would be at risk, and it was only after much debate and soul-searching that it was reported in December 1915 that: "... no further objection is to be raised by the Miners' Federation of Great Britain to the employment of Belgians underground provided that they are practical miners, understand English, and receive trade union rates of wages." Happily there had been no objections at all in Fleet Street to events leading to the announcement on 21 October 1914 that:

> *... this afternoon* L'Independance Belge, *Belgium's oldest newspaper, will be for the first time published in London. Within the last few*

weeks it has been published in succession at Brussels, Ghent and Ostend, leaving each town within a few hours of the Germans taking possession. The staff left Belgium among the last of the refugees, and will endeavour to carry on the work and propaganda of the journal from London until Belgium again provides a safe home.

Sadly, not all Belgian refugees were of Charles Bailey's "better class", nor as "nice and refined" as Ethel Bilbrough found them. On 12 April 1915, *The Times* reported that: "Mr Fordham, the West London Magistrate, again commented severely on the behaviour of certain Belgian refugees in this country when on Saturday several of them of them were brought up on charges of drunkenness." Two were fined 10s while a third, Jean de Pauw, got 14 days' hard labour and a harsh telling-off from Mr Fordham: "It seems a shame that a big strapping fellow like him should be over here when his country is in the state it is. There are such a number of these fellows at the Earl's Court [refugee] camp, big strapping fellows, who ought to be fighting for their country, but they skulk over here and give the police trouble. It looks as if we have the 'scum' of Belgium over here." Fordham's remarks were greatly resented, and in an attempt to undo the damage he later made a point of praising the Belgians for their part in Britain's war effort. But the press continued to feature items on the less-than-immaculate behaviour of certain Belgians. One such was pyromaniac Jean van Hoof, who in November 1915 was committed to the Hertfordshire Assizes by the Stevenage magistrates. He was charged with "setting fire to stacks of wheat at various times on Sunday October 24". "The prisoner", the magistrates were told, "was found in a hedge near the last fire." More fortunate was Le Mayeur de Merpris Jean, a Belgian painter who was arraigned for making a sketch of Tower Bridge and the River Thames "without permission of the competent naval or military authority". Happily, Lucien de Keyser of the Belgian Consulate "attended the Court on the Defendant's behalf, and said they were old artist friends. On Sunday afternoon they went to the Thames, and it was so beautiful that the defendant said, 'I will make a sketch.'" On hearing de Keyser's evidence, the court discharged de Merpris Jean, who had fought at Mons and Dixmude.

The plight of Belgian refugees in Britain sometimes gave the unscrupulous an opportunity to take advantage and make money. On 26 October 1914 at Bow Street Police Court, Jenny Lines, 24, described as an artist's model, was charged with obstructing the footway in Leicester Square. It was stated that she had appealed to passers-by to "help the poor Belgians" by purchasing leaflets about the Kaiser from her. Lines refused to go away when asked by the police and, when arrested, told them: "We have sold four dozen this morning. Gentlemen give us 2d [two pence] and 3d [threepence] each for them under the impression that they are helping the Belgians." It turned out that only 5 per cent of the takings went to the Belgian Relief Fund; the girls kept half and the remainder went to the Mirrorgraph Company which printed the leaflets. The magistrate was not impressed, remarking that: "The firm was flooding the streets with beggars and letting them make what they could from their begging." He fined Jennie Lines 10/- [ten shillings]. In December 1917 at Newcastle, a jury awarded £1,000 damages to Emile Beauvois, "a Belgian who came to England after the German invasion. The defendant was Joseph Richardson, of Tow Law, County Durham, described as a wealthy man, and the damages were for his seduction of Beauvois's daughter."

Soldiers from a more recent Ally – or rather Associated Power, as their President insisted on calling the United States – were much in evidence in parts of Britain during the summer of 1918. The coming of war in 1914 had shocked Americans. "Blood-mad monarchs prepare dread sacrifice. Fifteen millions facing death. Royalty forces wreck and ruin on fated lands. Stubborn rulers play subjects as pawns," was the verdict of one newspaper in Iowa. "If Europe insists on committing suicide, Europe must furnish the corpse for Europe's funeral," thought the *New York World*. And while it was true that the majority of Americans favoured the Allies above Germany, "peace-loving citizens", as the Chicago *Record-Herald* wrote, "will now rise up and tender a hearty vote of thanks to Columbus for having discovered America." American neutrality both puzzled and annoyed the British people, especially when President Woodrow Wilson made his "Too Proud To Fight" speech after the sinking of the *Lusitania*. But when, on 6 April 1917, the United States finally declared war on Germany there was a feeling of relief and thanksgiving, albeit tempered with "about time too". Typical of the official reaction was the service held at Birmingham's Cathedral Church on 23 April attended by the Lord Mayor and other local worthies. The Stars and Stripes was prominently hung from the pulpit and "The Battle Hymn of the Republic" sung by the congregation. Ethel Bilbrough recorded the news in her diary:

America has joined the fray! She couldn't well keep out of it any longer as the Germans have been calmly sinking her ships that came laden with grain to England; she certainly couldn't lay claim to her usual independence whilst that sort of thing went on. It will mean a big help to us, and a consignment of American nurses and surgeons have already arrived in England, and indeed we need them badly enough.

Annie Purbrook wrote how, after the sinking of the *Lusitania* in May 1915,

it was expected that America would join the struggle against Germany. Many notes passed before the great decision was arrived at. It was not lightly or hastily that America entered this frightful struggle. The allies rejoiced that at last we were to have her powerful help.... Russia was passing through a great internal revolution. The Czar and Czarina were dethroned and all law and order gave place to confusion and chaos. Of course the Russian Army became demoralized ... and the Allies were glad indeed at the prospect of help from America. Soon many shiploads of American troops were gladly welcomed in the fighting areas.

In fact the process of raising, training, arming and shipping the American Expeditionary Force was a less-than-speedy one, and the vast majority of the men eventually landed directly in France rather than in Britain. But quite a number did arrive at Liverpool and other ports, where they each received a facsimile letter from the King welcoming them to Britain. He had already extended a personal welcome to their commander General John Joseph "Black Jack" Pershing. Anticipating the Special Relationship, the King told Pershing and his staff: "It has always been my dream that the two English-speaking nations should some day be united in a great cause, and today my dream is realized. Together we are fighting for the greatest cause that people can fight. The Anglo-Saxon Race must save civilization."

In Britain in 1917, the Fourth of July had been celebrated in relatively modest fashion. But in 1918 the celebrations were on a much grander scale. The Stars and Stripes was flown from all public buildings alongside the Union Jack, and *The Times* enthused: "They flew together above Buckingham Palace, they flew together, also, from many a window in the humbler homes of London.... In the fight against the destroyers of the principles and ideals which to-day are cherished alike by the New World and all but a part of the Old, the Anglo-American peoples have found a new and lasting unity." In the streets of the capital,

> scores of vendors of small flags and button badges found a ready market among the throng, and as the day passed thousands of people wore the Stars and Stripes and the Union Jack in miniature. A woman wearing a dress of red, white, and blue stood outside the Gaiety Theatre with an armful of tiny flags, and did a particularly brisk trade. Taxicab drivers wore the flag; it flew gaily beside a woman on a mail van; a Chelsea pensioner had it pinned on his red coat. American soldiers wore it on their tunics … and although some of them may have missed the noises, cheerful and otherwise, with which they were wont to celebrate it at home, there could be no doubt that they were finding it enjoyable.

The highlight of the day was a baseball match between the US Army and Navy at Chelsea's football ground Stamford Bridge. It was attended by the King and Queen, the Asquiths, the Astors, the Churchills, Mrs Lloyd George and others of the Great and Good. The occasion "took us completely away to those distant times when we could rejoice under a blue sky without looking for Zeppelins and Gothas … [although] it passed in such a pandemonium as was perhaps never heard before on an English playing field; not even on a football ground". The noise temporarily subsided when "The Star Spangled Banner" and "God Save the King" were played by the band of the Welsh Guards and the "crowd awoke to consciousness that the afternoon had passed into the history of two great nations".

The King shook hands with both captains and autographed the ball which he handed over for play. However, that ball was swiftly substituted for another as it was to be sent to President Wilson in Washington. The US Navy won 2 to 1, but it was the symbolism of the match that struck *The Times* reporter, who saw it as "a wholehearted acceptance of America as a comrade in play and a near relation in the great work that lies before the two big English-speaking families".

Arriving in London that month, too late to see "his" navy team triumph over the army, was Assistant Secretary of the US Navy Franklin Delano Roosevelt. FDR had been pro-Allied from the start of the conflict and when America declared war had wanted to give up his post and go into uniform. But both President Wilson and his immediate chief Josephus Daniels thought him too valuable to be spared from Washington. He had now managed to wangle a trip to the war zone. The highlight of Roosevelt's time in Britain was an audience with King George on 29 July. Like everybody else, the King found his young American visitor "a charming man", who told him "everything his Navy was doing to help in the war, which is most satisfactory". The King, "who had a racy mind and enjoyed a doubtful joke so long as the point was obvious", told Roosevelt how during a visit to the wounded after the Battle of Jutland he had come across an injured sailor with a large tattooed portrait of the King on his chest. The King congratulated him on his patriotism whereupon the sailor pointed out that he also had tattoos of Queen Mary, the Prince of Wales and Princess Mary. Again the King congratulated him on his patriotism, to which the sailor replied: "That ain't the half of it your Majesty, you should see me behind. I 'ave two other portraits – I'm sitting on the Kaiser and Von Hindenburg!"

During his short stay in Britain, Roosevelt saw and experienced some of the changes that the war had brought about. On going to the menswear department of the Army and Navy stores, he found "… my old friends, the silk pyjamas, have gone up from 30 to 60 shillings & I only got 3 pairs instead of the 6 pairs I wanted". Weekending with Nancy and Waldorf Astor at Cliveden, FDR found his hostess, who was destined to be the first woman MP to take her seat in the Commons, "just the same, enthusiastic, amusing and talkative soul as always". Roosevelt wrote home that the Astors

> *live in the big house with only women servants – everything comfortable, food about like ours, only a scarcity of sugar and butter.*

FDR later recalled that on going down to breakfast he was unpleasantly surprised to find a hot dish piled high with bacon. The future President sternly told his hosts:

> *You know, I have gone without bacon for a year and a half, in order that you good people might have it.*

Roosevelt's fellow countrymen and the games they played exercised a considerable fascination over the British public during that last year of the war. A display of such games by "a hundred selected American soldiers, including 20 negroes" took place in Hyde Park in September 1918 and attracted several thousand spectators. A reporter was struck by how: "… the United States soldier possesses a beautiful faculty for letting his fun defy his years. The negroes, too, with their wide grins, delighted chuckles, and gurgling incantations, helped manfully to make the whole assembly, performers and spectators alike, realize that, after all, folks are only as old as they feel." But the presence in Britain of black American troops brought with it the problems of race relations and outbreaks of violence that would surface again, on a much greater scale, in the next war. A large number of American troops were stationed in Winchester and after the Armistice it was the site of a Repatriation Camp. On 28 April 1919, there was a major disturbance there among the men awaiting their return to America. According to a local correspondent, in the parlance of the day:

> *The trouble began between a negro and an American soldier in Winchester High-street over some woman. The negro drew his knife, but a local policeman intervened taking the knife from the negro, who turned and ran back towards the camp. On his way he collected some 50 or 60 other negroes, who, armed with cudgels cut from the hedges, went back to Winchester in search of any Americans they could find. They assaulted two or three, but were driven back to camp by the police and some British soldiers. In the camp they were met by a body of soldiers, mainly Americans. In the scuffle men on both sides were injured. An armed picket came out and the camp was soon quiet. The coloured men have now been put in a different part of the camp.*

On a happier note, a number of American soldiers married local English girls, and just as the GI brides of 1945 would journey to America on the *Queen Mary* and *Queen Elizabeth*, so the Doughboy brides of 1919 sailed on the crack liner the *Aquitania*.

In the summer and autumn of 1918, with victory in sight, Britain's war effort in all its manifestations showed no signs of slackening. In Dollis Hill, children from local schools raised £1,250 for the military hospital at Gladstone Park, Cricklewood, and at Colney Hatch Asylum patients collected 525 lb (240 kg) of horse chestnuts in the asylum grounds for the Ministry of Munitions. At Lord's, cricket teams from the Church and Stage played in a charity match to raise funds for the Church Army's recreation huts in France. After performing at a concert for the wounded at the South African Hospital in Richmond Park, George Robey was presented for all his efforts with a walking stick made of African buffalo horn, mounted with gold, with an engraved plate with a springbok badge. The miners of Northumberland agreed to work extra shifts themselves "to meet the dearth of labour" rather than employ "women labour battalions or German prisoners" at the pit bank as had been suggested. In Ilford the National Service Part-time Committee started a scheme for:

The collection of waste articles which can be used for national purposes. Circulars are being sent to householders giving a list of articles which can be used, and a house-to-house collection will be made. The articles asked for at present are paper, woollen and cotton garments, stockings, gloves, curtains, bottles, jars, leather, rubber, metal and bones. The proceeds will be handed over to the British Red Cross Society.

In Hackney, "to save paper, rags, old metal, bones, jars, broken glass, and pig food", the Council were being recommended to agree to the fixing of an experimental sorting grid at an estimated cost of £150. But Croydon had already stolen a march on Ilford and Hackney in the recycling stakes, with one ton of string, 1,040 pairs of boots and 112,200 bottles and jars being reclaimed from the borough's dustbins in the past year.

Still there were those who were not pulling their weight. Five munitions workers were each fined 5s (five shillings) at Enfield Police Court for gambling in the waiting room of the local railway station. The police reported that "hundreds of workers" had turned the waiting room "into a regular gambling rendezvous, and there were many complaints from the public as a consequence". In Glasgow, William Ernest Bounds, whose photograph as a military hero had appeared in the London press, was committed for trial. It was alleged that he had posed as a VC winner and to "have duped and defrauded many persons in Glasgow and the West of Scotland by telling tales of the non-arrival of cheques". And at Marlborough Street Police Court, 39-year-old clerk Horatio Nelson Hawkins was committed for trial on a charge of stealing and receiving from a trolley in Regent Street three parcels containing 21,000 false teeth valued at £800.

As the British and Allied armies advanced on the Western Front, in Windsor, Canon Foxell was wrestling with the bureaucratic intricacies of rationing. "Much of the morning", he recorded in his diary on 27 August, *was occupied in filling coal & gas ration application. I was a good deal perturbed to find how short our allotted amount falls below our last year's consumption. According to the scheme, we are to be allowed 9 tons of coal and 18,750 cubic feet* [5,310 cubic metres] *of gas in the year. Last year we consumed 150,000 cubic feet* [4,250 cubic metres] *of gas and 10½ tons of coal. By substituting equivalents I applied for 5 tons of coal, ¾ of coke and 71,250* [2,020] *of gas. I also applied for extra allowance on grounds of the children's needs.*

Economy was still very much the order of the day. In April, the Economy Section of the Petroleum Executive had issued a renewed appeal to the public for co-operation in saving petrol as "the demands of the fighting services for petrol are daily becoming greater". The public were "invited not to hire motor-cars, nor to use taxicabs when they can walk or avail themselves of public means of conveyance".

The Government Committee on War Savings mounted a campaign with the slogan "Don't be ashamed of wearing old clothes in wartime". But this advice was considered by Eastman and Son (Dyers and Cleaners) Ltd to be both "negative and theoretical". They declared: "There is no need to wear shabby clothes to save money. That is the policy of despair. The policy of courage and true economy is to have your clothes restored and repaired before they have 'gone too far' – and consult those who can assist you in doing this." The firm claimed that: "… silk dresses and blouses dyed by Eastman's dry process are the nearest approach to new yet offered and at one-tenth of the cost." Furthermore, "… corsets clean and repair well, and a complete restoration is made at a fraction of the cost of the new." Men's suits "should be dry-cleaned, pressed and repaired. Another method is to have them steamed and pressed and the spots removed, which is cheaper."

In a move that was to foreshadow the Utility scheme of the next war, standard clothing for British men together with standard blankets, flannels and hosiery was announced in January 1918 for delivery in June. Once again, King George set an example. On a visit to Leeds, the then centre of the British clothing industry, "after carefully consulting a pattern-book", the King gave an order for "a length of brown mixture cloth which, in a ready-made style, can be sold at £2 17s 6d [two pounds, seventeen shillings and sixpence]". At an exhibition of the standard clothing at Bradford Technical College, there was mention that "probably an experiment would be made in standard dresses for women", but nothing came of the idea before the war ended. There were, however, "luxury limits" on clothes for both men and women. A man's suit was to cost no more than £8 8s [eight pounds and eight shillings], while the price for "costumes for ladies i.e. coat and skirt, jacket and skirt, coat frock" should be no more than £7 7s [seven pounds and seven shillings], and "any other gown or dress" was fixed at £5 5s [five pounds and five shillings].

The Government that month had more serious things to worry about than the price of women's clothes. In his diary on 31 August, *Times* journalist Michael MacDonagh wrote in shocked tones, "The London police, Metropolitan and City, are on strike. About 14,000 constables 'came out' last night! Not a single policeman is on beat duty and only a few on point duty controlling traffic! This is the amazing news of the day." Lady Cynthia Asquith woke that same morning at 4.00 am and could not get back to sleep so she "… bicycled to my work for the first time. I didn't feel the lack of policemen (they were all out on strike) and I didn't know how to take advantage of their absence, which seems unimaginative." The strike had been called by the National Union of Police and Prison Officers after the dismissal of one of its key organizers PC Thomas Theil, and over the rejection of its demands for a pay increase, improved war bonuses, extension of pension rights to include policemen's widows, a shortening of the pension entitlement period, and an allowance for children of school age. But the most important demand was that the NUPPO be given official recognition as the representative of police officers. Unless that and the other demands were met by midnight on 29 August, its members would be called out. The strike caught the Government almost completely unawares, but the Guards were immediately deployed in Whitehall and the Special Constabulary called out *en masse*. There were a few ugly confrontations between the Specials and the striking policemen. In Whitehall, MacDonagh saw

> *a Special wearing gold spectacles being struck and striking back. Ultimately he emerged on to the roadway, bareheaded, without his glasses, with two deep rents in his tunic, and bleeding from the lips. Two soldiers among the spectators took him, one by each arm, to lead him away. Another soldier in hospital blue cried out to his assailants: "Don't strike a fellow-countryman. If you want to strike someone, go out to the Front and strike Germans."*

Lloyd George promptly met with the executive of the NUPPO to settle the strike. Very soon MacDonagh saw strikers rush from Downing

Street into Whitehall "cheering wildly and carrying shoulder-high their leaders", shouting out: "We've won! We've won!" "Yes," wrote *The Times* journalist, "Lloyd George has given way. On condition that the strikers return immediately to duty, they are to get an increase of thirteen shillings a week to their pay, and pensions are to be provided for widows." War bonuses were granted and the right to a pension was reduced from 30 years' service to 26. A grant of 2s 6d (two shillings and sixpence) for each child of school age was also given. No official recognition was given to the NUPPO but, as a strike leader told MacDonagh, "No matter. The Prime Minister has recognised our Union by consenting to meet us." And the heavy-handed Commissioner of Police Sir Edward Henry, *bête noire* to NUPPO, resigned and was replaced by General Sir Nevil Macready. Another threatened strike in Manchester was called off when the police there were offered and accepted the same terms as their London colleagues. MacDonagh was impressed: "… an outbreak of lawlessness had been feared. Not even a single shop had been pillaged." He concluded that the strike afforded proof of "London's ingrained respect for order and decorum". The police immediately resumed their usual duties such as the apprehending of 50-year-old Linton French, a porter at the Oxford Street store Bourne and Hollingsworth, for the thefts of silk, cloth and other goods. When arrested, French, who received 11 months' imprisonment, told the policeman that "he had been stealing goods nightly from the firm during the last two years, as he intended to set up business on his own account when the war was over".

It was not only the police that went on strike that summer as Sir Douglas Haig's men advanced steadily on the Hindenburg Line. In Birmingham, 100,000 engineers came out and in July a whole series of nationwide strikes broke out in munitions industries. The worst was at Coventry where, as Minister of Munitions Churchill wrote, "… we were confronted with a widespread cessation of work by the highly paid men engaged in the production of aircraft engines". Churchill, after obtaining Lloyd George's consent, "decided to take the step from which we had hitherto always abstained of withdrawing from men who would not work, their munitions protection against being taken for the Army". Churchill briefed representatives of the Newspaper Proprietors' Association and "despite their misgivings all undertook to sustain the national policy". Posters stating the Government's position and the threat to call up the strikers – "It is already hard that men between forty and fifty should be called up for the Army while younger men are left to earn high wages in the munitions factories" – were placed all over Coventry on Wednesday 17 July, and then "an anxious week-end intervened". On Monday "a cloud of speakers, propagandists and canvassers", including men from the Seamen and Firemen's Union, many of whom had been torpedoed, and women from former suffrage societies "under the fiery guidance of Miss Christabel Pankhurst", descended on the city. Patriotic meetings, complete with brass bands, were held, and "under these varied pressures the strike collapsed, and by Tuesday all Coventry was at work again".

Charles Balston was unsympathetic to those who took industrial action while the country was at war. Typical was his reaction to the Welsh miners' strike of July 1915 when 200,000 men came out. "It was this strike," he wrote,

> *which had the most important consequences – for the miners, conscious of their power, held the country to ransom and dictated terms. Mr Lloyd George, touched to the quick by the action of his own countrymen, met them.... But they were deaf to appeal and argument and insisted on a larger share of the profits of the mines.... The nation was at the miners' mercy and they took the fullest advantage of their opportunity.*

The next year, Balston was writing of "a considerable socialist or extremist minority who took advantage of their country's difficulties to breed strife ... on the Clyde ... [where] they had evolved a systematic & sinister plan for hindering the manufacture of guns urgently wanted for the front & home defence".

In May 1917, the National Executive of the Amalgamated Society of Engineers called a strike which earned not only Balston's condemnation but a fiery denunciation from the pulpit by Reverend George H. McNeal, the Superintendant of the Sheffield Wesleyan Mission. "The strikers", he told his congregation on 27 May, "should have remembered their privileges as well as their grievances. Grievances they had, but did they not think sufficiently of their privileges? Did they compare their position with the position of their brothers in the trenches – they themselves earning their four or six pounds a week (and that in perfect safety); their brothers on the battlefield targets for German guns day and night, and earning a shilling a day?" McNeal was in no doubt that "... the root cause in striking in the case of many young men of military age in munitions works was to preserve their privilege of exemption from military service". But "none of us [has] any right to claim absolute exemption. The existence of the empire, and civilization and world freedom are at stake." Reverend McNeal turned his attention to those he thought behind the strike, believing, like Balston, that: "… There is little doubt that men belonging to the anti-war party, the extreme syndicalists, and revolutionaries have been behind a good deal of the trouble." He had seen copies of a "crude Red Flag little journal entitled 'The Young Rebel' that has had a considerable circulation in Sheffield", which told its reader: "If you must have god to worship, then Labour is the god of all gods," and that: "the rich perform no useful function in society; they simply live on the working classes. Therefore they are parasites, and should be treated as such. Kings and queens are simply parasites." But, the congregation were told, "I believe that the majority of the strikers are at heart patriots." A view shared again by Balston, who wrote: "… whatever might be the feeling of the minority, Labour as a whole was determined to go with the conflict and 'Fight till Victory'."

Victory was in sight when a deadly influenza pandemic swept Britain and the rest of the world. Dwarfing the eight million killed on the battlefield, an estimated 50 million people died worldwide, and as *The Times* put it in December 1918: "Never since the Black Death has such a plague swept over the face of the world, and never, perhaps, has a plague been more stoically accepted." Britain escaped comparatively lightly with an estimated 228,000 deaths, but an unbelievable 18.5 million died in her Indian Empire and over 675,000 Americans perished. The pandemic, which was soon dubbed "Spanish flu" after a report of it first appearing in neutral Spain, came in three waves. The first lasted from March to August 1918, the second from September to December, and the final one from January to May 1919. It was no respecter of persons. Lloyd George went down with a particularly virulent form while visiting Manchester in September 1918 and President Wilson's right-hand man Colonel Edward House caught it three times. The President himself was taken seriously ill with flu in Paris on 3 April 1919, and the influential avant-garde poet Guillaume Apollinaire died of it there two days before the Armistice. War hero William Leefe Robinson VC, the "courageous young man who gave London its most dramatic war spectacle" when he shot down the SL-11 airship at Cuffley in September 1916, died of flu on the last day of 1918. He had been a prisoner of war in Germany, and the atrocious vindictive and brutal treatment meted out to him by his captors in "the damp, dark basement punishments cells at Holzminden had destroyed his health".

Britain had suffered from less deadly flu epidemics earlier during the war. In February 1915, one hit the London area. According to doctors, it was reported that: "… the West-end patient is particularly careless of his health, and is too frequently willing to sacrifice it to his social obligations. Women will especially lunch or dine in restaurants or visit theatres when the initial stages of influenza have clearly declared themselves."

Another bad outbreak of flu came in late 1916, and advertisers of restoratives were quick to come forward with their panaceas. In an advertisement which appeared in the papers on 4 December, Glaxo featured a telephone message that they claimed to have received from a doctor a few days before: "Do you know that the influenza epidemic this year is affecting the stomach, preventing the patients retaining nourishment? I find my patients can assimilate your Glaxo, due I suppose, to its flocculent curd. You ought to make this widely known at once." Readers were advised that "a flocculent curd is a soft pulverised formation. A hard, dense, leathery curd such as the curd of ordinary cow's milk would prevent the patient retaining nourishment." And if that failed to do the trick: "… influenza always upsets the digestive system – this year more than ever. The lightest and most nourishing diet is absolutely essential to allay the internal distress, and therefore Benger's is the food so often ordered by the doctor. Benger's food is retained when all other foods are rejected. It is prepared with fresh new milk, is dainty and delicious, highly nutritive, and the most soothing of all invalid foods."

With the coming of the 1918–19 pandemic, advertisers rose again to the occasion. Veno's Lightning Cough Cure was promoted as a veritable elixir, endorsed in an advertisement by a lance corporal of the Essex Regiment who had found "instantaneous relief" from Spanish flu by dosing himself with it. OXO was recommended to fortify "the system against influenza action. It will be apparent that a strong, healthy person will escape contagion when the ill-nourished one will fall, consequently, one's aim must be the maintenance of strength." Prevention is better than cure was the message from Jeyes Fluid: "Guard against influenza … spray the atmosphere of the office, factory, home and cinema … disinfect all lavatories, sinks and drains." The aristocracy was mobilized to praise the health-giving properties of Formamint, "the Germ Killing Throat Tablet".

Lady Manns felt "safe from infection of any kind when I have Formamint at hand and I have not had any throat trouble since I began to use the tablets". Lady Firbank had not used the tablets before but now they had "completely cured her throat, which owing to influenza has been left weak and painful". When it came to cures, during the first wave in July it was reported that: "… a somewhat serious situation has arisen, many chemists having sold their supplies of remedial medicines. Since it was stated that quinine and cinnamon possessed curative properties there has been a run on those articles which a Westminster chemist describes as 'terrific'."

Such cures were sought as doctors were rushed off their feet, as the son of one in Fleetwood, Lancashire remembered: "So many were ill that only the worst could be visited. People collapsed in their homes, in the streets and at work. Many never again regained consciousness. All treatment was futile." But the *News of the World* did its best, advising readers to "… wash inside the nose with soap and water each night and morning; force yourself to sneeze night and morning, then breathe deeply; do not wear a muffler; take sharp walks regularly and walk home from work; do not 'dope'; eat plenty of porridge".

On 4 July it was reported that the previous week there had been 67 fatalities from the flu in the capital, with "a large percentage of the victims being between 25 and 45 years of age". A younger fatality was 13-year-old William Charles Coats of Southwark. He had been taken ill on Wednesday 26 June and died just four days later. On 25 June, Hitchin Rural Council heard from the local medical officer that there were 600 cases of flu reported at two Letchworth factories. He advised that it was "a good precaution to avoid picture palaces and other crowded places and to keep the nasal passages purified". On the same day, in Cardiff at the Central Post Office 40 workers were taken ill, and 111 London teachers were reported to be down with the flu. Their pupils were soon heard singing a skipping rhyme:

I had a little bird
Its name was Enza
I opened the window
And in-flu-enza.

In Huddersfield so many teachers and pupils succumbed to the epidemic that the Education Committee was forced to close all the town's schools for ten days. In Belfast too, it was reported that "there is little abatement of the epidemic…. During the past nine days nearly 200 patients have been treated in the workhouse infirmary alone, 45 cases having been reported in a single day."

Statistics tended to obscure the human tragedies behind them. Frederick Lewis of Weston, Bath, had lost two sons in the war. At Christmas 1918, his two surviving sons Ernest and Walter came home on leave, only to die of influenza within hours of each other. Ernest passed away on Christmas Eve and Walter on Christmas Day. They were buried together in Chepstow Cemetery.

Bertram Copping, the ten-year-old son of an Islington newsagent, recalled how, when his father fell ill: "… our doctor came, looked at my father … and said he would call back in a day or two. When he did finally arrive, a week later, after repeated efforts on our part to reach him in the meantime, my father was dead." Bernard's mother was also seriously stricken with the flu, and it was left to him to make all the arrangements for the funeral and to choose a coffin. "That a small boy should come on such an errand," Bernard wrote nearly 60 years later, "caused no surprise to the undertaker – by that time he was used to it, and patiently took down all the details of time and place." When the funeral took place, Bernard found that it was just one of many that day; the coffins were stacked "one on top of the other" and the church was filled to overflowing with mourners. "It was," Bernard wrote, "at that moment at the age of ten that my boyhood ended."

As the second wave of flu took a turn for the worse in October 1918, the war news took a giant one for the better In Newark, would-be actor 16-year-old Donald Wolfit recorded the good news in his diary:

SATURDAY 2 NOVEMBER
Good news from Turkey. She has "caved" in after Austria and signed armistice.
SUNDAY 3 NOVEMBER
Good news from front. Germans retreating. Good biz.
THURSDAY 7 NOVEMBER
Good news from France.
FRIDAY 8 NOVEMBER
Queer rumours about Peace. It won't be long if things go on like this.

And then finally the news that everybody had been waiting so long to hear:

MONDAY 11 NOVEMBER
PEACE-PEACE-PEACE
Rag round the town in evening. Some game. Thank God for it.

That morning at 5.00 am in the railway carriage of Marshal Foch, the Allied supremo, located in the Forest of Compiegne, the Armistice had been signed. It was to come into effect at 11.00 am. Charles Balston wrote, "Evidently the enemy delegates did not have a happy time, either at their destination … or on their journey there for they appear to have been driven by a circuitous route so that they might see some of the wilful destruction done to France." Ethel Bilbrough sensed

> *a sort of feeling* in the air *that something was going to happen! And yet we all felt doubtful of Germany up to the very last, and half expected some new act of treachery at the eleventh hour. I was trying to write a coherent letter … when all of a sudden the air was rent by a tremendous BANG!! My instant thought was* a raid! *For our maroons have become so interwoven with the horrors of Gothas & bombs that it has become almost impossible to dissociate them. But when another great explosion shook the windows, and the hooters at Woolwich began to scream like things demented, and the guns started frantically firing all round us like an almighty fugue! I knew there was no raid, but the signing of the armistice had been* Accomplished. *Signal upon signal took up the news; the glorious pulverizing news – that the end had come at last, and* the greatest war in history was over.

The news of the Armistice was greeted with joy and, in some places, wild celebration. In Richmond, Surrey, guns were fired and church bells rung, businesses shut down for the day and "there was excitement everywhere", according to shopkeeper W. J. Hadow, writing to his daughter in India: "The wounded soldiers were parading down the streets with parasols, saucepan lids for cymbals, tin trays in fact anything they could lay their hands on that could make a noise while even ladies that otherwise are quite feminine & sedate were marching along the street like children at a day school treat." "Well thank God," Hadow piously continued. "He has pulled us through & I sincerely believe that if our Religion had been like the Germans' we should have gone under but our Prayers have been answered & that very quickly & now Righteousness has prevailed & we can look back at the war with clean hands. I think we shall see the fruits in a better and purer world." In Newton Abbot, the Graham family of Keyberry Park recorded how: "… the celebration of the Armistice was duly observed here. Those who had flags, no matter what nationality, hung them out, most of them upside down, and those who had none put their coloured, flannelled petticoats + combinations out to air; so it made a motley scene. The excitement was at its height when some boys came out with an air gun + a New Zealander fired off his revolver." Writing to her father, a chaplain in France, Ursula Horsley-Smith of Hunstanton, Norfolk, described how the Armistice had been celebrated there: "We had such excitement on the green on Monday. All the soldiers were there, and all the people. An officer got up on the steps on the green, and made a speech. After a long talk, he said 'First we will sing "God Save the King" then we will have three cheers, and *then* the soldiers will (with your permission) dance round the town!' They did!"

In the Midlands, "Leicester nearly went mad Monday," wrote Erwin Pepper to his parents from the town's Glen Parva barracks.

Thousands of people thronged the streets cheering. Flags were out and all the shops lit up without blinds being drawn. Motor cars decorated dashed about. A torchlight procession with band paraded the streets. The Municipal Buildings were decorated and illuminated. Girls wore red, white, blue ribbons around their hats (and) in their hair. Soldiers wore them on their caps. Twelve sailors marched along each one with a shrill toy trumpet. Restrictions were taken off the amusements. The wounded were given a free press till 7.30 an hour and a half longer than ordinary. Last night again was all life. The fire brigade turned out with flags and torches on the cars and all the firemen dressed up … fireworks going off.

In the next county, at St Peter and St Paul's Parish Church, Mansfield, Nottinghamshire, one of those ringing the joy bells on Armistice Day was 92-year-old William Gosling. A bell ringer for 70 years, he had performed the same happy task in 1856 and 1902 at the end of the Crimean and Boer Wars.

To their sibling in America, the McGuire sisters of Liverpool sent an exultant letter that day:

Hurrah! Hurrah! Hurrah! 'Der Tag' Peace at last. Such a day! I wish you could have seen Liverpool. All shops + offices closed immediately and the streets were thronged with people, soldiers in gangs, munitions girls, American Red Cross nurses. You could walk on their heads. Aunt Tilly has just come in out of the garden. She had decorated the summer house with flags & caught two boys stealing them. I think they have made off with one – little beggars!

Much better behaved was 13-year-old Streatham schoolgirl Olive Wells who:

came to school this morning hardly realizing what a great day this was going to be. Miss Bassett told us that the Armistice had been signed – we had received the news about 5 o' clock am. We cheered until we were hoarse! At 11 o' clock am the guns were fired, the church-bells were rung, the sirens were blown – we did not think of air-raids as we would have done on any other day. We went out into the road and cheered. The Union Jack was sent up the staff and there it fluttered in the breeze. Our home-work was excused for the week. It was not a bright day but very damp. The guns are booming while I am writing this. We are coming out of school at 12.30 pm instead of 12.45 pm this morning. Wherever we go, we see flags flying – big ones and small ones. This has started as a day of rejoicing and I am sure will end as happily.

It certainly did for Nurse Marjorie "Baby" Lean of the First Aid Nursing Yeomanry who married airman Reginald Manby at St Mary Abbots Church, Kensington: "'Baby' will not easily forget her wedding day which was also Armistice Day; escorted to the church by a cheering crowd, and shouts of 'Good luck to you Miss' etc." West Ham schoolboy D. L. Dewar "found a shop at the corner of the road that had been closed for years had suddenly opened and was giving away fireworks. The children however were not very happy. They were afraid of 'them bomb things'! They had never seen fireworks before." And for one civilian at least Armistice celebration fireworks brought tragedy: 46-year-old schoolmaster Joseph Dines of Kensal Rise died at St George's Hospital after being struck on the head by a rocket stick during a firework display in Hyde Park. Bad news also came from Ireland that day. Over 180 attendants at Ballinasloe Asylum had gone on strike at half an hour's notice, "leaving over 1,500 lunatics unguarded. There were in the asylum at the time over 280 cases of suicidal and homicidal tendencies." The strike had come about after the attendants had been offered and rejected a 10 per cent rise but without a war bonus. "Fifty patients, several of the most dangerous type" escaped and were still at large the following day, but after the intervention of the local priest and resident magistrate, the attendants "were prevailed upon to resume work".

Although the news of the Armistice was riotously celebrated all over Britain, London was the epicentre of rejoicing. The distinguished retired soldier Sir Percival Marling VC, who had fought in six campaigns before being invalided out of the army, decided to make the journey up from his Gloucestershire home. "The entire place seemed to have gone mad," he recorded in his diary. "Coming up from the Carlton Club into Piccadilly Circus with a pal we were each seized by two totally strange ladies and danced round till we couldn't dance any more. There was a seething mob in Piccadilly Circus, all dancing and singing at the tops of their voices. Thank God the War's over!" From his desk at the Ministry of Information, Evelyn Wrench joined the crowds and found too that: "London was a city gone mad.... For that one day we were all members of one great family." "Where is your British reserve?" an American asked Wrench. "We thought you were an unemotional nation. Why, Broadway couldn't go madder than this." Wrench heard Canadian soldiers chant:

> *Rah , rah, rah!*
> *Rah, rah, rah!*
> *This is the end of Bill Kaisah! –*
> *Did we win it?*
> *Well, I guess*
> *Canada! Canada! Yes, Yes, Yes!*

Other Canadian troops, in an excess of zeal, started a bonfire at the plinth of Nelson's Column, the scars of which are still visible nearly a century later. Wrench saw how "Australian troops, in response to the cheering of the crowds, gave coo-ees as had never been heard before in Whitehall". In Victoria Street, his sister saw another group of

> *Australian boys accompanied by a band and their girls decorated in*
> *red, white, blue were swinging down towards Whitehall to the huge*
> *delight of all spectators. Later I saw them in the Strand wheeling*
> *carefully at their head two legless companions in a bath chair. In*
> *Whitehall we got blocked, but what did it matter? We danced on*
> *the 'buses, we danced on lorries, we danced on the pavement, we*

shouted, we sang. I never knew before that a small car could carry twenty folk who did not mind how tight they sat, or that forty happy men and girls could caper on the roof of a 'bus, but so it was.... And the din! Everybody was making a noise; some soldiers on the top of the Admiralty had seized office coal scuttles and were banging them with sticks; the office boys and girls at the War Office yelled to their companions across the way; we cheered and cheered again and again, while the Church bells rang out a peal of jubilation.... As I passed down Charing Cross Road I noticed a Scot playing the bagpipes and some elderly charwomen and wounded 'Tommies' dancing in a circle to his tune – a crippled soldier was waving the Belgian flag from his crutch. Turning into the Strand – a sea of laughing, joking people – I came in the nick of the time to see the King and Queen drive by in a carriage escorted only by four mounted policemen.

That night the King, having dutifully stuck to his pledge to abstain from alcohol for the duration, ordered up a bottle of cognac laid down by the Prince Regent in 1815 to commemorate victory over Napoleon at Waterloo. Sadly, His Majesty, who had found the crowds' plaudits that day "indeed touching", considered it "very musty".

But there was also much sadness. Just back from France with a high decoration for gallantry, Duff Cooper "couldn't resist a feeling of profound melancholy, looking at the silly cheering people and thinking of the dead". Injured fellow officer 22-year-old Oswald Mosley, recently adopted as Conservative candidate for Harrow in the forthcoming General Election, was even more bitter. He recalled his disgust at the Ritz with the "smooth, smug people, who had never fought or suffered, [who] seemed to the eyes of youth – at that moment age old with sadness, weariness and bitterness – to be eating, drinking, laughing on the graves of our companions". And that morning in Hornchurch, Essex, Ernest and Florence Daniels received official notification that their 19-year-old son Ernest had died of wounds in France. On hearing the news, their neighbour Annie Purbrook wrote in her diary of Ernest, the Daniels' only son:

... stalwart, curly-haired and one of the kind who meet life with geniality and friendliness; expecting only good; and yet here at the onset he finds death, oblivion, before he has lived at all. How terrible! What waste; what must his father and mother feel – can they still

worship a God and believe in an all-wise Creator? Thinking thus I forgot the minutes of silence I had quite intended to devote to the most earnest thanksgiving....

In 1935, with a new world war threatening, Evelyn Wrench looked back to 11 November 1918. On that day, in common with so many millions of his fellow countrymen, he remembered how:

Mixed emotions swept through me. Great gratitude for peace, an outburst of pent-up excitement, a sensation of participating in mass consciousness, a feeling of uncertainty as to the future, an eager anticipation of a better world, a deep compassion for all who had suffered, and above all the lifting of a stupendous weight. The haunting fear —never admitted in words – that the forces of darkness might triumph and everything the English-speaking world stood for be swept away was banished once and for all.

But 22 years later, on 3 September 1939, the British people learned that they would have to do the whole job all over again.

BIBLIOGRAPHY

There are thousands upon thousands of books on the First World War in the Books Section of the Imperial War Museum, touching on every aspect of the conflict. Many have long been out of print. Listed below are hopefully the more accessible, (and others), of the many works that dealt with Britain's home front which I consulted and found most useful in the preparation and writing of this book:

Lady Cynthia Asquith Diaries 1915-18, Foreword by L P Hartley, London: Century 1987

Scrapbook 1900 to 1914 by Leslie Baily, London: Muller, 1957

Home Front 1914-1918: How Britain Survived the Great War by Ian Beckett, Kew, Richmond, Surrey: The National Archives, 2006

The Home Front in the Great War: Aspects of the Conflict 1914-1918 by David Bilton, Barnsley, South Yorks.: Leo Cooper/Pen and Sword, 2004

The Illustrated London News Social History of the First World War by James Bishop, London: Angus and Robertson, 1982

H H Asquith Letters to Venetia Stanley Selected and edited by Michael and Eleanor Brock, Oxford: Oxford University Press,1982

The Long Trail:Soldiers' Songs and Slang 1914-18 by John Brophy and Eric Partridge

The Imperial War Museum Book Of 1914 by Malcolm Brown, London: Pan Macmillan, 2005

Classified: The Secret History of the Personal Column by H G Cocks, London: Random House Book, 2009

Theatre at War 1914-1918 by L J Collins, Oldham: Jade, 2004

Working for Victory? Images of Women in the First World War, 1914-18 by Diana Condell and Jean Liddiard, London: Routledge & Kegan Paul, 1987

The Home Front: Civilian Life in World War One by Peter Cooksley, Stroud, Glos.: Tempus, 2006

A Durable Fire: The Letters of Duff and Diana Cooper 1913-1950 Edited by Artemis Cooper, London: Collins, 1983

Blighty: British Society in the Era of the Great War by Gerard J Degroot, London: Longman, 1996

A Brief Jolly Change:The Diaries of Henry Peerless, 1891-1920 Edited by Edward Fenton, Oxford: Day Books, 2003

The First Battle of Britain 1917/18 and the Birth of the Royal Air Force by Raymond H. Fredette, London: Cassell, 1966

BIBLIOGRAPHY

The Last Great War: British Society and the First World War by Adrian Gregory, Cambridge: Cambridge University Pres, 2011

First Blitz: The Secret German Plan to Raze London to the Ground in 1918 by Neil Hanson, London: Doubleday, 2008

George Robey and the Music Hall by James Harding, London: Hodder and Stoughton, 1990

Ivor Novello by James Harding, London: W H Allen, 1987

Keep the Home Fires Burning: Propaganda in the First World War by Cate Haste, London: Allen Lane, 1977

Myths and Legends of the First World War by James Hayward, Stroud, Glos.: Sutton, 2002

Oscar Wilde's Last Stand: Decadence, Conspiracy and the Most Outrageous Trial of the Century by Philip Hoare, New York: Arcade, 1998

Living With Enza: The Forgotten Story of Britain and the Great Flu Pandemic of 1918 by Mark Honigsbaum, London: Macmillan, 2009

Dope Girls: The Birth of the British Drug Underground by Marek Kohn, London: Granta Books,1992

The History of the British Film 1914-1918 by Rachael Low, London: Allen and Unwin, 1950

The Last Summer: May to September 1914 by Kirsty McLeod, London: Collins, 1983

The Virago Book of Women and the Great War Edited by Joyce Marlow, London: Virago, 2005

The Deluge: British Society and the First World (2nd Edition) by Arthur Marwick, London: Macmillan, 1991

Echoes of the Great War: The Diary of the Reverend Andrew Clark 1914-1919 Edited by James Munson, Oxford: Oxford University Press, 1985

The Home Front: A Mirror to Life in England During the First World War by E Sylvia Pankhurst, London: Cresset, 1987

The First World War and Popular Cinema: 1914 to the Present Edited by Michael Paris, Edinburgh: Edinburgh University Press, 1999

British Culture and the First World War by George Robb, Basingstoke, Hants.: Palgrave, 2002

Characters of Fitzrovia by Mike Pentelow and Marsha Rowe, London: Pimlico, 2012

Life in Kingston Upon Thames 1917 and 1918 from Cases at the Magistrates' Court by John Pink, Surbiton: Published by the author, 2006

Wilful Murder: The Sinking of the Lusitania by Diana Preston, London: Doubleday, 2002

The Flowers of the Forest: Scotland and the First World War by Trevor Royle, Edinburgh: Birlinn, 2006

Home Fires Burning: the Great War Diaries of Georgina Lee Edited by Gavin Roynon, Stroud, Glos.: Sutton Publishing, 2006

War Comes to York Summer 1914 by David Rubinstein, York: Quacks Books, 2011

Gramophone Records of the First World War: An HMV Catalogue 1914-1918 Introduced by Brian Rust, Newton Abbot: David and Charles, nd (circa 1975)

The Specials by Ronald Seth with a news section by Phillip Powell and Vivienne Catherall-Powell, Trowbridge, Wilts: The Cromwell Press, 2006

Kitchener's Army: The Raising of the New Armies 1914-1916 by Peter Simkins, Barnsley, South Yorks.: Pen and Sword, 2007

British Society 1914-1945 by John Stevenson, Harmondsworth, Middlesex: Penguin Book, 1984

Twentieth Century Maverick: The Life of Noel Pemberton Billing by Barbara Stoney, East Grinstead, West Sussex: Bank House Books, 2004

The Great War: Myth and Memory by Dan Todman, London: Hambledon and London, 2005

August 1914 by Barbara Tuchman, London: Macmillan Papermac, 1981

Dear Old Blighty by E S Turner, London: Michael Joseph, 1980

All Quiet on the Home Front: An Oral History of Life in Britain During the First World War by Richard van Emden and Steve Humphries, London: Headline, 2003

British Theatre in the Great War: A Re-Evaluatio by Gordon Williams, London: Continuum, 2003

The Rasp of War: The Letters of H A Gwynne to the Countess of Bathurst 1914-1918 Selected and edited by Keith Wilson, London: Sidgwick and Jackson, 1988

The Myriad Faces of War:Britain and the Great War 1914-1918 by Trevor Wilson, Cambridge: Polity Press, 1986

INDEX